D0301458

JIHADIST TERROR

I.B. TAURIS
Bloomsbury Publishing Plc
50 Bedford Square, London, WC1B 3DP, UK
1385 Broadway, New York, NY 10018, USA

BLOOMSBURY, I.B. TAURIS and the I.B. Tauris logo are trademarks
of Bloomsbury Publishing Plc

First published in Great Britain 2019

Cover design: Charlotte Daniels
Cover image © Sirikwan Dokuta / Shutterstock

A catalogue record for this book is available from the British Library.

A catalog record for this book is available from the Library of Congress

ISBN: HB: 978-1-7883-1553-1
PB: 978-1-7883-1554-8
ePDF: 978-1-7883-1555-5
eBook: 978-1-7883-1556-2

Typeset by Integra Software Services Pvt. Ltd.

To find out more about our authors and books visit www.bloomsbury.com
and sign up for our newsletters.

COMBATING JIHADIST TERRORISM AND EXTREMISM (COJIT)

In light of the London Bridge attack on 3 June 2017, the third of five jihadist-inspired terrorist assaults in the UK that year, concerned citizens across the country were asking three questions: why is this happening? Is there a solution? And if so, what is it?

The prime minister said we had shown 'too much tolerance' of extremism in the UK and that we must be prepared to have 'difficult' and 'embarrassing' conversations throughout our society to combat the influence of the nihilistic hatred that jihadist terrorism represents. Such conversations must involve all sectors of UK society, not just within and between minority segments.

CoJiT is an initiative designed to make a rapid, direct and high-profile contribution in responding to these difficult questions and to play a catalysing role in the 'national conversation' called for by the prime minister. It has brought together leading experts to look afresh at how we define the particular problem of jihadist terrorism and to discuss openly what has to be done to counter it and the extremist ideology that fuels it, not just in the UK but around the world. The initiative is focused on the active encouragement of practical policy engagement at all levels designed to affect both policy and operational change.

CoJiT will promote this engagement through an independent national dialogue with community individuals, local government and social and police leads, as well as with national government. It will focus on practical solutions identified by the initiative, such as CoJiT's recommendation for independent oversight of the government's Prevent programme, encouraging where possible their adoption and implementation.

CoJiT is conceived quite independently and begins with a problem-solving perspective: it is not our intention to duplicate any of the extensive and good analysis already in existence, but rather to offer an independent synthesis of it as a baseline of accepted evidence to initiate the sort of honest national dialogue the prime minister has called for.

The CoJiT-funded conference on *Combating Jihadist Terrorism in the United Kingdom*, held at the Royal Institution, London, in September 2018 under the Chairmanship of former RUSI Director, Professor Michael Clarke, of which this book is the product, was the first iteration of the independent national conversation that CoJiT is seeking to promote. CoJiT's objectives in light of the outcomes of that first conference are to:

- Promote an active, sustained national conversation primarily in the UK about jihadist terrorism and related extremism
- Develop further the body of analytical work contained in this first publication, summarizing the emerging conclusions with public presentations
- Support, contribute to and collaborate with other organizations involved in related endeavours

We hope you find much of value in the contributions in this volume and that you will wish to take an active part in the independent national conversation on combating terrorism and extremism in the months and years to come.

Ian Maxwell & Mohamed Amersi
CoJiT Founding Members & Directors

www.cojit.org

CONTENTS

1 INTRODUCTION

Anthony Richards

From March to September 2017 the UK endured a series of terrorist attacks on its mainland that killed thirty-six people and injured hundreds more. It was against the backdrop of these events that saw the formation of *Combating Jihadist Terrorism in the UK* (CoJiT-UK), an independent initiative designed to promote a national conversation on the causes of jihadist terrorism and what the most appropriate responses might be. Reconstituted in December 2018 and renamed *Combating Jihadist Terrorism and Extremism* (CoJiT), the project consists of two phases – Phase 1 has entailed bringing together leading national and international experts for their valuable contributions in understanding particular aspects of the phenomenon and their thoughts on potential responses. It is this first phase that culminated in a major conference in London in September 2018 and the publication of this edited volume. Phase 2 of the project aims to i) focus on the themes that have emerged from Phase 1 that have been identified as requiring further exploration and ii) generate a national conversation around the causes of, and responses to, jihadist terrorism.

Two elements in particular mark the CoJiT project and this book as distinctive: i) the project, from which this book has emerged, is independent and independently funded and therefore owes nothing to political sensitivities, institutional competition or preconceived ideas; and ii) the following contributions, rather than sharing new research, have adopted a synthesis approach in assessing the available evidence-based research to date. They are intended to determine, for each topic area, what we know, what we don't know and what we need to know in relation to terrorism carried out by those claiming to be acting on behalf of Islam.

The UK has sadly been no stranger to the threat of terrorism. It seems remarkable that, in fact, the country has been confronted by an almost uninterrupted threat from terrorism for the past fifty years – beginning with the outbreak of the 'Troubles' in Northern Ireland in the late 1960s, to the persistence of the dissident republican threat after the signing of the Good Friday Agreement in 1998, to the emergence of the Al-Qaeda threat, to the more subsequent threat posed by ISIS[1] inspired terrorism, to those who resorted to violence claimed to be on behalf of animal

2 DRIVERS OF JIHADIST TERRORISM: UNDERSTANDING THE IDEOLOGICAL ANTECEDENTS OF SALAFI-JIHADI TERRORISM

Shiraz Maher

Introduction

Although it may seem counterintuitive, on closer examination it is unsurprising that the terrorist attacks of 9/11 did not immediately spur wider discussion about the ideology or beliefs of those involved. There was instead a clamour to better understand the aims and objectives of this supposedly new group called Al-Qaeda, coupled with a desire to grasp its alleged grievances. Wars of ideas based around alternative and conflicting constructions of global order seemed to be over. That was, at least, what the post–Cold War consensus told us. The triumph of the liberal order was entrenched and conflicts would arise now only over struggles for resources or from heterodox non-state actors. The terrorists of Al-Qaeda belonged to the latter, an anomalous groupuscule of wanderer-warriors with a hangover from the Afghan–Soviet war of the 1980s. The anxieties of the intervening years have revealed that consensus to be under greater assault than at any other point since the end of the Second World War. Large swathes of the Muslim world continue to convulse under a febrile atmosphere of change. At the core of these struggles for dominance is a profound crisis over what role Islam should play in the modern world and how the temporal decline of its once vast fortunes can be reconciled with the ascendency – political, cultural, intellectual and material – of the West.

The intervening years since 2001 have revealed that anxieties about world order, our place within it, or the challenges of globalization – whether manifest through mechanization or multilateralism – are anything but limited to the Muslim world. What has emerged in the West is a comparable quest for meaning and renewed purpose, prompting a rise in populism, nativism and identitarianism, all of which

Al-Qaeda or the Islamic State (or associated movements) carry out acts of extreme violence, these outbursts are neither irrational nor whimsical. There is a broader soteriological doctrine around it, providing meaning and purpose.

Defining *salafi-jihadism*

The distinctions within *salafism* primarily stem from differences over how the different traditions view their relationship with power. The American scholar Quintan Wiktorowicz first theorized that the movement could be thought of as falling into one of three different categories – a system of codification that, although somewhat imperfect, suffices for the easy and quick conceptualization of *salafism*'s various strands.[11]

The first category is that of quietists who believe they should offer advice discretely and in private to those in positions of authority, in a process known as *naṣīḥa*. This is largely the official position of the Saudi clerical establishment who limit themselves to advising the House of Saud behind closed doors, where the monarch is free to embrace or disregard their counsel. Other groups of *salafis* – sometimes known as *ṣaḥwa salafis* (meaning 'awakening') – believe they should openly challenge the government over social issues while campaigning for reforms (in a process known as *iṣlāḥ*). Notably, they do not advocate rebellion or direct confrontation and see themselves merely as friendly critics. During the Arab uprisings of 2011 key *ṣaḥwa* figures from the Gulf, such as the Saudi cleric Salman al-Awda, repeatedly warned against popular protests while imploring the monarch of the time, King 'Abdullah, to grant ordinary Saudis a raft of social reforms ranging from the economic, to the social and political.

It is the final clustering of *salafis,* those who advocate jihad and violent confrontation, that is the most relevant for the purposes of this chapter. There are five essential and irreducible features of *salafi-jihadism* which give definition to the movement, based on a reading of its own texts. These are: *jihad, takfīr, al-walā' wa-l-barā', tawḥīd* and *ḥākimiyya.*[12] In a nutshell, these ideas can be defined as follows:

- **Jihad:** the legal concept of fighting in the cause (or path) of Allah; *fī sabīl Allah*;
- **Takfīr:** Excommunication of other Muslims, banishing them from the faith;
- **Al-walā' wa-l-barā':** To love and hate for the sake of Allah; loyalty and disavowal;
- **Tawḥīd:** The Islamic concept of monotheism; the core component of Islam and the single most important factor of *Salafism*;
- **Ḥākimiyya:** The rule of Allah; securing God's sovereignty in the political system.

There is a wealth of material from contemporary militant movements about the first three topics.[13] This is unsurprising given that they relate principally to battlefield concepts, requiring groups to justify and explain their actions. For example, Al-Qaeda long made the case for jihad against so-called 'crusader' nations – such as the United States or the United Kingdom – but was forced to launch a campaign around the principles of *takfīr* after 2003 so it could explain why it was so committed to the pursuit of a brutal sectarian war aimed against Shia Muslims.

The group similarly needed to marshal supporters in its cause, claiming that Muslims owed them loyalty or duty (*al-walā'*), even if they disagreed with Al-Qaeda's aims. By their reasoning, all Muslims are commanded to offer each other their fealty, whilst simultaneously disavowing their collective enemies, through the principles of *al-barā'*. Taken as a whole, the first three concepts therefore provide the framework for battlefield jurisprudence which guides and gives shape to the actions of *jihadi* non-state actors. After all, these are the ideas that must be sold to fellow Muslims if they are to find support for their actions. Without them, there is neither explanation nor justification for why *salafi-jihadi* groups act the way they do.

By contrast, the latter two ideas are more abstract and settled. *Tawḥīd* is not immediately relevant to battlefield tactics, although it plays an important role in the motivation of militants. Similarly, *ḥākimiyya* is an idea about which much has been written and whose advocates extend far beyond *jihadi* circles. Indeed, groups like the Muslim Brotherhood and Hizb ut-Tahrir have probably done more to popularize ideas of Islamic governance and the Caliphate than their more militant counterparts have. These realities mean *jihadi* groups view both *tawḥīd* and *ḥākimiyya* as ideas that require less of their attention. They are already well understood, popularized and have advocates that exist beyond the *jihadi* ecosystem.

Yet, either Muslims do not understand, or do not accept, militant interpretations of *jihad*, *takfīr* and *al-walā' wa-l-barā'*. Al-Qaeda consequently directed tremendous amounts of time and energy into explaining them during the years of the 9/11 wars in Afghanistan and Iraq.

The dichotomy of *salafi-jihadi* praxis

One notable feature of the way in which *jihadist* scholarship operates is that there are frequent tensions between those who actually fight on the ground and theorists. The latter have the luxury of operating in an abstract and intellectual realm, where ideas can gestate over time and the perfect conditions are imagined. For those on the ground, the privations of war mean that theoretical abstractions are often overlooked in favour of a less polished, more ad hoc real-time battlefield jurisprudence. This has often led to both sides criticizing the other for their lack of understanding.

Those tensions were accentuated by Islamic State which epitomized the triumph of praxis, placing very little emphasis on scholarship of any kind. One of the main criticisms against the movement from other *jihadi* actors was that it lacked true scholars within its ranks, perhaps with the exception of Turki al-Binali. Even then, he was not as widely lauded as he might have been. Although Binali pursued Islamic studies with scholars from within the *jihadi* orbit, including with important figureheads such as Abu Muhammad al-Maqdisi, he was not even thirty when he joined Islamic State, and in defiance of his tutor's opposition to the group.[14]

None of this has troubled Islamic State's supporters in any meaningful way, who continued to prioritize action over scholarship. As a result, Islamic State produced very little in terms of intellectual output. There are no foundational texts which fundamentally challenge or change the nature of *salafi-jihadi* thinking on core issues. Instead, the group contents itself with simply borrowing from existing ideas, and busies itself with their realization. This meant Islamic State was able to project itself as an attractive proposition through the sheer weight of its success: raising the black flag with the *shahada* emblazoned across it over new territories; staging military parades through freshly conquered town squares; implementing their arbitrary system of justice wherever their authority extended. That much was evident by their popular phrase – *bāqiyya wa tatamaddad*, which means 'remaining and expanding' – a catchall slogan chanted by the group whose members found themselves intoxicated by a succession of unlikely victories through 2013–2016.

For them, authenticity, authority and legitimacy are established through praxis. Less emphasis is placed on scholarship than on action. Consider, for example, the defiant images of *jihadi* leaders. They almost always appear in military fatigues, sprawling over military maps (presumably engaged in offensive attack-planning), or carrying weapons. The only significant exception to this has been the appearance of Islamic State's leader, Abu Bakr al-Baghdadi, at the Nouri mosque in Mosul, Iraq, where he attempted to project himself as much more than just the leader of a militant group. Standing upon the mosque's pulpit (*minbar*) in July 2014, Baghdadi declared himself the leader of the faithful, or *amīr al-mu'minīn*. Put another way, it was the first time anyone had seriously attempted to arrogate for themselves the seat of the Caliphate since the demise of the Ottoman Caliphate in 1924.[15]

Conclusion

Salafism is a broad and complex religious tradition. Based on the idea of reviving the Islamic traditions of the Prophetic generations, it is a doctrine of salvation that believes in literalist and unbending constructions of the faith. The practices of *salafism* are varied, with its distinct *jihadi* strand finding expression through the violent rejection of the existing political order, of which groups like Al-Qaeda and Islamic State represent its most potent forms.

Given that war serves as the primary driver of intellectual change in *salafi-jihadi* thought, it is the conflicts that have followed the terrorist attacks of 9/11 that have shaped so many of the destructive tendencies we ascribe to *salafi-jihadism* today. The invasion of Iraq in 2003 did more than perhaps any other event in recent times to help Al-Qaeda fashion the ideas of *jihad, takfīr* and *al-walā' wa-l-barā'* into something resembling a coherent warrior-doctrine.[16]

The disastrous implications of that evolution continue to reverberate across the Middle East today with increased sectarian tensions and militant violence. As conflicts continue to rage – not just in the Levant – but also in the southern Arabian Peninsula, Horn of Africa, Sahel, and in Libya, *salafi-jihadi* thought will continue to mould itself to the new realities in which it finds itself. If the last two decades have taught us anything about this ideology, it is that its malleability is its strength.

Notes

1 S. B. Smith, *The Cambridge Companion to Leo Strauss*, Cambridge: Cambridge University Press, 2009.

2 S. Maher, *Salafi-Jihadism: The History of an Idea*, London: Hurst & Co, Oxford University Press, 2016, pp. 25–27.

3 I have chosen to use the term 'salafi-jihadism' due to its understanding among Western audiences, although in absolutist terms, the correct Arabic translation would be 'jihadi-salafism' as the verb precedes the subject (and then object) in Arabic grammar.

4 The group known as 'Islamic State' has adopted various names throughout the Syrian conflict including: Islamic State of Iraq and Syria (ISIS); Islamic State of Iraq and the Levant (ISIL); and Daesh (an acronym of its name in Arabic). For the purposes of this chapter, I will refer to the movement as Islamic State (IS) and use the name as a proper noun. As such, the name Islamic State is applied as a marker of identity for a particular, identifiable and known group, and thereby avoids making any value judgements as to its subjective claims of constituting an actual Islamic state.

5 T. Gontier, 'From "Political Theology" to "Political Religion": Eric Voegelin and Carl Schmitt', *Review of Politics*, vol. 75, no. 1, 2013, pp. 25–43; E. Voegelin, *The New Science of Politics: An Introduction*, Chicago: University of Chicago Press, 1987.

6 Arabic terms have been transliterated with diacritic markings into English using the International Journal of Middle East Studies transliteration guide. Names of groups and individuals do not conform to this standard and adopt commonly recognized English spellings instead (Osama instead of Usama; Al-Qaeda instead of al-Qaida). The only exception is that an apostrophe to denote the *ayn* has been retained at the start of Arabic names.

7 *Sahih Muslim*, Book 31, Number 6159.

8 N. DeLong-Bas, *Wahhabi Islam: From Revival and Reform to Global Jihad*, Oxford: Oxford University Press, 2008.

9 Maher, *Salafi-Jihadism*, pp. 145–168.

10 'Abd al-'Aziz bin Baz, 'Speech during Sheikh Muhammad ibn 'Abd al-Wahhab week', *Fatwas of Bin Baz*, vol. 1, undated, p. 378.

11 Q. Wiktorowciz, 'Anatomy of the Salafi Movement', *Studies in Conflict & Terrorism*, vol. 29, 2006, p. 208.

12 Maher, *Salafi-Jihadism*, p. 14.

13 Maher, *Salafi-Jihadism*, p. 14.

14 It is worth noting that Maqdisi's opposition to Islamic State has occasionally waned, and that although he has broadly opposed the movement, he has also made appeals to them on kindred terms.

15 H. Kennedy, *The Caliphate*, United Kingdom: Penguin, 2016, p. 267 (although all of Chapter 11 is relevant to this discussion).

16 Maher, *Salaf-Jihadism*.

Recommended Readings

'Abd al-'Aziz bin Baz, 'Speech during Sheikh Muhammad ibn 'Abd al-Wahhab week', *Fatwas of Bin Baz*, vol. 1, undated, p. 378.

DeLong-Bas, N., *Wahhabi Islam: From Revival and Reform to Global Jihad*, Oxford: Oxford University Press, 2008.

Gontier, T., 'From "Political Theology" to "Political Religion": Eric Voegelin and Carl Schmitt', *Review of Politics*, vol. 75, no. 1, 2013, pp. 25–43.

Kennedy, H., *The Caliphate*, United Kingdom: Penguin, 2016.

Maher, S., *Salafi-Jihadism: The History of an Idea*, London: Hurst & Co, Oxford University Press, 2016.

Sivan, E., *Radical Islam: Medieval Theology and Modern Politics*, New Haven, CT: Yale University Press, 1990.

Smith, S. B., *The Cambridge Companion to Leo Strauss*, Cambridge: Cambridge University Press, 2009.

Voegelin, E., *The New Science of Politics: An Introduction*, Chicago: University of Chicago Press, 1987.

Wagemakers, J., 'The Transformation of a Radical Concept: al-wala' wa-l-bara' in the Ideology of Abu Muhammad al-Maqdisi', in Roel Meijer (ed.), *Global Salafism: Islam's New Religious Movement*, London: Hurst & Co, 2009.

Wiktorowciz, Q., 'Anatomy of the Salafi Movement', *Studies in Conflict & Terrorism*, vol. 29, 2006, pp. 207–239.

Wiktorowciz, Q., 'The New Global Threat: Transnational Salafis and Jihad', *Middle East Policy*, vol. VIII, no. 4, December 2001, pp. 18–38.

Wiktorowciz, Q., 'Introduction: Islamic Activism and Social Movement Theory', in Quintan Wiktorowicz (ed.), *Islamic Activism: A Social Movement Theory Approach*, Indiana: Indiana University Press, 2004.

3 THE IMPACT OF JIHADIST TERRORIST NARRATIVES AND HOW TO COUNTER THEM: A RESEARCH SYNTHESIS

Kurt Braddock

Jihadi narratives

Empirical work on terrorist narratives (including jihadi narratives) shows that these narratives have the potential to promote beliefs, attitudes, intentions, and behaviours consistent with terrorist ideologies – a process that some may call violent radicalization.[1] Given this, jihadi narratives can be potent vehicles for transmitting jihadi ideologies in a form that is easily accessible and interpretable by target audiences.

Although the smaller stories told by supporters of different terrorist groups (e.g. Islamic State, Al-Qaeda) differ slightly, all jihadi narratives tend to be characterized by four interrelated themes that collectively justify jihadi violence against civilian targets. These four themes respectively assert that:

- Only by practising the strictest interpretation of Islam (i.e. enacted through Sharia Law) can Muslim lands be peaceful and prosperous;
- Islam and its practitioners are under attack by Western forces and apostate regimes in the Middle East that support those forces;
- Only the jihadi group is capable of defending Muslims (and Islam) from attacks by Western forces and apostate regimes;
- Those who do not support jihadi groups' efforts to defend Islam and its practitioners are also apostates that should be punished.

The first theme is based on jihadi interpretations of Islamic history. In their narratives, jihadis often claim that prior to the emergence and growth of Islam, the world was a terrible place, particularly for vulnerable populations. Once Islam appeared, however, the Muslim world enjoyed an era of 'human rights, prosperity, and happiness for all'.[2] Moreover, Muslims' strict adherence to Islamic principles of behaviour was rewarded with victories over non-Muslims. Eventually, Muslims moved away from strict compliance with the tenets of Islam, and as a result, Allah revoked the blessings he had bestowed on the Muslim world. To return to the past days of glory, jihadi groups argue that it is necessary for Muslims to return to a strict interpretation of Islam,[3] which may include the establishment of a 'Sharia-governed polity to replace the corrupt governance structures of secular Western-backed regimes'.[4] By framing 'true' Islam as being diametrically opposed to Western regimes and governments that support them, jihadis depict an ideological conflict between 'true' Muslims and those who do not support Sharia law.

The second theme that defines jihadi narratives further emphasizes the necessity of Muslim resistance against the West. Specifically, jihadi narratives often contend that Muslims – and even Islam itself – are under constant attack by Western forces. Specifically, jihadi narratives characterize Muslims as a global community that is constantly oppressed and/or stigmatized.[5] Though these narrative claims are often exaggerated for persuasive effect among their intended audiences, Western intervention in the Middle East and other Muslim areas help fuel perceptions of the claims' legitimacy and corresponding grievances.[6] Halverson et al. argue that the narrative descriptions of these grievances indicate that a 'non-Muslim "other," typically Westerners, Zionists, and "Crusaders" are responsible, in collaboration with local dictators, for the mistreatment and humiliation of Muslims around the world'.[7] Through their narratives, jihadis group Western enemies with illegitimate governments, thereby arguing that local governance is incapable of providing Muslims with the freedoms and protection they want and deserve.

This, in turn, relates to the third theme that pervades jihadi narratives – that jihadi groups are the only ones capable of protecting Muslims, and that protection of Muslims must be achieved through violent activity against perceived aggressors. Jihadi narratives produced by both Islamic State and Al-Qaeda have argued that movement from the fundamental grievance (i.e. that Islam is under constant attack) to a righteous, peaceful society is possible only through violent struggle.[8] Moreover, these narratives also typically characterize the jihadi groups as the only ones capable of effectively engaging in this armed struggle.[9]

Finally, to foster support and minimize resistance to their ideology among those they purport to defend, jihadi groups often claim that Muslims who disapprove of their actions are not 'true' Muslims. Instead, they are apostates who should be punished in a manner similar to the Western aggressors and illegitimate governments against whom the jihadi group is fighting.[10] Through their narratives, jihadi groups provide audiences with a simplistic, black-and-white frame that defines actors as being either 'allied to Islam' or 'allied to those that fight against Islam'. In doing so, jihadi narratives contend that the only 'good Muslims' are those that support the violent actions of jihadis.[11]

By using these four themes as the foundational elements of their narratives, jihadi groups seek to justify violence as a necessary action undertaken by the only ones that are capable of defending Islam against foreign aggressors and traitorous supporters of those aggressors. Despite the appeal of these narrative themes, it can be possible to challenge them through carefully crafted counter-narratives. The following section summarizes the literature on counter-narratives and how they can be used to thwart the persuasive effectiveness of jihadi narrative themes.

Countering jihadi narratives

In response to jihadi narratives and their potential for fostering violent radicalization and support for terrorist groups, researchers and practitioners have offered strategic counter-messaging recommendations intended to dissuade support for the use of jihadi terror and the groups that engage in it. Although these recommendations are characterized by a variety of communicative strategies, the most heavily cited is the use of narratives that contradict, replace or otherwise challenge the themes that comprise jihadi narratives. Within the literature, these narratives are often referred to as *counter-narratives*. Given the degree to which researchers and security practitioners emphasize and utilize counter-narratives, this chapter will focus on counter-narrative development as a viable means of challenging jihadi narratives.

Terrorism researchers and security experts contend that a counter-narrative's effectiveness is contingent on two complementary factors. First, *counter-narrative content* must be specifically tailored to address the targeted jihadi narratives and the ideology that underpins them. Second, *the counter-narrative distribution method* must be informed by an understanding of the counter-narrative's intended audience(s) and their relationship with potential message sources. The following sections will synthesize research on these critical issues related to the use of counter-narratives for challenging jihadi narratives.

Content

Extant work on counter-narrative development provides an array of recommendations related to the kinds of content that should be incorporated into counter-narratives to ensure their effectiveness. Although these recommendations are as variable as the researchers that propose them, they can largely be classified into eight categories. These categories are:

- Proposing an alternative narrative rather than a confrontational narrative;
- Portraying alternative images of subjects within jihadi narratives;

- Avoiding generic content that is unspecific to any ideology;
- Understanding the ideological appeals that comprise terrorist narratives;
- Highlighting the stories of former jihadis;
- Highlighting the hypocrisies of terrorist actions relative to their messaging;
- Advocating non-violent forms of political dissent;
- Maintaining consistency between counter-narrative content and government actions.

First, several researchers indicate that rather than discrediting or discounting the themes that comprise jihadi narratives, effective messaging strategies can include narratives that provide alternative explanations or depictions than those offered by jihadi groups. Ashour argued that the content of effective counter-narratives should be 'attractive' while 'admitting the validity of some or all' jihadi grievances. At the same time, however, those counter-narratives should provide 'alternative ways to address those grievances'.[12] Beutel and his colleagues similarly argue that rather than confronting terrorist narratives or the ideologies that underpin them directly, counter-narratives should instead seek to 'reframe' the nature of the argument.[13] By doing so, developers of counter-narratives can avoid seeming dismissive of audience concerns while providing non-violent methods through which those concerns can be expressed.

Related to this, a second recommendation that emerges from within the literature on counter-narratives is the presentation of narrative characters in a different light than in the jihadi narratives. Counter-narrative researchers argue that the terrorists themselves, as well as those portrayed as enemies, should be redefined within effective counter-narratives. In the case of the former, many experts recommend challenging the common depiction of terrorists within jihadi narratives as stalwart fighters for Islam. Leuprecht et al. argue that counter-narratives must contest the perception 'that Muslim terrorists are defending Islam'.[14] Heffelfinger also highlights the importance of breaking down the 'Muslim hero' archetype in jihadi narratives, arguing that effective counter-narratives should undermine the notion that Al-Qaeda terrorists represent a 'fighting vanguard' that defends Islamic Law on behalf of a Muslim community.[15] Jacobsen argues for a more targeted approach to challenging the heroism imagery in many jihadi narratives, claiming that depicting terrorist leadership in a way that 'detracts from [the] leaders' authority and credibility is vital' for reducing support for the jihadi group. Moreover, it may be useful to depict jihadi terrorists as common criminals (e.g. emphasize jihadi groups' drug trafficking activities) to illustrate the 'impurity' of the jihadi ideology as practised by the target group.[16]

Other researchers have argued for the development of alternative images of those portrayed as enemies to the jihadi group. Braddock and Horgan[17] are straightforward in this recommendation, suggesting that counter-narrative authors offer 'an alternative view of the terrorist narrative's targets'. Others highlight the importance of countering jihadi narrative themes that paint Western actors as at war with Islam.[18] Instead, counter-narratives should highlight Western policies that have 'benefited Muslim interests,' including humanitarian aid, development work and the proliferation of education in Muslim communities.[19]

Third, multiple researchers argue that the content that comprises counter-narratives designed to challenge jihadi narratives should be nuanced and uniquely tailored to the ideology it targets. Ashour warned against generic counter-narratives, claiming that 'oversimplification, shallowness, and generic counter-narratives should be avoided, as these invite successful "strike-backs"'.[20] Others have also warned against the use of superficial, 'paint-by-numbers' counter-narratives, arguing that the use of generic messaging will do little to break down distrust felt by Muslims targeted by jihadi narratives.[21]

The fourth category of recommendations assists in the avoidance of the generic counter-narratives that extant research warns about. Many researchers argue that the development of an effective counter-narrative (i.e. involving the inclusion of content that is uniquely suited to challenge jihadi narrative propaganda) requires a thorough understanding of the ideological appeals that underpin jihadi narratives. In a report for Quilliam, Russell and Rafiq emphasized the need for this understanding, claiming that counter-narrative authors must understand not only the philosophical tenets of the Islamic narrative and the salafi-jihadi ideology, but also how that ideology is used to manipulate message targets' vulnerabilities.[22] Quiggin similarly argued that the effective countering of jihadist narratives requires knowledge related to the effectiveness of jihadis' ideological appeals.[23] Only by understanding the nature of the ideology that serves as the philosophical foundation on which jihadi narratives are built can effective counter-narratives be effectively tailored and developed.

Fifth, some researchers argue that the key to effective counter-narrative content is the use of stories by those who are likely to be perceived as experts in the jihadi ideology, and possibly, the targeted group. To these ends, some scholars argue that the stories of former ideological adherents (e.g. former members of the jihadi group) represent the most powerful counter-narrative content available. More specifically, recantations and refutations of the jihadi ideology on the part of those who used to belong to the jihadi group are potent weapons that can be embedded in counter-narratives.[24] In addition, it may be useful to develop counter-narratives that highlight the disappointing reality of life as a terrorist to effectively dissuade potential recruits.[25] This strategy is consistent with past work showing disillusionment with unmet expectations as one of the key motivators for past terrorists' disengagement from violence.[26]

One method for illustrating fighter disillusionment with engagement in jihadi terrorism is through the use of a sixth suggestion offered by existing work on counter-narratives – highlighting the hypocrisies and inconsistencies between adoption of jihadi ideologies and the extent that the latter can be used to challenge those ideologies. This brief synopsis of existing literature on these topics reveals that jihadi narratives (as developed by Al-Qaeda and the Islamic State) primarily comprise four themes. Perhaps more importantly, this literature also provides eight recommendations related to the incorporation of specific content into counter-narratives and three recommendations concerning the distribution of these counter-narratives. However, these findings should not be considered the final word on jihadi narratives and counter-narratives. As empirical work on jihadi narratives continues, our understanding of their effects will evolve. Our counter-narrative strategies intended to thwart the persuasive effects of jihadi narratives must evolve as well.

Notes

1 K. Braddock and J. Dillard, 'Meta-Analytic Evidence for the Persuasive Effect of Narratives on Beliefs, Attitudes, Intentions, and Behaviors', *Communication Monographs*, vol. 83, no. 4, 2016, pp. 446–467; K. Braddock and J. Horgan, 'Towards a Guide for Constructing and Disseminating Counternarratives to Reduce Support for Terrorism', *Studies in Conflict & Terrorism*, vol. 39, no. 5, 2016, pp. 381–404.

2 M. A. Upal, 'Confronting Islamic Jihadist Movements', *Journal of Terrorism Research*, vol. 6, no. 2, 2015, p. 64.

3 Upal, 'Confronting Islamic Jihadist Movements', p. 64.

4 J. Halverson, S. Corman, and H. L. Goodall, *Master Narratives of Islamist Extremism*, London: Palgrave MacMillan, 2011.

5 P. Lentini, *Neojihadism: Towards a New Understanding of Terrorism and Extremism*, Cheltenham, UK: Edward Elgar Publishing, 2013.

6 See E. Nugent, T. Masoud, and A. A. Jamal, 'Arab Responses to Western Hegemony: Experimental Evidence from Egypt', *Journal of Conflict Resolution*, vol. 62, no. 2, 2018, pp. 256–262.

7 Halverson, Corman and Goodall, *Master Narratives of Islamic Extremism*; see also D. Betz, 'The Virtual Dimension of Contemporary Insurgency and Counterinsurgency', *Small Wars and Insurgencies*, vol. 19, no. 4, 2008, p. 520.

8 P. Holtmann, 'Countering al-Qaeda's Single Narrative', *Perspectives on Terrorism*, vol. 7, no. 2, 2013, p. 145; A. P. Schmid, *Al-Qaeda's 'Single Narrative' and Attempts to Develop Counter-Narratives: The State of Knowledge*, The Hague, Netherlands: International Center for Counter-Terrorism, 2014, p. 6.

9 Upal, 'Confronting Islamic Jihadist Movements', p. 64.

10 Upal, 'Confronting Islamic Jihadist Movements', p. 64; see also J. Russell and H. Rafiq, *Countering Islamist Extremist Narratives: A Strategic Briefing*, London: Quilliam Foundation, 2016, p. 20.

11 Betz, 'The Virtual Dimension of Contemporary Insurgency and Counterinsurgency', p. 520.

12 O. Ashour, 'Online De-Radicalization? Countering Violent Extremist Narratives: Message, Messenger, and Media Strategy', *Perspectives on Terrorism*, vol. 4, no. 6, 2010, p. 17.

13 A. Beutel et al., 'Field Principles for Countering and Displacing Extremist Narratives', *Journal of Terrorism Research*, vol. 7, no. 3, 2016, p. 40.

14 C. Leuprecht et al., 'Winning the Battle but Losing the War? Narrative and Counter-Narratives Strategy', *Perspectives on Terrorism*, vol. 3, no. 2, 2009, p. 33.

15 C. Heffelfinger, 'Waiting out the Islamist Winter: Creating an Effective Counter Narrative to "Jihad"' (GTReC ARC Linkage Project on Radicalisation Conference, Melbourne, 8 November 2010), p. 4, available at http://1dneox4dyqrx1207m11b46y7tfi.wpengine.netdna-cdn.com/radicalisation/files/2013/03/conference-2010-counter-narratives-ch.pdf (accessed 21 January 2017).

16 M. Jacobsen, 'Terrorist Drop-Outs: One Way of Promoting a Counter-Narrative', *Perspectives on Terrorism*, vol. 3, no. 2, 2009, p. 13.

17 Braddock and Horgan, 'Towards a Guide', p. 390; see also Halverson, Corman, and Goodall, *Master Narratives of Islamist Extremism*.

18 Leuprecht et al., 'Winning the Battle but Losing the War?' p. 33.

19 Heffelfinger, 'Waiting out the Islamist Winter', p. 4.

20 Ashour, 'Online De-Radicalization?' p. 17.

21 Holtmann, 'Countering al-Qaeda's Single Narrative', p. 143.

22 Russell and Rafiq, *Countering Islamist Extremist Narratives*, p. 7.

23 T. Quiggin, 'Understanding al-Qaeda's Ideology for Counter-Narrative Work', *Perspectives on Terrorism*, vol. 3, no. 2, 2009, p. 24.

24 Heffelfinger, 'Waiting out the Islamist Winter', pp. 11–12.

25 Jacobsen, 'Terrorist Drop-Outs', p. 14.

26 J. Horgan, *Walking Away from Terrorism: Accounts of Disengagement from Radical and Extremist Movements*, London: Routledge, 2009.

27 Braddock and Horgan, 'Towards a Guide', p. 389.

28 Jacobsen, 'Terrorist Drop-Outs', p. 13; Leuprecht et al., 'Winning the Battle but Losing the War?' p. 33.

29 P. R. Neumann, *Victims, Perpetrators, Assets: The Narratives of Islamic State Defectors*, London: King's College, International Centre for the Study of Radicalisation and Political Violence, 2015, pp. 10–11.

30 Leuprecht et al., 'Winning the Battle but Losing the War?' p. 33.

31 Upal, 'Confronting Islamic Jihadist Movements', p. 66.

32 Russell and Rafiq, *Countering Islamic Extremist Narratives*, p. 8; Beutel et al., 'Field Principles for Countering and Displacing Extremist Narratives', p. 42.

33 Holtmann, 'Countering al-Qaeda's Single Narrative', p. 143.

34 Beutel et al., 'Field Principles for Countering and Displacing Extremist Narratives', p. 41.

35 Russell and Rafiq, *Countering Islamist Extremist Narratives*, p. 7.

36 Braddock and Horgan, 'Towards a Guide', p. 386; K. Braddock and J. Morrison, 'Cultivating Trust and Perceptions of Source Credibility in Online Counternarratives Intended to Reduce Support for Terrorism', *Studies in Conflict & Terrorism*, in press.

37 Beutel et al., 'Field Principles for Countering and Displacing Extremist Narratives', p. 42.

38 Ashour, 'Online De-Radicalization?' p. 18; A. Speckhard, A. Shajkovci, and A. S. Yahla, 'What to Expect Following a Military Defeat of ISIS in Syria and Iraq?' *Journal of Terrorism Research*, vol. 8, no. 1, 2017, p. 86; Neumann, *Victims, Perpetrators, Assets*, p. 14.

39 Hiffelfinger, 'Waiting Out the Islamist Winter', p. 5; Holtmann, 'Countering al-Qaeda's Single Narrative', p. 142; Braddock and Horgan, 'Towards a Guide', p. 393.

40 Russell and Rafiq, *Countering Islamist Extremist Narratives*, p. 8.

41 Beutel et al., 'Field Principles for Countering and Displacing Extremist Narratives', p. 42; Russell and Rafiq, *Countering Islamist Extremist Narratives*, p. 9.

Recommended Readings

Al-Raffie, D., 'Whose Hearts and Minds? Narratives and Counter-Narratives of Salafi Jihadism', *Journal of Terrorism Research*, vol. 3, no. 2, 2012, pp. 13–31.

Ashour, O., 'Online De-Radicalization? Countering Violent Extremist Narratives: Message, Messenger, and Media Strategy', *Perspectives on Terrorism*, vol. 4, no. 6, 2010, pp. 15–19.

Betz, D., 'The Virtual Dimension of Contemporary Insurgency and Counterinsurgency', *Small Wars and Insurgencies*, vol. 19, no. 4, 2008, pp. 510–540.

Beutel, A. et al., 'Field Principles for Countering and Displacing Extremist Narratives', *Journal of Terrorism Research*, vol. 7, no. 3, 2016, pp. 35–49.

Braddock, K., and J. Dillard, 'Meta-Analytic Evidence for the Persuasive Effect of Narratives on Beliefs, Attitudes, Intentions, and Behaviors', *Communication Monographs*, vol. 83, no. 4, 2016, pp. 446–467.

Braddock, K., and J. Horgan, 'Towards a Guide for Constructing and Disseminating Counternarratives to Reduce Support for Terrorism', *Studies in Conflict & Terrorism*, vol. 39, no. 5, 2016, pp. 381–404.

Braddock, K., and J. Morrison, 'Cultivating Trust and Perceptions of Source Credibility in Online Counternarratives Intended to Reduce Support for Terrorism', *Studies in Conflict & Terrorism*, 2018, pp. 1–25.

Corman, S. R., 'The Narrative Rationality of Violent Extremism', *Social Science Quarterly*, vol. 97, no. 1, 2016, pp. 9–18.

De Graaf, B., 'Counter-Narratives and the Unrehearsed Stories Counter-Terrorists Unwittingly Produce', *Perspectives on Terrorism*, vol. 3, no. 2, 2009, pp. 5–11.

El-Badawy, E., Comerford, M., and P. Welby, *Inside the Jihadi Mind: Understanding Ideology and Propaganda*, London: Tony Blair Institute for Global Change, 2015.

Glazzard, A., *Losing the Plot: Narrative, Counter-Narrative and Violent Extremism*, The Hague, Netherlands: International Centre for Counter-Terrorism, 2017.

Goodall Jr., H. L., *Counter-Narrative: How Progressive Academics Can Challenge Extremists and Promote Social Justice*, Walnut Creek, CA: Left Coast Press, 2010.

Halverson, J., Corman, S., and H. L. Goodall, *Master Narratives of Islamist Extremism*, London: Palgrave MacMillan, 2011.

Heffelfinger, C., 'Waiting out the Islamist Winter: Creating an Effective Counter Narrative to "Jihad"', (GTReC ARC Linkage Project on Radicalisation Conference, Melbourne, 8 November 2010), p. 4, available here: http://1dneox4dyqrx1207m11b46y7tfi.wpengine.netdna-cdn.com/radicalisation/files/2013/03/conference-2010-counter-narratives-ch.pdf (accessed 21 January 2017).

Holtmann, P., 'Countering al-Qaeda's Single Narrative', *Perspectives on Terrorism*, vol. 7, no. 2, 2013, pp. 141–146.

Horgan, J., *Walking Away from Terrorism: Accounts of Disengagement from Radical and Extremist Movements*, London: Routledge, 2009.

Jacobsen, M., 'Terrorist Drop-Outs: One Way of Promoting a Counter-Narrative', *Perspectives on Terrorism*, vol. 3, no. 2, 2009, pp. 12–17.

Lentini, P., *Neojihadism: Towards a New Understanding of Terrorism and Extremism*, Cheltenham, UK: Edward Elgar Publishing, 2013.

Leuprecht, C. et al., 'Containing the Narrative: Strategy and Tactics in Countering the Storyline of Global Jihad', *Journal of Policing, Intelligence and Counter Terrorism*, vol. 5, no. 1, 2010, pp. 42–57.

Leuprecht, C. et al., 'Winning the Battle but Losing the War? Narrative and Counter-Narratives Strategy', *Perspectives on Terrorism*, vol. 3, no. 2, 2009, pp. 25–35.

Neumann, P. R., *Victims, Perpetrators, Assets: The Narratives of Islamic State Defectors*, London: King's College, International Centre for the Study of Radicalisation and Political Violence, 2015.

Nugent, E., T. Masoud, and A. A. Jamal, 'Arab Responses to Western Hegemony: Experimental Evidence from Egypt', Journal of Conflict Resolution, vol. 62, no. 2, pp. 254–288.

Quiggin, T., 'Understanding al-Qaeda's Ideology for Counter-Narrative Work', *Perspectives on Terrorism*, vol. 3, no. 2, 2009, pp. 18–24.

Russell, J., and H. Rafiq, *Countering Islamist Extremist Narratives: A Strategic Briefing*, London: Quilliam Foundation, 2016.

Schmid, A. P., *Al-Qaeda's 'Single Narrative' and Attempts to Develop Counter-Narratives: The State of Knowledge*, The Hague, Netherlands: International Center for Counter-Terrorism, 2014.

Speckhard, A., Shajkovci, A., and A. S. Yahla, 'What to Expect Following a Military Defeat of ISIS in Syria and Iraq?' *Journal of Terrorism Research*, vol. 8, no. 1, 2017, pp. 81–89.

Upal, A., 'Alternative Narratives for Preventing the Radicalization of Muslim Youth', *Journal for Deradicalization*, vol. 15, no. 2, 2015, pp. 138–162.

Upal, M. A., 'Confronting Islamic Jihadist Movements', *Journal of Terrorism Research*, vol. 6, no. 2, 2015, pp. 57–69.

Vergani, M., 'Neo-Jihadist Prosumers and Al Qaeda Single Narrative: The Case Study of Giuliano Delnevo', *Studies in Conflict & Terrorism*, vol. 37, 2012, pp. 604–617.

Zahedzadeh, G., Barraza, J. A., and P. J. Zak, 'Persuasive Narratives and Costly Actions', *Terrorism and Political Violence*, vol. 29, no. 1, 2017, pp. 160–172.

4 THE IMPACT OF CONSPIRACY THEORIES AND HOW TO COUNTER THEM: REVIEWING THE LITERATURE ON CONSPIRACY THEORIES AND RADICALIZATION TO VIOLENCE

Amarnath Amarasingam

Introduction

The academic and popular literature on conspiracy theories is, in many ways, unimaginably varied, scattered and overwhelming. As such, this literature review is necessarily selective and focuses on a few key questions: definitional issues around conspiracy theories, debates about what causes people to believe in them, research into their individual and social consequences, and whether there is any evidence about their relationship to extremist radicalization and violence. In other words, this chapter focuses on streams of research in a variety of fields that may be useful for terrorism scholars' thinking about how to approach the question of extremism and conspiracism in their own work. For instance, research has shown that conspiracy theories are very much intertwined with particular events in history,[1] have noticeable impact on health outcomes and sexual activity,[2] affects parental willingness to vaccinate their children as well as their overall views about climate change and environmentalism,[3] and, of course, has an impact on an individual's social and political engagement, including their willingness to vote, donate and volunteer.[4]

Researchers have also repeatedly noted the presence of conspiratorial thinking when it comes to radical and violent movements across the ideological spectrum, from far-right conspiracies about the Middle East[5] to the ways in which skinheads invoke a host of negative emotions, which may help explain why belief in one conspiracy theory stimulates belief in other conspiracy theories.'[23]

Some studies into motivational forces behind conspiratorial thinking also suggest that the need for uniqueness is an important contributing factor. As Imhoff and Lamberty note, 'for some people and under some circumstances, going along with the crowd may be unsatisfactory as it violates individuals' need for uniqueness.'[24] Imhoff and Lamberty found in their study that some believers in conspiracy theories are more likely to agree with theories that have 'an aura of exclusiveness' to them rather than ones that are held by many in the population. This argument was tested in a series of studies by Lantian and colleagues. They attempted to find evidence for the idea that people who believe in conspiracy theories are more likely to believe they hold some special or secret information. In a second study, they tested whether individuals with a higher need for uniqueness were more drawn to conspiratorial thinking than others. In two subsequent studies, they tested the causal relationship between the need for uniqueness and conspiratorial thinking. Their results confirmed many of their assumptions and hypotheses. As they note, they were able to demonstrate that the 'need for uniqueness could have a causal impact on conspiracy beliefs'.[25]

In addition to the link between conspiratorial thinking and high-anxiety situations and the need for uniqueness, researchers have also conducted studies on the importance of individual predisposition. As Joseph Uscinski and his colleagues note, belief in conspiracy theories depends on more than simply exposure to information. Two other factors are also important: 'the political cues associated with that information vis-à-vis each individual's political disposition and each individual's predisposition toward seeing the world in conspiratorial terms'.[26] In other words, these studies point to a fairly obvious observation that while information about world events or incidents may circulate, how this information is received, filtered and understood by observers depends on their personal and political dispositions.[27] As Uscinski and his colleagues point out, 'The varying strengths of conspiratorial predispositions explain why some people resist conspiracy theories and believe in few, while other people accept conspiratorial logic and believe in many. All else equal, the more predisposed people are toward conspiratorial thinking, the more likely they will be to accept a specific conspiracy theory when given an informational cue that makes conspiratorial logic explicit.'[28] Relatedly, much research suggests that 'belief in one conspiracy theory is an excellent predictor of belief in a different, unrelated conspiracy theory'.[29]

Other important studies that are relevant for researchers trying to understand the link between conspiratorial thinking and extremist violence look at the ways in which an individual's loss of control, real or perceived, may influence their attachment to conspiracy theories. As Imhoff and Lamberty point out, 'individuals who suffer from enduring, long-lasting deprivation of control over important life outcomes (i.e., unemployment, bad financial prospects, and interpersonal control) show a higher tendency to belief in conspiracies in general.'[30] When individuals feel like they have lost control over important aspects of their life, certain 'sense-making' processes may kick in, and conspiracy theories have a tendency, as noted above, to provide all-encompassing explanations during high-anxiety situations. As Van Prooijen notes, 'Taken together, these findings suggest a prominent role for general uncertainty about the self – such as about one's abilities, one's attitudes, one's social value, or whether one meets the expectations of the social world – in the psychology of conspiracy beliefs.'[31]

Another important factor contributing to whether individuals may adopt conspiratorial beliefs is social concern for other people. This set of social psychological research is, of course, relevant for scholars of jihadism, who repeatedly note their self-sacrificial concern for their jihadist in-group, or the 'global ummah'. Indeed, research suggests that 'the extent to which people connect their own identity to victimized or threatened others is relevant for belief in conspiracy theories'.[32] This partly explains why conspiratorial beliefs tend to be more prevalent in marginalized communities and extremist movements, which tend to foster a heightened sense of in-group identification.[33] Studies conducted by Agnieszka Golec de Zavala and her colleagues also discuss this notion of 'collective narcissism', which ties together in-group identification and a belief in the 'exaggerated greatness of the ingroup' with the tendency to believe in conspiracy theories about the out-group.[34] In other words, most of these studies suggest that the stronger one's ties are to an established in-group, the more likely individuals will be suspicious of and attach conspiratorial intentions to a 'threatening' out-group.

Conspiracy theories: The research on impacts

Unlike the psychological and social psychological research on causes, the academic literature on the impact of conspiratorial thinking is somewhat constrained to a few trends: the ways in which this kind of thinking produces stress and anxiety, the ways in which it decreases trust in science, knowledge and expertise, and a tendency for these worldviews to act as an extremism multiplier. As discussed above, conspiratorial thinking may arise when individuals find themselves in high-anxiety situations, but these worldviews not only fail to assuage these anxieties, but tend to make them more pronounced. However, these anxieties can be linked to an overall view that one holds the truth, is being persecuted by outside enemies, and that salvation exists at the end of this difficult road.

Research by Dounia Bouzar suggests that this mechanism can be emotionally reinforcing for many youth.[35] Bouzar's research suggests that jihadist recruiters used conspiracy-laden narratives to further break apart existent trust youth had in societal institutions, in their families and friends, as well as education they had received up to that point. It was not conspiracy theories alone which accomplished this, but it was an important element:

> In the first case, recruiters would initially share YouTube videos that would show the young person that all adults lie to them: this includes the food they eat, vaccines, medications, history, politics, etc. The next step is to send related links that show that these are not isolated lies. The secret societies, the Illuminati, funded by Israel, apparently want to keep science and liberty for themselves; they buy and control all governments.[36]

Bouzar's interview with a sixteen-year-old named Norah is also indicative of how conspiratorial worldviews produce in young people the sense that they are 'awakened' to the truth, and how outside forces will try to contain and control their newfound knowledge. As Norah says, 'We knew we couldn't talk on the phone … So do we take out the SIM card? Or even the battery? It was obvious: our enemies were everywhere. Since we knew the truth, we were constantly under surveillance. And the more we felt under surveillance, the stronger became our conviction of knowing the truth. I saw this as belonging to an authentic group, in which we were the most "awakened" ones. We were being tracked because they wanted us asleep and indoctrinated.'[37] Bouzar rightly adds that 'The conspiracy theory and the sense of being persecuted can take on a sacred connotation' and accelerate the process by which individuals come to distrust and dismiss all information coming from outside the trusted in-group.[38]

This is an important and quite distressing aspect of conspiratorial thinking. Much research has suggested that espousal of conspiracy theories has real societal impact, such as the rejection of science,[39] a decrease in an individual's willingness to vote,[40] as well as an increase in hostility and aggression.[41] Other studies even suggest that exposure to conspiracy theories does not even have to be sustained. As Van Der Linden notes, even 'briefly exposing the public to conspiratorial thoughts about a specific issue may even decrease general pro-social tendencies'.[42] Other research also suggests that misinformation persists even after corrected information is provided to individuals: 'the encoding of misinformation suggests that false facts persist even when exposure to misinformation is weak (with few repetitions), and when the correction to that misinformation is strong (with many repetitions).'[43] In some ways, then, conspiracies may work closely with our natural risk averseness, in that the mere knowledge of competing worldviews is enough for many individuals to steer clear of activities they deem 'not worth the risk'.

An important study by Bartlett and Miller also reinforces much of what has been discussed so far. They argue that conspiracy theories often function as an 'extremism multiplier'. Based on their study of fifty extremist groups from all sides of the ideological spectrum, they point out:

> While it is not possible to demonstrate direct causal links between conspiracy theories and extremism, our findings suggest that the acceptance of conspiracy theories in contexts of extremism often serves as a "radicalising multiplier", which feeds back into the ideologies, internal dynamics and psychological

processes of the group. They hold extremist groups together and push them in a more extreme and sometimes violent direction.[44]

They argue that this happens because conspiracy theories do three things:

1. Create demonologies of us versus them. It is possible that through this self-aggrandizing siege mentality, conspiracy theories also reinforce a process called group polarization;
2. Delegitimize outside voices by painting them as part of the conspiracy. This is why, as Bartlett and Miller note, 'one of the greatest threats to the cohesion of extremist groups is criticism from former members and friends and family of current members';[45]
3. Portray violence as either necessary or as an obligation to protect the in-group against everyone else. As Bartlett and Miller note, violence comes to be seen as necessary because 'the group is under attack; its goals are unattainable through peaceful means; or there is some sense of impending, apocalyptic doom and a response is needed urgently'.[46]

Not only do conspiracy theories contribute to the idea that violence is the only remaining option for survival, they also create the impression amongst members that they are an embattled minority, holding on to a vital truth that can save and salvage society, and that by lashing out against the powerful and the corrupt, they will be rewarded or remembered at some point in the future. As Bartlett and Miller note, 'it places emphasis on a small, committed, tight-knit group of revolutionaries as the central agents in a struggle conducted on behalf of many others.'[47] This seems to be true among conspiracy theorists across the ideological spectrum. As Benjamin Lee's study of conspiracy theories amongst the counter-jihadist movement showed, 'the Islamisation conspiracy theory claims that we are living through an Islamic takeover of the West' and that it is their job to bring this reality to the sleeping masses.[48] As the interview with Norah above also showed, the feeling that you hold on to some hidden truth, a truth that will benefit society because it will unveil powerful and malicious forces that secretly control our world, can be enormously galvanizing and emotionally invigorating.

Recommendations and gaps in the research

The question of what society, or perhaps even governments, should do about conspiracy theories has no easy answers. Some have argued that these fringe ideas are not worth confronting, that a noisy minority in society will always hold bizarre beliefs and it is best to simply ignore them. Others counter that these ideas, if left to fester, will only grow and will eventually have real impacts on our democratic

10 J. Bartlett and C. Miller, *The Power of Unreason*, p. 16.

11 J. Bartlett and C. Miller, *The Power of Unreason*, p. 5; see also, B. Lee, '"It's Not Paranoia When They Are Really out to Get You": The Role of Conspiracy Theories in the Context of Heightened Security', *Behavioral Sciences of Terrorism and Political Aggression*, vol. 9, no. 1, 2017, pp. 4–20.

12 J. Pasek et al., 'What Motivates a Conspiracy Theory? Birther Beliefs, Partisanship, Liberal-Conservative Ideology, and Anti-Black Attitudes', *Electoral Studies*, vol. 40, 2014, pp. 482–489.

13 A. Amarasingam, 'Baracknophobia and the Paranoid Style: Visions of Obama as the AntiChrist on the World Wide Web', in *Network Apocalypse: Visions of the End in an Age of Internet Media*, Sheffield: Sheffield Phoenix Press, 2011, pp. 96–123.

14 C. Sunstein and A. Vermeule, 'Conspiracy Theories: Causes and Cures', *The Journal of Political Philosophy*, vol. 17, no. 2, 2009, pp. 202–227.

15 C. Sunstein and A. Vermeule, 'Conspiracy Theories', pp. 211–212.

16 C. Sunstein and A. Vermeule, 'Conspiracy Theories', p. 217.

17 M. Grzesiak-Feldman, 'The Effect of High-Anxiety Situations on Conspiracy Thinking', *Current Psychology*, vol. 32, 2013, pp. 100–118; see also, J. Parish, 'The Age of Anxiety', in J. Parish and M. Parker (ed.), *The Age of Anxiety: Conspiracy Theory and the Human Sciences*, Oxford: Blackwell Publishers, 2001, pp. 1–16.

18 W. Bergman, 'Anti-Semitic Attitudes in Europe: A Comparative Perspective', *Journal of Social Issues*, vol. 64, 2008, pp. 343–362; J. Byford and M. Billig, 'The Emergence of Anti-Semitic Conspiracy Theories in Yugoslavia During the War with NATO', *Patterns of Prejudices*, vol. 35, 2001, pp. 50–63.

19 J. W. Van Prooijen and K. Douglas, 'Conspiracy Theories as Part of History: The Role of Societal Crisis Situations', *Memory Studies*, vol. 10, no. 3, 2017, pp. 323–333.

20 C. McCauley and S. Jacques, 'The Popularity of Conspiracy Theories of Presidential Assassination: A Bayesian Analysis', *Journal of Personality and Social Psychology*, vol. 37, 1979, pp. 637–644.

21 R. A. LeBoeuf and M. I. Norton, 'Consequence-Cause Matching: Looking to the Consequences of Events to Infer Their Causes', *Journal of Consumer Research*, vol. 39, 2012, pp. 128–141.

22 J. W. Van Prooijen and E. Van Dijk, 'When Consequence Size Predicts Belief in Conspiracy Theories: The Moderating Role of Perspective Taking', *Journal of Experimental Social Psychology*, vol. 55, 2014, pp. 63–73; M. Abalakina-Paap et al., 'Beliefs in Conspiracies', *Political Psychology*, vol. 20, no. 3, 1999, p. 644.

23 J. W. Van Prooijen and K. Douglas, 'Conspiracy Theories as Part of History', pp. 328–329.

24 R. Imhoff and P. K. Lamberty, 'Too Special to be Duped: Need for Uniqueness Motivates Conspiracy Beliefs', *European Journal of Social Psychology*, vol. 47, 2016, p. 725; see also R. Imhoff and H. P. Erb, 'What Motivates Nonconformity? Uniqueness Seeking Blocks Majority Influence', *Personality and Social Psychology Bulletin*, vol. 35, 2009, pp. 309–320.

25 A. Lantain et al., '"I Know Things They Don't Know": The Role of Need for Uniqueness in Belief in Conspiracy Theories', *Social Psychology*, vol. 48, no. 3, 2017, p. 168.

26 J. E. Uscinski, C. Klofstad, and M. D. Atkinson, 'What Drives Conspiratorial Beliefs?' p. 57.

27 A. Berinsky, 'Rumors and Health Care Reform: Experiments in Political Misinformation', *British Journal of Political Science*, vol. 47, no. 2, 2015, pp. 241–262; J. Pasek et al., 'What Motivates a Conspiracy Theory?'.

28 J. E. Uscinski, C. Klofstad and M. D. Atkinson, 'What Drives Conspiratorial Beliefs?' p. 60.

29 J. W. Van Prooijen, 'Sometimes Inclusion Breeds Suspicion: Self-Uncertainty and Belongingness Predict Belief in Conspiracy Theories', *European Journal of Social Psychology*, vol. 46, 2015, p. 267; See also: T. Goertzel, 'Belief in Conspiracy Theories', *Political Psychology*, vol. 15, 1994, pp. 733–744.

30 R. Imhoff and P. K. Lamberty, 'Too Special to be Duped', p. 724.

31 J. W. Van Prooijen, 'Sometimes Inclusion Breeds Suspicion', p. 268.

32 J. W. Van Prooijen, 'Sometimes Inclusion Breeds Suspicion', p. 268.

33 P. A. Turner, *I Heard It through the Grapevine: Rumor in African-American Culture*, Berkeley: University of California Press, 1993; see also J. W. Van Prooijen and E. Van Dijk, 'When Consequence Size Predicts Belief in Conspiracy Theories'.

34 A. Golec De Zavala and A. Cichocka, 'Collective Narcissism and Anti-Semitism in Poland', *Group Processes and Intergroup Relations*, vol. 15, no. 2, 2012, p. 213.

35 D. Bouzar, 'A Novel Motivation-Based Conceptual Framework for Disengagement and Deradicalization Programs', *Sociology and Anthropology*, vol. 5, no. 8, 2017, p. 603.

36 D. Bouzar, 'A Novel Motivation-Based Conceptual Framework for Disengagement and Deradicalization Programs', p. 603.

37 D. Bouzar, 'A Novel Motivation-Based Conceptual Framework for Disengagement and Deradicalization Programs', p. 604.

38 D. Bouzar, 'A Novel Motivation-Based Conceptual Framework for Disengagement and Deradicalization Programs', p. 604.

39 S. Lewandowsky, K. Oberauer, and G.E. Gignac, 'NASA Faked the Moonlanding – Therefore, (climate) Science is a Hoax: An Anatomy of the Motivated Rejection of Science', *Psychological Science*, vol. 24, 2013, pp. 622–633.

40 D. Jolley and K. Douglas, 'The Social Consequences of Conspiracism: Exposure to Conspiracy Theories Decreases Intentions to Engage in Politics and to Reduce One's Carbon Footprint', *British Journal of Psychology*, vol. 105, 2014, pp. 35–56.

41 Abalakina-Paap et al., 'Beliefs in Conspiracies'.

42 S. Van Der Linden, 'The Conspiracy-Effect: Exposure to Conspiracy Theories (about Global Warming) Decreases Pro-Social Behavior and Science Acceptance', *Personality and Individual Differences*, vol. 87, 2015, p. 173.

43 K. L. Einstein and D. M. Glick, 'Do I Think BLS Data are BS? The Consequences of Conspiracy Theories', *Political Behavior*, vol. 37, 2015, p. 682; see also U. K. H. Ecker et al., 'Correcting False Information in Memory: Manipulating the Strength of Misinformation Encoding and its Retraction', *Psychonomic Bulletin and Review*, vol. 18, no. 3, 2011, pp. 570–578.

44 J. Bartlett and C. Miller, *The Power of Unreason*, pp. 4–5.

45 J. Bartlett and C. Miller, *The Power of Unreason*, p. 26.

46 J. Bartlett and C. Miller, *The Power of Unreason*, p. 29.

47 J. Bartlett and C. Miller, *The Power of Unreason*, p. 30.

48 B. Lee, 'It's Not Paranoia When They Are Really Out to Get You', p. 4.

49 Kou, Yubo, Xinning Gui, Yunan Chen, and Kathleen Pine, 'Conspiracy Talk on Social Media', *PACM on Human-Computer Interaction*, vol. 1, no. 2, 2017.

50 C. Sunstein and A. Vermeule, 'Conspiracy Theories: Causes and Cures', pp. 219–220.

51 J. Bartlett and C. Miller, *The Power of Unreason*, p. 37.

52 J. Bartlett and C. Miller, *The Power of Unreason*, pp. 39–40.

Recommended Readings

Amarasingam, A., 'Baracknophobia and the Paranoid Style: Visions of Obama as the AntiChrist on the World Wide Web', in *Network Apocalypse: Visions of the End in an Age of Internet Media*, Sheffield: Sheffield Phoenix Press, 2011, pp. 96–123.

Barkun, M., *A Culture of Conspiracy* (2nd ed.), Berkeley: University of California Press, 2013.

Bartlett, J. and C. Miller, *The Power of Unreason: Conspiracy Theories, Extremism and Counter-Terrorism*, London: Demos Report, 2010, p. 16.

Bergman, W., 'Anti-Semitic Attitudes in Europe: A Comparative Perspective', *Journal of Social Issues*, vol. 64, 2008, pp. 343–362.

Berlet, C. and M. Lyons, *Right-Wing Populism in America: Too Close for Comfort*, New York: Guilford, 2000.

Bogart, L. M. and S. Thorburn, 'Are HIV/AIDS Conspiracy Beliefs a Barrier to HIV Prevention among African Americans?' *JAIDS: Journal of Acquired Immune Deficiency Syndromes*, vol. 38, 2005, pp. 213–218.

Brotherton, R., *Suspicious Minds: Why We Believe Conspiracy Theories*, New York: Bloomsbury, 2016.

Cowan, D. E., 'Confronting the Failed Failure: Y2K and Evangelical Eschatology in Light of the Passed Millennium', *Nova Religio*, vol. 7, 2003, pp. 71–85.

Durham, M., 'The American Far Right and 9/11', *Terrorism and Political Violence*, vol. 15, no. 2, 2014, pp. 96–111.

Fekete, L., 'The Muslim Conspiracy Theory and the Oslo Massacre', *Race and Class*, vol. 53, no. 3, 2011, pp. 30–47.

Fenster, M., *Conspiracy Theories: Secrecy and Power in American Culture*, Minneapolis: University of Minnesota Press, 2008.

Goertzel, T., 'Belief in Conspiracy Theories', *Political Psychology*, vol. 15, 1994, pp. 733–744.

Goldberg, R. A., *Enemies Within: The Culture of Conspiracy in Modern America*, New Haven: Yale University Press, 2001.

Golec De Zavala, A., and A. Cichocka, 'Collective Narcissism and Anti-Semitism in Poland', *Group Processes and Intergroup Relations*, vol. 15, no. 2, 2012, p. 213.

Grzesiak-Feldman, M., 'The Effect of High-Anxiety Situations on Conspiracy Thinking', *Current Psychology*, vol. 32, 2013, pp. 100–118.

Hofstadter, R., *The Paranoid Style in American Politics and Other Essays*, New York: Knopf, 1966.

Jolley, D. and K. Douglas, 'The Social Consequences of Conspiracism: Exposure to Conspiracy Theories Decreases Intentions to Engage in Politics and to Reduce One's Carbon Footprint', *British Journal of Psychology*, vol. 105, 2014, pp. 35–56.

Imhoff, R. and P. K. Lamberty, 'Too Special to Be Duped: Need for Uniqueness Motivates Conspiracy Beliefs', *European Journal of Social Psychology*, vol. 47, 2016, p. 725.

LeBoeuf, R. A. and M. I. Norton, 'Consequence-Cause Matching: Looking to the Consequences of Events to Infer Their Causes', *Journal of Consumer Research*, vol. 39, 2012, pp. 128–141.

McCauley, C. and S. Jacques, 'The Popularity of Conspiracy Theories of Presidential Assassination: A Bayesian Analysis', *Journal of Personality and Social Psychology*, vol. 37, 1979, pp. 637–644.

Mole, P., '9/11 Conspiracy Theories: The 9/11 Truth Movement in Perspective', *Skeptic*, vol. 12, 2006, pp. 30–42.

Parish, J., 'The Age of Anxiety', in J. Parish and M. Parker (ed.), *The Age of Anxiety: Conspiracy Theory and the Human Sciences*, Oxford, Blackwell Publishers, 2001, pp. 1–16.

Pitcavage, M., 'Camouflage and Conspiracy: The Militia Movement From Ruby Ridge to Y2K', *American Behavioral Scientist*, vol. 44, no. 6, 2001, pp. 957–981.

Pollard, J., 'Skinhead Culture: The Ideologies, Mythologies, Religions and Conspiracy Theories of Racist Skinheads', *Patterns of Prejudice*, vol. 50, no. 4–5, 2016, pp. 398–419.

Sunstein, C. and A. Vermeule, 'Conspiracy Theories: Causes and Cures', *The Journal of Political Philosophy*, vol. 17, no. 2, 2009, pp. 202–227.

Turner, P. A., *I Heard It through the Grapevine: Rumor in African-American Culture*, Berkeley: University of California Press, 1993.

Uscinski, J. E., C. Klofstad and M. D. Atkinson, 'What Drives Conspiratorial Beliefs? The Role of Informational Cues and Predispositions', *Political Research Quarterly*, vol. 69, no. 1, 2016, pp. 57–71.

Van Prooijen, J. W. and K. Douglas, 'Conspiracy Theories as Part of History: The Role of Societal Crisis Situations', *Memory Studies*, vol. 10, no. 3, 2017, pp. 323–333.

Walker, J., *The United States of Conspiracy: A Conspiracy Theory*, New York: Harper Perennial, 2014.

Wiktorowicz, Q., *Radical Islam Rising*, Lanham: Rowman & Littlefield, 2005, p. 48.

Wood, M. J., K. Douglas, and R. M. Sutton, 'Dead or Alive: Beliefs in Contradictory Conspiracy Theories', *Social Psychological and Personality Science*, vol. 3, 2012, pp. 767–773.

5 THE INTERNATIONAL CONTEXT OF UK RADICALIZATION TRENDS: DEVELOPMENTS ABROAD THAT INSPIRE TERRORISM WITHIN THE UK

Petter Nesser

Introduction

'The current threat level for international terrorism in the UK is SEVERE', one can read from MI5's web portal.[1] In October 2017 the agency's director Andrew Parker spoke to British media about a 'dramatic upshift' in the level of jihadi terrorist plotting in Britain. He described the threat as 'multi-dimensional, evolving rapidly and operating at a scale and pace we have not seen before'.[2] He said terrorists targeting the UK were directed from within the country and abroad, that they employ diverse tactics and weapons, and comprise people of 'all ages, gender and backgrounds' united by 'toxic ideology'.

Parker's statements came after a year marked by three lethal attacks at Westminster, London Bridge, and the suicide bombing at an arena in Manchester. The attacks claimed thirty-six lives and injured well over 600. There was also a failed attempt to bomb a tube train at Parsons Green (which injured thirty people), and multiple thwarted plots attributed to transnational Islamist militants (jihadis). The MI5 director added that Britain's growing security service had foiled seven attack plots since April 2017 and twenty plots since 2013.

The severely amplified threat to the UK is part of an 'IS-effect' on European jihadism.[3] Since the announcement of the 'Caliphate' in the summer of 2014, there has been an escalation of attack plots linked to the Islamic State across Western Europe. The many plots and attacks have generated debates over why Europeans join the Islamic State and attack their home countries. These have mostly revolved around domestic issues in the countries under attack, such as immigration and integration.

However, the transnational terrorist threat from Al-Qaeda and the Islamic State in Europe is shaped by an intricate interplay between developments inside European countries and events abroad – particularly in conflict zones in the Muslim world. Through particular dynamics, which the author will discuss in the following, developments in the Muslim world influence the scope and nature of the threat in our region to a larger degree than domestic European affairs.

Based on evidence presented in Nesser (2018), the author argues that three main factors shape the jihadi threat to any given European country: (1) Interventions, (2) Networks and (3) Entrepreneurs. The chapter shall come back to what each factor entails and how they relate to one another, before then applying this framework to assess how the threat to the UK is influenced by developments abroad.

First, however, the author will describe how the rise of the Islamic State has affected the threat to Europe, and problematize the tendency to address terrorist cells merely as products of failed integration.

The IS effect (2014–2018)

Europe has witnessed an escalating threat from jihadi terrorism since the establishment of the Islamic State in 2014. The fast-rising threat has, at least for now, overwhelmed European security services. Never before have there been so many jihadi terrorist plots in Europe as in the period between 2014 and 2018. Never before have so many plots gone undetected and resulted in attacks. Never before have so many Europeans been killed by attacks. More people have died from this type of terrorism in Europe since the rise of the Islamic State than in the previous twenty years.[4]

Today's threat is dominated by the Islamic State. Most plots can be traced in some way or another to the group and its networks, and it has outcompeted Al-Qaeda as the main protagonist of jihadism in the region. The immediate reasons for the IS-effect are three-fold.

First, there have, in a very short time, become many more potential threats to monitor. This is linked to the large number of Europeans (4,000–7,000) who travelled to Syria as foreign fighters, most of them joining the Islamic State.[5] Since the rise of IS, the majority of plots in Europe have involved either returned foreign fighters, or extremists who never made it to Syria, but receive online instructions from IS operatives (oftentimes foreign fighters from the country under attack). The strength and nature of links from plotters to IS networks have varied, but as the author shall come back to, plots without any network contacts are very rare.[6]

Second, jihadi terrorists targeting Europe have modified their tactics and weapons. A higher proportion of attacks have involved simple weapons such as cars and knives rather than bombs, and almost half of the terrorist plots have involved single actors, rather than a group. Single actors with simple weapons are notoriously difficult to detect and stop. Adding to this, terrorists increasingly communicate via encrypted apps, which are challenging for security services to monitor.

A third factor contributing to the IS-effect is the exploitation of refugee streams to smuggle terrorists. The network behind the November 2015 Paris attacks and the 2016 attacks in Brussels (which also had links to the UK) transported several operatives from Syria to Europe disguised as refugees.[7]

Much of the debate concerning the escalating threat has revolved around socio-economic factors and integration. The focus on the immigrant-dominated suburb of Molenbeek after the attacks in Paris and Brussels is a case in point.[8] Because several of the attackers had lived in Molenbeek, it was declared Europe's 'terrorist capital' by media and experts. Investigations revealed, however, that the network behind the attacks and the terrorists' motives extended far beyond this suburb. It was a transnational plot involving cooperation between militants across Europe and links to the Islamic State in Syria and Iraq.

True, there are links between immigration and European jihadism. Equally true, there are links between socio-economic hardships and European jihadism.[9] Many militant Islamists who established networks for Al-Qaeda in Europe during the 1990s were refugees. And, as noted, in the last few years there have been examples of terrorists disguised as refugees. As for socio-economic factors, studies indicate overrepresentation of underprivileged and underemployed people from immigrant backgrounds among European jihadis. There is also overrepresentation of people with criminal records.[10]

At the same time, socio-economic factors and immigration are poor predictors of the emergence of jihadi cells in Europe. As reflected in MI5 chief Andrew Parker's statement that the UK threat involves 'all ages, gender and backgrounds', there is no fixed profile of the terrorists targeting Europe. While a majority may be underprivileged and underemployed, many are middle class, students and workers, and some are even from relatively wealthy backgrounds. Similarly, while many terrorists are young men in their twenties, they also include teenagers, people approaching their fifties, women and converts. For example, in April 2017, an all-female terrorist cell was disrupted in the UK, plotting knife attacks in London. The cell was composed of a mother, her daughter and their friend. The daughter was believed to be the main driving force and she had reportedly been in contact with British IS members online.[11]

It is also hard to see a systematic relationship between immigration and integration policy and threat levels in European countries. For example, if these were key factors, countries such as Sweden and Italy, with major challenges related to immigration and integration, would have experienced more plots and attacks than they do. Also, if integration policies were a main determinant, countries pursuing opposite policies such as Britain and France (multi-culturalism vs. assimilation) would face different threat levels. Yet, they do not. Britain and France face very similar threat levels – the highest in Europe.

If we look at what the terrorists say and do and examine the chains of events that bring about attack cells, it becomes clear that the main determinants of the jihadi threat to Europe can be traced to conflict zones in the Muslim world – rather than internal European affairs.

Interventions matter

When jihadis justify attacks in Europe, they stress two main factors: Western military interventions in Muslim countries and 'insults' against the Prophet Muhammad. Some also point to the ban on veils, arrests of Muslims (jihadis) and European support for Israel. Moreover, the colonial history of European countries is a recurrent topic. The interventions seem, however, to be at the top of the list of triggers. Statistics on jihadi plots in Europe since the 1990s show that attack activity increases and major attacks have been launched following Western military interventions in Muslim countries.

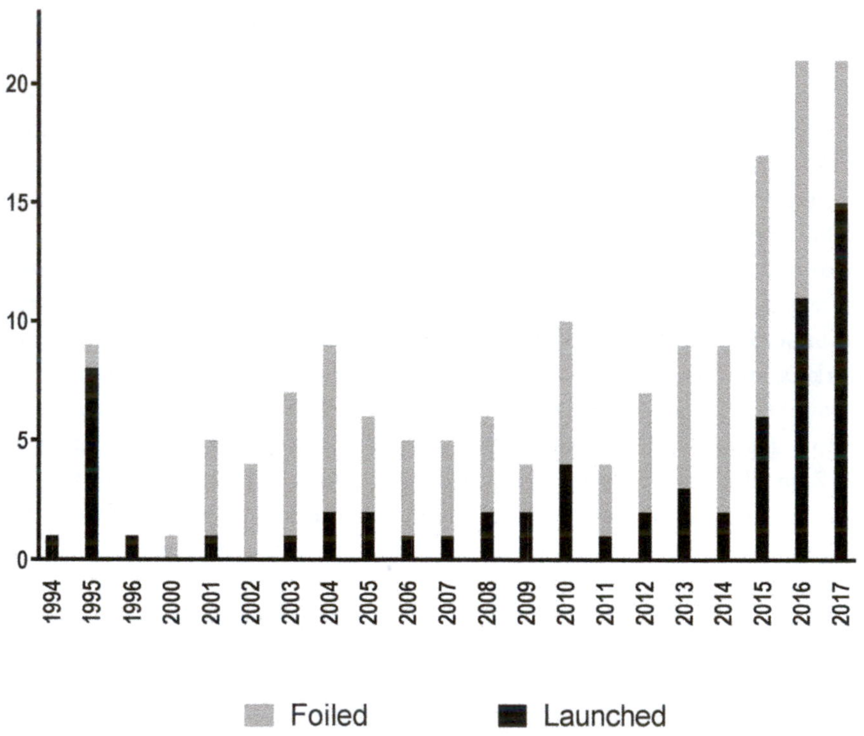

WELL-DOCUMENTED JIHADI TERRORIST PLOTS IN EUROPE 1994–2018. Graph based on open source data gathered at the Norwegian Defence Research Establishment (FFI) on jihadi terrorist plots in Western Europe. The dataset is maintained by the author and Anne Stenersen. It was last updated in December 2018.

The first increase came in the mid-1990s when France was accused of supporting the military regime against the Islamists during the Algerian civil war. The Al-Qaeda-linked Algerian terrorist group GIA declared war on France and executed a string of attacks in the country.

The next increase came in the mid-2000s following the US-led invasion and occupation of Iraq in 2003. Jihadis increasingly targeted European countries that were part of the invasion force and major attacks were launched: a Moroccan-based Al-Qaeda cell bombed commuter trains in Spain (2004) and a British-based Al-Qaeda cell bombed the London tube and a bus (2005).

Multiple attack plots were thwarted across Europe in the years following the invasion of Iraq. Several of the potentially most lethal plots targeted the UK, such as the 2004 fertilizer bomb plot, the 2006 plan to bomb trans-Atlantic passenger jets departing from Britain and the plot to bomb nightclubs in London linked to the Islamic State's forerunner, Al-Qaeda in Iraq (AQI).

The third increase in attack activity came with the establishment of the Islamic State and the launch of the anti-IS coalition in 2014. IS leaders swore to exact revenge against countries attacking the group, and IS terrorists have shouted 'this is for Syria' when they strike in Europe.

The geographical distribution of terrorist plots in Europe over time further shows that countries with heaviest military involvement in the Muslim world – France and the UK – are most targeted. Conversely, countries with less military involvement in Muslim countries such as Italy and Sweden are less targeted. This is despite the fact that all four of these countries experience high levels of Muslim immigration and that all of them face major challenges with regard to integration.

Another sign that military interventions motivate the terrorists is that many plots target military personnel, symbols or installations. Both Al-Qaeda and IS linked terrorists have sought military targets in the UK. Examples include (among others) the 2013 Lee Rigby murder, a 2014 plot by the medical student Tarik Hassane ('the surgeon') and fellow student Suhaib Majeed (they were reportedly instructed by IS via social media) to attack police stations and the Parachute Regiment Territorial Army Barracks at White City,[12] and a 2015 copycat plan by IS supporter and delivery driver for a pharmaceutical firm, Junead Khan (also reported to have communicated with British IS members via encrypted social media), to kill a soldier with a knife at a military base in East Anglia 'Lee Rigby-style'.[13]

Interventions surely trigger plots, but they can only partially explain the threat to European countries. Most European Muslims condemn Western interventions in Muslim countries, but very few resort to terrorism. Additionally, we have seen plots and attacks in countries with a relatively low-profile military contribution to the anti-IS coalition, for example Finland.

Networks matter more

Nearly all Al-Qaeda and IS cells targeting Europe can be traced to the networks that were established in the region from the early 1990s. These networks were set up by veteran Arab foreign fighters from the 1980s Afghan jihad. They had an international focus and aimed to support jihadis fighting regimes in the Muslim world with money and weapons, as well as fighters.

The UK became the nerve centre for the networks because the most important leaders and ideologues settled there, but the networks spread out transnationally across European countries. They grew larger and stronger through the recruitment of young European Muslims and cooperation with jihadi organizations in Algeria, Bosnia, Afghanistan, Pakistan, Somalia, Iraq, Syria and Libya.

When Al-Qaeda declared 'global jihad'[14] in 1998 the European jihadi networks became an important weapon against the United States' European allies. European jihadis, who travelled as foreign fighters to conflict zones, were recruited and trained by Al-Qaeda to execute attacks in their home countries. For this reason, the countries in Europe with most foreign fighters have been most targeted.

The threat to the UK strongly increased in the mid-2000s when Al-Qaeda in Afghanistan and Pakistan recruited British-Pakistani foreign fighters as terrorists. Another example is when Sweden experienced its first jihadi suicide bombing in 2010 after militants with long-time residence in Sweden rose to leadership positions in IS's forerunner, Al-Qaeda in Iraq.

The pattern has repeated itself with the Islamic State. A crucial reason why France and Britain have experienced so many IS plots is that French and British foreign fighters became influential within the group's section for international operations.[15] The wave of IS linked terrorism in Europe involves a new generation of European jihadis. This generation emanated from within Al-Qaeda's historical networks in the region, and particularly from the UK-based Al-Muhajiroun movement.

After being banned in the UK, this movement re-appeared under the name Islam4UK and branched out across Europe, establishing Sharia4Belgium, Sharia4Holland, Sharia4Spain, Sharia4Denmark (Kaldet til Islam), Sharia4Finland, Sharia4Italy, Sharia4France (Forsane Alizza), Millatu Ibrahim (Germany) and The Prophet's Umma (Norway).[16] Together, these Al-Muhajiroun spin-offs played a key role in mobilizing European foreign fighters for Syria and put them in touch with Al-Qaeda-affiliated militias, such as Jabhat al-Nusra.

When the Islamic State emerged as the strongest jihadi actor in Syria most of these European recruits sided with the 'Caliphate' rather than Al-Qaeda. The exact reasons why the Europeans preferred the Islamic State are unknown, but surely one significant factor is that the leader of the Islam4/Sharia4 movement, Anjem Choudary, announced his support for the 'Caliph', al-Baghdadi.

Choudary was sentenced to ten years in prison for supporting the Islamic State in 2016, but before that he was able to tour Europe and contribute to mobilizing foreign fighter networks, thereby elevating the threat in the region. Choudary played a significant role in establishing branches of his movement in Norway and Finland. These two countries, which hardly anyone thinks of as incubators of jihadism, ended up producing some ninety and eighty foreign fighters to Syria respectively, which are among the largest contingents in Europe (adjusted for general and Muslim population figures). There were, of course, multiple reasons why Norwegians and Fins joined the jihad in Syria, but the role of network builders like Choudary can hardly be overstated.

Entrepreneurs matter most

There is a recurring pattern in how people join jihadi networks in Europe, which points to the significance of ideology and the role of *entrepreneurs*, who are linked to groups abroad, in shaping the terrorists' actions. The entrepreneurs are the ones who build and direct networks and cells and recruit members. They are more resourceful, political and ideological than the people they recruit. They are experienced religious-political activists and most of them have spent time in jihadi conflict theatres. The entrepreneurs function as the link between networks and cells within Europe and groups abroad, thereby internationalizing the process through which attack plots occur.

Among the recruits, the *misfits* are characterized by personal grievance and problems. Here we find youths who have drifted into crime, substance abuse and that have become outsiders in society for different reasons. They are attracted by entrepreneurs who can offer a fresh start, community, spirituality and a political cause to fight for.

The *drifters* are random recruits - in this category we find underprivileged people, but also resourceful ones. It is mainly friendship, kinship or loyalty to someone inside networks that pull them inside.

The entrepreneurs are the minority, but they are also the ones who make things happen. Because they act as agents for jihadis in conflict zones threat patterns in Europe become more influenced by Muslim world events than most realize.

Due to jihadism's basis in an extreme form of Islam the terrorists must obtain approval from someone they look upon as a religious authority (an entrepreneur or ideologue) before launching an attack. This requires interaction with other extremists – within networks. Today, new, encrypted communication apps have made it possible for IS entrepreneurs to recruit online – to an extent that Al-Qaeda was never able to.[17]

IS's solo-terrorists in Europe are therefore rarely 'lone wolves'. Investigations reveal that they interact with networks physically and virtually. A case in point is that of the British-Libyan solo-terrorist who bombed the Ariana Grande concert in Manchester. Prior to the attack the perpetrator consulted with and received approval from an IS entrepreneur, probably a British foreign fighter, whom he addressed as a religious advisor (Sheikh).[18]

The UK has played a special role in European jihadism and has probably hosted more entrepreneurs than any other country in the region. Some, such as Abu Hamza al-Masri, Omar Bakri or his protégé Anjem Choudary, have functioned as ideologues and movement builders within the UK and Europe. Others, such as Abu Doha or Rashid Rauf, have organized networks of international terrorist cells for Al-Qaeda. In more recent times, Junaid Hussain and Raymond M. are reported to have sought to build attack cells targeting the UK on behalf of the Islamic State.[19]

Conclusion

Nowhere in Europe is jihadism more embedded than in Britain. The country has had more entrepreneurs and stronger networks than any other European country. The UK is the US' closest European ally and, alongside France, Europe's main contributor to military campaigns against Al-Qaeda and the Islamic State. Britain's colonial past is a visible theme in IS propaganda. Additionally, substantial immigration and challenges of integration imply no shortage of misfits and drifters for terrorist networks to enlist.

In the 1990s and 2000s, the UK was a hub for the mobilization of transnational jihadism in Europe and a transit point for foreign fighters joining jihadi groups in Muslim countries. With the invasion and occupation of Iraq, the UK became a target of priority for Al-Qaeda and likeminded movements and has remained so ever since. With the rise of the Islamic State and the UK's role in the fight against it, the threat has reached an unprecedented level.

The many plots and attacks fuel polarization over Muslim immigration across Europe and could in the worst case lead to political instability. It is, therefore, more important than ever to reduce the threat level. According to the framework presented here, this effort should primarily concentrate on entrepreneurs and networks, and on severing their connections (online and off-line) to foreign militant groups and would-be terrorists within Europe.

Longer prison sentences for entrepreneurs and a complete ban on any form of foreign fighting are probably the most effective measures to prevent the terrorist threat from growing further in the future. In addition to constraining future re-mobilizations it is necessary to increase efforts at de-radicalizing and reintegrating misfits and drifters who have come under the influence by extremist networks. Moreover, military interventions must avoid both harming civilians and taking the form of an invasion to the greatest extent possible. Only then will it be harder for entrepreneurs to convince recruits that there is a 'war on Islam'.

Better integration, increased social welfare benefits and reduction of socio-economic inequalities will not stop terrorist attacks in Europe. Yet, societies with functioning integration and just distribution produce fewer misfits for jihadis to recruit. Such societies will also be better equipped to deal with the effects of attacks.

Notes

1 MI5's website, January 2018, available here: https://www.mi5.gov.uk/threat-levels.

2 V. Dood, 'UK Facing Most Severe Terror Threat Ever, Warns MI5 Chief', *Guardian*, 17 October 2017, available here: http://www.theguardian.com/uk-news/2017/oct/17/uk-most-severe-terror-threat-ever-mi5-islamist.

3 For further explanation of what is meant by the 'IS-effect', consult P. Nesser, A. Stenersen, and E. Oftedal, 'Jihadi Terrorism in Europe: The IS-Effect', *Perspectives on Terrorism*, vol. 10, no. 6, 20 December, 2016, available here: http://www.terrorismanalysts.com/pt/index.php/pot/article/view/553. The article presents data on IS-related plots and attacks in Western Europe. It compares the modus operandi of plots in Europe in 2014–2016, with previous trends addressed in P. Nesser and A. Stenersen, 'The Modus Operandi of Jihadi Terrorists in Europe', *Perspectives on Terrorism*, vol. 8, no. 6, 2014, available here: http://www.terrorismanalysts.com/pt/index.php/pot/article/view/388/html.

4 Consult Nesser, Stenersen and Oftedal (2016) for data and statistics. We defined December 1994 as the starting point for jihadi terrorism in Europe, when the Al-Qaeda-affiliated Algerian terrorist group GIA hijacked an Air France jet in Algiers with the aim of crashing it into Paris. In the subsequent year the group launched a series of bombings in French cities.

5 For updated assessments of the European foreign fighters, consult e.g. Richard Barrett, 'Beyond the Caliphate: Foreign Fighters and the Threat of Returnees', *The Soufan Center*, October 2017, available here: http://thesoufancenter.org/wp-content/uploads/2017/11/Beyond-the-Caliphate-Foreign-Fighters-and-the-Threat-of-Returnees-TSC-Report-October-2017-v3.pdf., Thomas Renard and Rik Coolsaet, 'Returnees: Who Are They, Why Are They (Not) Coming Back and How Should We Deal with Them?: Assessing Policies on Returning Foreign Terrorist Fighters in Belgium, Germany, and the Netherlands', *Egmont Institute*, February 2018, available here: http://www.egmontinstitute.be/content/uploads/2018/02/egmont.papers.101_online_v1-3.pdf?type=pdf., and Pieter Van Ostaeyen and Guy Van Vlierden, 'The Role of Belgian Foreign Fighters in the Jihadification of the Syrian War from Plotting Early in 2011 to the Paris and Brussels Attacks', European Foundation for Democracy Counter Extremism Project, 2017, available here: http://europeandemocracy.eu/wp-content/uploads/2017/02/Belgian_fighters-DRAFT8-webversion.pdf.

6 The idea that terrorists can operate in complete isolation as 'lone wolves' has increasingly come under critique; for a recent contribution to debunking the lone wolf–myth, see e.g. Bart Schuurman et al., 'End of the Lone Wolf: The Typology That Should Not Have Been', *Studies in Conflict & Terrorism*, vol. 0, no. 0, 20 December, 2017, pp. 1–8, available here: https://doi.org/10.1080/1057610X.2017.1419554.

7 See Nesser, Stenersen and Oftedal and Anthony Faiola and Souad Mekhennet, 'Tracing the Path of Four Terrorists Sent to Europe by the Islamic State', *Washington Post*, 22 April 2016, available here: https://www.washingtonpost.com/world/national-security/how-europes-migrant-crisis-became-an-opportunity-for-isis/2016/04/21/ec8a7231-062d-4185-bb27-cc7295d35415_story.html.

8 P. Nesser, 'Molenbeek: One of Several Jihadi Hotspots in Europe', *Hurst Blog*, 19 November 2015, available here: http://www.hurstpublishers.com/molenbeek-one-of-several-jihadi-hotspots-in-europe/.

9 See e.g. T. Hegghammer, 'Revisiting the Poverty-terrorism Link in European Jihadism' (Society for Terrorism Research Annual Conference, Leiden, 8 November 2016), available here: http://hegghammer.com/_files/Hegghammer_-_poverty.pdf.

10 R. Basra and P. Neumann, 'Crime as Jihad: Developments in the Crime-Terror Nexus in Europe', *CTC Sentinel*, vol. 10, no. 9, 2017, pp. 1–6, available here: https://ctc.usma.edu/crime-as-jihad-developments-in-the-crime-terror-nexus-in-europe/ See also M. Hecker '137 Shades of Terrorism. French Jihadists Before the Courts', IFRI, Focus stratégique, No. 79 bis, April 2018, available here: https://www.ifri.org/en/publications/etudes-de-lifri/focus-strategique/137-shades-terrorism-french-jihadists-courts.

11 See e.g. N. Khomani, 'Members of All-Female Terror Cell Jailed over London Knife Plot', *Guardian*, 15 June 2018, available here http://www.theguardian.com/uk-news/2018/jun/15/all-female-terror-cell-rizlaine-boular-mina-dich-jailed-over-london-knife-plot. For a useful commentary on the role of women in IS attack activity see also Gartenstein-Ross, D., V. Hagerty and L. Macnair, 'The Emigrant Sisters Return: The Growing Role of the Islamic State's Women', *War on the Rocks*, 2 April 2018, available here: https://warontherocks.com/2018/04/the-emigrant-sisters-return-the-growing-role-of-the-islamic-states-women/.

12 R. Spillet and D. Gardham, 'Tarik Hassane and Suhaib Majeed Jailed for Life for ISIS-Funded Terror Plot' *Daily Mail Online*, 22 April 2016, available here: http://www.dailymail.co.uk/news/article-3553717/Tarik-Hassane-Turnup-Terror-Squad-jailed-life.html.

13 Press Association, 'Luton Delivery Driver Guilty of Planning Terror Attack on US Troops in Britain', *Guardian*, 1 April 2016, available here: http://www.theguardian.com/uk-news/2016/apr/01/luton-delivery-driver-junead-khan-guilty-planning-terror-attack-us-troops.

14 The declaration called for attacks against Americans and Jews, civilians as well as military personnel all over the world.

15 See e.g. K. Jackson and J-C. Brisard, 'The Islamic State's External Operations and the French-Belgian Nexus', CTC *Sentinel*, December 2016, available here: https://www.ctc.usma.edu/posts/the-islamic-states-external-operations-and-the-french-belgian-nexus. And N. Hamid, 'The British Hacker Who Became the Islamic State's Chief Terror Cybercoach: A Profile of Junaid Hussain', *CTC Sentinel*, April 2018, available here: https://ctc.usma.edu/british-hacker-became-islamic-states-chief-terror-cybercoach-profile-junaid-hussain/.

16 R. Pantucci, 'Al-Muhajiroun's European Recruiting Pipeline', *CTC Sentinel*, vol. 8, no. 8, 2015, pp. 21–24.

17 See e.g. D. Gartenstein-Ross and M. Blackman, 'ISIL's Virtual Planners: A Critical Terrorist Innovation', *War on the Rocks*, 4 January 2017, available here: https://warontherocks.com/2017/01/isils-virtual-planners-a-critical-terrorist-innovation/.

18 'Manchester Attack: Bomber "Received Permission" From ISIS in Syria and Recruiter in Dallas', *Newsweek*, 14 August 2017, available here: http://www.newsweek.com/manchester-attack-bomber-received-permission-isis-syria-recruiter-dallas-650300.

19 'Jihadist Who Left Manchester to Fight with Isis 'May Still Be Alive', *Guardian*, 26 September 2017, available here: https://www.theguardian.com/world/2017/sep/26/british-ally-of-jihadi-john-may-still-be-alive-raymond-matimba-raqqa.

Recommended Readings

Barrett, R., 'Beyond the Caliphate: Foreign Fighters and the Threat of Returnees', *The Soufan Center*, October 2017, available here: http://thesoufancenter.org/wp-content/uploads/2017/11/Beyond-the-Caliphate-Foreign-Fighters-and-the-Threat-of-Returnees-TSC-Report-October-2017-v3.pdf.

Basra, R. and P. Neumann, 'Crime as Jihad: Developments in the Crime-Terror Nexus in Europe', *CTC Sentinel*, vol. 10, no. 9, 2017, pp. 1–6, available here: https://ctc.usma.edu/crime-as-jihad-developments-in-the-crime-terror-nexus-in-europe/

Dood, V., 'UK Facing Most Severe Terror Threat Ever, Warns MI5 Chief', *The Guardian*, 17 October 2017, available here: http://www.theguardian.com/uk-news/2017/oct/17/uk-most-severe-terror-threat-ever-mi5-islamist.

Faiola, A. and S. Mekhennet, 'Tracing the Path of Four Terrorists Sent to Europe by the Islamic State', *Washington Post*, 22 April 2016, available here: https://www.washingtonpost.com/world/national-security/how-europes-migrant-crisis-became-an-opportunity-for-isis/2016/04/21/ec8a7231-062d-4185-bb27-cc7295d35415_story.html

Gartenstein-Ross, D. and M. Blackman, 'ISIL's Virtual Planners: A Critical Terrorist Innovation', *War on the Rocks*, 4 January 2017, available here: https://warontherocks.com/2017/01/isils-virtual-planners-a-critical-terrorist-innovation/.

Gartenstein-Ross, D., V. Hagerty, and L. Macnair 'The Emigrant Sisters Return: The Growing Role of the Islamic State's Women', *War on the Rocks*, 2 April 2018, available here: https://warontherocks.com/2018/04/the-emigrant-sisters-return-the-growing-role-of-the-islamic-states-women/.

Guardian, 'Luton Delivery Driver Guilty of Planning Terror Attack on US Troops in Britain', 1 April 2016, available here: http://www.theguardian.com/uk-news/2016/apr/01/luton-delivery-driver-junead-khan-guilty-planning-terror-attack-us-troops.

Hamid, N., 'The British Hacker Who Became the Islamic State's Chief Terror Cybercoach: A Profile of Junaid Hussain', *CTC Sentinel*, April 2018, available here: https://ctc.usma.edu/british-hacker-became-islamic-states-chief-terror-cybercoach-profile-junaid-hussain/.

Hecker, '137 Shades of Terrorism. French Jihadists Before the Courts', *IFRI Focus stratégique*, No. 79 bis, April 2018, available here: https://www.ifri.org/en/publications/etudes-de-lifri/focus-strategique/137-shades-terrorism-french-jihadists-courts.

Hegghammer, T., 'Revisiting the Poverty-Terrorism Link in European Jihadism' (Society for Terrorism Research Annual Conference, Leiden, 8 November 2016), available here: http://hegghammer.com/_files/Hegghammer_-_poverty.pdf.

Jackson, K. and J-C. Brisard, 'The Islamic State's External Operations and the French-Belgian Nexus', *CTC Sentinel*, December 2016, available here: https://www.ctc.usma.edu/posts/the-islamic-states-external-operations-and-the-french-belgian-nexus.

Khomami, N., 'Members of All-Female Terror Cell Jailed over London Knife Plot', *Guardian*, 15 June 2018, available here http://www.theguardian.com/uk-news/2018/jun/15/all-female-terror-cell-rizlaine-boular-mina-dich-jailed-over-london-knife-plot.

Moore, J., 'Manchester Attack: Bomber "Received Permission" From ISIS in Syria and Recruiter in Dallas', *Newsweek*, 14 August 2017, available here: http://www.newsweek.com/manchester-attack-bomber-received-permission-isis-syria-recruiter-dallas-650300.

Nesser, P. and A. Stenersen, 'The Modus Operandi of Jihadi Terrorists in Europe', *Perspectives on Terrorism*, vol. 8, no. 6, 2014, available here: http://www.terrorismanalysts.com/pt/index.php/pot/article/view/388/html.

Nesser, P., A. Stenersen and E. Oftedal, 'Jihadi Terrorism in Europe: The IS-Effect', *Perspectives on Terrorism*, vol. 10, no. 6, 2016, available here: http://www.terrorismanalysts.com/pt/index.php/pot/article/view/553/html

Nesser, P., *Islamist Terrorism in Europe*, Hurst: Oxford University Press, 2018 (2nd edition).

Nesser, P., 'Molenbeek: One of Several Jihadi Hotspots in Europe', *Hurst Blog* (blog), 19 November 2015, available here: http://www.hurstpublishers.com/molenbeek-one-of-several-jihadi-hotspots-in-europe/.

Neumann, P., *Radicalized: New Jihadists and the Threat to the West*, London and New York: I.B.Tauris, 2016.

Neumann, P., 'The Trouble with Radicalization', *International Affairs*, vol. 89, no. 4, July 1, 2013, pp. 873–893.

Pantucci, R., *'We Love Death as You Love Life': Britain's Suburban Terrorists*, London: Hurst & Company, 2015.

Pantucci, R., 'Al-Muhajiroun's European Recruiting Pipeline', *CTC Sentinel*, vol. 8, no. 8, 2015, pp. 21–24.

Ranstorp, M. (ed.), *Understanding Violent Radicalisation: Terrorist and Jihadist Movements in Europe*, London & New York: Routledge, 2010.

Reinares, F., *Al-Qaeda's Revenge: The 2004 Madrid Train Bombings*, New York: Columbia University Press, 2017.

Reinares, F., C. Garcia-Calvo, and Á. Vincente, 'Differential Association Explaining Jihadi Radicalization in Spain: A Quantitative Study', *CTC Sentinel*, vol. 10, no. 8, 2017, pp. 29–34, available here: https://ctc.usma.edu/differential-association-explaining-jihadi-radicalization-in-spain-a-quantitative-study/.

Renard, T., and Coolsaet, R. 'Returnees: Who Are They, Why Are They (Not) Coming Back and How Should We Deal with Them?: Assessing Policies on Returning Foreign Terrorist Fighters in Belgium, Germany, and the Netherlands', *Egmont Institute*, February 2018, available here: http://www.egmontinstitute.be/content/uploads/2018/02/egmont.papers.101_online_v1-3.pdf?type=pdf.

Schuurman, Bart et al., 'End of the Lone Wolf: The Typology That Should Not Have Been', *Studies in Conflict & Terrorism*, vol. 0, no. 0, 20 December 2017, pp. 1–8, available here: https://doi.org/10.1080/1057610X.2017.1419554.

Spillett, R. and D. Gardham, 'Tarik Hassane and Suhaib Majeed Jailed for Life for ISIS-Funded Terror Plot', *Mail Online*, 22 April 2016, available here: http://www.dailymail.co.uk/news/article-3553717/Tarik-Hassane-Turnup-Terror-Squad-jailed-life.html.

Steinberg, Guido W., *German Jihad: On the Internationalization of Islamist Terrorism*, New York: Columbia University Press, 2013.

Van Ostaeyen, P. and G. Van Vlierden, 'The Role of Belgian Foreign Fighters in the Jihadification of the Syrian War from Plotting Early in 2011 to the Paris and Brussels Attacks', *European Foundation for Democracy Counter Extremism Project*, 2017, available here: http://europeandemocracy.eu/wp-content/uploads/2017/02/Belgian_fighters-DRAFT8-webversion.pdf.

6 EVIDENCE FOR THE RELATIONSHIP BETWEEN NON-VIOLENT EXTREMISM AND VIOLENT RADICALIZATION: CONVEYOR BELT OR FIREWALL?

Emman El-Badawy

Introduction

In combating global terrorism, the advocacy and adoption of violence has historically been conceded as the primary threat, and a sufficient benchmark to determine degrees of extremism. Yet when developing a preventive response to terrorism, and when navigating motives in conflict zones, such as Syria, violence as a benchmark has proved inadequate – in both literature and practice. Instead, fixations on violence have increasingly shifted in favour of studying the milieu of ideas that accompany manifestations of extremist violence. Amidst this emerging trend, one debate overshadows all others: do political 'non-violent' Islamists – like the Muslim Brotherhood – discourage or prepare individuals for terrorism? Are 'non-violent' Islamists a firewall or a conveyor belt in radicalization? Whilst conveyor belt theorists argue that non-violent extremists are crucial enablers of terrorism and a precursor to violence, incubating religiously sanctioned intolerance that contributes to the justification for violent action,[1] firewall proponents insist that the doctrines and ideologies of violent and non-violent Islamists are radically different, and that the latter prevents otherwise vulnerable Muslims from descending down a path of terrorism.[2]

Shaping the discourse on the relationship between violent and non-violent extremist ideas, the conveyor belt–firewall dichotomy has left the study of radicalization and terrorism in a state of dispute. Regarding the relationship(s) between violent and non-violent radicalization, the reasons for such markedly disjointed scholarship is the consequence of too little evidence that can objectively trace the links and schisms between groups. Exacerbating the ambiguity in this debate is the inadequacy of working definitions and terminology. Where consensus has been reached, it has sought to distinguish tactics and methods from ideology and doctrine,[3] and mapped the interpersonal networks that exist across violent and non-violent movements.[4]

Contributions to the debate over the role non-violent ideas play in violent radicalization have varied widely according to whether emphasis is best placed on groups or individuals; and whether it is patterns of behaviour, or differences in ideology, that should inform categorization into violent or non-violent extremism.[5] Such variety in analytical frameworks, though not each exclusively distinct, has produced different assertions as to whether a relationship exists between violent radicalization and non-violent ideas.

Through a synthesis of relevant literature to date, this chapter challenges some developed habits in the discourse. In particular, it raises concerns of a tendency to interpret groups' attitudes towards violence through official rhetoric rather than sustained critical analyses of the shared intellectual and ideological resources and the fluidity of interpersonal networks between violent and non-violent groups. The long fixation on differing rhetoric between the leadership figures of violent and non-violent groups has resulted in the drawing of conclusions in favour of the firewall theory. Yet, little research acknowledges the motions at the peripheries, where individuals of non-violent groups too easily traverse into more explicitly violent factions of the Islamist movements. Research that traces the proximity of both the ideology and the networks is critical before attempting to draw conclusions on the relationship between violent and non-violent radicalization.

Behaviour versus ideology: A false dichotomy?

Where there has been sizeable consensus in the literature is on the value of distinguishing between a group's aims and objectives (typically timeless, consistent and ideologically determined) and the methods or tactics (practically determined but frequently justified through parameters dictated by ideological principles) used to achieve them. In this, views on the application of the doctrine of jihad are considered a key marker that separates the ideologies of so-called 'non-violent' Islamists and those of violent Islamists. When distinguishing between the Muslim Brotherhood (MB, Brotherhood) and Al-Qaeda, for example, experts have highlighted the MB's official position and its rejection of violent methods for the last three to four decades, and how the MB (and many affiliated public figures) immediately condemned the 9/11 attacks and Osama bin Laden's strategy. Brotherhood statements before and since then have denounced the legitimacy of terrorist acts, with rebuttals of Al-Qaeda violence driven from the group's own leadership and those associated with it.

Regarded as one of the Brotherhood's spiritual godfathers, Qatar-based Yusuf al-Qaradawi and his views, as published in his 2009 book titled *Fiqh ul-Jihad* (The Jurisprudence of Jihad), are frequently referenced as evidence the group is at odds with Al-Qaeda's methods. While Qaradawi upheld the spirit of jihad as an obligation, he ridiculed Al-Qaeda's 'mad declaration of war on the whole world'.[6] Similarly, analysts have noted the absence of the MB in the roster of suicide terror attacks for decades.[7] Due to such observations, a drive to distinguish between groups within the Islamist movement based on their advocacy for violence gained ground. In this framework, the likes of the Muslim Brotherhood, Hizb ut-Tahrir (HuT), Jamaat-e-Islami and their global affiliates became associated with 'non-violent' Islamism, while the likes of Al-Qaeda, Hezbollah, Hamas and organizations that maintained a militant capacity retained the 'violent Islamist' tag. Thus, tactics and violence, above all else, became the defining characteristic.

Such distinctions across groups, while instrumental in the designing of so-called *spectrums* of extremism versus 'moderation', have faced increased scrutiny. The period since 2011, marked by a series of events and developments that provided new opportunities for both violent and non-violent Islamists globally, has pressed the issue of whether non-violent Islamist activism can truly be regarded as a firewall to violent Islamist radicalization.[8]

Understanding the pressures in the UK requires knowledge of the major developments for Islamists groups internationally. The Middle East has proven to be the epicentre for highlighting the limitations of old binary narratives on Islamism, yet the implications have been felt far beyond; not least due to the coinciding of widespread and increased usage of social media platforms. The majority-Arab uprisings in 2011, mostly peaceful, was at first seen as a golden opportunity for Islamists prepared to work within existing political systems, and a major blow to violent Islamist terrorism in the form of Al-Qaeda. Political destabilization following the uprisings saw sudden formations of new (formerly apolitical) salafist groups establish political parties that challenged the monopoly of traditional Islamist actors in formal politics. Traditional Islamist opposition groups also saw demonstrable gains,[9] with Rachid Ghannouchi of the Islamist party Ennahda swiftly elected in Tunisia, and Mohammed Morsi of the Muslim Brotherhood's Freedom and Justice Party assuming power in Egypt.

Yet the eventual ousting of Islamists from government in Egypt by 2013, the eruption of civil war in Syria and the rise of Islamic State in Iraq and Syria (ISIS) exposed the inadequacy of spectrums of Islamism that distinguish between 'non-violent moderates' and 'violent extremists'. In the UK, the conflict in Syria attracted over 800 British fighters.[10] Galvanized by ISIS's proclamation of a Caliphate in 2014, many of these British jihadis were not new to the intelligence services, and were in fact either vocally prominent proponents of Islamist objectives well before 2014, or came into contact with pre-existing networks of influencers from both the Islamist and jihadist circles known in the UK.[11]

From 2013, the 'golden opportunity' for 'non-violent' Islamists was officially over, marked by the removal of Islamist Egyptian President Morsi, and the subsequent outlawing of the MB. The change in tide sent shockwaves through the group and deepened internal rivalries and generational divisions, with an empowered youthful membership calling to question the group's principle of non-violence during the days of clashes with the Egyptian military.[12] The failed Islamist project in Tunisia, following a showdown between Tunisia's secularists and Ghannouchi's Islamist party, proved a significant setback for non-violent factions of the global Islamist movement. In both cases, accusations were made that while in power, the Muslim Brotherhood and Ennahda glorified or turned a blind eye to radicalization taking place, as Islamist violence in Egypt's Sinai escalated, and Tunisia proved the most prominent country in the world for numbers of foreign fighters travelling to ISIS in Syria and Iraq.[13] The so-called 'Gulf crisis', which has largely centred around whether or not the MB should be designated a global terrorist organization, has deeply divided the political and academic communities, and raised the urgency of determining the absolutism of non-violence in the context of Islamism more broadly.

At the heart of this divergence in opinion has been the challenge of knowing definitively if so-called non-violent Islamist groups mean what they say regarding moderation towards violence. The tendency in the literature to create the category of 'non-violent' Islamists has been a response to the indisputable variance in behaviour of groups across the global Islamist movement. Yet, proponents of the 'non-violent' category typically regard tactics as distinguishable from the ideology – in other words, a detail drawn from the practical, not theological or philosophical, realm of decision making.

Yet for Islamist groups, Islam's doctrinal texts are instructive in determining behaviour and conduct: whether on the battlefield or at the ballot box. It is in fact the practical interpretation of the Qur'an and the Sunnah into a blueprint for political and social activism that makes Islamism an ideology, and Islam a religion. The tactics adopted by Islamists (violent or otherwise) cannot therefore be divorced from the ideology and the aims of the movement. While justification for methods might change and maintain a dynamism that can reflect new priorities or strategies, the ideologies of the groups – which articulate the group's objectives and the values upheld to achieve them – are necessarily static, reliable and thus consistent.

For Islamists of all varieties, the adoption of violence – often seen as inextricably tied to the theological interpretation of jihad – must be treated as a strategic decision rather than a matter of ideological debate. To avoid room for contradictions on sacred values that are seen as critical to the credibility of the ideology – including values relating to the 'spirit of jihad' – Islamist leaders have shied away from enabling an ideological debate on jihad. Debates have therefore centred on strategic factors rather than philosophical reflection. The implications of this are that behaviour may not always accurately represent the long-term ideological position of a group or movement.[14] Moderations away from violence may only therefore operate at a temporarily strategic level, yet the absence in the literature of *sustained* critical, and applied historical, analyses of groups' ideological gymnastics regarding fundamental principles as of yet prevents clarification either way.

Principled or strategic non-violence

The restriction of a tactics-based categorization of Islamism has resulted in a deeper debate over the ideological position with regard to violence across Islamist and violent Islamist groups. For example, where experts document the MB's condemnations of violence through the group's official documents, speeches and interviews over the last decades,[15] others have equally noted occasions where the group endorsed local insurgencies as a legitimate resistance to foreign occupation, such as the Iraq insurgency, and its support for Hamas violence against Israel.[16] Such incidences raise questions over the application of non-violence as a term to accurately depict Islamist groups that do not officially engage in violence, but are also not categorically 'anti-violent'. Across the literature, it is unclear where 'non-violence' refers to group positions that are *anti*-violent and thus explicitly challenges the notion of violence as a principle, and where groups are categorized as non-violent because of an absence in the use of violent methods. Such ambiguity can be the result of the typical behavioural-ideological binary, but it sits at the heart of the challenges in defining groups according to degrees of violence and the controversy over the conveyor belt–firewall dichotomy. Where principled non-violence applies, non-violent Islamist groups are more likely to be justifiably regarded as firewalls to terrorism; where strategic non-violence is a more accurate depiction, Islamists can justifiably be regarded as a staging post for terrorism. Principled non-violence is consistent and committed, while strategic non-violence is pragmatic and open to adaptation.

While evidence accumulates in favour of a long-term *strategic* non-violent stance by the likes of the MB (speeches, documents and participation in formal politics), there is much less convincing evidence of any principled stance towards non-violence. MB statements that are typically referenced in support for its advocacy for non-violence are in fact recreations of the group's 1980s revisionist literature that sought to correct past periods when its leaders not only advocated, but also mobilized, for violence. Few references, if any, serve as evidence of an effort to proselytize an explicit *anti*-violent reading of sacred scripture. Analysis comparing Islamist literature and salafi-jihadi literature in the stylistic application of the Qur'an on doctrinal concepts, including justifications for violence and the sanctity of jihad, has in fact revealed considerable overlap and significant departures from mainstream scholarly interpretation.[17] For this reason, cases that are made in support of the MB's designation of non-violent Islamism can and should only be read as evidence of a pragmatic moderation regarding violence.

Evidence that suggests a sustained *anti*-violent rhetoric in juxtaposition to salafi-jihadi thought would be, and is, far more challenging to collate.

There are few cases where principled non-violence accurately applies. At the most elementary level, today's non-militarized groups, including Hizb-ut-Tahrir, Jamaat-e-Islami, and the Muslim Brotherhood, each share with Al-Qaeda and ISIS a belief in the obligation – on theological and political lines – to establish and enforce an absolute reading of Islamic law as the underlying principle of public and state life, and they each are committed, in varying degrees, to the restoration of Muslim dignity through a return to a caliphate. What differentiates these groups from groups like Al-Qaeda and ISIS, however, is not their mission, and neither is it their choice of tactics as these are not, contrary to belief, fixed positions. Rather, it is the adoption of a subversive, gradualist strategy, with incremental but sustained gains, that sets apart today's so-called 'non-violent' groups from their violent comrades. Unlike the leaders of Al-Qaeda and ISIS, today's non-militarized groups choose to engage in a 'long war' and strive not for short-term gains, but for social and political reform that follows a widespread attitudinal shift in favour of Islamist ideals. Violence in this long-term strategy – so the argument goes – can be counter-productive to the long-term mission. It is therefore the sense of urgency, not the principles of engagement, that differentiates the violent and non-violent factions within the global Islamist movement.

Internal disagreements over whether to maintain a gradualist approach over the urgently and radically activist strategy adopted by groups like Al-Qaeda and ISIS have occurred at least once for each of today's most significant non-militarized Islamists, and typically resulted in splinters and enduring fault lines. The debates over violence, and whether to legitimize the doctrine of jihad for the cause, have been central to these disagreements. The so-called 'prison years' for the Muslim Brotherhood in Egypt, between 1954 and 1970, is an illustration of divergent views, not on violence but on the adoption of radical activist Islamism over a form of political conciliation with regimes. The Muslim Brotherhood's second *murshid*, or General Guide, Hasan al-Hudaybi (1951–1973) fought a long internal battle with the group's most militarized members, later dubbed the Qutbists.[18] Hudaybi spent much of his formative years as leader of the Brotherhood stemming the spread of Sayyid Qutb's ideological influence on the group, and securing his authority against Qutb's rising popularity in the group. Hudaybi's book, titled *Du'at la Qudat* (Preachers Not Judges), has been raised as the best-known criticism ever made against Sayyid Qutb's extreme interpretations of Islamic doctrine and was referenced by the Brotherhood in its submission to the UK government Select Committee inquiry into Political Islam and the Muslim Brotherhood Review in 2015–2016.[19]

Despite the Brotherhood describing the book as evidence for the group's 'peaceful teachings',[20] the book does not deal directly with the issue of violence and jihad, but rather critiques related issues such as *takfir* (excommunication of Muslims), neo-*jahiliyya* (the state of societal ignorance similar to that witnessed before the teachings of Islam) and *hakimiyyat Allah* (God's governance). While seen as supporting Hudaybi's vision of a non-violent Brotherhood opposition that influences the political system through negotiation and political manoeuvring, the book stops short of explicitly condemning the use of violence, allowing instead for a gradual increase in force if a ruler turns against Islamic law.[21] In fact, throughout the book, Qutb is not mentioned once, nor are his ideas explicitly addressed. This is partly because the book was primarily compiled to regain the loyalty of a polarizing Brotherhood membership, not to condemn the interpretations of Qutb's writings.

Though completed in 1969, the book was only published and distributed in 1977, by which time hardened Qutbists had already formed violent factions such as *al-Takfri wal Hijra* and *al-Jihad* groups. Similarly, Yusuf al-Qaradawi's book *Jurisprudence of Jihad*, published in 2009, has been frequently referenced as a repudiation against Al-Qaeda, and through his association with the Muslim Brotherhood, evidence that the latter is non-violent. Yet, a true reading of Qaradawi's book will find no evidence of any principled opposition to the violent interpretation of jihad in today's context. Instead he maintains that jihad is and must remain integral to Islam's traditions, and emphasized its role in the continuation of *muqawema*, or resistance, against efforts to secularize Islam and Muslim societies. He called on pragmatism, not restraint.

Despite evidence that rarely is *violence* the point of departure within the global Islamist movement, dividing the Islamist camp between those overtly violent and those that are not has played into the hands of groups that strategically obscure their messaging to operate within legal restraints. In the UK, the now-banned group al Muhajiroun enjoyed years of treading just outside of British terror legislation. Yet from the fertilizer bomb plotters in 2004, the 7/7 bombers in 2005, the Drummer Lee Rigby murderers in 2013 and the London Bridge attackers in 2017, the al-Muhajiroun network and its splinter groups proved a gateway to not only legitimizing violence but glorifying it. The group's notorious figurehead, Anjem Choudary, evaded prosecution for decades but was eventually convicted in July 2016 for 'inviting support' for ISIS.[22] Long evading the need to publicly and explicitly voice his views on jihad and violence, pressures after 2014 to declare allegiance to ISIS's caliphate or risk undermining his entire life's mantra pushed him to publish his support for the group, and in turn provided the opportunity to convict him for supporting terrorism.

From challenging ideas that justify or promote violence, to those that 'promote hatred', the UK 2018 Counter-Terrorism strategy states that: 'there is no precise line between what we [the government] have described [...] as terrorist ideology, and what we consider extremist ideology', and that 'aspects' of salafi-jihadi, violent Islamist, ideology is also shared by Islamist organizations.[23] Yet it remains that defining and identifying extremism, outside of the parameters of violence, requires a far deeper and sophisticated understanding of the values and objectives of Islamist ideologies and how they manifest in different groups. Policies and counter efforts have for long focused predominantly on the most extreme *symptoms* of Islamism (i.e. adoption of violence and terrorist tactics) over the roots of the arguments.

Individual networks

Evidence, and the interpretation of evidence on non-violence at the group level, is an ongoing challenge. This has reduced our ability to gather useful comparative evidence from across the broad Islamist movement, where analysis might be helpful on the varying degrees and positions towards violence. Where there is a sizeable archive of Muslim Brotherhood literature to analyse and identify membership from around the globe, there are considerably less resources to hand when studying small, local and lesser-known factions, either affiliated or independent. Consequently, the research community remains largely blinkered beyond the dominant groups, including the Muslim Brotherhood, Hizb-ut-Tahrir and Jamaat-e-Islami. As groups have grown and franchised, their leadership structures have also decentralized, meaning much of what can be gleaned from official documentation or interviews from spokesmen requires necessary caveats.

More recent studies have overcome such limitations by shifting towards analysing the relationship at the individual level.[24] Here, the evidence of the relationship between violent and non-violent ideas builds a different picture to group-centric models of analysis. Such studies have overall suggested that a relationship between violent and non-violent Islamist groups exists and stems more from centrifugal motions than from centripetal forces. The relationship, in other words, is most likely formed informally through personal kinship and networks of individuals between violent and non-violent factions.[25] Examples from Jamaat-e-Islami's links to Indonesia's Hidayatullah, to the Muslim Brotherhood's connections to Al-Qaeda, through network tracing and mapping suggest that ideas of militancy can permeate established networks of kin and alumni rooted or embedded in Islamist circles, and this is irrespective of a group's collective position or practice.[26]

For example, as the central Jamaat-e-Islami movement in India and Pakistan appeared to temporarily develop a more centred approach to democracy and secularism in the 1990s, a student offshoot, SIMI, simultaneously moved towards a militarized radicalization of Jamaat-e-Islami's ideology, attracting members over from the group. Similarly, just over half of the most prominent leaders of the global salafi-jihadist movement across the Middle East and Africa have been found to have entered terrorist networks via Islamist circles and groups.[27] Even more pronounced, among those who have travelled to Syria from the UK, research has found that a 77 per cent majority had traceable connections to non-violent Islamist groups.[28]

Such observations are hardly implausible if groups are regarded as a part of a broader movement. While documented and evidenced 'ties' or 'links' fall short of evidence of formalized coordination, there does appear to be more evidence mounting that individual-level networks across violent and non-violent groups are not exclusive, and that individuals assist and facilitate activity of violent groups.[29] In a UK parliamentary committee review of 'Political Islam', the evidence was clear that members of Muslim Brotherhood-affiliated groups in Libya, Yemen and Syria took part in the armed conflicts and civil wars since 2012.[30] Tracing individuals that traverse non-violent and violent Islamist groups highlights further the need to understand the relationship ideologically, not just behaviourally. Like all the world's activists – extreme or not – Islamists do not define themselves based on their tactics, but on the ultimate vision and objectives they set.

Conclusion

Non-violent extremism, unlike terrorism, has no semantic core to offer guidance on its meaning. To identify it and explain parameters, a benchmark is required; something that by comparison is more neutral or mainstream. Until now, the presence or absence of violence has been a guiding benchmark to determine degrees of extremism. Yet, the terminology of non-violence has been insufficient in capturing the areas of contradiction often unmasked of so-called non-violent Islamist groups, thereby undermining efforts to distinguish according to behaviour alone. Ideological synergies across violent and non-violent groups have long been acknowledged – where objectives have overlapped, tactics have been the key marker of distinction. Yet few attributions of non-violence across the literature distinguish between principled and strategic non-violence, which is critical to establishing a truer understanding of the exclusivity, or not, of the ideologies.

Greater clarity has been reached at the individual level over the group level, where interpersonal networks have been traced that suggest at least informal collaboration or cooperation. Yet, a tendency in the literature to regard behaviour and strategy as distinct from ideology has resulted in momentary observations of tactical shifts forming the basis of extremist spectrums, from moderation to extreme.

In sum, the evidence on the role of extremist non-violent Islamist ideas in violent radicalization is mixed and in short supply. Scholarly and policy debate is marred by arbitrary binaries and ambiguous terminology that has reduced the discourse to one either in favour of a conveyor belt theory where Islamists inevitably become terrorists, or a case for leveraging Islamists as a firewall in the fight against terrorism. Realities suggest that neither conclusion can be drawn from the evidence currently available. Research that purposefully sets to add clarity on this debate is urgently needed.

Notes

1 See A. Schmid, *Violent and Non-Violent Extremism: Two sides of the Same Coin*, The Hague, Netherlands: International Center for Counter-Terrorism, 2014; I. Bowen, *Medina in Birmingham, Najaf in Brent: Inside British Islam*, London: Hurst, 2014; M. Phillips, *Londonistan: How Britain Is Creating a Terror State Within*, London: Gibson Square, 2006; J. Bartlett, J. Birdwell, and M. King, *The Edge of Violence*, London: Demos, 2010.

2 See J. Githens-Mazer and R. Lambert, 'Quilliam on Prevent: The Wrong Diagnosis', *The Guardian*, 19 October 2009; J. Githens-Mazer, 'Mobilisation, Recruitment, Violence and the Street. Radical Violent Takfiri Islamism in Early Twenty-First-Century Britain', in R. Eatwell and M. J. Goodwin (ed.), *The New Extremism in 21st Century* Britain, Oxon: Routledge, 2010; J. Githens Mazer and R. Lambert, 'Why Conventional Wisdom on Radicalisation Fails: The Persistence of a Failed Discourse', *International Affairs*, vol. 86, 2010, pp. 889–901.

3 See L. Khalil, 'Al-Qa'ida and the Muslim Brotherhood: United by Strategy, Divided by Tactics', *Terrorism Monitor*, vol. 4, no. 6, 2006; C. Hamisch and Q. Mecham, 'Democratic Ideology in Islamist Opposition? The Muslim Brotherhood's "Civil State"', *Middle Eastern Studies*, vol. 45, no. 2, 2009, pp. 189–205; L. Vidino, *The Muslim Brotherhood in the United Kingdom*, Washington, DC: George Washington University, 2015; O. Ashour, *The De-Radicalisation of Jihadists: Transforming Armed Islamist Movements*, New York: Routledge, 2009.

4 See M. Lynch, 'Islam Divided between Jihad and the Muslim Brotherhood', in A. Moghadem and B. Fishman (ed.), *Fault Lines in Global Jihad: Organizational, Strategic, and Ideological Fissures*, Oxon, Routledge, 2011, pp. 161–183; L. Vidino, 'Sharia4: From Confrontational Activism to Militancy', *Perspectives in Terrorism*, vol. 9, no. 2, 2015, pp. 2–16; S. Hamdi, P. Carnegie and B. J. Smith, 'The Recovery of a Non-Violent Identity for an Islamist Pesantren in an Age of Terror', *Australian Journal of International Affairs*, vol. 69, no. 6, 2015, pp. 692–710; M. Ahmed, M. Comerford, and E. El-Badawy, *Milestones to Militancy: What the Lives of 100 Prominent Jihadis Tell Us about a Global Movement*, London: Tony Blair Institute for Global Change, 2016; R. Bryson, *For Caliph and Country: Exploring How British Jihadis Join a Global Movement*, London: Tony Blair Institute for Global Change, 2017.

5 J. Schwendler, 'Can Islamists Become Moderates? Rethinking the Inclusion-moderation Hypothesis', *World Politics*, vol. 63, no. 2, 2011, pp. 347–376.

6 See O. Ashour, *The De-Radicalisation of Jihadists*; M. Lynch, 'Islam Divided between Jihad and the Muslim Brotherhood'.

7 A. Moghadam, *The Globalization of Martyrdom: Al Qaeda, Salafi Jihad, and the Diffusion of Suicide Attacks*, Baltimore: John Hopkins University Press, 2008; M. Lynch, 'Islam Divided between Jihad and the Muslim Brotherhood'.

8 M. Gurses, 'Islamists, Democracy and Turkey: A Test of the Inclusion-Moderation Hypothesis', *Party Politics*, vol. 20, no. 4, 2012, pp. 646–653; J. Schwedler, 'Beyond Islamist Groups: Suggestions for a New Research Agenda on Islamist Politics', *POMEPS Briefings*, vol. 24, Project on Middle East Political Science, February 2014, pp. 47–49; A. Ranko and J. Nedza, 'Crossing the Ideological Divide? Egypt's Salafists and the Muslim Brotherhood after the Arab Spring', *Studies in Conflict and Terrorism*, vol. 39, no. 6, 2016, pp. 519–541.

9 K. al-Anani and M. Malik, 'Pious Way to Politics: The Rise of Political Salafism in Post-Mubarak Egypt', *Digest of Middle East Studies*, vol. 22, no. 1, 2013, pp. 57–73; D. A. Boehmer and J. P. Murphy, 'The Politicization of the Egyptian Salafiyya: Principled Participation and Islamist Competition in the Post-Mubarak Era', *IMES Capstone Paper Series*, 2012, passim.

10 'Who Are Britain's Jihadists?', *BBC News*, www.bbc.co.uk/news/uk-32026985.

11 R. Bryson, *For Caliph and Country*.

12 A. Ranko and J. Nedza, 'Crossing the ideological Divide?'; M. Awad, 'Understanding the Ideological Drivers Pushing Youth toward Violence in Post-Coup Egypt', *POMEPS Briefings* 24, Project on Middle East Political Science, 2014; E. Trager, 'Egypt's Muslim Brotherhood Gets a Facelift', *Foreign Affairs*, 20 May 2015, pp. 9–12.

13 I. Bremmer, 'The Top 5 Countries where ISIS Gets Its Foreign Recruits', Time, April 14 2017, available here: http://time.com/4739488/isis-iraq-syria-tunisia-saudi-arabia-russia/.

14 J. Schwendler, 'Can Islamists Become Moderates?', p. 371.

15 O. Ashour, *The De-Radicalisation of Jihadists*; B. Lia, *The Society of the Muslim Brothers in Egypt*, London: Ithaca Press, 1998; R. Mitchell, *The Society of the Muslim Brothers*, New York: Oxford University Press, 1989; M. Lynch, 'The Brotherhood's Dilemma', *Middle East Brief*, vol. 25, 2008.

16 M. Lynch, 'Islam Divided between Jihad and the Muslim Brotherhood'.

17 M. Comerford and R. Bryson, *Struggle over Scripture: Charting the Rift between Islamist Extremism and Mainstream Islam*, London: Tony Blair Institute for Global Change, 2017.

18 J. Gordon, 'Reviewed Work Of: The Muslim Brotherhood: Hasan al-Hudaybi and Ideology in Studies in Political Islam by Barbara H. E. Zollner', *International Journal of Middle East Studies*, vol. 43, no. 1, February 2011, pp. 147–148.

19 For example, see works by Giles Kepel and Emmanuel Sivan.

20 UK Government Foreign Affairs Select Committee inquiry on 'Political Islam and the Muslim Brotherhood Review', November 2016, p. 37, available here: https://publications.parliament.uk/pa/cm201617/cmselect/cmfaff/118/118.pdf.

21 B. Zollner, 'Prison Talk: The Muslim Brotherhood's Internal Struggle during Gamal Abdel Nasser's Persecution, 1954 to 1971', *International Journal of Middle East Studies*, vol. 39, no. 3, August 2007, pp. 411–433.

22 'Anjem Choudary: How Hate Preacher Was Finally Caught for Supporting ISIS after 20 Years of Spreading Extremism in UK', *Independent*, 17 August 2016, available here: https://www.independent.co.uk/news/uk/crime/anjem-choudary-how-hate-preacher-was-finally-caught-for-supporting-isis-after-20-years-of-spreading-a7195496.html.

23 CONTEST: The United Kingdom's Strategy for Counter-Terrorism, June 2018. Accessed at: https://assets.publishing.service.gov.uk/government/uploads/system/uploads/attachment_data/file/716907/140618_CCS207_CCS0218929798-1_CONTEST_3.0_WEB.pdf.

24 For example, M. Sageman, *Understanding Terror Networks*, Philadelphia: University of Pennsylvania Press, 2004, p. 69; J. Bartlett, J. Birdwell, and M. King, *The Edge of Violence*; S. Atran and J. Ginges, 'Religious and Sacred Imperatives in Human Conflict', *Science*, vol. 336, no. 6083, 2012, pp. 855–857; M. Ahmed, M. Comerford and E. El-Badawy, *Milestones to* Militancy; R. Bryson, *For Caliph and Country*.

25 M. Ahmed, M. Comerford and E. El-Badawy, *Milestones to* Militancy; R. Bryson, *For Caliph and Country*.

26 S. Hamdi, P. Carnegie and B. J. Smith, 'The Recovery of a Non-Violent Identity for an Islamist Pesantren in an Age of Terror'; H. Hassan, 'The Sectarianism of the Islamic State: Ideological Roots and Political Context', *Carnegie Endowment for International Peace*, 13 June 2016.; S. Lacroix, *Awakening Islam: The Politics of Religious Dissent in Contemporary Saudi Arabia*, Cambridge, MA: Harvard University Press, 2011.

27 M. Ahmed, M. Commerford and E. El-Badawy, *Milestones to* Militancy.

28 R. Bryson, *For Caliph and Country*.

29 M. Lynch, 'Islam Divided between Jihad and the Muslim Brotherhood'; A. Talimi, 'Departers from the Ikhwan: How, When, Why?', *Islam Online*, November 2008.

30 UK Foreign Affairs Select Committee inquiry into 'Political Islam and the Muslim Brotherhood Review', November 2016, p. 34. Accessed at: https://publications.parliament.uk/pa/cm201617/cmselect/cmfaff/118/118.pdf.

Recommended Readings

Ahmed, M., M. Comerford, and E. El-Badawy, *Milestones to Militancy: What the Lives of 100 Prominent Jihadis Tell Us about a Global Movement*, London: Tony Blair Institute for Global Change, 2016.

Al-Anani, K. and M. Malik, 'Pious Way to Politics: The Rise of Political Salafism in Post-Mubarak Egypt', *Digest of Middle East Studies*, vol. 22, no. 1, 2013, pp. 57–73.

Ashour, O., *The De-radicalisation of Jihadists: Transforming Armed Islamist Movements*, New York: Routledge, 2009.

Atran, S. and J. Ginges, 'Religious and Sacred Imperatives in Human Conflict', *Science*, vol. 336, no. 6083, 2012, pp. 855–857.

Awad, M., 'Understanding the Ideological Drivers Pushing Youth toward Violence in Post-Coup Egypt', *POMEPS Briefings*, vol. 24, Project on Middle East Political Science, 2014.

Bartlett, J., J. Birdwell, and M. King, *The Edge of Violence*, London: Demos, 2010.

Boehmer, D. A. and J. P. Murphy, 'The Politicization of the Egyptian Salafiyya: Principled Participation and Islamist Competition in the Post-Mubarak Era', *IMES Capstone Paper Series*, 2012, passim.

Bowen, I., *Medina in Birmingham, Najaf in Brent: Inside British Islam*, London: Hurst, 2014.

Bryson, R., *For Caliph and Country: Exploring How British Jihadis Join a Global Movement*, London: Tony Blair Institute for Global Change, 2017.

Comerford M. and R. Bryson, *Struggle over Scripture: Charting the Rift between Islamist Extremism and Mainstream Islam*, London: Tony Blair Institute for Global Change, 2017.

Githens-Mazer, J., 'Mobilisation, Recruitment, Violence and the Street. Radical Violent Takfiri Islamism in Early Twenty-First-Century Britain', in R. Eatwell and M. J. Goodwin (ed.), *The New Extremism in 21st Century* Britain, Oxon, Routledge, 2010.

Githens-Mazer, J. and R. Lambert, 'Quilliam on Prevent: the Wrong Diagnosis', *The Guardian*, 19 October 2009.

Githens-Mazer, J. and R. Lambert, 'Why Conventional Wisdom on Radicalisation Fails: The Persistence of a Failed Discourse', *International Affairs*, vol. 86, 2010, pp. 889–901.

Gurses, M., 'Islamists, Democracy and Turkey: A Test of the Inclusion-Moderation Hypothesis', *Party Politics*, vol. 20, no. 4, 2012, pp. 646–653.

Hamdi, S., P. Carnegie, and B. J. Smith, 'The Recovery of a Non-Violent Identity for an Islamist Pesantren in an Age of Terror', *Australian Journal of International Affairs*, vol. 69, no. 6, 2015, pp. 692–710.

Hamisch, C., and Q. Mecham, 'Democratic Ideology in Islamist Opposition? The Muslim Brotherhood's "Civil State"', *Middle Eastern Studies*, vol. 45, no. 2, 2009, pp. 189–205.

Hassan, H., 'The Sectarianism of the Islamic State: Ideological Roots and Political Context', *Carnegie Endowment for International Peace*, 13 June 2016.

Khalil, L., 'Al-Qa'ida and the Muslim Brotherhood: United by Strategy, Divided by Tactics', *Terrorism Monitor*, vol. 4, no. 6, 2006.

Lacroix, S., *Awakening Islam: The Politics of Religious Dissent in Contemporary Saudi Arabia*, Cambridge, MA: Harvard University Press, 2011.

Lia, B., *The Society of the Muslim Brothers in Egypt*, London: Ithaca Press. 1998.

Lynch, M., 'Islam Divided between Jihad and the Muslim Brotherhood' in A. Moghadem, and B. Fishman (ed.), *Fault Lines in Global Jihad: Organizational, Strategic, and Ideological Fissures*, Oxon: Routledge, 2011, pp.161–183.

Lynch, M., 'The Brotherhood's Dilemma', *Middle East Brief*, vol. 25, 2008.

Mitchell, R., *The Society of the Muslim Brothers*, New York: Oxford University Press, 1989.

Moghadam, A., *The Globalization of Martyrdom: Al Qaeda, Salafi Jihad, and the Diffusion of Suicide Attacks*, Baltimore: John Hopkins University Press, 2008.

Phillips, M., *Londonistan: How Britain is Creating a Terror State Within*, London: Gibson Square, 2006.

Ranko, A. and J. Nedza, 'Crossing the Ideological Divide? Egypt's Salafists and the Muslim Brotherhood after the Arab Spring', *Studies in Conflict and Terrorism*, vol. 39, no. 6, 2016, pp. 519–541.

Sageman, M., *Understanding Terror Networks*, Philadelphia: University of Pennsylvania Press, 2004, p. 69.

Schmid, A., *Violent and Non-Violent Extremism: Two sides of the Same Coin*, The Hague, Netherlands: International Center for Counter-Terrorism, 2014.

Schwedler, J., 'Beyond Islamist Groups: Suggestions for a New Research Agenda on Islamist Politics', *POMEPS Briefings*, vol. 24, Project on Middle East Political Science, February 2014, pp. 47–49.

Schwendler, J., 'Can Islamists Become Moderates? Rethinking the Inclusion-Moderation Hypothesis', *World Politics*, vol. 63, no. 2, 2011, pp. 347–376.

Talimi, A., 'Departers from the Ikhwan: How, When, Why?', *Islam Online*, November 2008.

Trager, E., 'Egypt's Muslim Brotherhood Gets a Facelift', *Foreign Affairs*, 20 May 2015, pp. 9–12.

Vidino, L., *The Muslim Brotherhood in the United Kingdom*, Washington, DC: George Washington University, 2015.

Vidino, L., 'Sharia4: From Confrontational Activism to Militancy', *Perspectives in Terrorism*, vol. 9, no. 2, 2015, pp. 2–16.

7 A DEMOGRAPHY OF BRITISH MUSLIMS: CROSS-SECTIONAL UNDERSTANDING OF MUSLIM COMMUNITIES AND THEIR HETEROGENEITY WITHIN THE UK

Tufyal Choudhury

Introduction

From being criticized for failing to condemn terrorism enough to being identified as potential partners for community policing and Prevent, British Muslim communities have been the focus of counter-terrorism policies in Britain since 2001. The aim of this brief chapter is to provide an outline of some of the basic demographic features of Muslims in the UK relevant to discussions of counter-terrorism policies.

The 2011 census counted 2,786,635 Muslims living in the UK, accounting for 4.4 per cent of the UK population. The Pew Research Center estimated that the UK Muslim population had increased to 4,130,000 by 2016. With zero net migration they projected that the number of Muslims would increase to 6,560,000 by 2050; with medium or high levels of net migration they estimated that the UK Muslim population would reach over 13 million by 2050.[1]

While there are almost 3 million Muslims in the UK today, there is no single, monolithic Muslim community; rather, there are a range of diverse communities shaped by differing patterns and experiences of migration, settlement and development. Furthermore, views and experiences are shaped and mediated by age, education, ethnicity, gender, geography and religious belief.

Evolution of Muslim communities in Britain

There has been contact between Muslims and the peoples of the British Isles since the early periods of Islam.[2] There are records of Muslims in England going back to the Tudor period.[3] Isolated from Europe following the ex-communication of Elizabeth I by Pope Pius V in 1570, and no longer bound by the Church's ban on trade with Muslims, England sought new trading relationships with the Ottoman and Persian Empires and rulers of North Africa. With trade came Britain's first Muslims: merchants and diplomats, their families and households. Imperial expansion led to the arrival from South Asia of Muslim sailors, known as lascars, working in the merchant navy, and who were joined (after the opening of the Suez Canal in 1869) by Muslim sailors from Yemen. This led to the establishment of Muslim communities in the port cities of London, Cardiff, Hull, Liverpool and South Shields.[4] By 1889, Woking became the site for the first purpose-built mosque in the UK. A year earlier, English Muslim convert Henry William Quilliam founded the Liverpool Muslim Institute.[5]

Over 400,000 Muslims were among the 1.2 million soldiers of the Indian army that fought for Britain during the First World War.[6] Some of those who arrived to fight in Europe settled in Britain after the Great War. However, it was after the Second World War that the Muslim population increased significantly with post-war migration and settlement made possible by Britain's imperial structures. Seeking to retain equality between all British Subjects of the Crown, the British Nationality Act 1948 guaranteed the right of all Subjects, whether British Citizens of the UK and Colonies or citizens of newly independent Commonwealth States, the right to travel, live and work in the UK, the metropolitan heart of the Commonwealth and Empire.

In the 1950s and 1960s this facilitated the migration of workers from the British Commonwealth and colonies, including Muslims from South Asia who came to work in factories and mills in the industrial conurbations of London, the West Midlands and Yorkshire and Lancashire. Increased migration led to calls for controls, linked to the perceived threat to social cohesion. Restrictions on immigration were argued as necessary in allowing new immigrants to be 'absorbed' or 'assimilated' into the host society. Black immigration from the 'new Commonwealth' was viewed as giving rise to tensions in relations between those of different 'racial' groups. Measures controlling or restricting immigration were justified as a prerequisite to adopting policies supporting integration.

This policy was most aptly described at the time by the Labour MP Roy Hattersley who said, 'Integration without (immigration) control is impossible, but (immigration) control without integration is indefensible.'[7] Until the introduction of controls and restriction on immigration from the Commonwealth, South Asian migration had been largely circular chain migration, as men worked several years and then returned, knowing that other members of their family could travel and work for a period and send remittances home. The introduction of immigration control forced those who were working in the UK to settle and establish families and communities here.

In the late 1960s and 1970s East African Asians, who were British Citizens of the UK and Colonies, began to arrive under pressure from the 'Africanisation' policies in Kenya and Tanzania, and, in the case of Uganda, as a result of forced expulsion.[8] The arrival of non-White British citizens led to restrictions on British nationals in the colonies, who found themselves exiled and banished as their citizenship was decoupled from the right of abode in the UK. This was not a revocation or deprivation of their citizenship but a curtailment on their rights as citizens to unrestricted access to the UK; through the partiality rule, only the children and grandchildren of British citizens born, adopted or naturalized in the UK enjoyed the same rights as British citizens born in the UK. The rule operated as 'a polite way of allowing whites in and keeping "coloureds" out'.[9] The British Nationality Act 1981 reinforced the racialized ethnic national identity. It applied a restrictive approach to British citizens from outside the UK, leaving British citizens in its former colonies, who could not claim an ancestral connection to Britain, exiled with either British Overseas Citizenship or British Dependent Territories Citizenship, both of which amounted to 'virtually worthless second-class citizenships' that gave them nowhere to go.[10]

From the 1970s oil wealth combined with political instability in the Middle East also attracted investors, students and professionals from that region. In the 1980s and 1990s Muslims also arrived as refugees escaping war and conflict in the Balkans, the Middle East, Iran, Turkey and Somalia. It was during this period that key figures connected to the subsequent radicalization of young people in Britain, such as Omar Bakri Mohammed[11] and Abu Qatada,[12] arrived in the UK seeking asylum. Since 2000, Somali Muslims, who had initially arrived as refugees in other parts of Europe and having secured EU citizenship, relocated to the UK as EU migrants.[13]

While the Muslim population has been developed and established through migration, the majority (78 per cent) are British citizens (by either naturalization or birth);[14] furthermore, by 2011 almost half (47 per cent) were born in the UK.[15]

There are important implications for counter-terrorism policies arising from this migration history and background. For some Muslims, their reading of the motives and actions of the British state today is shaped, in part, by their experiences, understandings and narratives of British history as colonial history. This informs their reading and response to calls for a focus on 'Fundamental British Values' as part of counter-terrorism policy. Furthermore, many Muslims have links, through family ties, to regions and areas of the world that have experienced the violence of the Islamic State, Al-Qaeda and the War on Terror. They are therefore aware of the lack of coverage and response in the media and by politicians to non-European deaths compared to the response to attacks in Europe or North America.

Demographics of the Muslim population today

Geographic distribution

Reflecting the migration patterns of their arrival, Muslims in Britain, although present in every nation and local area of the UK, are concentrated in urban areas. Three quarters live in Greater London, the West Midlands, the North West and Yorkshire and Humber. Although in 2011 only 4.4 per cent of the UK population, Muslims accounted for around one in four of the population in Blackburn and Darwen (27 per cent), Bradford (24.7 per cent), Luton (24.6 per cent) and Slough (23.3 per cent). They are also a fifth of the population in Birmingham (21.8 per cent), 15.8 per cent of the population in Manchester and 12.4 per cent of the population in London. Within London, the highest concentration of Muslims can be found in Tower Hamlets and Newham, where they account for one-third of the population. In 2011, 37 per cent of UK Muslims lived in London. Given the focus of terrorist attacks on London, this also means that Muslims are at significant risk of being victims of terrorist attacks. The experiences of the nature and dynamic of the Muslim populations in particular localities are also shaped by the ethnic, religious and socio-economic differences of those areas.

Ethnic diversity

Muslims make up about one-third of the UK's BME (Black and Minority Ethnic) population. Muslim communities are ethnically diverse; furthermore, that ethnic diversity is increasing. As noted above, the early post-war settlement of Muslims was largely from South Asia or Asians from East Africa. As a result, the majority of Muslims in 2011 were South Asian, mainly Pakistani (38 per cent), Bangladeshi (14.9 per cent) and Indian (7.3 per cent). However, the proportion of the Muslim population that is 'Asian' fell from 74 per cent in the 2001 census to 67 per cent in 2011. Of the one-third of Muslims that are not Asian, 10.7 per cent ticked the 'other' ethnicities category in the census (this includes 6.6 per cent Arab and 4.4 per cent 'other ethnic groups'); 10.1 per cent identified as Black Muslims, including 7.7 per cent who said they were Black Africans; 7.6 per cent of Muslims identified their ethnicity as White, including 2.9 per cent (77,272) who said they were White British.

Age profile

The age profile of Muslims is significantly younger than the general population. One-third of Muslims are of school age, that is, under the age of fifteen, compared to 19 per cent of the general population; half are under the age of twenty-four, compared to 31 per cent of the general population. The median age of Muslims is twenty-five; in the general UK population it is forty. The younger age groups are also likely to be more ethnically diverse. Thus, policies in relation to education and young people have a greater impact on Muslims than on the general population.

Education

Education is an area where important structural shifts and changes in Muslim populations are taking place. In 2011, 24 per cent of Muslims had a degree or equivalent, compared to 27.2 per cent of the whole population. However, participation in university education is higher among younger Muslims. Analysis of data from the Longitudinal Study of Young People finds that young Muslims have high educational aspirations compared to their peers. These aspirations are also supported by Muslim parents who have higher educational aspirations for their children than other parents in England, with aspiration for Muslim girls being higher than for Muslim boys.[16] Among eighteen to nineteen-year-olds, 42 per cent of Muslim women and 31 per cent of Muslim men were at university compared to 37 per cent of Christian White British women and 32 per cent of Christian White British men.[17] The increase in Muslim students has led to concerns about the risks of radicalization at universities. However, the Home Affairs Select Committee report *The Roots of Violent Radicalisation* found that there is 'much less direct' link between education and terrorist activity than was thought in the past, and that 'individuals involved in violent extremism are little different to others around them in terms of their education'.[18]

Religion and religious identity

The diversity of the different Muslim traditions, schools of thought and sects is present in the Muslim communities of Britain. The majority of Muslims are Sunni, with around 5 per cent estimated to be Shia.[19] Reflecting the dominance of Muslims with roots in the Indian subcontinent, the two largest groups are from the Barelwi and Deobandi traditions.[20] One group that has drawn particular attention in the context of counter-terrorism policy and policing have been salafi Muslims.[21] However, there is no reliable data on the size of different groups. A survey of 995 Muslims in the UK found that 5 per cent of Muslim respondents identified themselves as salafi and 10 per cent as either Deobandi or Barelvi.[22]

Analysis of data from the Ethnic Minority British Election Study 2010 also finds that over 90 per cent of Muslims have said that religion is 'extremely' (52 per cent) or 'very' (43 per cent) important to them; furthermore, UK graduates (62 per cent) were more likely than non-graduates (50 per cent) to say that religion was very important to them.[23] Religion is also important to Muslim children. In a survey of thirteen- to fourteen-year-olds, 79 per cent of Muslims said that religion is 'very important' to the way they live their lives.[24]

There are several studies that have aimed to understand the complex and diverse reasons for the foregrounding of religion as a marker of identity by Muslims. Stratham identifies two hypotheses put forward to explain mobilization by Muslims in the public space around their religious identity.[25] The first argues that there is something intrinsic to Islam that leads to greater demands being made for 'public' accommodation. The second hypothesis sees mobilization as a reaction to discrimination and socio-economic deprivation. Samad[26] and Saeed[27] see the increased salience of Muslim identity as, in part, a response to the public devaluation and disparagement of Muslims and Islam that has led to increased in-group solidarity. As well as constructing identities in response to external factors, identity is constructed as a mechanism for internal empowerment. For young Muslim women, Islamic identity can be an important resource for overcoming family objections and barriers, based on cultural traditions, to participation in employment or higher education.[28]

The importance of religious identity sits alongside a strong sense of belonging to Britain. An ICM poll in 2016 found that 93 per cent of Muslims had a very or fairly strong sense of belonging to Britain. In a ComRes poll in 2015, 95 per cent of Muslims said they felt loyalty to Britain. In fact, in a Survation poll in 2015, four out of five Muslims (82 per cent) said that their British identity was equally important or more important than their religious identity, and only 17 per cent placed their religious identity ahead of their British identity.[29] This interaction between religion and nationality is perhaps best illustrated by findings from the data in the Ethnic Minority British Election Study which found that 'the more British Muslims feel that they have in common with other Muslims the more they also feel they have in common with other Britons'.[30]

The importance of religion to the identity of Muslims means that perceptions and experiences of religious profiling in the implementation of counter-terrorism policies are particularly keenly felt – a source of identity that is seen as important and as a source of strength is felt to be misrecognized and treated as a source of suspicion.[31] Research on factors that impact on people's willingness to cooperate in counter-terrorism policing found that among Muslims in the UK, their religiosity or political beliefs had no impact; rather, the strongest predictor of willingness to cooperate in counter-terrorism efforts were perceptions of fair treatment in the implementation of legislation or policy by state authorities.[32] Furthermore, social or group identity plays an important role in the relationship between fair treatment and cooperative behaviour: individuals react not only to how they are treated, but also to how individuals belonging to a group that they identify with are treated. When they witness unfair treatment by the authorities making decisions concerning members of their social group, it affects their willingness to cooperate with those authorities.[33]

Conclusion

The Muslim population in the UK is growing in size and complexity. Attitudes, views and experiences of counter-terrorism policies are shaped by age, education, gender and geography. While there is no monolithic Muslim community, religion is an important part of identity for most Muslims, and one whose salience has, in part, increased as a response to experiences of discrimination and hostile public discourse. Perceptions that counter-terrorism policies and practices are unfairly profiling Muslims on the basis of their religion can increase in-group solidarity and reinforce Muslim religious identity. This, in itself, is not problematic as we know that a strong sense of Muslim religious identity sits comfortably alongside British identity. However, this can undermine efforts to increase community co-operation in counter-terrorism where an individual feels they, or members of a group they identify with, will not be treated fairly. This creates an opportunity for policy makers and those implementing policy to increase cooperation by ensuring norms of fair treatments are met, while at the same time it generates risks as experiences and perceptions of unfair treatment reduce cooperation.

Notes

1 Pew Research Center, *Europe's Growing Muslim Population*, 2017, available here: http://www.pewforum.org/192017/11/29/europes-growing-muslim-population/.

2 From the eighth century we have a gold coin from the Anglo-Saxon King Offa of Mercia – thought to be a copy of the gold dinar of the Abbasid Caliph, al-Mansur – containing the Islamic declaration of faith in Arabic.

3 J. Brotton, *This Orient Isle: Elizabethan England and the Muslim World*, London: Allen Lane, 2016.

4 H. Ansari, *The Infidel Within: Muslims in Britain since 1800*, London: Hurst and Co, 2004.

5 R. Geaves, *Islam in Victorian Britain: the Life and Times of Abdullah Quilliam*, Leicestershire, UK: Kube Publishing Limited, 2010.

6 Among them was Khuddad Khan, the first Indian to receive a Victoria Cross for his actions in halting a German advance during the battle of Ypres in October 1914. See L. Ferrier, *The Unknown Fallen: the Global Allied Muslim Contribution to the First World War*, The Forgotten Heroes 14–19 Foundation. https://unknownfallen.com/.

7 House of Commons Hansard, vol. 709, col. 378–385.

8 R. Hassen, *Citizenship and Immigration in Post-War Britain*, Oxford: Oxford University Press, 2000.

9 A. Kundnani, *The End of Tolerance: Racism in 21st Century Britain*, London: Pluto Press, 2007, p. 21.

10 B. Parekh, *The Future of Multi-Ethnic Britain*, London: Profile Books, 2000, p. 206.

11 Omar Bakri Mohammed sought asylum after arriving in the UK in 1986, and was subsequently granted indefinite leave to remain. He initially headed the organizations Hibz ut-Tahrir and then set up an offshoot, Al-Muhajirounn.

12 Abu Qatada, born Omar Mahoud Othman, was a Jordanian national who arrived in the UK in 1996, claiming asylum. He was convicted in terrorism in absentia by a court in Jordan. He is said to have influenced Richard Reid and Zacarias Moussaoui, both convicted of offences related to terrorism. He was placed under a Control Order in 2008 and eventually extradited to Jordan in 2013. In 2014, courts in Jordan cleared him of the terrorism charges that he faced there.

13 Open Society Foundations, *Somalis in Leicester*, New York: Open Society Foundations, 2014.

14 K. Kaur-Ballagan, R. Mortimer, and G. Gottfried, *A Review of Survey Research on Muslims in Britain*, London: IPSOS MORI, 2018, p. 11.

15 Census 2011, ONS table DC2207EW, cited in Muslim Council of Britain, *British Muslims in Numbers*, p. 22.

16 K. Kaur-Ballagan, R. Mortimer, and G. Gottfried, *A Review of Survey Research on Muslims in Britain*, p. 14.

17 N. Khattab and T. Modood, 'Accounting for British Muslim's Educational Attainment: Gender Differences and the Impact of Expectations', *British Journal of Sociology of Education*, 2017, p. 7.

18 House of Commons, *Roots of Violent Radicalisation*, Home Affairs Select Committee Nineteenth Report of Session 2010–12 HC 1446, London: The Stationary Office, 2012, p. 13.

19 See for example: Sunnis and Shias: What's the Story? Available at http://www.bbc.co.uk/guides/z373wmn.

20 S. Hamid, 'The Development of British Salafism', *ISIM Review*, vol. 21, 2008, pp. 10–11.

21 R. Lambert, 'Empowering Salafis and Islamists against Al-Qaeda: A London Counterterrorism Case Study', *Political Science and Politics* vol. 41, no. 1, 2008, pp. 31–35; R. Lambert, 'Salafi and Islamist Londoner: Stigmatised Minority Faith Communities Countering Al-Qaeda', *Crime, Law and Social Change*, vol. 50, no. 1, 2005, pp. 73–89; see also S. Hamid, *Sufis, Salafis and Islamists: the contested ground of British Islamic Activism*, London: IB Tauris, 2016.

22 L. Daniel-Staetsky, *Anti-Semitism in Contemporary Great Britain: A Study of Attitudes towards Jews and Israel*, London: Institute of Jewish Policy Research, 2016, p. 58.

23 K. Kaur-Ballagan, R. Mortimer, and G. Gottfried, *A Review of Survey Research on Muslims in Britain*, p. 17.

24 Longitudinal Study of Young People in England, Second Cohort Wave 1, cited in K. Kaur-Ballagan, R. Mortimer and G. Gottfried, *A Review of Survey Research on Muslims in Britain*, p. 18.

25 P. Statham, 'New Conflicts about Integration and Cultural Diversity in Britain', in R. Cuperus, K.A. Duffeck and J. Kandel (ed.), *The Challenge of Diversity: European Social Democracy Facing Migration, Integration, and Multiculturalism*, Studienverlag: Innsbruck, 2003.

26 Y. Samad, 'The Politics of Islamic Identity among Bangladeshis and Pakistanis in Britain', in T. Ranger, Y. Samad and O. Stuart (ed.), *Culture Identity and Politics: Ethnic Minorities in Britain*, Aldershot: Avebury 1996.

27 A. Saeed, N. Blain and D. Forbes, 'New Ethnic and National Questions in Scotland: Post-British Identities among Glasgow Pakistani Teenagers', *Ethnic and Racial Studies*, vol. 22, no. 5, 1999, pp. 821–844.

28 K.E. Brown, 'Realising Muslim Women's Rights: The Role of Islamic Identity among British Muslim Women', *Women's Studies International Forum*, vol. 29, no. 4, 2006, pp. 417–430.

29 Cited in K. Kaur-Ballagan, R. Mortimer and G. Gottfried, *A Review of Survey Research on Muslims in Britain*, p. 38.

30 Cited in K. Kaur-Ballagan, R. Mortimer and G. Gottfried, *A Review of Survey Research on Muslims in Britain*, p. 39.

31 L. Blackwood, N. Hopkins, and S. Reicher, '"Flying While Muslim": Citizenship and Misrecognition in the Airport', *Journal of Social and Political Psychology*, vol. 3, no. 2, 2015.

32 A. Huq, T.R Tyler, and S. Schulhofer, 'Mechanisms for Eliciting Cooperation in Counterterrorism Policing: Evidence from the United Kingdom', *Journal of Empirical Legal Studies*, vol. 8, 2011, pp. 728–761.

33 A. Cherney and K. Murphy, 'Policing Terrorism with Procedural Justice: The Role of Police Legitimacy and Law Legitimacy' *Australian & New Zealand Journal of Criminology*, vol. 46, 2013, pp. 403–421.

Recommended Readings

Ali, S., *British Muslims in Numbers: A Demographic, Socio-Economic and Health Profile of Muslims in Britain Drawing on the 2011 Census*. London: Muslim Council of Britain, (2015).

Ansari, H., *The Infidel Within: Muslims in Britain since 1800*, London: Hurst and Co, 2004.

Blackwood, L., N. Hopkins, and S Reicher, '"Flying While Muslim": Citizenship and Misrecognition in the Airport', *Journal of Social and Political Psychology*, vol. 3, no. 2, 2015.

Brotton, J., *This Orient Isle: Elizabethan England and the Muslim World*, London: Allen Lane, 2016.

Brown, K. E., 'Realising Muslim Women's Rights: The Role of Islamic Identity among British Muslim Women', *Women's Studies International Forum*, vol. 29, no. 4, 2006, pp. 417–430.

Cherney A. and K. Murphy, 'Policing Terrorism with Procedural Justice: The Role of Police Legitimacy and Law Legitimacy', *Australian & New Zealand Journal of Criminology* vol. 46, 2013, pp. 403–421.

Daniel-Staetsky, L., *Anti-Semitism in Contemporary Great Britain: A Study of Attitudes towards Jews and Israel*, London: Institute of Jewish Policy Research, 2016, p. 58.

Ferrier, L., *The Unknown Fallen: The Global Allied Muslim Contribution to the First World War*, The Forgotten Heroes 14-19 Foundation.

Geaves, R., *Islam in Victorian Britain: The Life and Times of Abdullah Quilliam*, Leicestershire, UK: Kube Publishing Limited, 2010.

Hamid, S., 'The Development of British Salafism', *ISIM Review*, vol.21, 2008.

Hamid, S., *Sufis, Salafis and Islamists: The Contested Ground of British Islamic Activism*, London: IB Tauris, 2016.

Hassen, R., *Citizenship and Immigration in Post-War Britain*, Oxford: Oxford University Press, 2000.

House of Commons Hansard, Volumes in Fifth Series (Commons)m vol. 709, Commons Sitting of 23 March 1965, col. 359.
House of Commons, *Roots of Violent Radicalisation*, Home Affairs Select Committee Nineteenth Report of Session 2010-12 HC 1446, London: The Stationary Office, 2012, p. 13.
Huq, A., T. R. Tyler, and S. Schulhofer, 'Mechanisms for Eliciting Cooperation in Counterterrorism Policing: Evidence from the United Kingdom', *Journal of Empirical Legal Studies*, vol. 8, 2011, pp. 728–761.
Kaur-Ballagan, K., R. Mortimer, and G. Gottfried, *A Review of Survey Research on Muslims in Britain*, London: IPSOS MORI 2018.
Khattab, N. and T. Modood, 'Accounting for British Muslim's Educational Attainment: Gender Differences and the Impact of Expectations', *British Journal of Sociology of Education*, vol. 39, no. 2, 2018, pp. 242–259.
Kundnani, A., *The End of Tolerance: Racism in 21st Century Britain*, London: Pluto Press, 2007, p. 21.
Lambert, R., 'Empowering Salafis and Islamists against Al-Qaeda: A London Counterterrorism Case Study', *Political Science and Politics*, vol. 41, no. 1, 2008.
Lambert, R., 'Salafi and Islamist Londoner: Stigmatised Minority Faith Communities Countering Al-Qaeda', *Crime, Law and Social Change*, vol. 50, no.1, 2005, pp. 73–89.
Open Society Foundations, *Somalis in Leicester*, New York, Open Society Foundations, 2014.
Parekh, B., *The Future of Multi-Ethnic Britain*, London: Profile Books, 2000, p. 206.
Pew Research Center, *Europe's Growing Muslim Population*, 2017, available here: http://www.pewforum.org/2017/11/29/europes-growing-muslim-population/
Saeed, A., N. Blain, and D. Forbes, 'New Ethnic and National Questions in Scotland: Post-British Identities among Glasgow Pakistani Teenagers', *Ethnic and Racial Studies*, vol. 22, no. 5, 1999, pp. 821–844.
Samad, Y., 'The Politics of Islamic Identity among Bangladeshis and Pakistanis in Britain', in T. Ranger, Y. Samad, and O. Stuart (ed.), *Culture Identity and Politics: Ethnic Minorities in Britain*, Aldershot: Avebury, 1996.
Statham, P., 'New Conflicts about Integration and Cultural Diversity in Britain', in R. Cuperus, K. A. Duffeck, and J. Kandel (ed.), *The Challenge of Diversity: European Social Democracy Facing Migration, Integration, and Multiculturalism*, Innsbruck: Studienverlag, 2003.

8 WILLINGNESS TO ENGAGE AND DISCUSS ISSUES ACROSS MUSLIM AND ETHNIC MINORITY COMMUNITIES: ATTITUDES TOWARDS MUSLIMS FROM NON-MUSLIMS IN THE UK

Maria Sobolewska

Introduction

As this chapter shows, existing literature converges on a picture of deteriorating attitudes towards Muslims in the UK, and on Muslims being the most prejudiced against group compared to other minority groups in the UK. Notably, negativity is directed towards Muslims not only from the white British majority, but also from other minority groups. Muslims are therefore at the bottom of the ethnic hierarchy in the UK.

A growing experimental literature reviewed in this chapter shows that these attitudes are likely to translate into every day discrimination against Muslims, including in the labour market. Survey experiments including questions about Muslims' access to certain rights and entitlements almost all show that Muslims are thought of as less deserving and as less entitled, even holding other factors constant. Although the evidence linking anti-Muslim sentiment with how the media cover Muslim-related affairs mostly hails from the United States, we can make a reasonable assumption that media negativity observable also in the UK forms part of the reason behind the growing hostility. In particular, misconstruing of Muslim public opinion, promulgating the view that Muslims fail to integrate and the link between Muslims and terrorist threat are the main areas where the media most likely impact on anti-Muslim sentiment.

Evidence on attitudes towards Muslims

Anti-Muslim sentiment, or prejudice against Muslims, can be (and is) measured in many ways. Some of these suffer from methodological problems, however, and will be excluded from this short review. An overview of what is available and whether it will be included or excluded, and why, is therefore necessary.

The first and most obviously relevant form of attitudinal measures are the questions about Muslims in polls and surveys. There are many available, commonly used attitudinal measures of out-group sentiment. Many have been used to measure negative sentiment against other non-Muslim groups and have a relatively long overtime trend, so they are of good validity and offer a useful comparison. These are the gold standard of measurement and will be used in this review.

Other attitudinal measures are more ad hoc and designed as a one-off measure – their validity is often unknown, but can be useful if the design is sound and data collection methods robust. These will be used in the review as, when collated over time, they offer a very good sense of overall trend in attitudes towards Muslims.

However, it is important to note that many direct attitudinal questions suffer from issues of social desirability bias: i.e. some respondents in surveys and polls, especially those conducted in person or on the phone (as opposed to online), will not admit readily to attitudes that might be considered socially undesirable, such as racism or prejudice. Which attitudes are thought to be undesirable is likely to vary across time, context and individual but it will almost certainly impact on the results.

A good method that overcomes issues of social desirability bias in the usual survey questions is the survey experiment. This is a relatively novel methodological technique and relies on the fact that it randomly allocates respondents to groups which are asked to express attitudes towards Muslims, and others as a control group that are asked about non-Muslims. As a result, we can be fairly certain that the attitudes expressed are genuine and are not a result of either individual or measurement variation. The commonly used vignette technique, where a question is longer and uses a more narrative approach, also presents a subtler way of asking about attitudes towards Muslims in a more unobtrusive manner – somewhat overcoming the issue of respondents trying to police and manipulate their answers on these questions. In this way survey experiments can also be treated as the gold standard form of measurement for attitudes towards Muslims.

Sometimes conclusions about attitudes towards Muslims are drawn from behavioural measures: these are often included to measure short-term increases in anti-Muslim sentiment, most often following terrorist attacks conducted by someone of Muslim origin or claiming to be conducting them for jihadist reasons. There are two common ones. The first, and slightly more robust measure, is the spike in violent attacks experienced by Muslims. The second is internet search trends.

Spike in violent attacks can be reported by either the police forces, or organizations such as Tell Mama UK which may in fact gather a wider range of data than the police given that reporting to the police might be skewed towards the more serious incidents. Both sources of data can give a useful insight into how often Muslims experience attacks and whether these are a response to media coverage that is negative towards Muslims, particularly following terrorist attacks. However, these data are not useful as measures of attitudes, despite their common treatment as such by the media. It is because it is entirely possible that the same number of people held stable negative attitudes about Muslims before and after attacks, and that the attacks simply mobilized into action those who were negative about Muslims already. It is thus impossible to discern if a small group of people conduct more attacks, or more people conduct attacks. As such, it is a good measure of mobilization of attitudes into action, but not of attitudes themselves.

Internet search trends are commonly used to report backlashes against Muslims following terrorist incidents. However, these suffer from huge methodological issues. Apart from the same problem as above – that they measure mobilization of attitudes into action and not attitudes themselves, and that individuals can and do search for similar things multiple times – they have other shortcomings. Principally it is very hard to differentiate the motivation for Google searches, even those negative in tone. Given the algorithms used by the different search engines to suggest searches and results, the conclusions from internet search trends are very hard to interpret.

Finally, some – like the influential Runnymede Islamophobia reports in 1997 and 2017 [1]– measure prejudicial attitudes against Muslims indirectly through outcomes. The first type of outcome is self-reported experience of prejudice, which suffers from similar limitations as attacks and internet search trends analysis. The second type assumes that prejudice must be behind any social, economic or political outcome gaps that cannot be explained by the usual relevant predictors. So, an analysis showing that on average, Muslim graduates with equal grades to non-Muslim graduates achieve lower employment success and lower income[2] would be included as an indicator of prejudicial treatment in these reports. These indirect measures give an excellent quality picture of disadvantage, but it is a leap and ultimately an untested assumption that these disadvantages are due to attitudinal factors, even if this is the most likely explanation. Therefore, such studies can be included only if they contain an element of a controlled experiment, which directly tests the conclusion that discrimination against Muslims is the explanatory force. The discriminatory behaviour in these studies is a good indicator for prejudicial attitudes.

Surveys and public opinion polls

There is some survey evidence that attitudes towards British Muslims are getting worse over time. British public opinion polls started asking about Muslims specifically relatively recently, following the Rushdie Affair in 1988, when his novel – thought by some Muslims to be offensive to their faith – was first published in Britain. Before that time, attitudes towards all Asian and black people were solicited as skin colour, and not religious affiliation, and were thought to be the basis for prejudice and discrimination from the white majority. Clive Field has collected all public opinion polls conducted since 1988 until 2006 and has painted a rather bleak picture of more and more Britons associating Muslims with terrorism and expressing a growing concern as to the degree of Muslim integration into British society and values.[3]

The worrying conclusion of Field's article[4] that the white public's suspicion that a non-negligible number of Muslims in Britain support terrorism and that Muslims do not integrate sufficiently may be well founded given that the picture painted by Muslim public opinion polls is problematic. A closer analysis of Muslim public opinion polls following the 2005 London terrorist attacks was conducted by Sobolewska and Ali.[5] What they show is that in the event of terrorist attacks linked to Muslims, the existing explanatory frame of poor integration outcomes leading to terrorist actions – one that has incidentally never received empirical support – is superimposed on Muslim opinion polls. In effect, in response to terrorist attacks, Muslim opinion polls ask British Muslims predominantly about their integration, rather than other relevant issues. As a result, the picture of what British Muslims think is skewed by how polls are conducted and there is a negative feedback loop between what is presented as what Muslims think and what the wider public thinks about Muslims.

How does the societal position of Muslims, even if it is declining, compare to other minority groups? Erik Bleich, looking at polls between 1988 and 2008, confirms Field's conclusion of deteriorating attitudes, but shows that Muslims are not yet the worst perceived minority group in Britain. Newer research, on the other hand, shows that they have become just that.[6]

Since the 1980s, the British Social Attitudes Survey (BSA) has been asking people if they would mind an in-law from a different ethnic group. Storm, Sobolewska and Ford[7] performed the overtime analysis of these data and showed that the British white majority has become considerably more tolerant towards black and Asian people, passing the ultimate test of welcoming them into their own family. However, against this positive picture, the attitudes towards Muslims stand out as exceptionally hostile. While only 24 per cent of BSA respondents in 2013 declared unease with a black or Asian in-law, 50 per cent expressed unease with a Muslim one.[8]

This huge anti-Muslim gap appears even more consequential when we break up the attitudes by different birth cohorts. It is a well-known finding that younger cohorts are more tolerant towards minority ethnic groups, but when we look at their sentiment towards Muslims we see that they are a lot more negative about this group than others.[9] Moreover, when we take the youngest adult cohort, those born in the 1990s, we see that they are becoming more negative towards Muslims, thus reversing the overall trend of falling prejudice among younger generations. This cohort, of course, is the one whose formative experiences included the 2001 WTC attacks and the 2005 London attack – indicating that there might be a link between perceived threat of terrorism and attitudes towards Muslims.

The picture of Muslims being placed at the bottom of the ethnic hierarchy in Britain is confirmed also when we look at the attitudes of other ethnic minority Britons. Muslims are universally perceived as the least desirable in-laws, among all black and Asian groups.[10]

Survey experiments

Although the evidence from surveys and polls is indicative, and the overtime picture is especially valuable, the public opinion polls used for the existing overtime accounts are of poor to moderate quality, particularly when it comes to question design. As indicated earlier, questions that directly ask about levels of prejudice suffer social desirability bias. It is therefore helpful to look at the relatively newer, but growing, experimental literature.

Experimental survey questions help distinguish two important aspects of public attitudes towards Muslims. Firstly, we can see the comparison of Muslims to other groups that are not contaminated by social desirability issues and the poll respondents' desire to be consistent, for example. Secondly, we can see which elements of the public perception of Muslims is causing hostility towards this group, as the experimental design can vary randomly as to which of these characteristics are made salient to the survey respondents.

In the first category of experimental studies the main two groups compared with Muslims are immigrants more generally, and then other ethnic minorities.[11] These studies measure both the direction of attitudes towards the groups in question as overall negativity or positivity and other indicative attitudes such as preference for immigrant admission into the country, or preference for Muslim access to political or social rights, including welfare and other benefits. The results are generally in agreement that Muslims are perceived more negatively than other racial and ethnic British-born minority groups[12] and worse or equally badly as other immigrants.[13] What is especially important in these studies is that they are testing important aspects of entitlement to enter and settle in Britain, and then to fully participate as equal citizens in the welfare provided by the state. Muslims being judged as less welcome to enter, and then subsequently as less deserving of welfare assistance, is an important indicator that negative sentiment translates into directly discriminatory attitudes, and then perhaps behaviour. Although experimental studies looking at discriminatory behaviour are relatively rare, and few look specifically at Muslims as opposed to ethnic minorities, there are a few studies that find discriminatory hiring practices directed against people from Muslim majority countries.[14]

In the second category of studies, the results are more mixed. While some studies indicate that Muslims' perceived religiosity is responsible for their negative public image,[15] others found that perceived levels of cultural assimilation and social contact trump religiosity.[16] This is the least well-developed area of study, but it is growing fast and is likely to bring important insights into how prejudicial attitudes are formed, and thus how they might be challenged and countered.

Influence of media coverage of Muslims

Although evidence of the direct influence of media on public opinion is scarce and predominantly based on research elsewhere,[17] the media narratives about Muslims in the UK likely shape, or at least reflect, wider attitudes. A lot of British research[18] offers exhaustive accounts of media biases against Muslims and the kind of stereotypes that may have originated with media misreporting. They document the promulgating of the stereotypes of Muslims' self-segregation, and direct falsehoods such as the now-proverbial banning of Christmas celebrations by a local city council.[19] Uniquely, and in contrast to the treatment of other minority groups, left-wing and independent media are as likely to promote negative stereotypes against Muslims as right-wing media.[20] Given that Muslims' perceived religiosity, self-segregation and differences in values have been shown to be important predictors of anti-Muslim sentiment in experimental studies, it is of rather obvious concern that the media choose these types of frames for so many discussions of British Muslims.[21]

Room for optimism?

Throughout this discussion, terrorism and its impacts on perceptions of Muslims have been present in the background almost invariably. Although a lot of the literature in this field agrees that the perceived threat of terrorism has had a negative influence on attitudes towards Muslims, it is important to inject some nuance into this picture. While it is true that over time the attitudes have worsened and that this rise in negativity coincided with the political salience of terrorism linked to jihadism, some evidence points to the fact that there is no direct or immediate link. For example, following the London 2005 attacks, some polls showed an improvement in attitudes towards British Muslims,[22] a finding that has been replicated in other countries.[23] More recently, unpublished research found that British attitudes to Muslims are remarkably resilient in the face of terrorism,[24] and comparative research also showed evidence that countries which experienced the vast majority of casualties from jihadist terrorist attacks in the West (including Britain) were among the least negative about Muslims.[25]

The willingness to spare the majority of British Muslims from the consequences of the actions of the few might indicate that while attitudes towards Muslims have been deteriorating, there might be room to counter this trend. One of the areas to investigate is the social responsibility of media reporting, which is too often ignored. An unusual instance where the regulator, the Independent Press Standards

Organisation, stepped in to force *The Sun* newspaper to correct its front-page story in which it claimed that one in five Muslims supported the Islamic State is a good indicator of what more can be done in this respect. Secondly, questions must be raised about Muslim leadership and how they represent the wider Muslim population. This problem has been highlighted in Saggar's seminal work,[26] which argues that without a widely accepted and respected Muslim leadership, coming from the more compromise-seeking, rather than the religiously radical, quarters, the situation of British Muslims is unlikely to improve. Such leadership is available among the various groups seeking to represent British Muslims, but it is not necessarily the leadership which gets the attention of the media and subsequently the air time.

Conclusion

Evidence synthesized for this chapter shows that British Muslims have been a controversial minority group since the 1980s, but their status in British society has likely deteriorated further following the modern wave of jihadist terrorism in the West. Attitudes towards Muslims in Britain also counter the general trend of falling racial and ethnic prejudice, with even younger British people feeling a considerable sense of social distance from Muslims. However, evidence also offers a glimmer of hope for future community relations as British attitudes towards Muslims are fairly resilient against short-term effects from single terrorist attacks and the new research from Ipsos Mori shows that Britain and France, the two countries that have experienced the most deaths from jihadist terrorism in Europe, are in fact the two most positive in Europe about their Muslim minorities.[27]

Notes

1 Runnymede Trust, 'Islamophobia: A Challenge for Us All', 1997, and 'Islamophobia: Still a challenge for us all', 2017, both available at: https://www.runnymedetrust.org/projects-and-publications/equality-and-integration/islamophobia.html.

2 Such studies traditionally group different groups of Muslim faith together and thus are not sensitive to difference by origin. In the UK, the majority of Muslims come from Pakistan and Bangladesh and increasingly from African countries (with a very small proportion from the Far East and other countries, Census 2011) and they are likely to have different experiences. Public opinion and thus attitudes are similarly measured towards Muslims as a homogenous group, which, of course, they are not.

3 C. Field, 'Islamophobia in Contemporary Britain: The Evidence of the Opinion Polls, 1998–2006', *Islam and Christian-Muslim Relations*, vol. 18, no. 44, 2007, pp. 447–477.

4 Field, 'Islamophobia in Contemporary Britain'.

5 M. Sobolewska and S. Ali, 'Who Speaks for Muslims? The Role of the Press in the Creation and Reporting of Muslim Public Opinion Polls in the Aftermath of London Bombings in July 2005', *Ethnicities*, vol. 15, no. 5, 2015, pp. 675–695.

6 E. Bleich, 'Where do Muslims Stand on Ethno-Racial Hierarchies in Britain and France? Evidence from Public Opinion Surveys, 1988–2008', *Patterns of Prejudice*, vol. 43, no. 3–4, 2008, pp. 379–400.

7 I. Storm, M. Sobolewska, and R. Ford, 'Is Ethnic Prejudice Declining in Britain? Change in Social Distance Attitudes among Ethnic Majority and Minority Britons', *The British Journal of Sociology*, vol. 68, no. 3, 2016, pp. 410–434.

8 Storm, Sobolewska and Ford, 'Is Ethnic Prejudice Declining in Britain'.

9 Storm, Sobolewska and Ford, 'Is Ethnic Prejudice Declining in Britain? Change in Social Distance Attitudes among Ethnic Majority and Minority Britons'.

10 Storm, Sobolewska and Ford, 'Is Ethnic Prejudice Declining in Britain? Change in Social Distance Attitudes Among Ethnic Majority and Minority Britons'.

11 Z. Strabac and O. Listhaug, 'Anti-Muslim prejudice in Europe: A Multilevel Analysis of Survey-Data from 30 Countries', *Social Science Research*, vol. 37, 2008, pp. 268–286; Z. Strabac, T. Aalberg, and M. Valenta, 'Attitudes towards Muslim Immigrants: Evidence from Survey Experiments across Four Countries', *Journal of Ethnic and Migration Studies*, vol. 40, no. 1, 2014, pp. 100–118; C. L. Adida, D. David and M. Valfort 'Region of Origin or Religion? Understanding Why Immigrants from Muslim-Majority Countries Are Discriminated against in Western Europe', 2013.

12 R. Ford and A. Kootstra, 'Do White Voters Support Welfare Policies Targeted at Ethnic Minorities? Experimental Evidence from Britain', *Journal of Ethnic and Migration Studies*, vol. 43, no. 1, 2017, pp. 80–101.

13 Strabac and Listhaug, 'Anti-Muslim prejudice in Europe'.

14 B. Lancee et al., 'Cultural Distance and Ethnic Discrimination in Hiring Behaviour. Results from a Cross-National Field Experiment', GEMM Project report, 2017; see also E. Zschirnt and D. Ruedin, 'Ethnic Discrimination in Hiring Decisions: A Meta-Analysis of Correspondence Tests 1990–2015', *Journal of Ethnic and Migration Studies*, vol. 42, no. 7, 2016, pp. 1115–1134.

15 M. Helbling and R. Traunmüller, 'What Is Islamophobia? Disentangling Citizens' Feelings towards Ethnicity, Religion and Religiosity Using a Survey Experiment', 2017.

16 M. Sobolewska, S. Galandini, and L. Lessard-Phillips, 'The Public View of Immigrant Integration: Multidimensional and Consensual. Evidence from Survey Experiments in the UK and the Netherlands', *Journal of Ethnic and Migration Studies*, vol. 43, no. 1, 2017, pp. 58–79.

17 See some American literature: S. K. Gadarian, 'The Politics of Threat: How Terrorism News Shapes Foreign Policy Attitudes', *The Journal of Politics*, vol. 72, no. 2, 2010, pp. 469–483; E. Das et al., 'How Terrorism News Reports Increase Prejudice against Outgroups: A Terror Management Account', *Journal of Experimental Social Psychology*, vol 45, no. 3, 2009, pp. 453–459.

18 P. Baker, C. Gabrielatos, and T. McEnery, *Discourse Analysis and Media Attitudes: The Representation of Islam in the British press*, Cambridge: Cambridge University Press, 2013.; E. Poole, and J. E. Richardson (ed.) *Muslims and the News Media*, London and New York: I.B. Tauris, 2006; E. Poole, *Media Representations of British Muslims: Reporting Islam*, London: I.B. Tauris, 2002.

19 Moore, Mason and Lewis. 'Images of Islam in the UK: The Representation of British Muslims in the National Print News Media 2000–2008', Cardiff School of Journalism: Media and Cultural Studies.

20 Sobolewska and Ali, 'Who Speaks for Muslims?'.

21 Poole, *Media Representations of British Muslims.*

22 L. Ridley, '7/7 Bombings Prompted An Outpouring of Unity That Britain Needs to Return To' 6th July', *Huffington Post*, 6 July 2015.

23 Pew Global, 'U.S. Views of Muslim Americans Improved after Sept. 11, 2001 Attacks', *Pew Research Center*, 2 June 2015; Pew Global, 'French Views of Muslims', 2014–15, *Pew Research Center*, 2 June 2015; P. M. Sniderman et al., *Paradoxes of Liberal Democracy: Islam, Western Europe, and the Danish Cartoon Crisis*, Princeton University Press, 2014.

24 Sobolewska, Ford, Sniderman 2015 'Democratic Resilience and Liberal Mobilisation in the Face of Terrorist Threat. Natural and Survey Experiment'. Paper presented at the American Political Association, Philadelphia.

25 Z. Strabac, T. Aalberg, and M. Valenta, 'Attitudes towards Muslim Immigrants: Evidence from Survey Experiments across Four Countries', *Journal of Ethnic and Migration Studies*, vol. 40, no. 1, 2014, pp. 100–118.

26 S. Saggar, *Pariah Politics: Understanding Western Radical Islamism and What Should Be Done*, Oxford: Oxford University Press, 2009.

27 Ipsos MORI 2018.

Recommended Readings

Adida, C. L., D. Laitin, and M.A. Valfort, 'Region of Origin or Religion? Understanding Why Immigrants from Muslim-Majority Countries Are Discriminated against in Western Europe', Working Paper, 2013.

Baker, P., C. Gabrielatos, and T. McEnery, *Discourse Analysis and Media Attitudes: The Representation of Islam in the British Press*, Cambridge: Cambridge University Press, 2013.

Bleich, E., 'Where Do Muslims Stand on Ethno-Racial Hierarchies in Britain and France? Evidence from Public Opinion Surveys, 1988–2008', *Patterns of Prejudice*, vol. 43, no. 3-4, 2008, pp. 379–400.

Das, E., et al., 'How Terrorism News Reports Increase Prejudice against Outgroups: A Terror Management Account', *Journal of Experimental Social Psychology*, vol. 45, no. 3, 2009, pp. 453–459.

Field, C., 'Islamophobia in Contemporary Britain: The Evidence of the Opinion Polls, 1998-2006', *Islam and Christian-Muslim Relations*, vol. 18, no. 44, 2007, pp. 447–477.

Ford, R. and A. Kootstra, 'Do White Voters Support Welfare Policies Targeted at Ethnic Minorities? Experimental Evidence from Britain', *Journal of Ethnic and Migration Studies*, vol. 43, no. 1, 2017, pp. 80–101.

Gadarian, S. K., 'The Politics of Threat: How Terrorism News Shapes Foreign Policy Attitudes', *The Journal of Politics*, vol. 72, no. 2, 2010, pp. 469–483.

Helbling, M. and R. Traunmüller, 'What Is Islamophobia? Disentangling Citizens' Feelings Towards Ethnicity, Religion and Religiosity Using a Survey Experiment', *British Journal of Political Science*, 2018, pp. 1–18.

IPSOS Mori, 'Britain Lags behind Canada and the U.S. in New Inclusiveness Index', 25 June 2018, available here: https://www.ipsos.com/ipsos-mori/en-uk/britain-lags-behind-canada-and-us-new-inclusiveness-index.

Jaspal, R. and M. Cinnirella, 'Media Representations of British Muslims and Hybridised Threats to Identity', *Contemporary Islam*, vol. 4, no. 3, 2010, pp. 289–310.

Lancee, B. et al., 'Cultural Distance and Ethnic Discrimination in Hiring Behaviour. Results from a Cross-National Field Experiment', GEMM Project Report, 2017, available here: http://gemm2020.eu/wp-content/uploads/2017/09/Report-on-Cultural-distance-and-ethnic-discrimination-in-hiring-behavior_v2.pdf.

Pew Global, 'U.S. Views of Muslim Americans Improved after Sept. 11, 2001 Attacks', *Pew Research Center*, 2 June 2015, available here: http://www.pewresearch.org/fact-tank/2015/06/03/ratings-of-muslims-in-france-and-us/ft_15-06-02_americanmuslims911/.

Pew Global, 'French Views of Muslims, 2014–15', *Pew Research Center*, 2 June 2015, available here: http://www.pewresearch.org/fact-tank/2015/06/03/ratings-of-muslims-in-france-and-us/ft_15-06-02_francemuslims/.

Poole, E., 'The Effects of September 11 and the War in Iraq on British Newspaper Coverage', in E. Poole and J. E. Richardson (ed.), *Muslims and the News Media*, London and New York: I.B. Tauris, 2006.

Poole, E. and J. E. Richardson (ed.), *Muslims and the News Media*, London and New York: I.B. Tauris, 2006.

Poole, E., *Media Representations of British Muslims: Reporting Islam*, London: I.B. Tauris, 2002.

Richardson, J.E., *(Mis)Representing Islam: The Racism and Rhetoric of British Broadsheet Newspapers*, Amsterdam: John Benjamins, 2004.

Ridley L., '7/7 Bombings Prompted An Outpouring Of Unity That Britain Needs to Return To' 6th July', *Huffington Post*, 6 July 2015, available here: http://www.huffingtonpost.co.uk/2015/07/05/77-bombings-reactions-muslims-islam_n_7730400.html.

Saggar, S., *Pariah Politics: Understanding Western Radical Islamism and What Should Be Done*, Oxford: Oxford University Press, 2009.

Sniderman, P. M. et al., *Paradoxes of Liberal Democracy: Islam, Western Europe, and the Danish Cartoon Crisis*, Princeton, New Jersey, United States: Princeton University Press, 2014.

Sobolewska, M. and S. Ali, 'Who Speaks for Muslims? The Role of the Press in the Creation and Reporting of Muslim Public Opinion Polls in the Aftermath of London Bombings in July 2005', *Ethnicities*, vol. 15, no. 5, 2015, pp. 675–695.

Sobolewska, M., S. Galandini, and L. Lessard-Phillips, 'The Public View of Immigrant Integration: Multidimensional and Consensual. Evidence from Survey Experiments in the UK and the Netherlands', *Journal of Ethnic and Migration Studies*, vol. 43, no. 1, 2017, pp. 58–79.

Sobolewska M., R. Ford, and P. Sniderman 'Democratic Resilience and Liberal Mobilisation in the Face of Terrorist Threat. Natural and Survey Experiment', (Paper presented at the APSA Conference, Philadelphia, 1–4 September 2016).

Storm, I., M. Sobolewska, and R. Ford, 'Is Ethnic Prejudice Declining in Britain? Change in Social Distance Attitudes among Ethnic Majority and Minority Britons', *The British Journal of Sociology*, vol. 68, no. 3, 2016, pp. 410–434.

Strabac, Z. and O. Listhaug, 'Anti-Muslim Prejudice in Europe: A Multilevel Analysis of Survey-Data from 30 Countries', *Social Science Research*, vol. 37, 2008, pp. 268–286.

Strabac, Z., T. Aalberg, and M. Valenta, 'Attitudes towards Muslim Immigrants: Evidence from Survey Experiments across Four Countries', *Journal of Ethnic and Migration Studies*, vol. 40, no. 1, 2014, pp. 100–118.

Zschirnt, E., and D. Ruedin, 'Ethnic discrimination in Hiring Decisions: A Meta-Analysis of Correspondence Tests 1990–2015', *Journal of Ethnic and Migration Studies*, vol. 42, no. 7, 2016, pp.1115–1134.

9 THE IMPACT OF STRUCTURAL INEQUALITIES, INTEGRATION, OTHERNESS AND DISCRIMINATION

Tahir Abbas

Introduction

This chapter concentrates on the struggles of British Muslim communities on matters of integration, participation and engagement, which are more pronounced than ever in the post-war history of migration, settlement and adaptation to Britain of Muslim minorities.[1] The equalities sector has dwindled, as social divisions, in general, continue to widen between the haves and have-nots. Moreover, diversity, ethnicity and difference are now presented as a threat to society rather than as an opportunity to improve the nature of the collective lived experience through enhanced understandings of the Other and the Self. There is also a wider national debate in relation to Brexit and the position of the UK within a European and global trade, exchange and distribution economic framework that is undecided. It has led to uncertainty, fear and doubt. During the Brexit referendum a virulent ethno-nationalism materialized on what it means to be English, British or European in today's inter-dependent, yet divided, world. The lack of a coherent answer is further destabilizing existing precarious ethnic relations in Britain.

While there are many nuanced studies of Islamism-inspired politics, research into the relationship between Muslims and militancy is often reliant on functionalist social-psychological approaches.[2] Ideology, deprivation and alienation cannot entirely explain what draws young people to violent Islamism. Religious belief interacts with other aspects of people's contextual experiences at various individual, group, institutional and state levels. It involves a fluid mix of variables that can align to influence how young Muslims join extremist groups. These can include racism, Islamophobia, anger at Western foreign policy, search for identity, status, adventure, justice or revenge – a range of perspectives that resonate with their perceptions of the world.[3] Nevertheless, a dominant analytical standpoint focuses on the role of ideology as the primary causal dynamic behind violent radicalization. However, sociological conditions at the level of the individual, the family, the neighbourhood, the city, the nation state and at a global level are argued to be more significant, where the quandaries of ethnic and racial inequality affect Muslim communities in disproportionate ways.[4]

Social, political and economic context

With a predominant youth profile of Muslims in Europe reflecting what are now third-generation minorities, the issues of educational underachievement, limited skills and training, underemployment, unemployment and discrimination continue to significantly affect their social mobility and opportunities for integration, including in, *and* through, the education system.[5] These predicaments suppress young Muslims further down the social hierarchy, leading to alienation, frustration, disenfranchisement and ultimately stress and anxiety.[6] For some, this leads to violence as a response to perceived *and* actual social conflict, emerging because of symbolic *and* actual violence through the 'biopolitics' of the state, which 'deals with the population, with the population as a political problem, as a problem that is at once scientific and political, as a biological problem and as power's problem'.[7]

Intergenerational disconnect also plays a role in dislocation. Grandfathers and fathers who were invited or migrated to Western European countries which now have large Muslim populations such as France, Britain, and Germany brought with them patriarchal values found in parts of South Asia, North Africa and Anatolian Turkey.[8] A cultural hierarchy maintains the male head of household as the final arbitrator in domestic decisions. While fathers maintain a certain level of influence over their sons in the home, wider society determines the social mobility of these fathers. This can result in young Muslim men being caught in a double bind. At one level, they are subject to the authority of the male head of household who is, simultaneously, demonized or rendered invisible in the public sphere. This can create a sense of psychological dislocation among European-born young Muslim men and women who wish to attain a certain degree of individuality and cultural affinity with the host society that, at the same time, does not fully accept who they are or what they represent, allowing the radicalizers to take advantage of this malaise.[9]

Western European societies and economies have transformed profoundly since the deregulation of the financial sector and the dominance of privatization of public utilities and economic neoliberalism that began in the 1980s.[10] The inner cities, oft-forgotten by urban planners and policymakers until the conditions facing disadvantaged 'underclass' groups could not be neglected any further, are sites of diverse communities. Post-war ethnic minorities cluster in specific urban areas to utilize social, economic and cultural capital for group survival. Simultaneously, the spatial concentration of deprived marginalized majorities is also an opportunity to protect group norms and values associated with group identity, which, in the light of present politics, perceives a threat from the dominant (or subordinated) other. The general overriding discourse, however, is to present 'self-styled segregation' among ethnic minorities as a self-induced rejection of integration. This discourse is ultimately harmful for many minorities who are on the receiving end of frequent vilification, alienation and discrimination.[11]

The separation between white indigenous and Muslim minority groups in relation to differences in identity formations emerges at the local and global levels. It reveals a distinct layer of conflict, locking both groups in an intense struggle for the least in society. A crucial feature in the radicalization of far-right and Islamist extremists is, therefore, the search for an alternative, 'pure' identity.[12] It affected the Brexit vote in the UK, which was, in part, motivated by negative discourses on immigration, refugees and questions of national political identity. Majority white-British communities also suffer from the predicaments that lead to extremism, radicalization and violence, but media and political discourses concentrate less on such groups, markedly skewing the debate.[13] Deindustrialization, post-industrialization and globalization affect Muslim minority groups in the inner cities of Western Europe, but these concerns also affect majority groups who may turn to far-right political views.[14] In general, there is limited discussion on the associations between extremist far-right and radical Muslim groups. Developments in such thinking would help to explore the synergies between arguably two parallel and similar radicalization and violent extremism outcomes.[15]

Symbiotic radicalizations

In 2017, there were five terrorist attacks. The Westminster Bridge, Manchester Arena, Borough Market and the failed Parsons Green attacks received extensive coverage. However, following the Finsbury Park Mosque attack, which was perpetrated by forty-eight-year-old Darren Osborne who drove a van into and killed fifty-one-year-old Makram Ali, much of the media and political response to the attack reflects the 'institutionalization of Islamophobia' in Britain, acting as a driver of far-right extremism in as much as far-right extremism thrives on Islamist radicalization.[16] Arguably, Darren Osborne would not have been radicalized if Muslims did not receive consistent demonization in the media. While yet unclear, it appears he had no other motivation than wanting to 'kill all Muslims'. Osborne faces charges of the terrorism-related murder of Makram Ali and for injuring eleven others. In under-exposing the objective explanations behind the political or ideological motivations behind attacks, it intimates a far greater demographic capable of such acts. Here, Islamism supposedly thrives among radicalized

Muslims who use it to legitimize violence. It avoids all nuances. In the case of far-right extremists, not only is there limited recognition of the wide-ranging problem of far-right extremism and terrorism, over-emphasizing the 'loner' angle distracts from implicating the wider negative structural and cultural forces at play. Meanwhile, Islamophobia has become normalized in society to such an extent that even to evoke it is to suggest that groups challenging the status quo, in particular Muslims, are being disingenuous, at best, or downright treacherous, at worst.[17]

In reporting on responses to attacks, Islamist extremists are purely ideological, while English or other white ethnic groups have social and psychological problems. This suggests a general degree of acceptance on the part of society that their violence towards Muslims is somehow legitimate – i.e. because of something that Muslims espouse or adhere to, e.g. their faith, or because they are somehow responsible, as an entire faith community, for the actions of a limited few. Orientalism, scientific racism and now racialization based on an ethnic, cultural and religious category suggests institutionalized Islamophobia: wholesale, widespread, menacing and omnipotent.[18] If plans go ahead to introduce Islamophobia as a counter-terrorism or countering violent extremism issue it has the potential to take attention away from structural racism, which potentially further institutionalizes Islamophobia. A deeper understanding of Muslim differences in society would reorient this thinking away from the counter-terrorism/countering violent extremism space, while Muslims outside of this realm are not only rendered homogenous but, crucially, invisible. This homogeneity is not open-ended, diverse or layered with class, racial, sectarian and cultural characteristics but rather a representation of Muslims as various threats to society. Engagement with Muslims is restricted to a focus on problems seemingly emanating from a Muslim cosmos – now potentially relegating anti-Muslim hatred to the realm of counter-terrorism, further absolving the state's responsibility in relation to Muslims everywhere else in society.

In spite of the growth of 'Islamophobia studies', problems of classification, categorization and generalization still afflict the term. Some regard the term as a *process*, although others see it as a *product*. The former relates to prejudice and marginalization measured as distinct patterns of racial, cultural and religious discrimination. The latter manifests itself in history as well as contemporary politics. As such, there remains an analytical gap between conception, perception and ultimately realization.[19] For others, the ambiguity of the concept is its strength as Islamophobia takes many different shapes and forms depending on context and opportunity. These have local and global manifestations found within spheres of intellectual, political, cultural and social ontologies.[20] Other scholars have come to interpret its relationship to existing patterns of xenophobia, Orientalism and imperialism that affect liberal democracies and constructions of multiculturalism found within them.[21] Racism is the preserve of not only far-right groups or institutionalized in the workings of state apparatus – 'Islamophobia, like other forms of racism, can be colour-coded, i.e. it can be biological (normally associated with skin colour) and can be cultural (not necessarily associated with skin colour), or it can be a mixture of both'.[22] Islamophobia is not only a lived social and political experience facing British Muslims. Rather, the reality of anti-Muslim sentiment has the power to generate a reactionary response on the part of beleaguered young Muslims, conflated with a paradigm of anti-multiculturalism, which in recent periods seeks to abandon a critical acceptance of differences in society and replace it with an outmoded, reductive and exclusive notion of English nationalism, especially in the post-Brexit referendum era.[23]

Islamophobia today is the normalization of anti-Muslim hatred that has grown exponentially since the onset of the war on terror culture that began after the events of 9/11.[24] During this time intolerance, bigotry and the development of alt-right, far-right, radical left and religious extremist groups have found succour in the vacuum and absence of dominant discourses to stabilize societies that provide opportunities, as well as outcomes, for the many, not the few. Cumulative extremisms at the margins of society incubate the discourses of intolerance and hate that allow these subgroups and their ideas to foment. Islamophobia and radicalization are intimately tied up with each other.[25]

Conclusion

To understand radicalization, context and perspective are crucial. In some respects, radicalization refers to pathways. In others, it relates to outcomes. Furthermore, radicalization does not always equate with terrorism.[26] This lack of clarity over what constitutes radicalization distorts understandings of violent extremism,[27] in particular where there is confusion over clearly problematic social outcomes that are high-priority security threats. No two countries define 'radicalization' or 'extremism' in the same way. For some, violence is the main concern. For others, an ideology that may or may not lead to violence is the primary focus. All definitions, nevertheless, recognize the notion as a highly individualized and largely unpredictable process.[28] For the purposes of this discussion, radicalization refers to both the *processes* and *outcomes* of violent extremism.

This chapter has shown that issues of structure are important to take into consideration when attempting to understand the nature of radicalization among those who engage in extremism and eventually terrorism. While all efforts to help reduce the likelihood of radicalization leading to terrorism are extremely important, the new Commission for Countering Extremism needs to do a great deal to build bridges, improve ethnic relations and generate a positive story in relation to difference and diversity in the UK context. There is a risk that the Commission represents a particular ideology that seeks to focus on values, identity and even religious principles as the precursors for extremism, radicalization and terrorism in the UK. This would be genuinely reductive, simplistic and hugely problematic given the serious nature of anti-Muslim sentiment, widespread inequality and racism, and a global hostility to a faith tradition that is constantly demonized. Everywhere in the world people are radicalized because they are responding to injustices, whether it is individually or collectively perceived, or locally, nationally or globally realized.

Since the events of 9/11 the response from certain Muslim individuals and groups involved in presenting a counter-argument to the logic of the 'war on terror' as defined by the state has been to decry state institutions and co-opted individuals supporting the dominant motif. However, there is a great deal of nuance as these divisions are not equally split between the idea of a world separated by light and dark, or that evil and good forces are in a constant battle. External forces have broken down Islam as a faith tradition and the lived Muslim social experience, with many nations seeking to take full advantage of the resources available to them through colonialism, imperialism and, today, globalization. However, the main problem with such a perspective is that it denies Muslim agency. Where confidence and trust in politics are at an all-time low, Muslims still have a positive role to play in society. While a proportion of upwardly mobile, professional, technologically savvy, internationally travelled, well-read British Muslims represent the paradigm of *Generation M* – a mobilization on the part of Muslims engaging actively with the *halal* economy[29] – many Muslim groups, having lost their confidence, remain suspicious of what they regard as a betrayal by the state.

The collective ownership of the problem and the solutions can help abate patterns of radicalization and terrorism through improved relations, interactions and engagements between and within communities combined with an open, informed and meaningful mode of engagement with the state by being a critical friend. In addition, the state needs to move on from the inadequate perspective that ideology is the cause and the solution to extremism and terrorism. It merely exacerbates existing problems.

Notes

1 L. Casey, *The Casey Review A Review into Opportunity and Integration*, London: Department of Communities and Local Government, 2016.

2 Q. Wiktorowicz, (ed.), *Islamic Activism: A Social Movement Theory Approach*, Bloomington: Indiana University Press. 2004.

3 L. Lorne and A. Amarasingam, 'Talking to Foreign Fighters: Insights into the Motivations for Hijrah to Syria and Iraq', *Studies in Conflict & Terrorism*, vol. 40, no. 3, 2017; 191–210; O. Roy, *Globalized Islam: The Search for a New Ummah*, New York: Columbia University Press, 2002.

4 A. Heath and J. Martin, 'Can Religious Affiliation Explain "Ethnic" Inequalities in the Labour Market?', *Ethnic and Racial Studies*, vol. 36, no. 6, 2013, pp. 1005–1027.

5 T. Abbas, 'Editorial' as Guest Editor of the Special Edition, 'Educating British Muslims: Identity, Religion and Politics in a Neoliberal Era', *British Journal of Sociology of Education*, forthcoming, March 2018, pp. 1–3.

6 T. Abbas, *Islamic Radicalism and Multicultural Politics: The British Experience*, London and New York: Routledge, 2011.

7 M. Foucault, 'Lecture 11, 17 March 1976', in M. Foucault (ed.), *Society Must Be Defended: Lectures at the College de France*, London and New York: Picador, 2003, p. 245.

8 M. Anwar, *The Myth of Return: Pakistanis in Britain*, London: Heinemann Educational, 1979.

9 E. Pearson, 'The Case of Roshonara Choudhry: Implications for Theory on Online Radicalization, ISIS Women, and the Gendered Jihad', *Policy and Internet*, vol. 8, no. 1, 2016, pp. 5–33.

10 M. Ferrera, 'Ideology, Parties and Social Politics in Europe', *West European Politics*, vol. 37, no. 2, 2014, pp. 420–448.

11 C. Peach, 'The Meaning of Segregation', *Planning Practice and Research*, vol. 11, no. 2, 1994, pp. 137–150.

12 D. Pisoiu, 'Subcultural Theory Applied to Jihadi and Right-Wing Radicalization in Germany', *Terrorism and Political Violence*, vol. 27, no. 1, 2015, pp. 9–28.

13 H. Beider, *White Working Class Voices: Multiculturalism, Community-Building and Change*, Bristol: The Policy Press, 2015.

14 H-G Betz, 'The Two Faces of Radical Right-Wing Populism in Western Europe', *The Review of Politics*, vol. 55, no. 4, 1993, pp. 663–685; R. Saull, 'Capitalism, Crisis and the Far-Right in the Neoliberal Era', *Journal of International Relations and Development*, vol. 18, no. 1, 2015, pp. 25–51; D. Dorling, *Inequality and the 1%*, London and New York: Verso, 2015.

15 M. Goodwin, *The Roots of Extremism: The English Defence League and the Counter-Jihad Challenge*, London: Chatham House Briefing Paper, 2013.

16 T. Abbas, 'Ethnicity and Politics in Contextualising Far Right and Islamist Extremism', *Perspectives on Terrorism*, vol. 11, no. 3, 2017, pp. 54–61.

17 S. Waarsi, *The Enemy Within: A Tale of Muslim Britain*, London: Allen Lane, 2017.

18 A. Kundnani, *The Muslims Are Coming! Islamophobia, Extremism, and the Domestic War on Terror*, London and New York: Verso, 2014.

19 C. Allen, *Islamophobia*, Farnham: Ashgate, 2010.

20 S. Sayyid and A.V. Vakil (ed.), *Thinking through Islamophobia: Global Perspectives*, London and New York: Hurst and Columbia University Press, 2011.

21 J. Esposito and I Kalin (ed.), *Islamophobia: The Challenge of Pluralism in the 21st Century*, New York: Oxford University Press, 2011.

22 M. Cole, 'Critical Race Theory comes to the UK: A Marxist Response', *Ethnicities*, vol. 9, no. 2, 2009, pp. 246–284, quoted from pp. 251–252.

23 T. Abbas, 'The Symbiotic Relationship between Islamophobia and Radicalisation', *Critical Studies on Terrorism*, vol. 5, no. 3, 2012, pp. 345–358.

24 Esposito and Kalin, *Islamophobia*.

25 J. Ebner, *The Rage: The Vicious Circle of Islamist and Far-Right Extremism*, London and New York: IB Tauris, 2018.

26 R. Borum, 'Radicalization into Violent Extremism I: A Review of Social Science Theories', *Journal of Strategic Security*, vol. 4, no. 4, 2011, pp. 7–36.

27 M. Sedgwick, 'The Concept of Radicalization as a Source of Confusion', *Terrorism and Political Violence*, vol. 4, no. 4, 2010, pp. 479–494.

28 G. Bailey and P. Edwards, 'Rethinking "Radicalisation": Microradicalisations and Reciprocal Radicalisation as an Intertwined Process', *Journal for Deradicalisation*, Spring issue, no. 10, 2017, pp. 255–281.

29 S. Janmohamed, *Generation M: Young Muslims Changing the World*, London and New York: IB Tauris, 2017.

Recommended Readings

Abbas, T., 'Editorial' as Guest Editor of the Special Edition, 'Educating British Muslims: Identity, Religion and Politics in a Neoliberal Era', *British Journal of Sociology of Education*, forthcoming, March 2018, pp. 1–3.

Abbas, T., 'Ethnicity and Politics in Contextualising Far Right and Islamist Extremism', *Perspectives on Terrorism*, vol. 11, no. 3, 2017, pp. 54–61.

Abbas, T., 'The Symbiotic Relationship between Islamophobia and Radicalisation', *Critical Studies on Terrorism*, vol. 5, no. 3, 2012, pp. 345–358.

Abbas, T., *Islamic Radicalism and Multicultural Politics: The British Experience*, London and New York: Routledge, 2011.

Allen, C., *Islamophobia*, Farnham: Ashgate, 2010.

Anwar, M., *The Myth of Return: Pakistanis in Britain*, London: Heinemann Educational, 1979.

Bailey, G. and P. Edwards, 'Rethinking "Radicalisation": Microradicalisations and Reciprocal Radicalisation as an Intertwined Process', *Journal for Deradicalisation*, Spring issue, no. 10, 2017, pp. 255–281.

Beider, H., *White Working Class Voices: Multiculturalism, Community-Building and Change*, Bristol: The Policy Press, 2015.

Betz, H-G., 'The Two Faces of Radical Right-Wing Populism in Western Europe', *The Review of Politics*, vol. 55, no. 4, 1993, pp. 663–685.

Borum, R., 'Radicalization into Violent Extremism I: A Review of Social Science Theories', *Journal of Strategic Security*, vol. 4, no. 4, 2011, pp. 7–36.

Casey, L., *The Casey Review A Review into Opportunity and Integration*, London: Department of Communities and Local Government, 2016.

Cole, M., 'Critical Race Theory comes to the UK: A Marxist response', *Ethnicities*, vol. 9, no. 2, 2009, pp. 246–284.

Dorling, D., *Inequality and the 1%*, London and New York: Verso, 2015.

Ebner, J., *The Rage: The Vicious Circle of Islamist and Far-Right Extremism*, London and New York: IB Tauris, 2018.

Esposito, J. and I Kalin (ed.), *Islamophobia: The Challenge of Pluralism in the 21st Century*, New York: Oxford University Press, 2011.

Ferrera, M., 'Ideology, Parties and Social Politics in Europe', *West European Politics*, vol. 37, no. 2, 2014, pp. 420–448.

Foucault, M. 'Lecture 11, 17 March 1976', in M. Foucault (ed.), *Society Must Be Defended: Lectures at the College de France*, 239–264, London and New York: Picador, 2003, p. 245.

Goodwin, M. *The Roots of Extremism: The English Defence League and the Counter-Jihad Challenge*, London: Chatham House Briefing Paper, 2013.

Heath, A. and J. Martin, 'Can Religious Affiliation Explain "Ethnic" Inequalities in the Labour Market?', *Ethnic and Racial Studies*, vol. 36, no. 6, 2013, pp. 1005–1027.

Janmohamed, S. *Generation M: Young Muslims Changing the World*, London and New York: IB Tauris, 2017.

Kundnani, A. *The Muslims Are Coming! Islamophobia, Extremism, and the Domestic War on Terror*, London and New York: Verso, 2014.
Lorne, L. and A. Amarasingam, 'Talking to Foreign Fighters: Insights into the Motivations for Hijrah to Syria and Iraq', *Studies in Conflict & Terrorism*, vol. 40, no. 3, 2017; pp. 191–210.
Peach, C., 'The Meaning of Segregation', *Planning Practice and Research*, vol. 11, no. 2, 1994, pp. 137–150.
Pearson, E., 'The Case of Roshonara Choudhry: Implications for Theory on Online Radicalization, ISIS Women, and the Gendered Jihad', *Policy and Internet*, vol. 8, no. 1, 2016, pp. 5–33.
Pisoiu, D. 'Subcultural Theory Applied to Jihadi and Right-Wing Radicalization in Germany', *Terrorism and Political Violence*, vol. 27, no. 1, 2015, pp. 9–28.
Roy, O., *Globalized Islam: The Search for a New Ummah*, New York: Columbia University Press, 2002.
Saull, R. 'Capitalism, Crisis and the Far-Right in the Neoliberal Era', *Journal of International Relations and Development*, vol. 18, no. 1, 2015, pp. 25–51.
Sayyid, S. and A.V. Vakil (eds.), *Thinking through Islamophobia: Global Perspectives*, London and New York: Hurst and Columbia University Press, 2011.
Sedgwick, M., 'The Concept of Radicalization as a Source of Confusion', *Terrorism and Political Violence*, vol. 4, no. 4, 2010, pp. 479–494.
Waarsi, S., *The Enemy Within: A Tale of Muslim Britain*, London: Allen Lane, 2017.
Wiktorowicz, Q. (ed.), *Islamic Activism: A Social Movement Theory Approach*, Bloomington: Indiana University Press. 2004.

10 THE ROLE OF COMMUNITY ENGAGEMENT AND THE PRACTICAL ROLE OF MODERATE AND NON-VIOLENT EXTREMIST MOVEMENTS IN COMBATING JIHADIST TERRORISM

Basia Spalek and Salwa El-Awa

Introduction

Scholars in terrorism studies have, for many years, written about the importance of considering communities when understanding, responding to and preventing politically, religiously and other ideologically motivated violence. Terrorists are in competition with communities and socio-political-religious movements for proactive and passive support for their causes, membership and resources. In the aftermath of a series of jihadist terror attacks, alongside terror acts committed by far-right extremists, in the UK there has been an increased emphasis upon the role of communities in combatting terrorism. 'Communities can defeat terrorism' has become a well-known mantra. With this in mind, this chapter comprises a short research synthesis of recently published work on the role of community engagement, and the practical role of moderate and non-violent extremist movements, in combating jihadist terrorism.

The chapter is divided into three separate sections. The first section sets out the key debates within the research literature on the challenges of engaging communities and moderate and non-violent extremist movements in the UK. Section two explores some of the key Islamist movements from an historical and ideological perspective and what the research tells us about these movements in relation to their involvement in violence and its prevention. This section particularly focuses upon our understanding of Islamist movements in relation to their involvement in perpetuating and/or combating jihadist terrorism nationally and internationally. Section three presents research evidence of the practical involvement of non-violent 'extremist' movements in combating jihadist terrorism.

Section One: Engaging Communities and Moderate and Non-Violent Extremist Movements in the UK for Countering Jihadist-Linked Terrorism

The terror attacks of 9/11 are viewed as a significant turning point in counter-terrorism policies and practices[1] in the UK alongside other international contexts, partly because governments have increasingly become concerned by the threat posed by citizens from within their own countries.[2] This has helped to create a 'hearts and minds' approach to counter-terrorism, whereby community engagement in preventing terrorism is seen as a beneficial and even essential aspect.[3]

Community engagement is a broad notion that includes drawing upon the knowledge, skills and credibility of members of particular ethnic/cultural/religious/political communities alongside involving a wide range of professionals working within health/mental health, housing, educational and other sectors.[4]

The research suggests that engaging Muslim communities for countering jihadist terrorism can have a number of important benefits. Individuals within Muslim communities may have knowledge about colleagues, friends, family members and others that is not available to policing, security and other statutory bodies.[5] As established by a large body of research, there is no one pathway to terrorism[6] and as such drawing upon knowledge about communities can help police and security services and others to risk assess a particular person or network or group of individuals and to take appropriate action as required.[7] Much research has been conducted looking at community engagement in relation to community policing within a counter-terrorism arena. Although this can be both controversial and debatable, some research suggests that community members can be the 'eyes and ears' of the police, passing on information that can help prevent or investigate a terror attack.[8] However, the research suggests that community members will not pass on information to policing, security and other statutory agencies unless there is trust.[9]

The research literature places a large emphasis upon community engagement as a critical way of building and maintaining trust.[10] The literature suggests the following stressors to building and maintaining trust: where community engagement is seen by community members as being there only for information-sharing reasons rather than to empower and support communities; where there are no information sharing protocols[11]; where any trust that is developed is placed under strain as a result of policies and practices that stigmatize and potentially harm community members; and where there is a high turnover of staff within policing units/divisions and of other professionals.[12]

Research indicates that counter-terrorism policies and practices, including initiatives brought in under the label of 'community engagement', have stigmatized entire communities. The literature suggests that in the aftermath of 9/11 it is Muslim communities in particular that have become 'suspect communities',[13] involving the securitization of their identities, 'hard' policing and security practices, and community penetration by informants.[14] This can detrimentally impact upon any community engagement that is subsequently instigated. The research indicates that Muslim community members voluntarily cooperate with police to combat terrorism when they see tangible benefits that outweigh any negative effects of engagement, and when they have a belief that the police are a legitimate authority, where police legitimacy depends upon the perceived fair and accountable application of the rule of law.[15]

Community members can help the authorities make a risk assessment of any individuals or groups that have been flagged up as being of concern; they can work with individuals deemed at risk, as mentors, to reduce the risk; and they also may have access to persons that police would struggle to engage with – those sections within communities that are particularly distrustful or fearful of police services.[16] This raises the issue of engaging non-violent extremist movements, which has raised considerable research and policy attention in the UK and internationally.

In the UK considerable research highlights that non-violent extremists can play an important preventative and divertive role in that they provide identity, belonging and political/religious frameworks of understanding and practices and in this way take potential recruits away from violent extremist groups.[17] Indeed, there may be no direct link between extremism and violent extremism.[18] On the other hand, some commentators raise concerns about the involvement of non-violent extremist groups in combating jihadist terrorism. They argue that non-violent extremist groups can provide the space within which extremist ideologies and practices can flourish, making it easier for people to transition to violent extremism.[19] Section two is a synthesis of research findings on the question of which groups of Islamists could be good partners in countering violent extremism and their historical and ideological foundations that justify this argument.

Section Two: Research Findings on the History and Ideology of Violent and Non-Violent Political Islamists

Research suggests that political Islamic[20] activists who seek change within their communities, countries or internationally can be roughly divided into three broad categories.[21] First, the jihadi approach which resorts to violent means to achieve its aims, and which, in turn, splits into various political and theological sects mainly divided around the question of who is the enemy (national or international).[22] Those groups include small local militants whose acts of violence are directed towards their countries' regimes, but also those affecting civilians, groups such as the former jihad organization (*Tanzim al-Jihad*) of Egypt with its many offspring groups[23] and the newly emerging *Harakat Hasm*; and transnationally active groups such as Al-Qaeda and the Islamic State; or those active both locally and internationally such as Boko Haram in Nigeria, Chad, Niger and Cameron.[24]

There are two approaches that refuse to endorse violence on a theological basis and, thus, offer the alternative to jihadists' violent extremism. These are namely the non-jihadi 'radical' approach of Wahhabi salafism and the 'moderate' or rather 'centrist'[25] reformist approach of the Muslim Brotherhood (henceforth MB) global movement.[26] Both approaches are widespread and largely represented in both Muslim and non-Muslim countries.[27]

Looking at the ideologies and theological basis of the two movements shows that they can pose a threat to violent extremism because they are both founded on a theological basis that is contradictory to the ideas adopted by the global jihadi movement, and their ideologues explicitly oppose its activities as well as principles and engage in direct theological and jurisprudential polemicism with their jihadist counterparts.[28]

The aims of political Islamist activism have often been to achieve individual, social and political reform through recourse to a pure form of religion.[29] However, contemporary radical salafism rooted in Wahhabism discourages political participation altogether because of the movement's strong association with the Saudi State. There is much debate about Wahhabi salafism and a relatively widespread perception that it is the same as jihadi salafism.[30] However, a large body of research into the history and ideology of Wahhabism concludes that this is not necessarily the case.[31] Muhammad ibn 'Abd al-Wahhab's theology was embraced by the Saudi state in the 1970s and the doctrine that forbids opposition to the state and any form of political engagement, be it violent or peaceful, has since become a part and parcel of this ideology.[32]

Non-violent radical salafis around the world have worked both alone and with the state to reduce political activism of all kinds, particularly jihadist activism, based on a presumed resemblance of the current time for Muslims to the earlier years of Prophet Muhammad's mission (the Meccan period), when jihad and political confrontation with opponents were no longer a requirement for Muslims because Islam and Muslims were not in a position to win such battles. This, along with the principle of *tahrim alkhuruj 'ala al-hakim* (forbidding rebellion/opposition against rulers), led to the conclusion that contemporary Muslims should live at a stage of *da'wa* (preaching and teaching religion) rather than jihad (offensive).[33] Therefore, to the Wahhabis, the jihadi solution in Islam is by default contrary to a non-violent solution.[34]

However, with the growing interest in global jihad, and the empowerment of young people through modern means of communication as well as the recent shock to Arab states through the Arab Spring uprising, in which many young salafists participated along with all sectors of Arab societies, the case against the legitimacy of engaging in politics weakened gradually. The salafis' participation in politics after the political scene had changed gave rise to criticism and cynicism about their former theological stance and hence undermined the credibility of their ideologues and preachers.[35]

The controversial global social movement known as the Muslim Brotherhood (MB) has often raised debate as to its position regarding the issue of jihad. To summarize a very lengthy debate, the following points should be noted.[36] The MB's struggle against colonialism ended in the early 1950s, but it did involve the use of armed struggle against occupying forces. That was followed later on by the group's leadership publicly distancing it from extremist factions evolving under persecution in Nasser's prisons in the 1960s (the Qutbies and *al-Tanzim al-Khass*). Since then, the reformative political approach has become the only official position of the MB outside occupied territories.[37] The movement aspired to participation in democratic processes as a way of achieving wider popular acceptance following the repeated persecutions of the movement's members in Egypt (in 1954, 1962 and recently in 2013). Thus, the global Muslim Brotherhood movement repeatedly calls upon its members around the world to be active within the legal and political systems of their countries and, also, to reject all means of violent activism.[38]

An interesting example that highlights the lack of compatibility between violent and non-violent political activism in contemporary Islamic ideologies is a local non-violent political group in Egypt, *al-Jama'a al-Islamiyya* (the Islamic Group, EIG henceforth). The recent history of the EIG shows that the group was able to participate in the political process, from an ideological point of view, only after it had denounced violence in the name of jihad in 2001, which was the fruit of a prolonged process of theological revision followed by a large-scale in-prison de-radicalization program facilitated by the State.[39] More co-operation between the Egyptian State and the EIG in in-prison de-radicalization has been repeatedly reported since 2001 to the present day.[40]

The EIG's self-imposed theological revisions denounced the group's old belief that the State and the Regime are 'disbelievers' who should be fought against, and, instead, called for reconciliation and gradual reform through participation in the political process and '*dafiwa*' (Islamic education and preaching).[41] This current position is almost identical to that of the MB. Subsequently, the group's ideologues have also engaged in theological debates with their jihadist counterparts about the validity and permissibility of their violent struggle from an Islamic jurisprudential point of view, calling upon groups such as Al-Qaeda and the Islamic State to denounce violence against the state and civilians alike.[42] The ideologies of these movements have a wide influence on Islamist activists across the globe and have therefore been invested in to counter jihadi ideologies in various parts of the world.[43]

Section Three: Research Evidence of the Practical Involvement of Members of Non-Violent Extremist Movements in Combating Jihadist-Linked Terrorism

Two particular case studies of partnership approaches to counter-terrorism involving members of non-violent extremist movements and police officers have been researched in depth within the UK. Both of these will be the focus here.

The first case study is that of an initiative that took place between members of a salafi community based at a mosque in Brixton in London and police after 9/11. The initiative comprised salafi community members working in partnership with police officers in order to risk-assess vulnerable individuals, to provide interventions to make vulnerable individuals less likely to use violence (whether politically/religiously motivated or gang-related violence), and to flag up those individuals who had moved from non-violent to violent extremism with the police so that these individuals could be disrupted and prevented from committing acts of terrorism. It is important to highlight that this initiative between community members and the police involved a particular policing unit – the Muslim Contact Unit (MCU). The MCU was a specialist community-based counter-terrorism policing unit whose particular remit was to build trusting relationships with wide-ranging Muslim communities across London, including moderate and non-violent extremist groups.

The second case study of partnership between members of non-violent extremist movements and the police in London focuses on the involvement of community members linked to the Muslim Brotherhood at Finsbury Park mosque and the MCU. Again, the MCU set out to build trust with Muslim community members at the mosque, which had at one time been associated with the extremist cleric Abu Hamza. Both of these cases have been documented at length.[44] The key findings from this body of research are as follows:

- It is important to facilitate community participation as mutually beneficial, even if forms of participation are not routinely of direct police interest.
- Trust building is key, particularly between the police and members of communities who have been previously marginalized or alienated.
- There can be conflicting values to negotiate between different partners: as the values and goals of police and community members are not always in concordance it is vital that conflicts are addressed to the satisfaction of all partners and that commonalities are used to consolidate partnerships.
- Information gathering, particularly through good police–community relations, should be viewed as a secondary benefit of partnership work, which seeks primarily to empower communities to develop approaches to tackling violent extremist ideology and its propagators.

- It is important to provide Reassurance Policing in the context of racist and Islamophobic attacks.
- It is important to acknowledge grievances on both sides, for example the frustration with foreign policy for some community members and the perception by some police officers that community members may apportion too much responsibility regarding political matters on to the police rather than politicians.[45]

On an international level also, these findings have been reinforced. Trust-based cooperation between state actors such as special police units and Islamist group leaders in combatting violent ideologies has been successful in the de-radicalization of thousands of imprisoned EIG members in Egypt[46] and in de-radicalizing emerging groups of radicals outside prisons in remote areas such as Sinai.[47] The co-operation has also involved empowering freed leaders of the group to identify individuals deemed at risk of adopting violent extremism, working with them on a theologically based de-radicalization program and flagging up cases that they deemed to be in need of police intervention.[48] This work continues to this day, although trust issues have arisen due to the change of administration that took place recently in Egypt.[49]

The empowerment of the MB since the 1980s and the Wahhabi-type salafi preachers in the late 1990s led to the formation of a large social and political force of people seeking in-depth religious education and social and political change (particularly for the MB). The long and intensive efforts were successful in mobilizing hundreds of thousands of Egyptians of various age groups and social and professional backgrounds towards meaningful activism and away from what were seen as destructive and religiously illegitimate jihadi ideologies.[50] Such social empowerment is considered to be a key factor in the uprising that the Arab World witnessed in 2011, choosing non-violent methods over militancy to change the ruling regime, particularly in Egypt and Tunisia. In more recent years, when Egypt's military seized power by the removal of the elected MB president in 2013, the widely prosecuted members and supporters of the MB remained faithful to their peaceful (non-violent) ideology and, despite continued pressure from angry and disillusioned young Muslims opposed to the new regime, the group's leadership continued to be publicly outspoken against the various calls to adopt violence to defeat the oppressive regimes both in Egypt and elsewhere.[51]

To conclude, there is historical evidence that the two approaches to Islamic activism, the jihadi and the non-jihadi, negate each other and are non-complementary. The empowerment of communities called for by researchers yet again has been most effective, as seen from the research discussed above, when it relied on non-violent Islamists being able and free to provide a viable and legitimate channel to which active young Muslims could resort instead of violence.[52]

Notes

1 Counter-terrorism policies and practices are dominated by 'hard' approaches involving surveillance and disruption activities and building technical and structural resilience. See for example J. Coaffee, *Terrorism, Risk and the Global City*, London: Routledge, 2009, pp. 1–10.

2 A. Cherney and J. Hartley, 'Community Engagement to Tackle Terrorism and Violent Extremism: Challenges, Tensions and Pitfalls', *Policing and Society*, vol. 7, no. 27, 2017, pp. 750.

3 R. Briggs, C. Fieschi, and H. Lownsbrough, *Bringing It Home: Community-Based Approaches to Counterterrorism*, London: Demos, 2006, p. 12.

4 B. Spalek, *Terror Crime: Prevention with Communities*, London: Bloomsbury, 2013; B. Spalek, 'Introducing Counter-Terrorism Studies', in B. Spalek (ed.), *Counter-Terrorism: Community Based Approaches to Preventing Terror Crime*, Hampshire: Palgrave Macmillan, 2012, pp. 10–15; A. Huq, 'Community-Led Counter-Terrorism', *Studies in Conflict and Terrorism*, vol. 40, no. 12, 2017, pp. 1043–1048; R. Lambert and T. Parsons, 'Community-Based Counter Terrorism Policing: Recommendations for Practitioners', *Studies in Conflict and Terrorism*, vol. 40, no. 12, 2017, p. 1055.

5 A. Huq, 'Community-Led Counter-Terrorism', *Studies in Conflict and Terrorism*, vol. 40, no. 12, 2017, p. 1041.

6 J. Githens-Mazer and R. Lambert, 'Why Conventional Wisdom on Radicalization Fails: The Persistence of a Failed Discourse', *International Affairs*, vol. 86, no. 4, 2010, pp. 889–901.

7 R. Briggs, 'Community Engagement for Counter-Terrorism: Lessons from the United Kingdom', *International Affairs*, vol. 86, no. 4, 2010, pp. 972–974; A. H. Baker, 'Engagement and Partnership in Community-Based Approaches to Counter-Terrorism', in B. Spalek (ed.), *Counter-Terrorism: Community-Based Approaches to Preventing Terror Crime*, Basingstoke: Palgrave Macmillan, 2012, p. 80; B. Spalek and D. Weeks, 'The Role of Communities in Counter Terrorism: Analysing Policy and Exploring Psychotherapeutic Approaches within Community Settings', *Studies in Conflict and Terrorism*, vol. 40, no. 12, 2017, pp. 992–994.

8 M. Innes, 'Policing Uncertainty: Countering Terror through Community Intelligence and Democratic Policing', *The Annals of the American Academy of Political and Social Science*, vol. 605 no. 1, 2006, p. 230; J. Klausen, 'British Counter-Terrorism after 7/7: Adapting Community Policing to the Fight against Domestic Terrorism', *Journal of Ethnic and Migration Studies*, vol. 35, no. 3, 2009, pp. 410–412; D. Ramirez et al., 'Community Partnerships Thwart Terrorism', in D. Silk, B. Spalek, and M. O'Rawe (eds.), *Preventing Ideological Violence: Communities, Police and Case Studies of Success*, New York: Palgrave Macmillan, 2013, pp. 158–160; Spalek and Weeks, 'The Role of Communities in Counter Terrorism', pp. 994–995.

9 B. Spalek, 'Community Engagement for Preventing Violence: The Role of Connectors', *Conflict and Terrorism Studies*, vol. 37, no. 10, 2014, pp. 830–836.

10 B. Spalek, 'Community Policing, Trust and Muslim Communities in Relation to "New Terrorism"', *Politics and Policy*, vol. 38, no. 4, 2010, p. 793.

11 A. H. Baker, 'Engagement and Partnership in Community-Based Approaches to Counter-Terrorism', in B. Spalek (ed.), *Counter-terrorism: Community-based Approaches to Preventing Terror Crime*, Basingstoke: Palgrave Macmillan, 2012, p. 80.

12 Spalek, 'Community Policing, Trust and Muslim Communities in Relation to "New Terrorism"', pp. 799–804.

13 P. Hillyard, *Suspect Community: People's Experience of the Prevention of Terrorism Acts in Britain*, London: Pluto Press, 1993, pp. 1–320; P. Hillyard, 'The Role of Communities in Counter Terrorism The "War on Terror": Lessons from Ireland', *Essays for Civil Liberties and Democracy in Europe, European Civil Liberties Network*, vol. 12, January, 2018, pp. 1–4.; C. Pantazis and S. Pemberton, 'From the "Old" to the "New Suspect" Community: Examining the Impacts of Recent UK Counter-Terrorist Legislation', *British Journal of Criminology*, vol. 49, no. 5, 2009, pp. 53–57.

14 A. Kundnani, *Spooked: How Not to Prevent Violent Extremism*, London: Institute of Race Relations, 2009, pp. 13–15; T. Choudhury and H. Fenwick, *The Impact of Counterterrorism Measures on Muslim Communities in Britain*, London: Equality and Human Rights Commission, 2011, pp. 30–65; F. Vermeulen, 'Suspect Communities- Targeting Violent Extremism at the Local Level: Policies of Engagement in Amsterdam, Berlin and London', *Terrorism and Political Violence*, vol. 26, 2014, p. 303.

15 T. Tyler, S. Shulhofer, and A. Huq, 'Legitimacy and Deterrent Effects in Counter Terrorism: A Study of Muslim Americans', *Policing Law and Society Review*, vol. 44, no. 2, 2010, pp. 365–402.

16 A. H. Baker, *Extremists in our Midst: Confronting Terror*, Basingstoke: Palgrave Macmillan, 2011, pp. 38–62; R. Lambert, *Countering Al-Qaeda in London: Police and Muslims in Partnerships*, London: Hurst and Co, 2011.; R. Lambert, 'Empowering Salafis and Islamists against Al-Qaeda: A London Counterterrorism Case Study', *Political Science and Politics*, vol. 41. no. 1, 2008, pp. 31–35.

17 Baker, *Extremists in Our Midst: Confronting Terror*, pp. 38–62. R. Lambert, *Countering Al-Qaeda in London: Police and Muslims in Partnerships*, London: Hurst and Co., 2011; Lambert, 'Empowering Salafis and Islamists against Al-Qaeda', pp. 31–35.

18 R. Briggs, 'Community Engagement for Counter-Terrorism', pp. 971–981.

19 E. Husain, *The Islamist*, London: Penguin 2007; M. Phillips, *Londonistan: How Britain Is Creating a Terror State Within*, London: Gibson Square, 2006, p. 1; M. Gove, *Celsius 7/7*, London: Phenoix, 2006, pp. 5–8.

20 This is to exclude spiritual and non-political groups that do not aspire to achieve 'change' such as the purely spiritual *sufi* approach or the purely classical educational/ scholarly approach of *madrasa*s and *darul 'ulum*, for example.

21 This division is not meant as the ultimate and definitive division. Each of the three categories split internally into a large number of other groups sometimes varying in ideology and practice. Also, the social and political situations they react to are in a state of constant change and therefore new groups keep emerging and ideologies are consequently revised.

22 F. A. Gerges, *The Far Enemy: Why Jihad Went Global*, Cambridge: Cambridge University Press, 2005, pp. 119–184.

23 For more on the small local jihadi groups in Egypt: Abdul Mun'im Munib, *Kharitat al-Harakat al-Islamiyyah fi Misr* (*Map of the Islamic Movements in Egypt*), Cairo: Al-Shabaka al-'Arabiyyah Lima'lümat Hqüq al-Insan, 2009, pp. 10–15, available here: http://www.anhri.net/reports/islamic-map/islamic-map.pdf For more on international Jihadist networks:Dia' Rashwan and Muhammad Fayiz Farahat (ed.), *Dalil al-Harakat al-Islamiyyah fi l-'Alam (A guide to Islamic Movements around the*

World), Cairo: Markaz al-Ahram Liddirasat Al-Istratigiyyah, 2006. M. Sageman, *Understanding Terror Networks*, Philadelphia: University of Pennsylvania, 2004; M. Sageman, *Leaderless Jihad: Terror Networks in the Twenty-First Century*, Philadelphia: University of Pennsylvania, 2008; M. Sageman, 'Understanding Jihadi Networks', *Strategic Insights*, vol. 5, no. 4, 2005. https://www.iwp.edu/docLib/20140819_SagemanUnderstandingJihadiNetworks.pdf (accessed 1 February 2018).

24 For more on Boko Haram, its activities and links with other international organizations: A. R. Mustapha (ed.), *Sects & Social Disorder: Muslim Identities & Conflict in Northern Nigeria*, Suffolk & New York: Boydell & Brewer Ltd, 2014, pp. 147–198; M. A. Pérouse de Montclos (ed.), *Boko Haram: Islamism, Politics, Security, and the State in Nigeria*, Los Angeles: Tsehai Publishers, 2015.

25 For the origin and implications of the term 'centrist', R. W. Baker, *Islam without Fear*, USA: Harvard University Press, 2003.

26 By the MB's global movement, the authors do not mean just the organizational members of the Muslim Brotherhood, but rather the many groups across the globe adopting the peaceful political approach of Hassan El-Banna, founder of the MB, such as the Jamaat Islami in India and Pakistan and groups tied with it in Bangladesh, Kashmir and elsewhere as well as other more recent ideologies developing within groups such as the EIG in Egypt.

27 See: Dia' Rashwan (ed.), *The Spectrum of Islamist Movements*, H. Schiler Berlin, 2007. Ahmad Salim Abu Fihr, *Ikhtilaf al-Islamiyyin: halat Misr unamudhajan* (*Differences among Islamists: Egypt as a case study*), Cairo: Markaz Nama' lil-Buhüth wa Al-Dirasat, 2013.

28 Muhammad Mustafa al-Muqri', *Hukm Qatl Al-Madanyyin fi Al-Shari'a Al-Islamiyya: (The Ruling on Killing Civilians in Islamic Sharia)*, London: Al-Markaz al-Duwali li-Ddirasat wa al-I'lam, (1418 h). Karam Zuhdi et al, *Istratijiyyat Tafjirat Al-Qa'ida: al-akhta' wa al-akhtar* (*Al-Qaeda's Attack Strategy: mistakes and dangers)*, Riyadh: Al-'Ubaykan, 2005.Nagih Ibrahim, *Al-Jihad: ghaya am wasila (Jihad: aim or means?)*, Cairo: Dar al-Haytham, 2016.Hisaham Al-Najjar and Nagih Ibrahim, *Da'ish* (*ISIS*), Cairo: Dar al-Shuruq, 2014. 'Ismat Al-Sawi, *Hiwar Hadi' ma'a Da'ishi* (*A Calm Dialogue with a Member of ISIS)*), Cairo: Mu'assasat Rawa'i' li-thaqafa, 2017. Yusuf Al-Qaradawi, *Al-Islam wa Al-'Unf* (*Islam and Violence)*, Cairo: Dar al-Shuruq, 2005.

29 A. Hijazi, *Dirasat fi Al-Salafiyya Al-Jihadiyya* (*Studies in Jihadi Salafism)*, Cairo: Madarat lil-Abhath wa Al-Nashr, 2013, pp 33–36.T. Stanley, 'Understanding the Origins of Wahhabism and Salafism', *Terrorism Monitor*, vol. 3, 2005.

30 The Telegraph Reporters, 'What Is Wahhabism? The Reactionary Branch of Islam from Saudi Arabia Said to Be "The Main Source of Global Terrorism"', *The Telegraph*, London, 19 May 2017, available here: http://www.telegraph.co.uk/news/2016/03/29/what-is-wahhabism-the-reactionary-branch-of-islam-said-to-be-the/; C. Moniquet, *The Involvement of Salafism/Wahhabism in the Support and Supply of Arms to Rebel Groups around the World*, Belgium: European Union, 2013.

31 A. Hijazi, *Dirasat fi Al-Salafiyya Al-Jihadiyya* (*Studies in Jihadi Salafism)*, pp 33–36. Trevor Stanley 2005, URL:https://jamestown.org/program/understanding-the-origins-of-wahhabism-and-salafism/; M. Ali and M.S.A.S. Sudiman, 'Salafism Vs Wahhabism: Are They the Same?', *Eurasia Review*, 2016. URL: https://www.sott.net/article/330853-Salafism-vs-Wahhabism-Are-they-the-same (accessed 29 January 2018).

32 For various *fatwas* and discussions of 'democracy as a forbidden form of *shirk*' (polytheism) by prominent Wahhabi Salafi Sheikhs: https://islamqa.info/ar/107166 (accessed 01 February 2018). The same source also includes references to *fatwas* by various prominent scholars of the Saudi Permanent Committee: Abdul Aziz bin Baz, Abdullah bin Ghadhyan, Abdullah bin Qa'ud and Abdurrazzaq 'Afifi. For further Salafi discussions of the legitimacy of political participation: https://www.sahab.net/forums/index.php?app=forums&module=forums&controller=topic&id=126009.

33 A. Ibn Baz, *Majmu' al-Fatawa* (*Collection of Fatwas*), vol. 8, pp. 204–202 http://shamela.ws/browse.php/book-21537#page-3769 Ibn 'Uthaymın, *Majmu' al-Fatawa* (*Collection of Fatwas*), vol. 18, p. 388. http://shamela.ws/browse.php/book-12293#page-7099 (accessed 03 February 2018). For a further detailed discussion: Sadiq ibn Muhammad Al-Baydani, 'Hal al-Jihad fi hadha al-'asr farida 'ala kul Muslim?' (Is Jihad Incumbent on every Muslim in this Era?), available here: http://albidhani.com/home/هل-الجهاد-في-هذا-العصر-فرض-عين-على-كل-مس/ (accessed 02 February 2018).

34 They are different alternatives that could exist only in different conditions and therefore are mutually exclusive in any given situation.

35 G. Fahmi, 'Mustaqbal al-Salafiyya al-Siyasiyya fi Misr wa Tunus', *Carnegie Middle East Centre*, available here: http://carnegie-mec.org/2015/11/16/ar-pub-61954 (accessed 13 February 2015). Also see, for example: https://www.almesryoon.com/story/1044151/الدعوة-السلفية-من-تحريم-الديمقراطية-إلى-مدحها-مراجعات-أم-تراجعات (accessed 01 February 2018). This gave greater credence to the MB's approach, which later won wide popular support in elections that followed in several Arab countries.

36 For more details on this issue: Foreign Affairs Committee, Political Islam and the Muslim Brotherhood Review, London: House of Commons, 2016. file:///Users/SE/Documents/Research/Co-Jit%20paper%20-%20BS%20&%20SE%20Dec17-Jan%2018/CoJit%20-%20Lit/House%20of%20Commons%20-%20'Political%20Islam'%20and%20the%20Muslim%20Brotherhood%20Review%20-%20Foreign%20Affairs%20Committee.webarchive (accessed 20 December 2017). H. Tammam, *Al-Ikhwan al-Muslimun: Sanawat ma Qabla al-Thawra* (*The Muslim Brotherhood: Pre-revolution Years)*, Cairo: Dar al-Shuruq, 2013 pp 137–161.

37 O. Al-Tilmisani, *Du'a la Quda* (*Preachers Not Judges)*, Cairo: Dar al-Tawzi' wa al-Nashr al-Islamiyya, 1977. Notably here, this is the MB's current position as regards all forms of political violence, except for that which is directed against foreign, non-Muslim occupiers in occupied territories, where they continue to use warfare against the occupiers, e.g. that carried out by Hamas.

38 Y. Al-Qaradawi, *Fiqh al-Jihad* (*The Jurisprudence of Jihad)*, Qatar: Markaz al-Qaradawi lil-Wasatiyya al-Islamiyya wa al-Tajdid, 2008. Ahmad Fawzi Salim, Qabla 'Hasm': Limadha Taraddada al-Ikhwan?', https://www.ida2at.com/before-hasam-why-did-the-muslims-brotherhood-hesitate-to-declaere-their-opinion-on-violent-groups/.

39 S. El-Awa, *Al-Jama'a al-Islamiyya al-Musallaha fi Misr 1974–2004* (*The Militant Islamic Group in Egypt 1974–2004*) Cairo: Maktabat al-Shuruq al-Duwaliyya, 2006, pp. 146–186. Mu̧ammad Abu 'Atiyya Al-Sandabisi, *al-Inqilab al-Fikri lil-Jama'a al-Islamiyya* (*the Intellectual Coup of the Islamic Group)*, Cairo: Awraq Li-nnashr wa al-Tawzi', 2012, pp 163–245.

40 S. El-Awa, *The Relation between the EIG and the Egyptian State Security*, Cairo: Unpublished study, 2009.

41 For details of their revised theology: K. Zuhdi et al, *Tashih al-Mafahim* (Reformation of Concepts) (series), Riyadh: al-'Ubaykan, 2001.

42 See footnote 28 above.

43 For example, see the works of The *Jamaat Islami* in India and Pakistan, the Izalah movement in Nigeria.

44 Baker, *Extremists in Our Midst: Confronting Terror*, pp. 38–62. Lambert, *Countering Al-Qaeda in London;* Lambert, 'Empowering Salafis and Islamists against Al-Qaeda', pp. 31–35; B. Spalek, S. El-Awa, and L. McDonald, *Police-Muslim Engagement and Partnerships for the Purposes of Counter-Terrorism Summary Report*, Birmingham: University of Birmingham, 2008, pp. 11–18.

45 Spalek, El-Awa, and McDonald, '*Police-Muslim Engagement and Partnerships for the Purposes of Counter-Terrorism Summary Report*', pp. 11–14.

46 See: S. El-Awa, *al-Jama'a al-Islamiyya al-Musalla͏̦a fi Misr (1974–2004)*, Cairo: Maktabat al-Shuruq al-Duwaliyya, 2007.

47 For example: 'Amr Al-Naqib, 'Al-Sujun al-Misriyya Wazza'at Kitab '*Hiwar ma'a Da'ishi*' 'ala al-Jihadiyyin li Muwajahat al-Takfir' ('Egyptian Prisons Distribute "*A Dialogue with a Member of ISIS*" to Jihadis in an Attempt to Combat *Takfir*'), 24, 26.04.2017, http://24.ae/article/343379/مصادر-أمنية-لـ-24السجون-المصرية-وزعت-كتاب-
%22حوار-مع-داعشي-%22على-الجهاديين-لمواجهة-التكفير (accessed 03 February 2018).

48 El-Awa, *The Relation between the EIG and the Egyptian State Security.*

49 The previously exemplar successful relation between the EIG and the Egyptian state has been shaken after the recent change in Egyptian politics and is in a state of flux that is currently difficult for researchers to access. For more on the EIG after the 2011 uprising, see: Mu͏̦ammad Abu 'Atiyyah al-Sandabisi, 2012, pp. 319–329.

50 See, C. R. Wickham, *Mobilizing Islam: Religion, Activism and Political Change in Egypt*, New York: Columbia University Press, 2002.

51 R. Dandachli, 'Fighting Ideology with Ideology: Islamism and the Challenge of ISIS'. *Brookings*, 5 January, 2017, available here: https://www.brookings.edu/opinions/fighting-ideology-with-ideology-islamism-and-the-challenge-of-isis/; see also: footnote no 35 above.

52 B. Spalek, S. El-Awa and L. McDonald, *Police-Muslim Engagement and Partnerships for the Purposes of Counter-Terrorism Summary Report*, Birmingham: University of Birmingham, 2008; King's College London, Recruitment and Mobilisation for the Islamist Militant Movement in Europe, 2007, p.5. Study carried out by King's College London for the European Commission (Directorate General Justice, Freedom and Security).

Recommended Readings

Baker, A. H., 'Engagement and Partnership in Community-Based Approaches to Counter-terrorism', in B. Spalek, (ed.), *Counter-terrorism: Community-Based Approaches to Preventing Terror Crime*, Basingstoke: Palgrave Macmillan, 2012, pp. 74–99.

Baker, R.W., *Islam without Fear*, USA: Harvard University Press, 2003.

Bergen, P., 'Do NSA's Bulk Surveillance Programs Stop Terrorists?', *New America Foundation*, 2014.

Bjorgo, T., *Strategies for Preventing Terrorism*, Basingstoke: Palgrave Macmillan, 2013.

Briggs, R., 'Community Engagement for Counter-Terrorism: lessons from the United Kingdom', *International Affairs*, vol. 86, no. 4, 2010, pp. 971–981.

Cherney, A. and J. Hartley, 'Community Engagement to Tackle Terrorism and Violent Extremism: Challenges, Tensions and Pitfalls', *Policing and Society*, vol. 7, no. 27, 2017, pp. 750–763.

Choudhury, T. and H. Fenwick, *The Impact of Counterterrorism Measures on Muslim Communities in Britain*, London: Equality and Human Rights Commission, 2011, pp. 1–105.

El-Awa, S., *Al-Jama'a al-Islamiyya al-Musalla¸a fi Misr 1974-2004* (*The Militant Islamic Group in Egypt 1974-2004*) Cairo: Maktabat al-Shuruq al-Duwaliyya, 2006.

Foreign Affairs Committee, *Political Islam and the Muslim Brotherhood Review*, London: House of Commons, 2016.

Githens-Mazer, J. and R. Lambert, 'Why Conventional Wisdom on Radicalization Fails: The Persistence of a Failed Discourse', *International Affairs*, vol. 86, no. 4, 2010, pp. 889–901.

Gunaratna, R., J. Jerard, and S. M. Nasir, *Countering Extremism: Building Social Resilience Through Community Engagement*, London: Imperial College Press, 2013.

Hijazi, A., *Dirasat fi Al-Salafiyya Al-Jihadiyya (Studies in Jihadi Salafism)*, Cairo: Madarat lil-Abhath wa Al-Nashr 2013.

Hillyard, P., *Suspect Community: People's Experience of the Prevention of Terrorism Acts in Britain*, London: Pluto Press, 1993.

Huq, A., 'Community-Led Counter-Terrorism', *Studies in Conflict and Terrorism*, vol. 40, no. 12, 2017, pp. 1038–1053.

Ibrahim N., *Al-Jihad: ghaya am wasila (Jihad: means or end?)*, Cairo: Dar al-Haytham, 2016.

Innes, M., 'Policing Uncertainty: Countering Terror through Community Intelligence and Democratic Policing', *The Annals of the American Academy of Political and Social Science*, vol. 605, no. 1, 2006, pp. 222–241.

Lambert, R., *Countering Al-Qaeda in London: Police and Muslims in Partnerships*, London: Hurst and Co, 2011.

Lambert, R. and T. Parsons 'Community-Based Counter Terrorism Policing: Recommendations for Practitioners', *Studies in Conflict and Terrorism*, vol. 40, no. 12, 2017, pp. 1054–1077.

Pérouse de Montclos, M. A. (ed.), *Boko Haram: Islamism, Politics, Security, and the State in Nigeria*, Los Angeles: Tsehai Publishers, 2015.

Pantazis, C. and S. Pemberton, 'From the 'Old' to the "New Suspect" Community: Examining the Impacts of Recent UK Counter-Terrorist Legislation', *British Journal of Criminology*, vol. 49, no. 5, 2009, pp. 46–66.

Qaradawi, Y. *Al-Islam wa Al-'Unf (Islam and Violence)*, Cairo: Dar al-Shuruq, 2005.

Ramirez, D., et al., 'Community Partnerships Thwart Terrorism', in D. Silk, B. Spalek, and M. O'Rawe (ed.), *Preventing Ideological Violence: Communities, Police and Case Studies of Success*, New York: Palgrave Macmillan, 2013, pp. 151–169.

Rashwan, D. and M. F. Farahat (ed.), *Dalil al-Harakat al-Islamiyyah fi l-'Alam (A guide to Islamic Movements around the World)*, Cairo: Markaz al-Ahram Liddirasat Al-Istratigiyyah, 2006.

Sageman, M., *Leaderless Jihad: Terror Networks in the Twenty-First Century*, Philadelphia: University of Pennsylvania, 2008.

Sandabisi, M. A., *Al-Inqilab al-Fikri lil-Jama'a al-Islamiyya (The Intellectual Coup of the Islamic Group)*, Cairo: Awraq, 2012.

Sawi,'I., *Hiwar Hadi' ma'a Da'ishi (A Calm Dialogue with a Member of ISIS)*, Cairo: Muassasat Raw'i' li-Thaqafa, 2017.

Silk, D., B. Spalek and M. O'Rawe, *Preventing Ideological Violence: Communities, Police and Case Studies of 'Success'*, New York: Palgrave Macmillan, 2013.

Spalek, B., S. El-Awa, and L. McDonald, *Police-Muslim Engagement and Partnerships for the Purposes of Counter-Terrorism Summary Report*, Birmingham: University of Birmingham, 2008.
Spalek, B., 'Community Engagement for Preventing Violence: The Role of Connectors', *Conflict and Terrorism Studies*, vol. 37, no. 10, 2014, pp. 825–841.
Spalek, B., *Terror Crime: Prevention with Communities*, London: Bloomsbury, 2013.
Spalek, B. and L. Davies, 'Mentoring in Relation to Violent Extremism: A Study of Role, Response, Purpose and Outcome', *Studies in Conflict & Terrorism*, vol. 35, no. 5, 2012.
Spalek, B. and D. Weeks, 'The Role of Communities in Counter Terrorism: Analysing Policy and Exploring Psychotherapeutic Approaches within Community Settings', *Studies in Conflict and Terrorism*, vol. 40, no 12, 2017, pp. 991–1003.
Hussam Tammam, *Al-Ikhwan al-Muslimun: Sanawat ma Qabla al-Thawra* (*The Muslim Brotherhood: Pre-revolution Years)*, Cairo: Dar al-Shuruq, 2013.
Omar Al-Tilmisani, *Du'a la Quda* (*Preachers Not Judges)*, Cairo: Dar al-Tawziʻ wa al-Nashr al-Islamiyya, 1977.
Weeks, D., 'Doing DeRad: an analysis of the UK System', *Studies in Conflict and Terrorism*, vol. 41, no. 7, 2018, pp. 523–540.
Zuhdi K. et al., *Istratıjiyyat Tafjirat Al-Qa'ida: al-akhta' wa al-akhtar (Al-Qaeda's Attack Strategy: Mistakes and Dangers)*, Riyadh: Al-'Ubaykan, 2005.

11 THE ROLE AND IMPACT OF WOMEN'S INFLUENCE IN RADICALIZATION AND COUNTER-RADICALIZATION

Katherine Brown

Introduction

Over the past decade governments and security services have become more aware of the role and impact of women in terrorism and radicalization. In part this is because of the seemingly unprecedented levels of success that the 'so-called Islamic State' – also referred to as Daesh[1] – had in recruiting women from all over the world. Estimates placed as much as 20 per cent of their membership as being women, a figure usually found only among socialist and anarchist groups.[2] The Islamic State used this recruiting success as part of their overarching propaganda and as a means to further radicalize women. Violent Islamic extremist groups are not the only groups to maximize the power of women in order to radicalize and recruit others. Parallels have been drawn with international recruitment to the Spanish Civil War.[3] In the UK the fascist movement also had extensive involvement of women.[4] Moreover, women have been involved in all sides of the conflict in Northern Ireland.[5] Another reason for this awareness of women in radicalization follows successive UK governments' attempts to minimize the risk of terrorist activity by investigating and prosecuting 'everything that happens before the bomb goes off'.[6] Consequently, women's complex and often 'back-room' roles have become visible to the State. This corresponds with a widening range of activities criminalized because of their association with terrorism and an increase in women's convictions for related offences. In the year ending 31 December 2017, 15 per cent (61) of those arrested were women.[7] This is an increase of 4 percentage points on the year ending December 2016. Since September 2001, when the collection began, women have accounted for 9 per cent of arrests.[8]

Background/Key terms

Radicalization, much like the term *terrorism*, has proven to be difficult to define in law, policy circles, and in practice. However, in short, radicalization is a process that in the end produces an individual willing to actively support and potentially engage in violent extremist actions.[9] What that process looks like is trickier to establish, with a report from RAND identifying over 200 separate variables.[10] Moreover, an additional challenge when considering radicalization in relation to women is that our models purport to be gender-blind whereas in reality they rely heavily on a male-centric worldview and set of assumptions. This bias has occurred because original datasets focused on those who had a direct role in political violent attacks rather than the broader range of actors involved in terrorist groups. Understanding gender in the radicalization process is more than 'adding women and stirring' – although this is an important first step. Gender-aware approaches also require considering how gender roles, relationships and norms constitute radicalization and associated social phenomena. With this in mind, in a previous report for the UK High Court concerning a young woman's radicalization, Andrew Silke and this author highlighted a number of individual-level factors: a quest for significance; support for altruism and willingness for self-sacrifice; mortality salience; self-esteem and importance of identification with a collective/group. The significant environmental factors we highlighted are: role of family and peers; connections and social bonds within communities; experience directly or vicariously of grievances; and the influence of charismatic online or local radical speakers.[11] Importantly these variables are also relevant for men in the radicalization process as gendered influences and experiences. From these we see that radicalization is therefore about extreme beliefs, extreme behaviours and extreme belonging. Understanding the relationship between the three components allows us to generalize while also acknowledging the variety of individual motivations for joining extremist groups and the multiple pathways, and to do so without diminishing women's participation or their agency.

Countering radicalization using such a broad framework – especially given the definitional ambiguity of 'extremism' – can make it difficult to delineate these efforts from other counter-terrorism policies or social interventions. Nevertheless, a widely used definition of counter-radicalization is: 'the use of non-coercive means to dissuade individuals or groups from mobilizing towards violence and to mitigate recruitment, support, facilitation or engagement in ideologically motivated terrorism by non-state actors in furtherance of political objectives'.[12] These efforts are divided into two different categories: the first is countering violent extremism (CVE), and the second preventing violent extremism (PVE). CVE tends to be security driven and responds to specific groups or known threats. In contrast PVE is more holistic, and focuses on underlying structural factors that contribute to violent extremism. These efforts contrast with 'de-radicalization' efforts that target individuals who are already radicalized and that seek to rehabilitate them. The focus in this chapter is on the broad range of initiatives linked to CVE – which are associated with the Prevent strand in the UK counter-terrorism strategy CONTEST.[13]

There are two main phases of Prevent to date, the first ran until 2011, and relied on the Department of Communities and Local Government (DCLG) to deliver programmes focused on building Muslim community capacity. At the same time those delivering services in Muslim communities came under pressure to identify and report those 'at risk' of radicalization, and there was increased influence and funding for policing in this area. In its second phase (still in operation) DCLG has been mostly removed from CVE policies and addressing community needs has largely been side-lined in policy. These have been replaced with a more narrowly defined remit focusing on minimizing and reducing risk from vulnerable individuals, with projects and initiatives commissioned accordingly by the Office for Security and Counter-Terrorism (OSCT). The majority of CVE effort is on training all 'front line' public servants to identify those at risk of, or in the process of, radicalization. This training is presented as 'safeguarding' vulnerable persons and places a 'duty of care' to report any individual who matches the 'signs' of radicalization outlined in training videos and other material. In both phases Prevent has been contested, challenged and criticized from a range of participants and viewpoints.[14]

Role and Impact of Women in Radicalization

Throughout history women have been visible and have influenced all aspects of the process of radicalization; however, these have been mostly through informal and unofficial means. It is important to remember that while there is considerable focus on the role of *Muslim women*, and this is the focus of this review, the ideas and experiences of radicalization can be used beyond this demographic. As radicalization incorporates a journey towards someone holding extreme belief, extreme belonging and extreme behaviours, this is how research on women's roles and impact on radicalization will be organized.

Extreme belief – The research shows there are three key ways gender is important to understanding extreme belief. First, women help to generate and perpetuate extreme beliefs through acting as online and offline propagandists. Evidence from social media analysis reveals women share and re-tweet more material than do accounts associated with men.[15] It is also known that the online space is more important to women's radicalization than that of men.[16] Women are also at protests, rallies, and run study circles to promote the beliefs associated with radical groups. Women are involved in the production of material, such as Samina Malik (the self-titled 'lyrical terrorist', although her terrorism conviction was quashed in 2008). They are also involved in the creation of women's magazines and pamphlets addressing women (such as *The Way of Khaula*, from the Tehrik-e

Taliban Pakistan (TTP) in Pakistan, the Arabic-only so-called *Women's Manifesto of ISIS* reportedly by the predominantly European-run Al-Khansa women's brigade; and Hayat Boumeddiene (girlfriend of the French Charlie Hebdo attacker Amedy Coulibaly) was interviewed for *Dabiq*). In their writings they reinforce the extremist groups' messages that attract individuals to their cause.

Second, women's lives shape and frame extreme narratives. The author argues that it is important to pay attention to the gender ideology of extremist groups, especially as they relate to hyper femininity and masculinity.[17] For example, women's extreme behaviours (such as suicide bombing) are used to shame men into action; perceived violations against women's honour are used as reasons for the group to take the action that it does.[18]

Third, women are often seen as among the most fervent members – they are seen as less likely to be motivated by 'reason', legitimate political grievances or material concerns.[19] Rather, belief and emotions are seen to drive membership. Importantly, men are also driven by emotion and belief, but these are not a dominant part of their narrative of participation, and while researchers prioritize men's accounts of their actions and belonging, researchers tend not to pay such close attention to women's own accounts.[20] This framing of women's radicalization, emphasizing belief and emotions, makes women appear as victims and denies them agency in their decision-making (they become brainwashed, seduced or groomed instead of radicalized).[21]

Extreme belonging – Contrary to studies that focus on men, in research on women's radicalization the importance of social networks in radicalization processes seems downplayed – although it features as a 'promise of sisterhood' that the Islamic State makes to new recruits.[22] This might be because of assumptions that women's radicalization happens online or from stereotypes that women live isolated lives in *purdah*.[23] However, like men, when we look at women who have travelled to Iraq or Syria, we see that they often have friends or family who have also attempted to travel – the 'Bethnal Three Girls' being typical examples. Women form a 'sisterhood' for the cause – building communities of women who become closed groups. These groups are often gender segregated – especially if the group espouses a socially conservative or right-wing ideology. In these groups they foster rituals and regulations and modes of dependency to further group coherence. One example is the provision of child-care during study circles and activities for children after protests. Through these groups those involved depend upon an increasingly narrow range of individuals for information, social and welfare services, and advice. This builds trust and isolation from alternatives that are essential in most radicalization processes. Also, women of these groups are often encouraged to marry men within the same group or family to facilitate male group cohesion and radicalization.[24]

Extreme action – There has been considerable debate over the significance of women's violent action and its likelihood. While women remain less likely to participate in 'front line' extremist action, they nevertheless do – for example the recent cases of women involved in the failed Paris Notre Dame attack, in the

Nairobi attacks and the five London women prosecuted in 2017 for planning a terror attack. There appears to be an increase in women's extreme violent action, which has led to debates about whether or not the women who are radicalized are radical feminists, wanting to engage in the same forms of violence and have the same empowerment as men.[25] However, it is notable that terrorist organizational support for women's violent actions is less than it is for men and women's participation is often a divisive issue for the groups involved.[26] This means that any tactical advantage (more likely to succeed and gain more publicity) may be outweighed by factionalism and the risk of undermining overarching extremist gender narratives (i.e. that women need protecting as a frequent trope deployed by extremist groups).[27] In the main, evidence demonstrates that women are more likely to carry out supporting roles – financing, logistics; communications and coordination roles; reconnaissance; provision of alibis and other support.[28] They rarely hold leadership or decision-making roles, and so claims about women's empowerment from their participation may be questioned.[29]

Role and Impact of Women in Counter-Radicalization

Women have been identified as the 'missing link' in UK counter-terrorism since 2006.[30] Despite this claim, very few CVE programmes address women or include women as designers, leaders, practitioners or deliverers.[31] Women are treated as passive targets of these programmes and policies rather than as co-producers. The exceptional appointment of Sara Khan in 2018 as the Lead Commissioner for Countering Extremism has led to controversy with many seeing her as a 'token' and that her close allegiance to government has made many doubt her ability to be independent.[32] Second, the presumption of women as primarily located in the domestic realm dominates counter-radicalization programming. As a result we find women's roles are focused on parenting, counter-narratives and promoting women's informal community leadership. This is in contrast to women's potential roles in 'hard' security measures to counter-terrorism, such as in formal policing, intelligence and security services, and the military. The focus in this section is therefore on the areas where women are visible.

Parenting and family approaches – Across CVE programmes there remains a presumption that women's primary influence is as mothers and wives – rather than as citizens or as potentially radicalized individuals.[33] The home is an important site for parenting and the power of 'motherhood' is something that women have tapped into in politics worldwide. However, this framing prioritizes the security and non-radicalization of youth, and pathologizes teenagers by encouraging mothers to consider deviance as a 'sign' of radicalization.[34] Second, this approach fails to recognize that women's power and voice may be limited in the home (especially vis-à-vis teenagers who mostly listen to their peers). As Surinder Guru and Imran Awan's research demonstrates, such approaches also fail to consider the negative effects of counter-terrorism and counter-radicalization programmes on women as mothers or heads of households.[35]

Community approaches – Originally, community cohesion programmes were welcomed because they addressed underlying material and social exclusion in marginalized communities that are linked to radicalization. These often included programmes to train women in civic leadership as, and as noted in the UN PVE Plan of Action,[36] societies that have higher levels of gender inequality are more vulnerable to extremism. In the UK this also translated into more broadly defined projects to empower and *inspire* Muslim women.[37] However, as Rashid notes:

> The association between initiatives to empower Muslim women and Prevent [UK counter-terrorism policy] is only intelligible through an understanding of a wider policy trajectory in which an imagined, essentialized Muslim community is pathologised.[38]

Muslim women are assumed to suffer 'death by culture': Muslims are 'driven' by cultural traditions and practices that compel them to behave in particular ways.[39] This becomes highly apparent when there is no consideration or policies to address the gender inequalities in far-right movements or white poor communities. Additionally, even though these women's leadership empowerment programmes may be seen as social goods, and as intrinsic to the UK commitment to human rights conventions on their own terms, they were not resourced from new funds but from diverted resources from a new securitized agenda. This meant that when Prevent was re-orientated away from community towards policing approaches the funding did not stay with social cohesion and women's empowerment programmes but went to the police instead. This has meant a serious reduction in services for women, and the instrumentalization of women's rights.[40]

The second way in which women feature in community approaches are where they have been 'responsibilized' and co-opted in counter-radicalization programmes and policies through the new Prevent obligations placed upon front-line state institutions.[41] These include requirements to train 'front line' staff by requiring them to attend 'workshops to raise awareness of Prevent' (known as WRAP), and to report any signs of radicalization in those they encounter while carrying out their work. Mostly unreported is that the majority of these individuals are women – GPs, teachers, nursery workers, social workers, nurses, health workers. This might lead to the conclusion that otherwise unpalatable coercive measures are being 'women-washed' to facilitate compliance and acceptability.[42]

Counter-narrative approaches – Women's rights are seen as a key battleground for counter-radicalization.[43] The Islamic State claims that Western society has failed Muslim women and it presents an alternative 'female Utopia'.[44] Oddly, it would appear that UK policies have accepted this claim but for different reasons – whereas the Islamic State argues that it is Western feminism that harms Muslim women in the UK, the UK government argues that weak adherence to Western feminism in Muslim communities and its demonization in Islamic extremist narratives harm Muslim women. In both cases Muslim women are presented as without agency and power. Highlighting Muslim women's rights and opportunities while living in the West as a counter-narrative is undermined by a popular press and public discourse that also demonizes feminism, is littered with sexism, uses stereotypes to fuel Islamophobia and reinforces a 'them and us' framing – as discussed above.[45] Moreover, there is a notable say-do gap in policy regarding promises to advance the rights and lives of Muslim women – not least because of the reduction in funding for women's services over the years – that diminishes the credibility of the counter-narrative.[46] The intermittent engagement with the National Muslim Women's Advisory Group (NMWAG) also gives the impression of a lack of commitment to Muslim women's rights.[47]

Another approach in counter-narratives is to emphasize the harms inflicted upon women by extremist groups in order to undermine the claims of such groups that they offer a better life for women. The London Metropolitan Police video interviewing 'Syrian Mothers'[48] and also using the testimony of mothers of 'formers' to stress the emotional harms suffered by families[49] are two different ways in which this occurs. The idea of women as 'victims' also frames responses to women in de-radicalization policies.

Policing, governmental and judicial approaches – At the level of national government and policy, there are frequent reviews of counter-terrorism legislation and a new commission has been set up to review policies and programmes. The UK carries out gender impact assessments for new policies and laws but the remit is always narrowly defined.[50] For example, reviews fail to highlight how rendering the university as a 'radicalising space' makes it less likely that Muslim women will attend,[51] and fail to consider how terrorism financing regulations have led to a decline in the services that women's organizations can deliver (because they are often cash driven, rely on anonymity of clients and service providers, and are often smaller in scale, relying heavily on volunteers who are intimidated by new regulations).[52]

Human security and restorative approaches are not meaningfully considered in the UK. In the UK the concern with countering radicalization has not been linked to broader conflicts, despite a history in Northern Ireland. Instead counter-radicalization efforts have been divorced from broader discussions about what a lasting outcome for UK society might appear to be. As a result counter-radicalization programmes do not consider victims, conflict resolution or peace-building initiatives as comparable. Given the developments in women's involvement in these areas this is a wasted opportunity.

Conclusion

When reviewing the research and policy on women's roles and impact on radicalization we see that women are involved in every component (extreme belief, extreme belonging, extreme action). However because of the tendency to prioritize the function of 'extreme belief' in radicalization processes, and the association of women as irrational beings, there is a lack of complexity and nuance in our understanding. Consequently, women's roles and impact are sometimes exaggerated or overlooked in stereotypical ways in counter-radicalization policy and programming. This leads to the instrumentalization and bartering of women's rights and a failure to consider the differential gendered impact of these programmes and policies. Significantly, evaluations of countering radicalization programmes are generally poor and are woefully lacking consideration of gender in their analysis.

Notes

1 Daesh is an insulting term that is based on an acronym of the Arabic name for the so-called Islamic State group. For further discussions, please refer to https://www.freewordcentre.com/explore/daesh-isis-media-alice-guthrie.

2 B. Boutin et al., *The Foreign Fighters Phenomenon in the EU – Profiles, Threats & Policies*, The Hague, Netherlands: International Centre for Counter-Terrorism, 2016.

3 L. Tarras-Wahlburg, *Seven Promises of ISIS to its Female Recruits,* The International Center for the Study of Violent Extremism, 2017; A. P. Schmid, *Foreign (Terrorist) Fighter Estimates: Conceptual and Data Issues*, The Hague, Netherlands: International Centre for Counter-Terrorism, 2015.

4 W. Yeom, 'Between Fascism and Feminism: Women Activists of the British Union of Fascists', in J. H. Lim, K. Petrone (ed.), *Gender Politics and Mass Dictatorship. Mass Dictatorship in the 20th Century*, London: Palgrave Macmillan, 2010, pp. 107–124.

5 S. McEvoy, 'Loyalist Women Paramilitaries in Northern Ireland: Beginning a Feminist Conversation about Conflict Resolution', *Security Studies*, vol. 18, no. 2, 2009, pp. 262–286; N. Gilmartin, '"Without Women, the War Could Never Have Happened": Representations of Women's Military Contributions In Non-State Armed Groups', *International Feminist Journal of Politics*, vol. 19, no. 4, 2017, pp. 456–470.

6 P. R. Neumann, *Perspectives on Radicalisation and Political Violence*, (ICSR First International Conference on Radicalisation and Political Violence, London, 17–18 January 2008), p. 4.

7 N. Dempsey, G. Allen, and B. Politowski, *Terrorism in Great Britain: The Statistics*, Commons Briefing papers CBP-7613, London: House of Commons, 2017.

8 Office of National Statistics, Home Office, 'Operation of police powers under the Terrorism Act 2000 and subsequent legislation: Arrests, outcomes, and stop and search, Great Britain, quarterly update to December 2017' *Statistical Bulletin Update* 8th March 2018, available here: https://assets.publishing.service.gov.uk/government/uploads/system/uploads/attachment_data/file/686342/police-powers-terrorism-dec2017-hosb0518.pdf.

9 Revised Prevent Duty Guidance for England and Wales, issued on 12th March 2015 and revised on 16th July 2015, offers a definition as 'the process by which a person comes to support terrorism and extremist ideologies associated with terrorist groups'; please refer to https://www.gov.uk/government/publications/prevent-duty-guidance.

10 P. K. Davis and K. Cragin (eds.), *Social Science for Counterterrorism: Putting the Pieces Together*, Santa Monica, CA: RAND Corporation, 2009.

11 Silke, A. and K.E Brown, 'Expert Witness Report', [2016] EWHC 1707 (Fam) London Borough of Tower Hamlets and B, 2016.

12 Report to the General Assembly, A/HRC/31/65, 2016, available here: https://documents-dds-ny.un.org/doc/UNDOC/GEN/G16/088/68/PDF/G1608868.pdf?OpenElement.

13 Available here: https://www.gov.uk/government/collections/contest.

14 For example: T. O'Toole et al., 'Governing through Prevent? Regulation and Contested Practice in State–Muslim Engagement', *Sociology*, vol. 50, no. 1, 2016, pp.160–177.

15 E. Pearson, 'Online as the New Frontline: Affect, Gender, and ISIS-Take-Down on Social Media', *Studies in Conflict & Terrorism*, vol. 41, no. 11, 2018, pp. 850–874; L. Windsor, 'The Language of Radicalization: Female Internet Recruitment to Participation in ISIS Activities', *Terrorism and Political Violence*, 8 Jan 2018.

16 R. Briggs and A. Strugnell, *Radicalisation: The Role of the Internet*, Policy Planners' Network Working Paper, London: Institute for Strategic Dialogue, 2011.

17 K. E. Brown, 'Gender and Terrorist Movements', in R. Woodward and C. Duncanson (ed.), *The Palgrave International Handbook of Gender and Military*, Basingstoke: Palgrave Macmillan, 2017; K. E. Brown, 'Islamic State as a Proto-state', in S. Parashar, A. Tickner and J. True (eds.), *Revisiting Gendered States*, Oxford: Oxford University Press, 2018, Chapter 11.

18 N. Lahoud, 'Can Women be Soldiers of Islamic State', *Survival*, vol. 59, no. 1, 2017, pp. 69–78.

19 L. Sjoberg and C. Gentry, *Beyond Mothers, Monsters, Whores: Thinking about Women's Violence in Global Politics*, London/New York: Zed Press, 2015.

20 E. Pearson and E. Winterbotham, 'Women, Gender and Daesh Radicalisation', *RUSI Journal*, vol. 162, 2017, pp. 60–72; M. Loken and A. Zelenz, 'Explaining Extremism: Western Women in Daesh', *European Journal of International Security*, vol. 3, no. 1, 2018, pp. 45–68.

21 S. M. Edwards, 'Cyber Grooming Young Women for Terrorist Activities: Dominant and Subjugated Explanatory Narratives', In E. Viano (ed.), *Cybercrime, Organized Crime and Society Responses*, Cham: Springer, 2016, pp. 23–46.

22 This observation is based on the lack of discussion on social networks in research on women and radicalization and the lack of discussion of gender on research on social networks in radicalization research. For examples of a social networks approach (with no discussion of gender/women): J. Day and S. Kleinmann, 'Combating the Cult of ISIS: a Social Approach to Countering Violent Extremism', *The Review of Faith and International Affairs*, vol. 15, no. 3, 2017, pp. 14–23. M. Hafez and C. Mullins, 'The Radicalization Puzzle: A Theoretical Synthesis of Empirical Examples of Homegrown Extremism', *Studies in Conflict and Terrorism*, vol. 38, no. 11, 2015, pp. 958–975.

23 E. Saltman and M. Smith, *Til Martyrdom Do Us Part – Gender and the ISIS Phenomenon*, London: Institute for Strategic Dialogue, 2015; A good discussion of women's online roles (and how they relate to action) can be found here: K. Rachel, 'Jihad and Hashtags: Women's Roles in the Islamic State and Pro-Jihadist Social Networks', Western University MA Research Paper, 2017, p. 13; see also L. Huey and E. Witmer, '#IS_Fangirl: Exploring a New Role for Women in Terrorism', *Journal of Terrorism Research*, vol. 7, no. 1, 2016, pp. 1–10.

45 P. Baker, C. Gabrielatos, and T. McEnery, *Discourse Analysis and Media Attitudes: The Representation of Islam in the British Press*, Cambridge: Cambridge University Press, 2013; K. West and J. Lloyd, 'The Role of Labelling and Bias in the Portrayals of Acts of "Terrorism": Media Representations of Muslims vs. Non-Muslims', *Journal of Muslim Minority Affairs*, vol. 37, no. 2, 2017, pp. 211–222; A. Mondon and A. Winter, 'Articulations of Islamophobia: From the Extreme to the Mainstream?', *Ethnic and Racial Studies*, vol. 40, no. 13, 2017, pp. 2151–2179; C. Chambers et al., '"Sexual Misery" or "Happy British Muslims"?: Contemporary Depictions of Muslim Sexuality," *Ethnicities*, vol. 19, no. 1, 2019, pp. 66–94; K. Mendes, *Feminism in the News: Representations of the Women's Movement since the 1960s*, Basingstoke: Palgrave, 2011; J. Martinson, *Seen but Not Heard: How Women make Front Page News*, Women In Journalism, 2012.

46 Not helped by the decision to remove feminism from politics A level syllabus. S. Cassidy, 'Feminism to be Dropped from A-level Syllabus under Department for Education Plans', *The Independent*, 19 November 2015, available here: http://www.independent.co.uk/news/education/education-news/feminism-to-be-dropped-from-a-level-politics-syllabus-under-department-for-education-plans-a6740881.html; or by L. Bates, *Everyday Sexism*, London: Simon & Schuster, 2014.

47 C. Allen and S. Guru, 'Between Political Fad and Political Empowerment: a Critical Evaluation of the National Muslim Women's Advisory Group (NMWAG) and Governmental Processes of Engaging Muslim Women', *Sociological Research Online*, vol. 17, no. 3, 2012, pp. 1–9.

48 K. E. Brown, 'Gender and Countering Islamic State', *E-International Relations*, 18 February 2016, available here: https://www.e-ir.info/2016/02/18/gender-and-countering-islamic-state-radicalisation/.

49 *Families for Life* was set up by Mrs Benyahia whose nineteen-year-old son was killed in Syria fighting with Islamic State, available here: http://www.familiesforlife.org.uk.

50 HM Government, *Prevent Strategy: Equality Impact Assessment 2011*, available here: https://www.gov.uk/government/uploads/system/uploads/attachment_data/file/97979/prevent-review-eia.pdf; on the general challenges of evaluation of programmes please refer to C. Mastroe, 'Evaluating CVE: Understanding the Recent Changes to the UK's Implementation of Prevent', *Perspectives on Terrorism*, vol. 10, no. 2, 2016, pp. 49–60.

51 T. Saeed, *Islamophobia and Securitization Religion, Ethnicity and the Female Voice*, Basingstoke: Palgrave Macmillan, 2016.

52 K. E. Brown, 'Gender and Anti-Radicalisation: Women and Emerging Counter-Terrorism Measures', in M. Satterthwaite and J. Huckerby (ed.), *Gender, National Security and Counter-Terrorism: A Human Rights Perspectives*, London: Routledge, 2012, pp. 36–59; J. Huckerby and S. Adamczyk, 'Tightening the Purse Strings: What Countering Terrorism Financing Costs Gender Equality and Security', Duke Law International Human Rights Clinic and Women Peacemakers Program, 2017.

Recommended Readings

Ahram, A. I., 'Sexual Violence and the Making of ISIS', *Survival*, vol. 57, no. 3, 2015, pp. 57–78.

Bates, L., *Everyday Sexism*, London: Simon & Schuster, 2014.

Brown, K. E., 'Gender and Terrorist Movements', in R. Woodward and C. Duncanson (ed.), *The Palgrave International Handbook of Gender and Military*, Basingstoke: Palgrave Macmillan, 2017, pp. 419–436.

Buril, F., 'Changing God's Expectations and Women's Consequent Behaviours – How ISIS Manipulates "Divine Commandments" to Influence Women's Role in Jihad', *Journal of Terrorism Research*, vol. 8, no. 3, 2017, pp.1–10.

Coppock, V. and M. McGovern, 'Dangerous Minds? Deconstructing Counter-Terrorism Discourse, Radicalisation and the "Psychological Vulnerability" of Muslim Children and Young People in Britain', *Children and Society*, vol. 28, no. 3, 2014, pp. 242–256.

Day, J. and S. Kleinmann, 'Combating the Cult of ISIS: A Social Approach to Countering Violent Extremism', *The Review of Faith and International Affairs*, vol. 15, no. 3, 2017, pp. 14–23.

Eggert, J. P., *The Roles of Women in Counter-Radicalisation and Disengagement (CRaD) Processes*, Berlin: Berghof Foundation, 2018.

Fink, N.C., S, Zieger, and R. Bhulai (eds.), *A Man's World Exploring the Roles of Women in Countering Terrorism and Violent Extremism*, Abu Dhabi: Hedayah and The Global Center on Cooperative Security, 2016.

Gilmartin, N., '"Without Women, the War Could Never Have Happened": Representations of Women's Military Contributions in Non-State Armed Groups', *International Feminist Journal of Politics*, vol. 19, no. 4, 2017, pp. 456–470.

Giscard d'Estaing, S., 'Engaging Women in Countering Violent Extremism: Avoiding Instrumentalisation and Furthering Agency', *Gender & Development*, vol. 25, no. 1, 2017, pp. 103–118.

Huey, L. and E. Witmer, '#IS_Fangirl: Exploring a New Role for Women in Terrorism', *Journal of Terrorism Research*, vol. 7, no. 1, 2016, pp. 1–10.

Lahoud, N., 'Can Women Be Soldiers of Islamic State" *Survival*, vol. 59, no. 1, 2017, pp. 69–78.

Margolin, D., 'A Palestinian Woman's Place in Terrorism: Organized Perpetrators or Individual Actors?' *Studies in Conflict & Terrorism*, vol. 39, no. 10, 2016, pp. 912–934.

Musial, J., 'My Muslim Sister, Indeed You Are a Mujahidah: Narratives in the Propaganda of the Islamic State to Address and Radicalise Western Women. An Exemplary Analysis of the Online Magazine Dabiq', *Journal for Deradicalization*, vol. 9, 2017.

Ní Aoláin F. and J. Huckerby, 'Gendering Counterterrorism: How to, and How Not to – Part 1', *Just Security*, May 2018, available here: https://www.justsecurity.org/55522/gendering-counterterrorism-to/.

O'Toole, T., et al., 'Governing through Prevent? Regulation and Contested Practice in State–Muslim Engagement', *Sociology*, vol. 50, no. 1, 2016, pp. 160–177.

Pearson, E. and E. Winterbotham, 'Women, Gender and Daesh Radicalisation', *RUSI Journal*, vol. 162, 2017, pp. 60–72.

Rashid, N., 'Giving the Silent Majority a Strong Voice: Initiatives to Empower Muslim Women as Part of the UK's 'War on Terror'', *Ethnic and Racial Studies*, vol. 34, no. 4, 2014, pp. 589–604.

Saeed, T., *Islamophobia and Securitization Religion, Ethnicity and the Female Voice*, Basingstoke: Palgrave Macmillan, 2016.

Silke, A. and K.E. Brown, 'Expert Witness Report', [2016] EWHC 1707 (Fam) London Borough of Tower Hamlets and B.

Sjoberg, L. and C. Gentry, *Beyond Mothers, Monsters, Whores: Thinking about Women's Violence in Global Politics*, London/New York: Zed Press, 2015.

Thomas, P., 'Changing Experiences of Responsibilisation and Contestation within Counter-Terrorism Policies: The British Prevent Experience', *Policy & Politics*, vol. 45, no. 3, 2017, pp. 305–321.

Windsor, L., 'The Language of Radicalization: Female Internet Recruitment to Participation in ISIS Activities', *Terrorism and Political Violence*, 8 Jan 2018.

12 PSYCHOLOGICAL DIMENSIONS OF TERRORISM: PROFILING IMPOSSIBLE BUT PATTERNS DISCERNIBLE

Max Taylor

Introduction

In the context of concern here, psychological profiles are a form of offender profiling (including terrorists) that emphasize psychological, rather than social or contextual, qualities of the offender, as descriptive and possibly predictive qualities. Offender profiles should be essentially evidence based. At its simplest, an offender profile refers to making predictions about offender qualities from the way an offender might have behaved whilst committing a crime using the evidence available at a crime scene. This might mean deducing, from such evidence that might be available, an offender's qualities and personality characteristics, perhaps extending to a broader and more ambitious attempt to quantify risk and threat of future offending. Whilst it might be argued that investigators have always used crime scene evidence to make inferences about criminals (as, for example, Sherlock Holmes might), the systematic development and use of this evidence to guide investigators has its origins in the work of the FBI Behavioral Science Unit during the 1960s.[1] This early work tended to focus on violent crime, and particularly serial offending, but what made it distinctive was that it was evidence-based, rather than experience-based, intuition. Terrorism as essentially a violent crime, therefore, might be thought to fall within this framework.

However, profiles based on crime scene evidence are not the only way insights into offender behaviour might be gained, and the term 'profile' has been extended into less clearly evidence-based activities. Offenders live in society and are subject to the same social forces we are all subjected to. So, quite appropriately, alongside psychological analyses of behaviour based on crime scene analysis, other forms of descriptive aggregate categorization that may be much less securely tied to evidence bases have emerged, drawing on concepts such as social advantage (or disadvantage), background, class and economic factors. This has recently been extended as people share data online, into the analysis of personal data available through disclosure whilst using social media, which can then be used to generate an individual's profile using computerized algorithms. More recently, these analyses have also been extended to include the neurosciences.[2] With such a rich array of potential information available, it is therefore not surprising that analysts of terrorism and terrorist behaviour have sought to develop predictive models or profiles of terrorists based on aggregate qualities (including psychological) that might aid detection, prevention, risk assessment or at least improved understanding of terrorist behaviour.

This chapter is primarily concerned with psychological approaches to understanding terrorism and terrorists; and at the outset we can assert that the literature is replete with failures to construct terrorist profiles based on personality traits, psychopathology, religious orientation, or racial and/or economic background.[3] That is to say, the evidence strongly suggests that whilst an array of factors associated with engagement with terrorism might be detected for any given individual and across other individuals, the evidence suggests that there are no common qualities that would enable actual or potential terrorists to be identified from the general population based solely on these qualities. As Roy notes, individuals who have been involved in recent attacks in Europe are not necessarily the poorest or even particularly poor, the most humiliated or those excluded from society.[4] It might be further argued that even the assumed links between radicals and their real or imagined constituency is largely in fact an imaginary construct;[5] some 25 per cent of those involved in recent jihadi attacks, for example, are converts, and have at best a tenuous link with the community they allegedly align with.

Logical and methodological constraints

It perhaps isn't too surprising that aggregate qualities fail to adequately characterize terrorist behaviour given the methodologies employed to gather data. Almost all studies are essentially correlational in character, in that typically the incidence of some quality (a variable such as, for example, authoritarianism or a measurement of social disadvantage) is explored from within a defined representative population (people convicted of terrorism for example). Some measure of the incidence of that variable is then estimated which might describe the relative incidence of the variable within that specific population compared to the population as a whole. But regardless of the extent of incidence or relationship, such a methodology does not allow the inference of causal qualities to any relationship identified – this is to commit the logical fallacy of confusing correlation with causation – *cum hoc ergo propter hoc*, Latin for 'with this, therefore because of this,' and 'false cause.'

There is a similar fallacy that can be identified limiting inferences based on aggregate qualities; this particularly relates to complex causal accounts where it is assumed that an event that follows another is necessarily a consequence of the first event. This is termed the *post hoc ergo propter hoc* (Latin for ' … after this, therefore because of this.') fallacy.

We can express this in a slightly different way. A necessary condition for some state of affairs S is a condition that must be satisfied in order for S to obtain. A sufficient condition for some state of affairs S, in contrast, is a condition that if satisfied guarantees that S obtains. There is broad agreement that the factors that lead to terrorism are complex, and whilst there may well be many necessary conditions that relate to its incidence for some people in some circumstances, rarely, if ever, is it possible to identify a sufficient set of conditions that guarantees a terrorist act. What this means in terms of the development of psychological profiles of terrorists is that whatever other constraints there may be, there are structural impediments given current methodologies to generating data on which to build a meaningful predictive profile. These methodological weaknesses might be addressed using alternative methods emphasizing experimental approaches, for example, but the practical and ethical problems this might give rise to necessarily limit this route.

Patterns rather than profiles

Whilst these methodological constraints limit what can be inferred from studies, it does not follow that meaningful or useful accounts can't be developed. But it is important to recognize constraints; not the least of which is that there are arguably many different types of terrorist acts, all of which might have some commonalities in terms of intention, context, physical and social situation, but in behavioural or psychological terms might be quite different. The IS suicide bomber, for example, seems to be arguably very different from the risk-averse PIRA bomb maker, and arguably the 'lone wolf' attacker[6] lacking a clear organizational structure to which he or she belongs is perhaps different from both of these. It is also plausible to suggest that different routes into terrorism might well influence the significance of causal accounts that might be inferred. These concerns may suggest a need for exploring different and more discriminating kinds of methodologies that might yield a more robust causal account; Moore et al. offer a useful review of methodologies appropriate for exploring complex process evaluations.[7]

Monahan has reviewed psychological risk factors for terrorism and he identifies a number of potential factors that might contribute to our understanding of risk of becoming involved in terrorism.[8] These include ideologies, affiliations, grievances and moral reasoning. We will explore these further in the following, because each of these factors in a sense represents elements of a potential psychological pattern for terrorist engagement, rather than a profile. For some individuals, all of these may be necessary conditions for involvement; for others only some, or some particular and idiosyncratic combination, but it is important to note that in aggregate or individually none offers a sufficient account; features of all are more widely distributed in the general population than those who become terrorists.

Ideology is often regarded as a primary motivating factor in terrorism, given terrorism's avowed political aspirations. Ideology might be regarded as a reflection or cause of an individual's belief system that shapes understanding of the social and physical world. At one level ideology might be thought of as a form of rule governance[9] that guides or even controls behaviour; at other levels, it might be seen in much more general terms as recommending, justifying or endorsing collective action aimed at preserving or changing political practices and institutions. A useful focused definition on a role of ideology as militant extremism has been offered by Saucier et al.: 'zealous adherence to a set of beliefs and values, with a combination of two key features: advocacy of measures beyond the norm (i.e., extremism) and intention and willingness to resort to violence (i.e., militancy).'[10] This definition has clear relevance to thinking about terrorism and has formed the basis of the Fanatical/Extremist Thinking Pattern Scale which offers a potentially psychometrically valid assessment tool.

Monahan suggests this tool may be a way of extending and exploring Borum's notion of mindset[11] as 'a relatively enduring set of attitudes, dispositions, and inclinations – and worldview as the basis of a psychological "climate," within which various vulnerabilities and propensities shape ideas and behaviours in ways that can increase the person's risk or likelihood of involvement in violent extremism.'[12] Adherence to what seem to be militant ideologies seems to be sufficiently widespread to limit predictive qualities, but notions like 'mindset' might offer a way of exploring specific psychological vulnerabilities within this framework that lead towards active engagement, rather than passive support, to terrorism.

On the other hand, some qualities of ideologies do seem to be particularly facilitating of engagement with violence. One particular quality relates to a sense of millenarianism, and particularly a sense of millenarian imminence and individual agency to affect or make more effective the millenarian event.[13] This seems to be a particularly powerful driving force towards extreme behaviour and a disregard for social norms; Saucier et al.'s analysis clearly relates to this.[14]

Ideology might be best seen as setting the framework for behaviour, but it does not necessarily push or cause extreme behaviour, and the factors involved in determining specific behaviour may be quite different from such general dispositions. It may be useful to explore this broad distinction further; it is similar to that made by Cornish and Clarke with respect to criminal behaviour where they distinguish between criminal involvement and criminal events – we might therefore say terroristic involvement and terrorist events.[15] Terrorist involvement is a very general social lifestyle state of affairs – terrorist events in contrast relate to actually conducting a terrorist act. The importance of this distinction is that the ways we might address these elements in understanding the process of terrorism are different, and investment in managing or influencing terrorist involvement, for example, might have little or nothing to do with changing terrorist events – the commission of violent acts. Events are situational specific, and heavily influenced by environment; in contrast involvement factors are much more general lifestyle-/social-/contextually related. Following through on both these qualities of process may be worthwhile but won't work in the same way.

There is a sense in which many examples of terrorism seem to be communal activities, or have communal qualities. Kinship and/or friendship seem to be common qualities of terrorist groupings and the role of the internet and social media might even enhance the relationship qualities of affiliation.[16] Ginges, Hansen and Norenzayan have explored this by noting the power of religion to strengthen coalitional identities and to foster 'parochial altruism' in the context of suicide bombings.[17] The concept of parochial altruism was developed by Choi and Bowles and combines a sense of parochialism, i.e. hostility towards individuals who are not members of one's own group, with altruism, i.e. benefitting in-group members at a tremendous cost to oneself.[18] Reeve has extended this idea as an underlying feature of engagement and involvement in Islamist terrorism more generally.[19] Reeve argues that 'Islamist terrorist grievances can be considered as perceptions of evolutionarily relevant threats, whilst terrorism itself is an example of parochial altruistic behaviour. It is further proposed that features associated with engagement in terrorism (including exposure to ideology, propaganda, socialisation, etc.) enhance and guide parochial altruism, that is, perceptions of intergroup threat, and violent responses to it'. The concept of altruism expressed in these terms may well merit further exploration as a process variable underlying individual differences in susceptibility to engagement with terrorism.[20]

A sense of interpersonal closeness implied by altruism, therefore, seems to be a further factor that might contribute to the process of vulnerability to engagement with terrorism. A related sense of affiliation also may underpin notions of grievance, which are so commonly referred to as a causal factor by terrorists and supportive commentators. Grievance may be construed in personal or group terms (or both) and may be a quality of an objective event that has happened to an individual (such as an assault by security personnel) or as a product of a more general process (such as a concern with the plight of Palestinians). One way of bringing this more clearly into a psychological context is to think of grievance in the context of self-esteem – the sense of how we feel about ourselves, and how we relate to the outside world. Thus, striving to maintain an image of oneself fits as a further element of a pattern of engagement with terrorism. An important element of this may be the experience of loss of either loved ones, friends or acquaintances, or even role model figures through actions of a hated or despised enemy. Particularly in the context of cultures where there is a strong sense of honour, where retribution is seen as an appropriate response to assault, insult or dishonour, this may be a further powerful factor influencing vulnerability to engagement with terrorism.[21]

The idea of retribution introduced above also focuses attention on the moral context to terrorism, and a relationship to ideology or religion becomes plausible when values (particularly sacred values)[22] become compromised or challenged by another group's violence against you or your group. Sacred values are those that command 'unbounded and infinite commitment' from the believer.[23] Thus, notions of morality may be a further bridge within an ideological context to understanding the process of engagement with terrorism. Whether this is essentially a post facto explanation remains less clear.

Patterns?

Psychological conceptualization of terrorism and terrorists might be argued to be what Davies[24] has called a wicked problem[25] – there are multiple legitimate ways of framing questions about psychological qualities and parameters, but any solution has unintended consequences that are likely to spawn new problems. It is therefore a problem that is difficult or impossible to solve in aggregate because of incomplete, contradictory and changing and challenging requirements that are often difficult to recognize. Given the uncertainties surrounding what we mean by terrorism, this seems even more pertinent. However, if what has been described here is a reasonable way of looking at psychological approaches to terrorism, then we can also say with confidence that we are not looking at a state as implied by a notion of profile, but at a process where pattern becomes of critical significance.

A helpful way of characterizing what a psychological understanding of terrorism could be is to see terrorism as the product of a complex adaptive system, reflecting environment, psychological and social content, and particularly recognizing the significance of *time*. Each process acts on others, leading not to a stable system, but to a changing and dynamic process. Perhaps to develop these ideas further, we need to draw on the complexity sciences to identify methodologies that will enable systematic exploration and conceptual development. Notions such as tipping points, reflecting combinations of pattern elements, may be worth exploring further. Methodologies have been developed for process evaluations of complex medical and public health interventions which seem appropriate to moving this debate forward.[26]

Notes

1 D. Canter, 'Offender Profiling and Investigative Psychology', *Journal of Offender Profiling and Investigative Psychology*, vol. 1, 2004, pp. 1–15.

2 J. Decety, R. Pape, and C.I. Workman, 'A Multilevel Social Neuroscience Perspective on Radicalization and Terrorism', *Social Neuroscience*, vol. 13, no. 5, 2018, pp. 511–529.

3 Please see: S. Atran, 'Genesis of Suicide Terrorism', *Science*, vol. 299, no. 5612, 2003, pp. 1534–1539; J., Horgan, *The Psychology of Terrorism* (2nd edn.), New York, NY: Routledge, 2014; A. W. Kruglanski, et al., 'The Psychology of Radicalization and Deradicalization: How Significance Quest Impacts Violent Extremism', *Political Psychology*, vol. 35(Suppl.1), 2014, pp. 69–93; and J. Victoroff, 'The Mind of the Terrorist: A Review and Critique of Psychological Approaches', *Journal of Conflict Resolution*, vol. 49, no. 1, 2005, pp. 3–42.

4 O. Roy, *Jihad and death: The Global Appeal of Islamic State*, London: C. Hurst & Co, 2017.

5 Roy, *Jihad and Death*.

6 J. D. Simon, 'What Can Be Done about the Lone Wolf Terrorist Threat', *Georgetown Journal of International Affairs*, 4 April 2017.

7 G. F. Moore, et al., *Process Evaluation of Complex Interventions: Medical Research Council Guidance*, vol. 350: h1258, 2015.

8 J. Monahan, 'The Individual Risk Assessment of Terrorism: Recent Developments', Virginia Public Law and Legal Theory Research Paper No. 57, 2015, *Social Science Research Network Electronic Paper Collection*.

9 Please see: S.C. Hayes, 'Rule Governance: Basic Behavioral Research and Applied Implications', *Current Directions in Psychological Science*, vol. 2, no. 6, 1993, pp. 193–197; and M. Taylor and J. Horgan, 'The Psychological and Behavioural Bases of Islamic Fundamentalism', *Terrorism and Political Violence*, vol. 13, 2001, pp. 37–71.

10 G.L. Saucier, *et al.*, 'Patterns of Thinking in Militant Extremism', *Perspectives on Psychological Science*, vol. 4, 2009, p. 256.

11 R. Borum, 'Psychological Vulnerabilities and Propensities for Involvement in Violent Extremism', *Behavioral Sciences and the Law*, vol. 32, 2014, pp. 286–305.

12 J. Monahan, 'The Individual Risk Assessment of Terrorism'.

13 Please see: M. M. and Taylor, *The Fanatics. A Behavioural Approach to Political Violence*, London: Brasseys, 1991; and B. Schuurman and M. Taylor, 'Reconsidering Radicalization: Fanaticism and the Link between Ideas and Violence', *Perspectives on Terrorism*, vol. 12, no. 1, 2018.

14 Saucier, *et al*, 'Patterns of Thinking in Militant Extremism', p. 256.

15 D. Cornish and R. V. Clarke, 'Introduction', in D. Cornish and R., Clarke (eds.), *The Reasoning Criminal*, New York: Springer-Verlag, 1986, pp. 1–16.

16 K. K. Cetina, 'Complex Global Microstructures: The New Terrorist Societies', *Theory Culture Society*, vol. 22, 2015, pp. 213–234.

17 J. Ginges, I. Hansen, and A. Norenzayan, 'Religion and Support for Suicide Attacks', *Psychological Science*, vol. 20, 2009, pp. 224–230.

18 J. Choi and S. Bowles, 'The Coevolution of Parochial Altruism and War', *Science*, vol. 318, 2007, pp. 636–640.

19 Z. Reeve, 'Islamist Terrorism as Parochial Altruism', *Terrorism and Political Violence*, 2017, DOI: 10.1080/09546553.2017.1346505.

20 C. McCauley and S. Moskalenko, *Friction: How Radicalization Happens to Them and Us*, New York: Oxford University Press, 2011.

21 For a discussion see: R. Nibbett and D. Cohen, *The Culture of Honor: The Psychology of Violence in the South*, Boulder, CO: Westview Press, 1996 and A. Fiske and T.S. Rai, *Virtuous Violence: Hurting and Killing to Create, Sustain, End, and Honor Social Relationships*, Cambridge: Cambridge University Press, 2014.

22 J. Ginges, S. Atran, Sachdeva, and Medin, 'Psychology out of the Laboratory: The Challenge of Violent Extremism', *American Psychologist*, vol. 66, 2011, pp. 507–519.

23 P.E. Tetlock, 'Thinking the Unthinkable: Sacred Values and Taboo Cognitions', *Trends. Cogn. Sc.*, vol. 7, 2003, pp. 320–324.

24 Davies, L., 'Wicked Problems: How Complexity Science Helps Direct Education Responses to Preventing Violent Extremism', *Journal of Strategic Security*, vol. 9, no. 4, 2016, pp. 32–52.

25 Rittel, H., 'Dilemmas in a General Theory of Planning', *Policy Sciences*, vol. 4, no. 2, 1973, pp. 155–169.

26 G.F. Moore, *et al*, *Process Evaluation of Complex Interventions UK Medical Research Council (MRC) Guidance Council*, 2015.

Recommended Readings

Atran, S., 'Genesis of Suicide Terrorism', *Science*, vol. 299, no. 5612, 2003, pp. 1534–1539.

Borum, R., 'Psychological Vulnerabilities and Propensities for Involvement in Violent Extremism', *Behavioral Sciences and the Law*, vol. 32, 2014, pp. 286–305.

Canter, D., 'Offender Profiling and Investigative Psychology', *Journal of Offender Profiling and Investigative Psychology*, vol. 1, 2004, pp. 1–15.

Cetina, K.K., 'Complex Global Microstructures: The New Terrorist Societies', *Theory Culture Society*, vol. 22, 2015, pp. 213–234.

Cornish, D. and R. V. Clarke, 'Introduction', in Cornish, D. and R. Clarke (eds.), *The Reasoning Criminal*, New York: Springer-Verlag, 1986, pp. 1–16. ISBN 3-540-96272-7.

Davies, L., 'Wicked Problems: How Complexity Science Helps Direct Education Responses to Preventing Violent Extremism', *Journal of Strategic Security*, vol. 9, no. 4, 2016, pp. 32–52.

Decety, J., R. Pape, and C.I. Workman, 'A Multilevel Social Neuroscience Perspective on Radicalization and Terrorism', *Social Neuroscience*, vol. 13, no. 5, 2018, pp. 511–529. https://doi.org/10.1080/17470919.2017.1400462

Fiske, A. and T. S. Rai, *Virtuous Violence: Hurting and Killing to Create, Sustain, End, and Honor Social Relationships*, Cambridge: Cambridge University Press, 2014.

Ginges, J., I. Hansen, and A. Norenzayan, 'Religion and Support for Suicide Attacks', *Psychological Science*, vol. 20, 2009, pp. 224–230.

Ginges, J., S. Atran, Sachdeva, and Medin, 'Psychology out of the Laboratory: The challenge of Violent Extremism', *American Psychologist*, vol. 66, 2011, pp. 507–519. doi: 10.1037/a0024715

Horgan, J., *The Psychology of Terrorism* (2nd edn.), New York, NY: Routledge, 2014.

Hayes, S.C., 'Rule Governance: Basic Behavioral Research and Applied Implications', *Current Directions in Psychological Science*, vol. 2, no. 6, 1993, pp. 193–197.

Kruglanski, A. W., M.J. Gelfand, J.J. Bélanger, A. Sheveland, M. Hetiarachchi, and R. Gunaratna, 'The Psychology of Radicalization and Deradicalization: How Significance Quest Impacts Violent Extremism', *Political Psychology*, vol. 35 (Suppl.1), 2014, pp. 69–93.

McCauley, C., and S. Moskalenko, *Friction: How Radicalization Happens to Them and Us*, New York: Oxford University Press, 2011.

Monahan, J., 'The Individual Risk Assessment of Terrorism: Recent Developments', Virginia Public Law and Legal Theory Research Paper No. 57, *Social Science Research Network Electronic Paper Collection*, http://ssrn.com/abstract=2665815

Moore, G.F., S. Audrey, M. Barker, L. Bond, C. Bonell, W. Hardeman, L. Moore, A. O'Cathain, T. Tinati, D. Wight, and J. Baird, 'Process Evaluation of Complex Interventions: Medical Research Council Guidance', *BMJ*, vol. 350, h1258, 2015. Doi:10.1136/bmj.h1258

Moore, G.F., S. Audrey, M. Barker, L. Bond, C. Bonell, W. Hardeman, L. Moore, A. O'Cathain, T. Tinati, D. Wight, and J. Baird, *Process Evaluation of Complex Interventions UK Medical Research Council (MRC) Guidance Council*, 2015. https://www.ncbi.nlm.nih.gov/pubmed/25791983.

Nibbett, R. and D. Cohen, *The Culture of Honor: The Psychology of Violence in the South*, Boulder, CO: Westview Press, 1996.

Rittel, H., 'Dilemmas in a General Theory of Planning', *Policy Sciences*, vol. 4, no. 2, 1973, pp. 155–169.

Roy, O., *Jihad and Death: The Global Appeal of Islamic State*, London: C. Hurst & Co, 2017.

Saucier, G., L. Akers, S. Shen-Miller, G. Knežević, and L. Stankov, 'Patterns of Thinking in Militant Extremism', *Perspectives on Psychological Science*, vol. 4, 2009, pp. 256–271. Doi: 10.1111/j.1745-6924.2009.01123.x

Schuurman, B. and M. Taylor, 'Reconsidering Radicalization: Fanaticism and the Link Between Ideas and Violence', *Perspectives on Terrorism*, vol. 12, no. 1, 2018.

Simon, J.D., 'What Can Be Done about the Lone Wolf Terrorist Threat', *Georgetown Journal of International Affairs*, April 4, 2017.

Taylor, M., The Fanatics, A Behavioural Approach to Political Violence, London: Brasseys, 1991. ISBN 978-0-08-036274-8.

Taylor, M. and J. Horgan, 'The Psychological and Behavioural bases of Islamic Fundamentalism', *Terrorism and Political Violence*, vol. 13, 2001, pp. 37–71.

Victoroff, J., 'The Mind of the Terrorist: A Review and Critique of Psychological Approaches', *Journal of Conflict Resolution*, vol. 49, no. 1, 2005, pp. 3–42.

PART TWO

METHODS AND MODALITIES OF JIHADIST TERRORISM AND COUNTER-MEASURES

13 NEIGHBOURHOOD EFFECTS – HOW JIHADIST RECRUITMENT REALLY WORKS

Jytte Klausen

Introduction

There is now, it would seem, a lull in the global war on terror. Terrorist recruiters no longer recruit Western youths on social media. ISIS's para-state has gone. Al-Qaeda has not launched a major attack in the West for years. That was left to ISIS (also known as ISIL and the Islamic State), but the sophisticated commando-style attacks carried out by ISIS veterans in Paris in November 2015 have not been repeated. The cyber attack capabilities of the jihadists have turned out to be limited to website defacement. ISIS is known to have used mustard gas captured from Syrian military depots in Syria but no such attacks have materialized in the West.[1]

And yet, the jihadists are regrouping. Taking the long view, it is apparent that Al-Qaeda remains the movement leader. Groups associated with Al-Qaeda have been quietly building up military capabilities in an arc stretching from the Sahel to Libya, from Somalia to Yemen, and from Syria into Pakistan and Afghanistan. Hayat Tahrir al-Sham (HTS), an Al-Qaeda-aligned fighter group, has an estimated 20,000 fighters under its control in Northern Syria alone.[2] Al-Qaeda's bases are geographically and ethnically diverse, and localized affiliates blend insurgency tactics and terrorism in conflict zones in the Middle East, Africa and Asia.

ISIS, meanwhile, much diminished, has shown that it too still has global ambitions. It has affiliates operating in at least six other locations stretching from South East Asia to Northern Africa. A CNN analysis from February 2018 identified 143 attacks in 29 countries that were carried out by ISIS loyalists.[3] The number has continued to grow. The incidents have varied from knife attacks carried out by a single individual to the primitive, but terrifying, truck attacks in Barcelona, Berlin, London and Nice, to suicide bombings in Syria and Afghanistan, and in January 2019, a strike against a cathedral on Jolo island in the island group of Mindanao, the Philippines. As at January 2019 estimates of ISIS strength were that it may have been down to 3,000 fighters in Syria and Iraq, but that it still controlled thousands of fighters across several continents.[4]

The Paris attacks and the subsequent attacks in March 2016 in Brussels brought into focus the threat to European domestic security presented by extremists who had migrated to ISIS and been trained and managed in Syria and Iraq by the organization's military cadre. The attackers were men whose loyalty to each other was forged in renegade prayer rooms in Brussels's Molenbeek district and in the Syrian insurgency. They represent the future face of jihadist terrorism in the West. The next cycle in the fight against jihadist extremism will not be fought online. It will be fought locally, neighbourhood by neighbourhood.

Jihadists on the internet

The social media giants – Facebook, Twitter and Google, which owns YouTube – were widely blamed for facilitating the rise of ISIS. Thousands of European volunteers travelled to join ISIS. Many have died but many more have returned home or are still embedded with fighter groups.[5] Thousands who stayed at home continue to give support to those who leave. Twitter and Facebook have been blamed for enabling terrorist recruitment. True, digital media facilitated the rise of ISIS. Twitter, YouTube and Facebook were a gift to terrorist recruiters who suddenly could trawl for recruits everywhere.

Yet, the social reality of terrorist recruitment has been more complex than the stereotyped image of teenagers being radicalized as they surf the internet in the isolation of their bedrooms. Seamus Hughes, who served as a counter-terrorism expert in the Obama administration and transitioned into academia, bluntly describes the obsession with internet radicalization as 'overblown'.[6] In practice, extremist radicalization and recruitment is an exceptional event, and one that rarely occurs purely online. Radicalization and recruitment occur within an integrated loop formed by real-life local and global – 'glocal' – social networks, salafi-jihadist hubs and insurgent fighter groups.[7]

Twitter was the platform favoured by ISIS in 2013, when the group began the offensive that led to its spectacular rise.[8] Volunteers from around the world who wished to travel to the insurgency and, by 2014, to migrate to the self-declared caliphate used Twitter as a bridge to transport themselves in their imagination from home to the warzone and, then, when they were ready to leave, to solicit travel instructions. Phone-based, the app could be used with ease in the insurgent territories. Teams of foreign fighters broadcast their atrocities and presented themselves as heroes to followers back home.

This propaganda campaign was anything but spontaneous. In ISIS-controlled territories access to the use of phones and the internet was strictly controlled and content was monitored.[9] However, ISIS's social media campaign became a weapon of war and not merely an instrument of mass conversion.[10] Propaganda was directed at locals in the insurgent zones in Syria and Iraq, who were willing to credit what they read online while rejecting the messages broadcast by state media from Damascus and Baghdad. Videos of executions of captured army regulars, and of soccer games played with the severed heads of soldiers, were uploaded to terrify local residents and soldiers. In June 2014 ISIS took control of Mosul and Tikrit after the Iraqi army melted away.[11]

The 'Big Three' tech giants – Twitter, Google and Facebook – were slow to recognize the risks that online extremism represented for their consumer-oriented business model. Twitter was first to act. In late 2016 Twitter's suspensions began to degrade ISIS's presence on the platform.[12] ISIS responded by diversifying its online activities. New accounts were opened, using similar names to the old accounts, and followers were directed to cross-postings on other platforms. The tactic proved resilient to suppression.[13] The artificial intelligence (AI) algorithms used by the tech companies to flag extremist content often stumbled upon the use of innocuous-sounding or non-English names and headings.[14] Posters started to use Arabic letters for names or posed as ostensibly neutral observers or journalists. Another tactic was to post content simultaneously on multiple platforms. These techniques are still used, with some success.

Pressured by public opinion and complaints from the US Congress and the European Union, the big service providers promised to take down jihadist content on their social media platforms. When it was revealed, in 2017, that jihadists were making money from digital advertising on the platform, Google's stock took a nosedive and corporate advertisers withdrew.[15] Speaking before the US Senate in April 2018, Mark Zuckerberg promised Congress that Facebook's artificial intelligence algorithms removed 99 per cent of all content posted on the site by ISIS and Al-Qaeda followers 'before any human sees it'[16] (in fact, however, it is not possible for Facebook to know the total volume of jihadist content hosted on its platform).[17]

In recent months attention has turned to 'fake news' campaigns and to Russian and Iranian agents exploiting social media platforms for misinformation campaigns. But the jihadists are also still engaging in this. The spread of encryption technology and platforms has made policing the online presence of extremists of all types far more difficult. Over several days in April 2018 law enforcement agencies from eight countries seized computers and network servers and blocked internet portals used by ISIS's online radio broadcaster, *al-Bayan*, and its official news agency, *Amaq*.[18] The coordinated online and offline police action aimed to put the propaganda machinery out of business. It did not. ISIS's news agency migrated to new servers and was soon up again. The proliferation of 'grey' servers and file-sharing platforms catering to gamers, pornographers, neo-Nazis and online copyright piracy has undermined efforts to control online jihadism. In a press statement, Europol could claim only that the ISIS propaganda machine had been 'compromised'.[19]

In May 2018, Digital Citizens Alliance, an activist watch group, reported finding masses of postings glorifying jihadist violence.[20] WIRED magazine was able to replicate most of the searches and found that while some of the pictures and threads had been removed, others remained intact.[21] The content was no longer found through Twitter and Facebook, but was uploaded on sites hosted by Google+. The experiment showed that terrorist news agencies now make cross-postings on multiple platforms, saturating the monitors and the takedown algorithms. This tactic is an online version of what in military parlance is known as 'swarming' whereby the capabilities of the target are overwhelmed by saturating their defences. An experimental study from December 2018 similarly found ISIS postings on Facebook in Albanian, Arabic, English and Turkish. The postings showed decapitations, promoted the 'caliphate' and extolled recent atrocities and 'victories' claimed by ISIS.[22]

For more than twenty years Al-Qaeda and other jihadist organizations have maintained their own news agencies online. More outlets have been added and online tactics have changed. Typically, messages go out on Telegram, a privately held encrypted messaging and file-sharing platform (https://telegram.org/) that was launched in 2013. Telegram is designed to resist regulation and government surveillance.[23] However, the classic imprints are still in use. What has changed is the way in which the press releases, sermons and official announcements are pushed out. For instance, in August 2018, ISIS used one of its established online news agencies, *al-Furqan* Media, to release an audio recording featuring Abu Bakr al-Baghdadi. The release came with a list of fourteen different online locations for followers to access. In the same month, Al-Qaeda's emir, Ayman al-Zawahiri, uploaded a video speech using Uptobox.com, another file-sharing platform that appeals to gamers and other online customers who wish to obscure their log-in information.

A widely used tactic to foil surveillance is to programme posts to self-destruct within a short time. An online cloud server popular with the jihadists, dropjiffy.com, automatically deletes all archived material after thirty days. When an announcement goes up followers are alerted to download it and they are simultaneously directed to cross-lateral postings and backup servers. Another tactic is to use host domains that are the online equivalent of ungoverned territories. A popular domain is risala.ga.[24] The .ga domain code is the country code for Internet Service Providers (ISPs) registered to Gabon, a tiny West African country (Tuvalu, a small nation in Micronesia, using the .tv domain, was another domain of choice for jihadist sites). The point of Gabon is that American or European authorities have no practical avenue for serving an order to shut an account down or to solicit information that may lead to prosecution. For the same reason, Russian service providers are also popular with the jihadists.

It is worth noting that the tech giants are also in this market. Facebook owns WhatsApp, a popular encrypted messaging app that can also be used for streaming. Given the growth of encrypted messaging apps and file-sharing platforms designed to evade regulation by authorities, the suppression of jihadist sites on Twitter, YouTube and Facebook is not a big win in the fight against jihadist terrorism.

In any case, the single-minded focus on social media ignores the fact that these platforms are no longer as necessary as they once were to the global strategists of jihadism. Getting terrorists off Facebook and Twitter will not degrade the real-life local hubs of jihadist extremists that are linked to international networks of experienced fighters.

The European recruitment pipeline

Contemporary jihadist organization relies on the integration of global and local networks. Their manifestations in the West are networked offshoots of ISIS and Al-Qaeda, and, occasionally, other Islamist terrorist groups. The hubs appear as localized small-world networks clustering around a charismatic leader.[25] On closer inspection, it is evident that they are rooted in local social networks and neighbourhoods.

The local jihadist landscape has changed radically in the last five years. Three principal factors have driven the changes: (1) the galvanizing effect of ISIS's declaration of a 'righteous' para-state founded on the doctrines advocated by salafi-jihadism; (2) the role played by local recruiters, who operate as networked travel agents for the *jihad*; and (3) the lowering of barriers to join, as a consequence of the open-door policy adopted by ISIS during the period of the 'caliphate', and the efficiency gains made possible by social media. The new networks grew from the old but both the architecture and the scope of the networks have changed. Before the ISIS surge, the western clusters counted membership in the hundreds. Now the jihadist community at large is counted in the thousands with a presence in more cities and countries.

Today the local hubs of Western jihadist networks are clusters of militants who are joined together by multiple overlapping social connections. They are brothers and cousins, school friends, neighbours, connected by friendships forged in person and through family associations.[26] These clusters, in turn, are woven together by online networks and by real-world networks that are sustained and amplified by the travels of members and animated by charismatic preachers, and by an online community of extremist dating sites, chat rooms and encrypted exchanges of manuals and evangelizing *communiques*.

Mapping jihadism-related arrests and incidents onto a map of Europe highlights the importance of on-the-ground hubs and clusters in the jihadist recruitment pipeline. Data from the Western Jihadism Project, a decade-long data collection project, supports the use of geo-location to map the hometowns of convicted terrorists and travellers to the ISIS-controlled territories.[27] Using this method, we are able to rank the cities most affected by jihadist recruitment for terrorist incidents and for travel to join terrorist organizations abroad. In recent years, eighteen of the top twenty western cities that have been home to known Syrian foreign fighters are in western Europe. Minneapolis is the only American city on the list. Melbourne, Australia, is the second city outside western Europe on the list. The surprise is that half of the places in the top twenty are taken by secondary cities with populations of 500,000 or less.

The locational concentration of recruitment hubs reaches down to neighbourhoods. One hundred and fifty ISIS fighters came from the Angered district and the adjacent neighbourhood in Gothenburg, a mid-sized city with a population of about 500,000. Two dozen volunteers and 10 per cent of all the French ISIS soldiers killed in action came from Lunel, a small French town near Montpellier.[28] Birmingham, Britain's second largest city, has been home to so many jihadists that the tabloid press refers to the city as 'the jihadi capital of Britain'.[29] Most came from just four wards in the city. Brussels, the centre of the European Union, is a contender for the European title of jihadi capital.[30] One district within the city, Molenbeek, was home to a plurality of the Belgian travellers to Syria and Iraq and to the infamous French–Belgian network responsible for the commando-style attacks in Paris in November 2015 and the suicide attacks in Brussels in March 2016[31] (the same network was also responsible for a long list of other but less well-known plots, some of which were foiled). Across North Africa, recruitment has also been highly localized – for example, Tunisia exhibits a similar pattern of localized networks of militants.[32]

Intergenerational contagion is part of the picture. Surviving preachers and organizers from the halcyon days of Al-Qaeda's European networks before the 9/11 attacks are often found at the core of today's tangled networks. An example is Bassam Ayachi. A Syrian who obtained French nationality through marriage, he founded the Belgian Islamic Centre in Molenbeek in the early 1990s. For years this was a known meeting place for jihadists travelling through Europe. The men responsible for the assassination of anti-Taliban leader Ahmad Shah Massoud in Afghanistan (on the orders of Osama bin Laden) met there two days before the 9/11 attacks.[33]

Ayachi proved that travelling to the new Jihadistan in Syria was not only for the young. Taking a tour to visit the 'liberated' cities in Syria, Ayachi posted jubilant travel snapshots on Facebook from the insurgent-controlled zones in 2013 and 2014. Accompanying him was his son and grandson, and his long-time bodyguard, Oliver 'Hamza' Dassy. Dassy was a member of Sharia4Belgium, an offshoot of a chain of continental European organizations linked to Anjem Choudary and the proscribed Al Muhajiroun group. Ayachi lost an arm in a car bomb incident in Syria in 2015. He was later arrested in Turkey while shopping for a prosthetic and extradited to France in April 2018, where he is awaiting trial.[34] His son and the bodyguard are both dead.

The single most important institution in the recruitment network was the trans-European network associated with the British-based *Al Muhajiroun*. Omar Bakri Muhammed, a Syrian salafist and self-described sheikh, who had moved to London in 1986, formed the group in 1996. Bakri Muhammed and his organization came to the attention of law enforcement agencies in the United States and the UK after the 9/11 attacks. The organization was proscribed by the UK Government in 2006 after it was found that Mohammed Siddique Khan, the ringleader of the London Underground suicide attacks on 7 July 2005, was an *Al Muhajiroun* follower. Since then a series of aliases of the group have been banned.[35]

Bakri Muhammed left the UK one month after the 7/7 attacks and settled in Lebanon, from where he continued to evangelize via the internet. He appointed Anjem Choudary, a British-educated solicitor, to be his *emir*. The organization continued to prosper under Choudary's leadership. Groups formed under Choudary's auspices are often branded with variants of the 'Sharia4UK' label, which was once used by Choudary, and other recognizable branding names.[36]

Between one-quarter and one-third of all the Western foreign fighters who travelled to join the jihadist insurgent groups in Syria and Iraq are thought to have belonged to one of the group's British incarnations or branch organizations in Belgium, Denmark, France, Germany, the Netherlands and Norway, and other affiliates.[37]

Case study: The family and friends plan

Anjem Choudary's Scandinavian recruits and their tangled biographical histories illustrate the 'small-world' phenomenon driving the social contagion mechanisms behind localized recruitment. Four Swedish-Lebanese-Palestinian brothers from the El-Hassan Dib (or Deeb) family died fighting for Al-Qaeda-linked groups in Lebanon, Syria and Iraq. The family comes from the Ein Al Hilwah refugee camp in Tripoli. Part of the family emigrated to Sweden and settled in Borås, near Gothenburg, in the 1980s.

The first brother to die, *Rabih*, was born in Kuwait and became a permanent resident of Sweden. He was killed fighting in Tripoli, Libya, in 2012. The second and the third brothers to die were *Hassan*, twenty, and *Moatassem*, nineteen. Moatassem died in a suicide bombing attack against Syrian army barracks near Homs in late July 2013.[38] A fourth brother, a half-brother, *Al-Monzer Khaldoun al-Hassan*, twenty-four, a Swedish resident with a Lebanese passport, was killed in a raid on his apartment in Tripoli by the Lebanese army on 20 July 2014. He was wanted by the Lebanese authorities in connection with his involvement in a suicide attack by two Saudi jihadists on 25 June 2014 against the Duroy Hotel in Beirut.[39]

Cousins and uncles of these brothers have also given their lives for violent jihad, in insurgent combat or as suicide bombers, or have been imprisoned on charges related to terrorism. *Khaled*, an uncle who was also based in Borås, was arrested in 2012 in Beirut on suspicion of terrorist activity. He was carrying military night goggles and other combat equipment but was later released. His current location is not known. Another family member, *Yusef Mohammed al-Hajj Dib*, was convicted in 2008 in connection with an attempt in 2006 to bomb two trains departing from Cologne, Germany.[40] Technically an uncle to the four dead brothers from Borås, *Yusef* was twenty-one years old when he was arrested. An older brother of Yusef, *Saddam el-Hajdib*, and another uncle of the Swedish brothers, died in a suicide bombing in May 2007. He was allegedly the fourth highest leader in Fatah al-Islam, a jihadist organization operating in Palestinian refugee camps in Lebanon.[41] The suicide bombing caused a flare-up of the Lebanese civil war when, in retaliation, the Lebanese army bombed the Palestinian refugee camp where the militants belonging to the jihadist group resided.[42] Another uncle, *Othman*, is in prison in Lebanon, serving a seven-year sentence on charges also linked to Fatah al-Islam.

The train bombings were planned to avenge the publication of caricatures portraying the Prophet Muhammad in a Danish newspaper in 2005, and the death of Abu Musab al-Zarqawi, the leader of Al-Qaeda in Iraq (AQI), a predecessor to ISIS, in June 2006. Choudary visited Nordic fan groups several times. The Norwegian branch organization, Profetens Ummah, played host in late 2012. Choudary's followers from Denmark and Norway travelled to Oslo for the event and celebrated the visit by posting pictures of themselves on Facebook (see Figure 1).

FIGURE 1 Anjem Choudary meets with his Scandinavian followers in 2012.
Sources: Gudmundson.blogspot.com taken from Facebook (now closed); Norsk TV2.

Note: Left photo: Choudary (left) photographed with Omar Bakri Muhammed's Swedish nephew taken during a visit to Oslo, Norway, in 2012. Right photo: Group picture taken in Oslo in front of a store located on Tøyengata in the Grønland neighbourhood in Oslo. Choudary is in the centre wearing a long black coat over a shin-length white shirt. The index finger pointing towards the sky is a symbol for 'tawhid,' which in the jihadist playbook refers to monotheism under the Islamic State and its caliphate.

In 2012, back in Sweden, a young cousin, known only as '*Abu Dujanah Al Lubnani*', ran a website linked to Anjem Choudary and the proscribed British Al-Muhajiroun. When Choudary attended the launch of the Norwegian 'Profeten's Ummah' in Oslo in 2012, 'Abu Dujanah' was photographed with Choudary who also posed for a group portrait.[43] Many of the men in the photo subsequently joined the Norwegian migration to ISIS. Al-Muhajiroun has no formal affiliate in Sweden but it has another connection. Omar Bakri Mohamad's nephew, Mohamed Fostok Aboyakoub, lives in Borås. He managed a jihadist website, www.islam-tawhid.se (the site no longer exists). The owner of that site, Jiro Mehho, died fighting for ISIS in Syria in August 2013.[44] Completing the loop, back in Tripoli, Lebanon, Omar Bakri Mohammed, the emir of al-Muhajiroun, in exile after being denied re-entry to the UK in 2005, praised the martyrdom of the young Swedish brothers.[45]

Choudary met with his followers freely and openly as he travelled Europe and held press conferences. By 2010, British media cooled their interest in broadcasting interviews with Choudary when Islam4UK and several other brand names of his organization were, once again, listed as proscribed organization – but no such bans were in place in other European countries. As a result, Choudary was able to travel freely and conduct press conferences and appear on TV everywhere[46] (the videos from these events and interviews are now widely redacted but may still be found on YouTube) as his controversial statements were of particular interest to producers.[47]

Strategies for countering the next phase

Have the right lessons been drawn from the successes and failures in the fight against Al-Qaeda and ISIS? What works, and what doesn't work? Governments are now being tempted, once again, to declare victory in the war on terror. Why not? Domestic attacks are down. The irony of counter-terrorism is that it can count on the full support of elected officials and the voting public only when it fails.

New challenges have emerged that require European governments to blend domestic policing and prevention into a broader overarching strategy of global containment and targeted military operations against jihadist strongholds. The global picture is worrying. The diffusion of terrorist settlements – both small and large – across Africa, Asia and the Middle East poses a direct threat to local populations and to Western NGO workers, diplomats, businesses and travellers in a growing number of locations. During its reign, ISIS became the wealthiest terrorist organization ever and is believed to have smuggled vast amounts of money out of Syria and Iraq. Raids on military depots in Syria and Iraq provided it with caches of Russian and American weaponry.[48] And Al-Qaeda is stronger than ever. The lull in Al-Qaeda operations in Europe should not be taken as a sign of weakness. Bruce Hoffman argues that Al-Qaeda has the capacity to mount attacks in Europe. Its low profile is a tactic designed to avoid attracting attention during a phase of expansion.[49]

The transformation of ISIS from a territorial para-state back to an insurgent guerrilla organization adds new elements to the threat picture, even as Europe is struggling to cope with women, men and families returning from ISIS's so-called caliphate. Advertising on public social media accounts was useful to the terrorist organizations only as long as the travel routes to the jihadist insurgency in Syria were open. The struggle moves on, but with far more armed and experienced fighters under the control of the foreign terrorist organizations and from a much enlarged and more diffuse base in Europe and North Africa.

Attacks and arrests declined across Europe as well as globally in 2017 and, although the final numbers have yet to be confirmed, the downturn continued in 2018.[50] Yet, the structural underpinnings for a jihadist comeback are strong. Europe is probably more at risk now than at any time since the 1990s.

The ISIS 'bulge' dramatically increased the size of the radicalized population in Europe. Intelligence and police officials are rightly concerned. Estimates of the number of returnees vary, but experts agree that the risk posed is significant.[51] Not all of the returnees come back as hardened extremists but experience from previous migrations between Europe and jihadist insurgencies is that many will return to form a cadre around whom new recruits will congregate. Their personal, real-life connections to comrades from the insurgent combat zones will become the pathways through which the networks regenerate and undertake further recruitment. Porous borders and Europe's proximity to jihadist strongholds in Syria, Yemen and North Africa are another risk factor.

Cracking down on the consumer-oriented tech companies has only marginal effect on terrorist capabilities in a highly decentralized online communications environment, where encryption technologies are widely available. But that does not mean that Western governments should give in to another temptation, which is to crack down on immigrant Muslim communities, ramping up surveillance and counter-propaganda.

It is important not to lose sight of the fact that jihadist extremism is a marginal, low-prevalence phenomenon. Several thousands and even tens of thousands of jihadist extremists are a serious problem but they represent only a tiny fraction of Europe's Muslim populations (following the public health logic, the incidence rate is 1/2000, assuming a total Muslim population of 20 million in the European Union).[52] Given that converts comprise 15–20 per cent of the extremist offenders, the fallacy of a population-based approach to the prevention of jihadist extremism is yet more apparent.

There is also a grave risk that the application of CVE policies may have seriously adverse consequences for social cohesion. Olivier Roy, a French sociologist, has argued that the jihadists are revolutionaries by another name. He describes jihadism as a 'generational nihilistic radicalized youth revolt'.[53] There is, however, no compelling evidence that social alienation is the root cause of terrorist extremism. By painting violent extremism as a social problem, broadly conceived CVE policies often imply that jihadist extremism is a problem produced by Muslim identities or by Islam itself.

Concerns about stereotyping Muslims lead to the argument that the authorities should take a general public health approach to the mitigation of all types of violent extremism. This gets good marks for fairness but is based on the erroneous assumption that all extremist ideologies are in some measure 'the same'. The reality is that extremist ideologies may be very different. Particular social strata are susceptible to specific appeals, and the action scripts for who to hate and how to hate are very various.

A more sophisticated policy response should start from a rather different understanding of the process of radicalization. The key drivers of violent extremism are prolonged exposure to real-life local extremist networks and grooming by recruiters who offer to men and women – the young and the not so young, Muslim-born and converts to Islam – membership of a mighty global community, and the promise of eternal life, marriage, status and opportunities for travel, adventure and heroic exploits.

This message is brought home to local youth in local networks. Jihadist recruitment should be understood as a process of *networked social contagion*.[54] Political sociologists and behavioural economists have used the concept of social contagion to capture the process by which riots spread, cults grow or financial panics take hold.[55] The contagion effect drives the patterns of recruitment that are best described as neighbourhood effects, highly localized real-world clusters or hubs of extremists. If you lived in Molenbeek or Angered – or in Sparkbrook, Birmingham – contact with ISIS's migratory network might be one friend away, or made through a cousin who knows somebody. The key to the success of the ISIS recruitment wave was the bringing together of old and new adherents in real-world centres. The next generation of jihadists is being tapped through networks of friends and former fighters in predominantly immigrant neighbourhoods. Local recruitment is the work of clandestine, real-world, *local* networks.

Given that jihadist recruitment is a small-world phenomenon, combating further network growth requires a coordinated and concentrated effort on the part of a multinational alliance of law enforcement and antiterrorism professionals to target leaders and local cadres. The implications for counter-terrorism are clear – target the hubs and focus on neutralizing recruiters, jihadist evangelists and influencers who capitalize on their status and know-how gained through membership of insurgent fighter groups. This is a task for law enforcement, prosecutors and courts. Among the priorities should be the provision of better probation services, more options for mandatory juvenile engagement programs and the improvement of coordination and detection techniques on the part of police agencies. Counter-terrorism is the business of the police rather than that of teachers and social workers.

Arguments that the returnees should be rehabilitated and reintegrated into society rather than prosecuted and sent to prison often overlook the fact that some of them have committed grave crimes. Europe – and Britain – is responsible for holding its citizens accountable for the crimes that they have committed against Iraqis and Syrians who were subjugated by ISIS's willing executioners and foot soldiers from Birmingham, Brussels, Gothenburg and beyond.[56] The Nobel Peace Prize recipient Nadia Murad, who was captured and sold as a sex slave by ISIS, has eloquently made the case for the survivors' right to justice.[57] Prosecutions of returnees on charges of crimes against humanity or specific crimes committed in a civil war may be difficult, but there are cases where they must be undertaken, if at all possible. For reasons of justice and prudence, returnees should be investigated to discover whether they have committed crimes, and to assess whether or not they represent a threat to community cohesion and public safety.

To be sure, there are many circumstances where compassion is called for. France is working to repatriate 150 children of French ISIS fighters who are currently held in Kurdish detention camps. Most are under the age of six.[58] Their mothers are expected to stand trial in Iraq. One French mother, Melina Boughedir, agreed to the repatriation of three of her children after she was sentenced to life in an Iraqi prison for being an ISIS member.[59]

Notes

1 E. Schmitt, 'ISIS Used Chemical Arms at Least 52 Times in Syria and Iraq, Report Says,' *The New York Times*, 21 November 2016, https://www.,ytimes.com/2016/11/21/world/middleeast/isis-chemical-weapons-syria-iraq-mosul.html (accessed 27 January 2019).

2 B. Hoffman, 'Al-Qaeda's Resurrection', *Expert Brief*, Council on Foreign Relations, 6 March 2018, https://www.cfr.org/expert-brief/al-qaedas-resurrection (accessed 24 August 2018).

3 T. Lister et al., 'ISIS Goes Global', *CNN*, 12 February 2018, available here: https://www.cnn.com/2015/12/17/world/mapping-isis-attacks-around-the-world/index.html (accessed 27 January 2019).

4 *Worldwide Threat Assessment of the US Intelligence Community*, Daniel R. Coats, Director of National Intelligence, Senate Select Committee on Intelligence, 29 January 2019, https://www.intelligence.senate.gov/sites/default/files/documents/os-dcoats-012919.pdf, p. 11 (accessed 30 January 2019).

5 T. Renard and R. Coolsaet, eds., *Returnees: Who are They, Why Are They (Not) Coming Back and How Should We Deal with Them? Assessing Policies on Returning Foreign Terrorist Fighters in Belgium, Germany and the Netherlands*, Brussels, Egmont Paper no. 101, February 2018, available here: http://www.egmontinstitute.be/content/uploads/192018/02/egmont.papers.101_online_v1-3.pdf?type=pdf (accessed 29 January 2019).

6 S. Hughes, 'To Stop ISIS Recruitment, Focus Offline', *Lawfare*, 7 August 2016, available here: https://www.lawfareblog.com/stop-isis-recruitment-focus-offline (accessed 29 January 2019).

7 J. Klausen, 'Tweeting the Jihad: Social Media Networks of Western Foreign Fighters in Syria and Iraq', *Studies in Conflict & Terrorism*, vol. 38, no. 1, 2015, pp. 1–22.

8 J. M. Berger and J. Morgan, *The ISIS Twitter Census: Defining and Describing the Population of ISIS Supporters on Twitter*, The Brookings Project on US Relations with the Islamic World no. 20, 2015, available here: https://www.brookings.edu/wp-content/uploads/2016/06/isis_twitter_census_berger_morgan.pdf (accessed 27 January 2019).

9 Klausen, 'Tweeting the Jihad'.

10 B. I. Koerner, 'Why ISIS Is Winning the Social Media War', *WIRED*, March 2016, availabe here: https://www.wired.com/2016/03/isis-winning-social-media-war-heres-beat/ (accessed 27 January 2019).

11 M. Chulow, 'Iraq Faces the Abyss after Its Military Melts Away', *The Guardian*, 13 June 2014, available here: https://www.theguardian.com/world/2014/jun/13/baghdad-faces-the-abyss-after-its-military-melts-away (accessed 27 January 2019).

12 J. M. Berger and H. Perez, *ISIS's Diminishing Returns on Twitter: How Suspensions Are Limiting the Social Networks of English-Speaking ISIS Supporters*, George Washington University, 2016.

13 J. Klausen, C. E. Marks, and T. Zaman, 'Finding Extremists in Online Social Networks', *Operations Research*, vol. 66, no. 4, July-August 2018, pp. 893–1188, available here: https://doi.org/10.1287/opre.2018.1719 (accessed 27 January 2019).

14 J. Koebler and J. Cox, 'The Impossible Job: Inside Facebook's Struggle to Moderate Two Billion People', *VICE*, 23 August 2018, available here: https://motherboard.vice.com/en_us/article/xwk9zd/how-facebook-content-moderation-works (accessed 27 January 2019).

15 R. Cookson, 'Jihadi Website with Beheadings Profited from Google Ad Platform', *The Financial Times*, 17 May, pp. 2–16, available here: https://www.ft.com/content/b06d18c0-1bfb-11e6-8fa5-44094f6d9c46 (accessed 27 January 2019); A. Mostrous, 'Big Brands Fund Terror through Online Adverts', *The Times*, 9 February 2017, available here: https://www.thetimes.co.uk/article/big-brands-fund-terror-knnxfgb98 (accessed 27 January 2019).

16 'Transcript of Mark Zuckerberg's Senate Hearing', *The Washington Post*, 10 April 2018, available here: https://www.washingtonpost.com/news/the-switch/wp/2018/04/10/transcript-of-mark-zuckerbergs-senate-hearing/?utm_term=.6fac03d83f7e (accessed 27 January 2019).

17 M. Bickert and B. Fishman, 'Hard Questions: Are We Winning the War on Terrorism Online?', *Facebook News Room*, November 2017, available here: https://newsroom.fb.com/news/2017/11/hard-questions-are-we-winning-the-war-on-terrorism-online/ (accessed 27 January 2019).

18 J. Warrick, 'In Fight Against ISIS's Propaganda Machine, Raids and Online Trench Warfare', *Washington Post*, 19 August 2018, available here: https://www.washingtonpost.com/world/national-security/in-fight-against-isiss-propaganda-machine-raids-and-online-trench-warfare/2018/08/19/379d4da4-9f46-11e8-8e87-c869fe70a721_story.html?utm_term=.39c14e771efb (accessed 2 February 2019)

19 Europol, 'Islamic State Propaganda Machine Hit by Law Enforcement in Coordinated Takedown Action', *Press Release*, 27 April 2018, available here: https://www.europol.europa.eu/newsroom/news/islamic-state-propaganda-machine-hit-law-enforcement-in-coordinated-takedown-action (accessed 27 January 2019).

20 Digital Citizens Alliance, *Fool me once…*, May 2018, [website]. Available at https://digitalcitizensalliance.org/clientuploads/directory/Reports/DigitalCitizens_FoolMeOnce-Final.pdfm (accessed 27 January 2019).

21 I. Lapowski, 'Gruesome Jihadi Content Still Flourishes on Facebook and Google+', *WIRED Magazine*, 17 May 2018, available here: https://www.wired.com/story/jihadi-content-still-on-facebook-google/, (accessed 27 January 2019).

22 A. Speckhard and A. Shajkovci, 'Is ISIS Still Alive and Well on the Internet?', *Homeland Security Today.US*, 14 January 2019, available here: https://www.hstoday.us/subject-matter-areas/terrorism-study/is-isis-still-alive-and-well-on-the-internet/ (accessed 29 January 2019).

23 For a description of the advantages that Telegram presents to jihadists and other illicit users, see N. Robins-Early, 'How Telegram Became The App of Choice for ISIS', *The Huffington Post*, 25 May 2017, available here: https://www.huffingtonpost.com/entry/isis-telegram-app_us_59259254e4b0ec129d3136d5 (accessed 29 January 2019).

24 For examples of recent jihadist leadership uploads using the described distribution pathway, go to Jihadology.net, a digital archive managed by Aaron Y. Zelin.

25 In network theory, small-world networks comprise actors and entities (known as nodes) that are not direct neighbours of each other but in which any given node can reach out and have contact with most other nodes in the network through a small number of steps or links. These are, in other words, not random graphs or control-and-command vertical networks but rather clusters exhibiting high internal communicative transitivity. The phenomenon is often confused with the well-known 'six degrees of separation' parable that 'everybody is connected to everybody else on the planet' popularized by the American psychologist Stanley Milgram and the playwright John Guare and numerous TV shows playing on the (erroneous) idea.

26 M. Kenney, S. Coulthart, and D. Wright, 'Structure and Performance in a Violent Extremist Network: The Small-World Solution', *The Journal of Conflict Resolution*, vol. 61, no. 10, 2017, pp. 2208–2234.

27 J. Klausen, *The Western Jihadism Project Database and Archive*. Web-based computer file. Brandeis University. For information about the project, see http://www.brandeis.edu/klausen-jihadism. Access available by request for qualified researchers and research teams.

28 A. Higgins, 'A French Town Linked to Jihad Asks Itself Why', *The New York Times*, 16 January 2015, available here: https://www.nytimes.com/2015/01/17/world/europe/french-town-struggles-over-departures-for-jihad.html (accessed 27 January 2019).

29 P. Bracchi, 'So How DID Birmingham Become the Jihadi Capital of Britain? "Connection" of London Terror Attacker to Britain's Second City Is More than Just a Coincidence', *The Daily Mail*, 23 March 2017, available here: https://www.dailymail.co.uk/news/article-4344300/How-DID-Birmingham-jihadi-capital-Britain.html (accessed 27 January 2019).

30 ABC News, 'Molenbeek: Life Inside the So-Called "Jihadi Capital of Europe"', 2015, available here: https://abcnews.go.com/International/video/molenbeek-life-inside-called-jihadi-capital-europe-35533055 (accessed 27 January 2019).

31 J. Klausen, 'The Myth of Homegrown Terrorism', *Special Issue: What the New Administration Needs to Know About Terrorism and Counterterrorism, The Georgetown Security Studies Review*, 24 February 2017, pp. 50–60, available here: http://georgetownsecuritystudiesreview.org/wp-content/uploads/192017/02/Klausen-Te-Myth-of-Homegrown-Terrorism.pdf (accessed 29 January 2019).

32 A. Y. Zelin, *Your Sons Are at Your Service: Tunisia's Missionaries of Jihad*, New York: Columbia University Press, forthcoming.

33 *The 9/11 Commission Report: Final Report of the National Commission on Terrorist Attacks upon the United States*, Washington DC: National Commission on Terrorist Attacks upon the United States, 2004, p. 214.

34 P. Van Ostaeyen and G. Van Vlierden. 'Separating Facts from Fiction about Belgium's Oldest Foreign Fighter, Bassam Ayachi', *Blogspot*, 4 September 2018, available here: https://www.bellingcat.com/news/uk-and-europe/2018/04/09/separating-facts-fiction-belgiums-oldest-foreign-fighter-bassam-ayachi/ (accessed 27 January, 2019); E. Jacob, 'L'imam Bassam Ayachi, figure de l'islamisme belge, écroué en France', *Le Figaro*. 4 April 2018, available here: http://www.lefigaro.fr/actualite-france/2018/04/04/01016-20180404ARTFIG00314-l-imam-bassam-ayachi-figure-de-l-islamisme-belge-ecroue-en-france.php (accessed 27 January 2019).

35 Home Office (UK), *Proscribed Terrorist Organisations*, 20 August 2014, available here: https://assets.publishing.service.gov.uk/government/uploads/system/uploads/attachment_data/file/354891/ProscribedOrganisationsAug14.pdf, p. 7, (accessed 29 January 2019).

36 Organizational Map of Anjem Choudary's affiliates, no date, [website] Available at https://www.hopenothate.org.uk/research/investigations/is-ambassador-at-large/choudarys-international-network/, (accessed 29 January 2019).

37 Estimates based on the author's own research. See also N. Lowles and J. Mulhall, *Gateway to Terror. Anjem Choudary and the al-Muhajiroun Network*, [website], London: Hope Not Hate. Ca., 2014, available here: https://www.hopenothate.org.uk/wp-content/uploads/2018/10/gateway-to-terror-2013-11.pdf (accessed 27 January 2019).

38 AFP, 'Lebanese-Swedish Brothers Killed in Syria', *Fox News*, [Online], updated 10 December 2015, available here: https://www.foxnews.com/world/lebanese-swedish-brothers-killed-in-syria (accessed 29 January 2019).

39 AFP, 'Swedish- Lebanese Bomb Suspect Killed in Raid', *The Local*, [Online], 20 July 2014, available here: https://www.thelocal.se/20140720/swedish-lebanese-bomb-suspect-killed-in-raid (accessed 29 January 2019). For the Lebanese government's release of identifying information see, http://nna-leb.gov.lb/en/show-news/28970/nna-leb.gov.lb/en, (accessed 29 January 2019).

40 'Train Plotter Jailed in Germany', *BBC News*, 9 December 2008, available here: http://news.bbc.co.uk/2/hi/europe/7772817.stm (accessed 29 January 2019).

41 G. W. Steinberg, *German Jihad*, New York: Columbia University Press, 2013, p. 131;

'Slain Lebanese Militant Was Suspect in Failed German bombing', *The New York Times*, 21 May 2007, available here: https://www.nytimes.com/2007/05/21/world/africa/21iht-suspect.4.5811521.html (accessed 29 January 2019).

42 C. Chassay, 'Army Pounds Refugee Camp as Death Toll Rises in Conflict with Islamist Militants', *The Guardian*, 21 May 2007, available here: https://www.theguardian.com/world/2007/may/22/syria.topstories3 (accessed 29 January 2007).

43 K. Person and B. Skjærstad, 'Her er islamister fra Europa samlet i Oslo', *Norsk TV2*, 2 February 2013, available here: https://www.tv2.no/a/4157868#.UoqHHOf3S_h.twitter (accessed 29 January 2019); P. Gudmundson, 'The Swedish Foreign Fighter Contingent in Syria', *CTC Sentinel*, vol. 3, no. 9, September 2013, note 58.

44 The site was estimated to have about ninety visitors daily before it was discontinued, Statens Medieråd, *Våldsbejakande och antidemokratiska budskab på internet*, Stockholm, Regeringskanseleriet, May 2013, p. 212.

Renard, T. and R. Coolsaet, eds. *Returnees: Who Are They, Why Are They (Not) Coming Back and How Should We Deal with Them? Assessing Policies on Returning Foreign Terrorist Fighters in Belgium, Germany and the Netherlands*, Egmont Paper no. 101, Brussels, February 2018.

Sageman, M., *Leaderless Jihad: Terror Networks in the Twenty-First Century*, Philadelphia: University of Pennsylvania Press, 2008.

Schmitt, E. 'ISIS Used Chemical Arms at Least 52 Times in Syria and Iraq, Report Says', *The New York Times*, 21 November 2016.

Steinberg, G. W., *German Jihad*, New York: Columbia University Press, 2013.

Symons, E.-K. 'ISIL Is Really a Revolt by Young Muslims against Their Parents' Generation', Interview with Olivier Roy, *Quartz*, 3 December 2015.

The Washington Post, Transcript of Mark Zuckerberg's Senate Hearing, 10 April 2018.

Worldwide Threat Assessment of the US Intelligence Community. Daniel R. Coats, Director of National Intelligence, Senate Select Committee on Intelligence, 29 January 2019.

Zelin, A. Y., *Your Sons Are at Your Service: Tunisia's Missionaries of Jihad*, New York: Columbia University Press, forthcoming.

14 THE ROLE AND IMPACT OF ENCRYPTION AS FACILITATOR AND PROS AND CONS OF THE ENCRYPTION INTERVENTION DEBATE

Carl Miller

Introduction: The crypto-wars

A small, brown tablet excavated from the banks of the Tigris River was found to hide in its lettering a craftsman's treasured recipe for pottery glaze from 1500 BCE. The Incans tied knots in Llama hair as a way to secretly exchange information. In 800 AD, the Arab Mathematician Al-Kindi wrote a 'Manuscript for Deciphering Cryptographic Messages'. The process of 'encrypting' information into code in order to protect it is a very old craft, as is the race to crack it.

From its ancient origin all the way up until the 1970s, encryption has been based on the idea of a single 'key'. This key was used by both sender and receiver, necessary to both lock the message as code and unlock it again. Single-key encryption suffered an enduring problem: how do you transmit the key securely if you want to transmit information securely?

In 1976, two MIT mathematicians, Whitfield Diffie and Martin Hellman, wrote a paper describing 'public key encryption'.[1] They proposed a cipher system where each user was given two keys, different but mathematically related to each other. A user could share their public key with anyone, and a message could be encrypted with it that only their private key could unscramble. It transformed encryption; for the first time, people were able to send encrypted messages to each other without having to exchange a single key, indeed without even having to ever meet at all. Senders could secure messages for a single receiver. A receiver could ensure the message was from a given sender. It allowed someone to encrypt their own identity. It was a seminal breakthrough and the modern internet, indeed modern life, would be impossible without it.

Public key encryption had actually been discovered by GCHQ cryptographers some years before, but Diffie and Hellman's re-discovery meant that now it was no longer the sole preserve of governments. In the same year, 1976, the United States classified powerful encryption as a 'munition' and made its export illegal without a license.

So began the 'crypto-wars'.[2] In 1991, activist and programmer Phil Zimmerman released 'Pretty Good Privacy' – PGP – a programme that used Diffie and Hellman's idea to allow emails, files, even entire computers to be encrypted. Whilst Zimmerman was still being investigated for allegedly violating the Arms Control Act, in 1993 the US government announced the 'Clipper Chip': a chip developed by the National Security Agency (NSA) to use a form of encryption that the NSA themselves could break. PGP and the Clipper Chip were only early battles in an enduring struggle over whether and how cryptography should be used outside governments.

Encryption as a commodity

The crypto-wars continued, but it was the 2013 revelations of Edward Snowden that began to change the role of encryption in everyday life. In their aftermath, public anxiety about the scale and scope of government surveillance increased, and a significant cohort of the public began to look towards more privacy-conscious ways of using the internet. This was the 'Snowden Effect', and it marked the emergence of encryption into the mainstream.[3]

As part of Snowden's revelations, in June 2013 *The Guardian* published a document wherein the US National Security Agency claimed they had 'direct access' to the networks of Apple, Google, Microsoft and Facebook through a program called PRISM.[4] A senior security engineer at Google, Mike Hearn, described it as 'industrial-scale subversion of the judicial process'.[5]

As consumer confidence in the tech giants decreased, they began to react.[6] 'We therefore do what Internet engineers have always done,' Mike Hearn continued, 'build more secure software. The traffic shown in the [leaked, NSA] slides below is now all encrypted.' Encryption became a 'privacy' feature, a commodity-offering for users. About a year and a half after the disclosures, Apple implemented a form of encryption on its mobile operating system, iOS 8, that, 'end-to-end', was designed to prevent the sort of hacking described in the NSA leaks.[7] 'E2E', as it was called, meant the data was encrypted when it was stored locally, in transit, and on Apple's servers, but the decryption keys were stored only on the phone itself. Apple, themselves, could not decrypt the data; only the user could. Google then announced that Lollipop, its next version of Android OS, would enable device encryption by default. Then later in 2014 WhatsApp announced it would support TextSecure, an end-to-end encryption protocol.

Alongside the tech giants, a market of smaller, specialized encrypted services also quickly grew. After Snowden, the number of people connecting to TOR – a form of anonymous web browser – rocketed from 1 million to 6 million.[8] In 2014 the encrypted messaging app Telegram became the top of the App Store charts in forty-six countries, reaching 180 million users by 2017.[9] Signal allowed people to make encrypted phone calls. Dust allowed users to delete messages as soon as they were read. There was MailPile and Dark Mail, email services that automatically encrypted traffic. Silent Circle launched the Blackphone in 2014, an encrypted mobile phone.

ZixGateway, Cryptocat, Folder Lock, Secure IT, TAILS, Kruptos 2, CryptoForge, SafeHouse, SensiGuard and Privacy Drive, Namecoin, Bitmessage, Twister, Viber, … the list of encrypted services kept getting bigger, spanning everything from chats, group conversations, proprietary applications, encrypted operating systems, phone messages and text files. Encryption was available for free, required no training to use, was often present in services by default and, as implemented by companies like Apple, was so seamlessly integrated that users might not even tell it existed. By the end of 2015 it was estimated that 3.2 billion people used some kind of encryption globally.[10]

Use of encryption by violent extremists

In his memoir, *The Great War of Our Time*, the former CIA Deputy Director Michael Morrell wrote that 'within weeks of the leaks, terrorist organizations around the world were already starting to modify their actions in light of what Snowden disclosed. Communications sources dried up, tactics were changed'.[11]

There is significant evidence that violent extremists – like everyone else – make use of modern encryption and indeed customize and develop it. The Snowden Effect didn't just change how the public used encryption. Perhaps even more dramatic was how it changed the habits of serious criminals and violent extremists. Analysts at the security firm Recorded Future observed an increased pace of innovation, new competing jihadist platforms and three major new encryption tools. 'There's no doubt that use of encryption is part of terrorist tradecraft now,' FBI Director James Comey told the US Senate Judiciary Committee on 9 December 2015.

Ways of evading surveillance and detection are – predictably enough – frequently discussed on forums and websites by terrorists and serious and organized criminals of all types. Extremist groups across the political spectrum have created online tutorials, videos and how-to recommendations for their online followers on the software and hardware to use to escape detection.[12] Anders Breivik, the Norwegian terrorist who murdered seventy-seven people in 2011, wrote a manual that set out best practice recommendations regarding the use of TOR and Virtual Private Network services. In another example, a post from the blog 'al khalifah aridat' ('the caliphate has returned') was entitled 'Remaining Anonymous Online'.[13] 'We see that the tyrants have invested in methods by which they can monitor every single particle of data that goes across the web,' the author wrote. The entry then

Table 1 Encryption-Related Software Developed by Violent Extremist Groups and Related Properties[16]

Product	Release Date	Organization	Key Feature	Execution Platform	Messaging Platform	Crypto Method	Delivery
Mujahideen Secrets (Asrar al-Mujahideen)	2007	GIMF (AQ main)	Encryption of messages or file exchange	Windows with recent instructions for Mac porting	Primarily email	Public/Private key, RSA based, 2048 bit	Windows app
Asrar al-Dardashah	6 February 2013	GIMF (AQ main)	Encryption of instant message traffic	Pidgin platform, Windows installer	Messaging (Pidgin): Yahoo, Google, AOL,etc.	Based on MujahideenSecrets encryption	Pidgin plugin
Tashfeer al-Jawwal (Mobile EncryptionProgram)	4 September 2013	GIMF (AQ main)	Encryption of SMS traffic	Android/Symbian	SMS	Twofish, use SSL for transport	Android/ Symbian apps
Asrar al-Ghurabaa	27 November 2013	ISIS (AQ adversary)	Pure text encryption	Website, accessible via TOR	Platform Independent, just encrypts	'A special or unique encryption algorithm'	Website
Amn al-Mujahid	10 December 2013	Al-Fajr Technical Committee (FTC)	Text encryption	Windows OS	Email, SMS, instant messaging	AES/Twofish	Windows app
Amn al-Mujahid (Mobile)	7 June 2014	Al-Fajr Technical Committee (FTC)	Text encryption	Android	SMS	AES/Twofish	Android app

lists counter-surveillance technologies, including Virtual Private Networks, TOR, encrypted email, the encrypted TAILS operating system and secure messaging services. Researchers Aaron Brantly and Muhammad al-`Ubaydi discovered a thirty-four-page 'OPSEC' guide from the Islamic State forums and a more general pattern of forum-based activity they characterize as 'online technical support communities'. They concluded that it showed a 'mid-level understanding of digital operational security'.[14]

In January 2015, an IS supporter known online as 'al-Khabir al-Taqni' created a 'scorecard'. Summarized by the *Wall Street Journal*, it placed thirty-three messaging applications into one of four categories, from 'safest' to 'unsafe'. 'Signal', an encrypted messaging application was considered 'safe' for instance, whilst the scorecard warned against the use of Viber, WhatsApp, WeChat and fourteen other applications as 'unsafe'.[15]

Violent extremist groups have also developed their own bespoke software that uses encryption. Asrar al-Mujahedeen, the first purpose-made Islamist encryption software, was released in 2007 by Al-Qaeda's Global Islamic Media Front (GIMF), primarily used for email communications. More recently, the Al-Qaeda-associated al-Fajr Technical Committee has released Amn al-Mujahid for Windows, which encrypts emails, instant messages and SMS. In 2014, Christopher Ahlberg compiled a table of six distinct products reproduced in Table 1.

Facilitation of terrorist attacks

Although naturally difficult to independently verify, security officials have made a number of both specific and more general claims about the role of encryption in facilitating terrorism, and routinely point to the role of encryption in terrorist attacks in their aftermath.

After the November 2015 attacks in Paris US intelligence officials indicated that the Islamic State probably used secure messaging applications, specifically SnapChat and Telegram, to coordinate the attacks,[17] although this has been contested by journalists who emphasize the use of burner phones over encrypted services.[18] In the May 2015 attacks in Garland, Texas, the suspect reportedly exchanged 109 encrypted messages with a known terrorist overseas before his attack.[19] On 2 December 2015, a mass shooting and attempted bombing attack at the Inland Regional Center in San Bernardino led to a notorious stand-off between the FBI and Apple. The FBI sought to examine the contents of the attacker's smartphone, an Apple iPhone 5c, but whilst the FBI sought a court order, the end-to-end encryption present on the device meant that Apple was unable to decrypt it.[20]

After the March 2016 attacks in Brussels, NYPD deputy commissioner John Miller stated, 'I think the real point here is we're looking at we call [*sic*] "going dark" ... entire communication systems that are designed to be impenetrable, and we're seeing those become the primary tools of terrorists.'[21]

The Westminster attack of 2017 was another case where the attacker used WhatsApp shortly before he began the attack.[22] The last message was finally recovered from the phone and in it the attacker, Khalid Masood, declared that he was waging jihad in revenge against Western military action in Muslim countries in the Middle East.[23]

Impact on counter-terrorism

The widespread adoption of encryption has impacted a large number of different law enforcement activities, from child protection to the policing of organized crime and counter-terrorism. Across these different domains encryption caused a gap to emerge between the legal privileges of law enforcement agencies to intercept communications and their technical ability to actually do it.

In a major 2016 overview of seventy-five IS-linked plots against the West, the US Homeland Security Committee argued, 'Terrorists are "going dark", making it harder in some cases to prevent attacks. The Islamic State followers have widely distributed guidance on securing their communications, which appears to be having an effect. A number of prominent cases have involved IS-linked attackers encrypting their communications or making their data inaccessible to authorities'.[24]

The statements from law enforcement officials around the world indicate a consistent anxiety that surveillance is becoming less effective, either for stopping attacks, gathering information for criminal trial, or to identify other individuals or networks involved in attack preparation, encouragement or future illicit activity. However, based on open sources alone, it is impossible to fully establish what this means for counter-terrorism: how much more difficult it is to disrupt terrorist networks that exist online, or to detect active plots, or to conduct post-attack or post-arrest investigations.

It is not true, of course, that anything that uses encryption is completely secure. An international policing operation, for instance, closed two large cryptographically secured markets on the dark net in 2017. The dynamic of encryption and cryptanalysis is constantly evolving and, set against this background, debates amongst security researchers over whether any given standard, app or software is secure are constant. Many allege that they have found weaknesses and bugs in popular encryption apps and there are always rumours about whether a service has created a backdoor or some other relationship with law enforcement.

In 2014 the security consultancy Praetorian claimed they had found several weaknesses in the implementation of encryption within WhatsApp that made it vulnerable to several well-known attacks. 'This is the kind of stuff the NSA would love,' they wrote.[25] Another vulnerability in WhatsApp was found in 2018 that allowed unauthorized users to enter group chats.[26] Bitlocker, an encryption service for hard drives, was shown to have a serious vulnerability in 2015.[27] Illicit users of TOR have, too, been identified and arrested, although the nature of the vulnerability has not been released.[28]

In 2016, the Berkman-Klein Centre at Harvard produced a major report assessing the implications of encryption to surveillance.[29] Entitled 'Don't Panic: Making Progress on the Going Dark Debate', the report's authors painted a significantly different picture to the statements of law enforcement officials on the overall impact of encryption. 'The "going dark" metaphor does not fully describe the future of the government's capacity to access the communications of suspected terrorists and criminals,' they concluded.[30] They argued that encryption was not an impermeable barrier to surveillance, and that other trends in technology were opening up new and different opportunities for it to be done:

- The use of end-to-end encryption would be limited by market forces: the ability for companies to read data is exactly what provides the revenue streams for lots of online services;
- Cloud-based services increasingly hold data in a centralized architecture and are not necessarily encrypted end-to-end. iCloud, for instance, can be decrypted by Apple;
- Networked sensors and IoT will offer new opportunities for surveillance through devices;
- Meta-data (location, destination and time of the message) are unencrypted, and often have significant intelligence value, sometimes beyond the content of the communication itself.

In an appendix to the report one of its authors, Jonathan Zittrain, wrote: 'The label is "going dark" only because the security state is losing something that it fleetingly had access to, not because it is all of a sudden lacking in vectors for useful information.'[31]

Interventions

The original intervention suggested by law enforcement back in 1993 was the Clipper Chip, a way of weakening encryption through the obligatory use of a standard that could be decrypted by the NSA. This is the use of a 'backdoor' and it has been a common suggestion since then, alongside the banning of any encryption standard, especially 'end-to-end' architectures, that law enforcement are unable to break (or so it is claimed). As recently as January 2015 David Cameron (notoriously) proposed an outright ban on end-to-end encryption technologies following the January 2015 attacks at the *Charlie Hebdo* offices in Paris. A number of countries have indeed introduced legislation requiring companies to retain readable user data and provide access to government authorities on request. Saudi Arabia, Russia and the UAE use pre-emptive legal mandates for data retention and decryption by technology providers. The Chinese government has required companies selling computers to banks to turn over source code and introduce backdoors to their systems.[32] In 2015 there were also reports that the European Commission has considered introducing new legislation[33] and in 2017 EU Justice Commissioner Věra Jourová threatened to introduce legislation to weaken encryption.[34]

From the very beginning any attempt to weaken encryption on the basis of security arguments has been fiercely criticized and outrightly technologically opposed. Any legislative response would apply only to services operating under the jurisdiction where it applied, and general encryption standards – like PGP – exist outside of any legal entity. It would also, of course, not prevent terrorists developing their own uses of encryption. Any intervention in encryption itself struggles with a core dilemma: encryption does not just protect terrorists; it also protects everyone else too. Strong, uncompromised encryption is used across the internet, from online banking to legitimate journalism. Weakening it does not only expose terrorists to surveillance, but also harms the basis of much of cybersecurity.

Backdoors, when they exist, are routinely exploited. Vodafone built backdoor access into Greece's cell phone network for the Greek government; it was used against the Greek government in 2004–2005. Dubbed the 'Athens Affair', an unknown attacker was discovered to have exploited Vodafone's lawful intercept system to listen to the phone calls of Greek politicians, including their President.[35] Google kept a database of backdoor accesses provided to the US government under surveillance legislation; the Chinese breached that database in 2009.[36] And in an embarrassing leak in 2015 3D blueprints of the TSA's master-keys for 300 million pieces of luggage appeared online.[37]

US and UK security officials have therefore avoided pursuing a legislative response. The White House declared in October 2015 that it would not pursue a legislative fix in the near future. 'To be very clear – Government supports strong encryption and has no intention of banning end-to-end encryption,' Amber Rudd claimed in 2017.[38] Jonathan Evans, a former head of MI5, echoed this after he retired: 'I'm not personally one of those who thinks we should weaken encryption … Within the broader context of cybersecurity, encryption in that context is very positive.'[39]

Instead, two other different interventions are being pursued. First, Western governments have sought to engage with the major technology companies, hoping for greater cooperation and voluntary change rather than legislative coercion. In 2016 the Director of GCHQ gave a speech calling for a new relationship with tech firms over encryption and dismissed the idea of mandatory backdoors.[40] Likewise former FBI Director Comey has also called on the private sector for help in identifying solutions that provide the public with security without frustrating lawful surveillance efforts.

The second intervention has been to increase capability and legal authority for 'equipment interference'. For the first time, the Investigatory Powers Bill, introduced in 2016, explicitly gave legal authority for security services to hack into phones, computers and networks, including for individuals living outside the UK. Exploiting a device makes it possible to both seize encryption keys and access clear-text forms of messages before or after they have been encrypted. It is likely that this reflects an operational shift within security and intelligence services towards such techniques as the result of the widespread use of encryption.

Conclusion

The debate over encryption sits at the core of many of the fundamental logics currently affecting security and intelligence work. It has arisen because violent extremist actors continue to exploit new technology for illicit ends, as they have always done. In part, it is a question of how to apply enduring legal principles within a world that is rapidly changing but it is also a clash of the world of laws and warrants with technical possibility.

Opinion has settled firmly, the author suspects, on the recognition that strong encryption is a feature of modern life and indeed is necessary for modern life. Whilst in this sense the 'crypto-wars' may be coming to an end, the arms race between securing communications and finding ways to access them will continue.

Notes

1 W. Diffie and M. Hellman, 'New Directions in Cryptography', *IEEE Transactions on Information Theory*, vol. IT-22, no. 6, 1976, pp. 472–492.

2 For a description of the crypto-wars, see J. Bartlett, *Dark Net*, London, William Heinemann, 2015.

3 Almost 90 per cent of Americans surveyed indicated they had heard something about 'the government surveillance program', and of those who had, 25 per cent had changed their use of communications technologies either 'a great deal' or 'somewhat' – M. Madden, 'Americans' Privacy Strategies Post-Snowden', *Pew Research Center*, 16 March 2015, available here: http://www.pewinternet.org/2015/03/16/americans-privacy-strategies-post-snowden/.

4 G. Greenwald, 'NSA Prism Program Taps in to User Data of Apple, Google, and Others', *The Guardian*, 7 June 2013, available here: http://www.theguardian.com/world/2013/jun/06/us-tech-giants-nsa-data.

5 M. Masnick, 'Pissed Off Google Security Guys Issue FU to NSA, Announce Data Center Traffic Now Encrypted', *TechDirt*, 6 November 2013, available here: https://www.techdirt.com/articles/20131106/00235225143/pissed-off-google-security-guys-issue-fu-to-nsa-announce-data-center-traffic-now-encrypted.shtml.

6 M. Madden, 'Americans' Attitudes About Privacy, Security and Surveillance', *Pew Research Center*, 20 May 2015, available here: http://www.pewinternet.org/2015/05/20/americans-attitudes-about-privacy-security-and-surveillance/.

7 R. Fingas, 'Edward Snowden Hails Apple as "Pioneering" for iOS 8 Security Measures', *Apple Insider*, 5 June 2015, available here: http://appleinsider.com/articles/15/06/05/edward-snowden-hails-apple-as-pioneering-for-ios-8-security-measures.

8 TOR Metrics, 'Estimation of User Numbers (2012–2018)', [website], available here: https://metrics.torproject.org/userstats-relay-country.html?start=2012-11-15&end=2018-02-13&country=all&events=off.

9 Statista, Number of Active Telegram Users Worldwide from March 2014 to December 2017, [website], available here: https://www.statista.com/statistics/234038/telegram-messenger-mau-users/.

10 P. Strassman, 'Readily Available Encryption Tools Proliferate', Personal Website, August 2016, available here: http://www.strassmann.com/pubs/afcea/2016-8.html.

11 S. Harris, 'CIA's Ex-No.2 says ISIS Learned from Snowden', *DailyBeast*, 5 June 2016, available here: http://www.thedailybeast.com/articles/2015/05/06/cia-s-ex-no-2-says-isis-learned-from-snowden.html.

12 M. Coker, 'How Islamic State Teaches Tech Savvy to Evade Detection', *Wall Street Journal*, 17 November 2015, available here: https://www.wsj.com/articles/islamic-state-teaches-tech-savvy-1447720824.

13 The blog is reproduced in full at, J. Bartlett and A. Krasodomski-Jones, *Online Anonymity: Islamic State and Surveillance*, London: Demos, 2015, pp. 10–12.

14 A. Brantly and Muhammad al-`Ubaydi, 'Extremist Forums Provide Digital OpSec Training', *CTC Sentinel*, vol. 8, no. 5, 2015. pp. 10–13.

15 Coker, M., Schechner, S., and Flynn, A., 'Islamic State Teaches Tech Savvy', *Wall Street Journal*, November 17 2015.

16 Table from C. Ahlberg, 'How al-Qaeda uses Encryption Post-Snowden', *Recorded Future*, 1 August 2014, available here: https://www.recordedfuture.com/al-qaeda-encryption-technology-part-2/.

17 E. Perez, 'Paris Attackers Likely Used Encrypted Apps Officials Say', *CNN*, 17 December 2015, available here: http://www.cnn.com/2015/12/17/politics/paris-attacks-terrorists-encryption/.

18 G. Moody, 'Paris Attackers used Burner Phones Not Encryption to Avoid Detection', *Arstechnica*, 21 March 2016, available here: https://arstechnica.com/tech-policy/2016/03/paris-terrorist-attacks-burner-phones-not-encryption/.

19 Homeland Security Committee, *#Terror Gone Viral*, March 2016, available here: https://homeland.house.gov/wp-content/uploads/2016/03/Report-Terror-Gone-Viral-1.pdf, p. 7.

20 The FBI eventually used third-party assistance to unlock the phone. See E. Pettersson, 'U.S. Drops Apple Case after Getting into Terrorist's iPhone', *Bloomberg*, 28 March 2016, available here: http://www.bloomberg.com/news/articles/2016-03-28/u-s-drops-apple-case-after-successfully-accessing-iphone-data-imcj88xu.

21 CBS New York, 'Top NYPD Official: "Technology Is Becoming a Big Enabler" In Terrorists Secretly Planning Attacks', *CBS New York*, 22 March 2016, available here: http://newyork.cbslocal.com/2016/03/22/john-miller-nypd-brussels-attacks/.

22 R. Price, 'The Westminster Terror Attack Has Reignited a Furious Row over Encryption in the UK', *Business Insider*, 27 March 2017, available here: http://

uk.businessinsider.com/westminster-terror-attacks-encryption-whatsapp-messaging-uk-2017-3.

23 K. Sengupta, 'Last Message Left by Westminster Attacker Khalid Masood Uncovered by Security Agencies', *The Independent*, 27 April 2017, available here: http://www.independent.co.uk/news/uk/crime/last-message-left-by-westminster-attacker-khalid-masood-uncovered-by-security-agencies-a7706561.html.

24 Homeland Security Committee, *#Terror Gone Viral*.

25 D. Goodin, 'Crypto Weaknesses in WhatsApp "The Kind of Stuff the NSA Would Love"', *Arstechnica*, 21 February 2014, available here: https://arstechnica.com/information-technology/2014/02/crypto-weaknesses-in-whatsapp-the-kind-of-stuff-the-nsa-would-love/.

26 A. Greenberg, 'WhatsApp Security Flaws Could Allow Snoops to Slide into Group Chats', *Wired*, 10 January 2018, available here: https://www.wired.com/story/whatsapp-security-flaws-encryption-group-chats/.

27 L. Constantin, 'BitLocker Encryption Can Be Defeated with Trivial Windows Authentication Bypass', *PCWorld* 13 November 2015, available here: https://www.pcworld.com/article/3005182/encryption/bitlocker-encryption-can-be-defeated-with-trivial-windows-authentication-bypass.html.

28 J. Cox, 'Court Docs Show a University Helped FBI Bust Silk Road 2', *Child Porn Suspects*, 11 November 2015, available here: https://motherboard.vice.com/en_us/article/gv5x4q/court-docs-show-a-university-helped-fbi-bust-silk-road-2-child-porn-suspects.

29 J. L. Zittrain, et al, *Don't Panic: Making Progress on the 'Going Dark Debate'*, Berkman Center's Berklett Cybersecurity Project, The Berkman Center Research Publication, 2016.

30 Berkman Center for Internet & Society, *Don't Panic*.

31 Berkman Center for Internet & Society, *Don't Panic*.

32 P. Mozur, 'New Rules in China Upset Western Tech Companies', *New York Times*, 28 January 2018, available here: https://www.nytimes.com/2015/01/29/technology/in-china-new-cybersecurity-rules-perturb-western-tech-companies.html.

33 P. Hockenos, 'Europe Considers Surveillance Expansion after Deadly Attacks', *The Intercept*, 20 January 2015, available here: https://theintercept.com/2015/01/20/europe-considers-surveillance-expansion/.

34 K. McCarthy, 'Europe to Push New laws to Access Encrypted Apps Data', *The Register*, 30 March 2017, available here: https://www.theregister.co.uk/2017/03/30/ec_push_encryption_backdoors/.

35 T. Timm, 'The Athens Affair Shows Why We Need Encryption without Backdoors', *The Guardian*, 30 September 2015, https://www.theguardian.com/commentisfree/2015/sep/30/athens-affair-encryption-backdoors.

36 E. Nakashima, 'Chinese Hackers Who Breached Google Gained Access to Sensitive Data, U.S. Officials Say', *The Washington Post*, 20 May 2013, https://www.washingtonpost.com/world/national-security/chinese-hackers-who-breached-google-gained-access-to-sensitive-data-us-officials-say/2013/05/20/51330428-be34-11e2-89c9-3be8095fe767_story.html?utm_term=.e638054de705.

37 K. McCarthy, '3D Printer Blueprints for TSA Luggage-Unlocking Master Keys Leak Online', *The Register*, 10 September 2015, available here: https://www.theregister.co.uk/2015/09/10/tsa_master_key_blueprints_leaked/.

38 A. Rudd, 'Encryption and Counter-Terrorism: Getting the Balance Right', *UK Government*, 31 July 2017, available here: https://www.gov.uk/government/speeches/encryption-and-counter-terrorism-getting-the-balance-right.

39 P. Muncaster, 'Ex-MI5 Boss Evans: Don't Undermine Encryption', *InfoSecurity Magazine*, 14 August 2017, https://www.infosecurity-magazine.com/news/exmi5-boss-evans-dont-undermine/.

40 E. MacAskill, 'GCHQ Boss Calls for New Relationship with Tech Firms over Encryption', *The Guardian*, 7 March 2016, available here: https://www.theguardian.com/uk-news/2016/mar/07/gchq-boss-new-relationship-tech-firms-encryption.

Recommended Readings

Ahlberg, C., 'How al-Qaeda Uses Encryption Post-Snowden', *Recorded Future*, 1 August 2014, available here: https://www.recordedfuture.com/al-qaeda-encryption-technology-part-2/.

Bartlett, J., *Dark Net*, London: William Heinemann, 2015.

Bartlett, J. and A. Krasodomski-Jones, *Online Anonymity: Islamic State and Surveillance*, London: Demos, 2015, pp. 10–12.

Brantly, A., and Muhammad al-'Ubaydi, 'Extremist Forums Provide Digital OpSec Training', *CTC Sentinel*, vol. 8, no. 5, 2015. pp. 10–13.

CBS New York, 'Top NYPD Official: "Technology Is Becoming a Big Enabler" in Terrorists Secretly Planning Attacks', *CBS New York*, 22 March 2016, available here: http://newyork.cbslocal.com/2016/03/22/john-miller-nypd-brussels-attacks/.

Coker, M., 'How Islamic State Teaches Tech Savvy to Evade Detection', *Wall Street Journal*, 17 November 2015, available here: https://www.wsj.com/articles/islamic-state-teaches-tech-savvy-1447720824

Constantin, L., 'BitLocker Encryption Can Be Defeated with Trivial Windows Authentication Bypass', *PCWorld* 13 November 2015, available here: https://www.pcworld.com/article/3005182/encryption/bitlocker-encryption-can-be-defeated-with-trivial-windows-authentication-bypass.html

Cox, J., 'Court Docs Show a University Helped FBI Bust Silk Road 2', *Child Porn Suspects*, 11 November 2015, available here: https://motherboard.vice.com/en_us/article/gv5x4q/court-docs-show-a-university-helped-fbi-bust-silk-road-2-child-porn-suspects.

Diffie, W., and M. Hellman, 'New Directions in Cryptography', *IEEE Transactions on Information Theory*, vol. IT-22, no. 6, 1976, pp. 472–492.

Fingas, R., 'Edward Snowden Hails Apple as 'Pioneering' for iOS 8 Security Measures', *Apple Insider*, 5 June 2015, available here: http://appleinsider.com/articles/15/06/05/edward-snowden-hails-apple-as-pioneering-for-ios-8-security-measures.

Goodin, D., 'Crypto Weaknesses in WhatsApp "The Kind of Stuff the NSA Would Love"', *Arstechnica*, 21 February 2014, available here: https://arstechnica.com/information-technology/2014/02/crypto-weaknesses-in-whatsapp-the-kind-of-stuff-the-nsa-would-love/.

Greenberg, A., 'WhatsApp Security Flaws Could Allow Snoops to Slide into Group Chats', *Wired*, 10 January 2018, available here: https://www.wired.com/story/whatsapp-security-flaws-encryption-group-chats/.

Greenwald, G., 'NSA Prism Program Taps in to User Data of Apple, Google, and Others', *The Guardian*, 7 June 2013, available here: http://www.theguardian.com/world/2013/jun/06/us-tech-giants-nsa-data

Harris, S., 'CIA's Ex-No.2 says ISIS Learned from Snowden', *DailyBeast*, 5 June 2016, available here: http://www.thedailybeast.com/articles/2015/05/06/cia-s-ex-no-2-says-isis-learned-from-snowden.html.

Hockenos, P., 'Europe considers Surveillance Expansion after Deadly Attacks', *The Intercept*, 20 January 2015, available here: https://theintercept.com/2015/01/20/europe-considers-surveillance-expansion/.

Homeland Security Committee, *#Terror Gone Viral*, March 2016, available here: https://homeland.house.gov/wp-content/uploads/2016/03/Report-Terror-Gone-Viral-1.pdf, p. 7.

MacAskill, E., 'GCHQ Boss Calls for New Relationship with Tech Firms over Encryption', *The Guardian*, 7 March 2016, available here: https://www.theguardian.com/uk-news/2016/mar/07/gchq-boss-new-relationship-tech-firms-encryption.

Madden, M., 'Americans' Privacy Strategies Post-Snowden', *Pew Research Center*, 16 March 2015, available here: http://www.pewinternet.org/2015/03/16/americans-privacy-strategies-post-snowden/.

Madden, M., 'Americans' Attitudes About Privacy, Security and Surveillance', *Pew Research Center*, 20 May 2015, available here: http://www.pewinternet.org/2015/05/20/americans-attitudes-about-privacy-security-and-surveillance/

Masnick, M., 'Pissed Off Google Security Guys Issue FU To NSA, Announce Data Center Traffic Now Encrypted', *TechDirt*, 6 November 2013, available here: https://www.techdirt.com/articles/20131106/00235225143/pissed-off-google-security-guys-issue-fu-to-nsa-announce-data-center-traffic-now-encrypted.shtml

McCarthy, K., 'Europe to Push New Laws to Access Encrypted Apps Data', *The Register*, 30 March 2017, available here: https://www.theregister.co.uk/2017/03/30/ec_push_encryption_backdoors/

McCarthy, K., '3D printer blueprints for TSA Luggage-Unlocking Master Keys Leak Online', *The Register*, 10 September 2015, available here: https://www.theregister.co.uk/2015/09/10/tsa_master_key_blueprints_leaked/

Moody, G., 'Paris Attackers Used Burner Phones Not Encryption to Avoid Detection', *Arstechnica*, 21 March 2016, available here: https://arstechnica.com/tech-policy/2016/03/paris-terrorist-attacks-burner-phones-not-encryption/.

Mozur, P., 'New Rules in China Upset Western Tech Companies', *New York Times*, 28 January 2018, available here: https://www.nytimes.com/2015/01/29/technology/in-china-new-cybersecurity-rules-perturb-western-tech-companies.html

Perez, E., 'Paris Attackers Likely Used Encrypted Apps Officials Say', *CNN*, 17 December 2015, available here: http://www.cnn.com/2015/12/17/politics/paris-attacks-terrorists-encryption/

Pettersson, E., 'U.S. Drops Apple Case after Getting into Terrorist's iPhone', *Bloomberg*, 28 March 2016, available here: http://www.bloomberg.com/news/articles/2016-03-28/u-s-drops-apple-case-after-successfully-accessing-iphone-data-imcj88xu

Price, R., 'The Westminster Terror Attack Has Reignited a Furious Row over Encryption in the UK', *Business Insider*, 27 March 2017, available here: http://uk.businessinsider.com/westminster-terror-attacks-encryption-whatsapp-messaging-uk-2017-3

Rudd, A., 'Encryption and Counter-Terrorism: Getting the Balance Right', *UK Government*, 31 July 2017, available here: https://www.gov.uk/government/speeches/encryption-and-counter-terrorism-getting-the-balance-right

Sengupta, K., 'Last Message Left by Westminster Attacker Khalid Masood Uncovered by Security Agencies', *The Independent*, 27 April 2017, available here: http://www.independent.co.uk/news/uk/crime/last-message-left-by-westminster-attacker-khalid-masood-uncovered-by-security-agencies-a7706561.html

Statista, Number of Active Telegram Users Worldwide from March 2014 to December 2017, [website], available here: https://www.statista.com/statistics/234038/telegram-messenger-mau-users/

Strassman, P., 'Readily Available Encryption Tools Proliferate', Personal Website, August 2016, available here: http://www.strassmann.com/pubs/afcea/2016-8.html

TOR Metrics, Estimation of User Numbers (2012–2018), [website], available here: https://metrics.torproject.org/userstats-relay-country.html?start=2012-11-15&end=2018-02-13&country=all&events=off

Zittrain, J. L., et al, *Don't Panic: Making Progress on the "Going Dark Debate"*, Berkman Center's Berklett Cybersecurity Project, The Berkman Center Research Publication, 2016.

15 PHYSICAL FACILITATING ENVIRONMENTS – PRISONS AND MADRASSAS AS MECHANISMS AND VEHICLES OF VIOLENT RADICALIZATION?

Andrew Silke

Introduction

A consistent element of the UK's counter-terrorism strategy since 2011 has been the proposal that certain physical spaces represent a significant risk of radicalization. As argued in the government's Prevent Strategy:

> Radicalisation tends to occur in places where terrorist ideologies, and those that promote them, go uncontested and are not exposed to free, open and balanced debate and challenge. Some of these places are the responsibility of Government, some are Government funded but have considerable autonomy and others are both privately owned and run.[1]

The institutions particularly singled out in this regard have been education and health-care providers, universities, faith groups, charities and prisons. Following from this perception, the Counter-Terrorism and Security Act 2015 duly required a range of organizations – including local authorities, schools, universities, prisons and health bodies – to fulfil a duty of care to detect and prevent radicalization within their settings.

The government position has been supported by several theoretical models of the radicalization process. For example, an early model by Precht flagged the importance of 'Opportunity Factors' in the radicalization process, drawing attention to the degree of, or exposure to, extremist ideas in an individual's environment, including physical spaces such as mosques and prisons.[2] The exposure theme also appears in subsequent frameworks, including, for example, Kruglanski et al.'s quest for significance model of radicalization which has a role for physical spaces such as mosques and madrasas as places where individuals can 'encounter the terrorism-justifying ideology'.[3] This framework stresses that other factors are also critical in the process and that exposure to the ideology alone, while important, is by itself not enough. Other radicalization models note that physical spaces are important in terms of providing an arena where groups of individuals can meet and interact. For example, Helmus notes the importance of 'bottom-up peer groups' in the radicalization process, highlighting the importance of venues. He identifies religious settings advocating violence and prisons as particularly important in these terms.[4] Neumann and Rogers referred to such venues as 'places of vulnerability' and as 'gateways' which can facilitate exposure to extremist ideology and also create and sustain social connections to people who endorse such ideologies.[5]

Collectively these models have had considerable influence on government policy, but the evidence around the specific role of physical spaces is often ambiguous. Crucially, the evidence supporting such a link is often anecdotal and is usually much more conceptual than empirical.[6] More recent assessments have increasingly questioned the degree to which such physical spaces can be accurately viewed as incubators of radicalization.

Prisons

Prisons are frequently portrayed and widely viewed as 'hotbeds' of radicalization and an increasing amount of research has focused on understanding the risks and dynamics behind prisoner radicalization.[7] Speaking in 2016, the then Prime Minister David Cameron warned that in England and Wales there were 1,000 prisoners who were radicalized or assessed as potentially vulnerable to radicalization.[8] In 2017 this figure was revised down to approximately 700 prisoners, of whom 180 had been convicted of terrorism-related offences or were on remand for such offences.[9] The remaining 520 prisoners comprise those who were radicalized within prison and those assessed as vulnerable. While exact figures have not been released, it is generally accepted that the vulnerables make up the overwhelming majority of the 520, and those who have actually been radicalized are small in number. To set the wider context, in 2017 the prison system held over 86,000 prisoners, of whom 13,244 were classified as Muslim.[10] Thus, terrorist prisoners, radicalized 'ordinary' prisoners and prisoners identified as potentially vulnerable to radicalization represented 0.8 per cent of the prison population.

The spread of radicalization among 'ordinary' prisoners has been a recurring obsession with authorities, for understandable reasons. High-profile (albeit very isolated) cases such as the Spaniard José Emilio Suárez Trashorras and the American José Padilla stand as a warning about the potential danger posed by such prisoners.[11] More evidence-based reviews of prison systems in the West, including those of England and Wales, have found that such radicalization is relatively rare.[12] As highlighted in a recent United Nations report:

> There is a concern that if left unchecked, prisons may serve as locations in which violent extremism can thrive and where prisoners can be radicalised to violence or where violent extremist prisoners who are co-located can form closer relationships, more cohesive networks and mutual reinforcement of violent extremist beliefs. However, recent research suggests that such risks are overstated and that there is limited evidence for suggesting that significant numbers of prisoners are being radicalised to violence and proceed with committing violent extremist acts upon release.[13]

Theories on prison radicalization argue that when it does occur, it primarily stems from a combination of institutional, social and individual factors, such as overcrowding and deprivation, violence and group dynamics, and a desire for protection and belongingness.[14] The role of charismatic leaders is also often emphasized. Mark Hamm, for example, stresses how charismatic leaders select vulnerable inmates and use one-on-one proselytization to recruit groups of followers.[15] Liebling and colleagues describe a similar dynamic in the UK, where charismatic Muslim 'key-players' target searching or 'lost' inmates and offer themselves as trustworthy guides, propagating Islam as a means to find an identity and meaning in life.[16] In the Liebling context, however, the aim of the recruiters was conversion to Islam, not radicalization.

One problem, however, with the discussion around the causes of radicalization within prison is that the evidence base has tended to be anecdotal. Current theories on prison radicalization are almost entirely based on an analysis of a small number of case studies, combined with a theoretical assessment of likely drivers which draws primarily on the wider literature on radicalization and also frequently on the literature around prison gangs.[17]

Nevertheless, a shortage of actual cases has not stopped frequent claims that radicalization is a serious problem in UK prisons. Most notable in this regard was the recent Acheson Review into the threat of Islamist extremism to prisons and probation services. Overall, the review concluded that 'Islamist Extremism (IE) was a growing problem within prisons',[18] though the statistics to support this conclusion were not released. Acheson reported that

> We believe that there are a small but significant number of people in custody who either have become radicalised themselves in custody or who have been imprisoned for Islamist extremist-related offences … They are not being imprisoned in the high-security estate, where there is a higher level of understanding and surveillance, but in the category B, C and D estates. There is an issue with them.[19]

The main conclusions made by the review were that: (1) staff training needed to be improved particularly outside the high-security prisons, (2) National Offender Management Service (NOMS)[20] senior leadership was too complacent about the threat; and (3) the recruitment, training and supervision of prison imams were poor.

It is perhaps not surprising that such conclusions were not shared by NOMS which could highlight the very low re-offending rate for former terrorist prisoners, and the extreme rarity of cases of individuals actually radicalized in prison in England and Wales who are subsequently convicted of terrorist offences. In some respects the Acheson conclusions were more about the perceived *potential* for radicalization rather than *actual* radicalization.

Nevertheless, the Acheson conclusions chimed with public perceptions and ultimately a receptive government introduced one of the key recommendations: the creation of specialist 'separation centres' to isolate terrorist prisoners from the rest of the prison population.[21] Three centres were established, each located in a high-security prison, and with a combined capacity for up to twenty-eight prisoners.

Researchers quickly raised concerns. For example, drawing on interviews with former British jihadi prisoners, Tam Hussein highlighted that the ability of terrorist prisoners to radicalize other prisoners in British jails was widely overestimated, and what was significantly underestimated was how exposure to other prisoners actually moderated the views of most extremist prisoners.[22] Overseas research added further concerns. For example, after evaluating the Dutch policy of concentrating terrorist prisoners in specialized 'terrorism wings', Veldhuis found that there was no substantial evidence that concentration was a necessary and helpful response to violent extremism.[23] Moreover, concentration policies can produce undesired side effects, such as intensification of extremist ideologies and networks. They can also enhance the prisoners' ability to plan and orchestrate activities both within the prison and with elements beyond the prison walls (as the case of Northern Ireland, for example, highlights).[24]

Madrassas

As with prisons, madrassas have been frequently flagged as potential locations of radicalization. In a UK context, it has been estimated that there are about 2,000 madrassas with about 250,000 Muslim children attending them.[25] According to the Muslim Council of Britain there are three main types of madrassas: (1) madrassas attached to mosques, (2) madrassas run by volunteers who teach Islamic classes in hired-out community centres or school halls, and (3) informal classes run in people's homes. The degree to which there is independent oversight of the activities of these madrassas also varies. For example, the Department of Education has reported that a location would not count as a school if it does not teach classes in subjects such as maths, English or science. Further, if children at the site are taught less than eighteen hours a week again it would not count as a school. Thus, primarily religiously focused sites do not technically fall under Department of Education oversight, inspection and guidelines.[26] This has resulted in concerns that exclusively religious 'schools' are effectively an unregulated space, with fears raised about the quality of teaching and child welfare standards. Such concerns apply to Jewish and Christian sites, for example, but an additional element with regard to madrassas is anxiety around the potential for radicalization.

This issue was highlighted in March 2018 with the conviction of Umar Ahmed Haque for a range of terrorism offences, including attempts to radicalize children.[27] Haque had worked as a classroom assistant at a school and was also involved in running evening classes in a madrassa connected to a mosque. He exposed students to extremist propaganda and had engaged students in terrorist role-playing. The police believe that he attempted to radicalize at least 110 children, with thirty-five of these identified as needing long-term support in the aftermath of the case.[28]

The Haque case highlighted that madrassas could be hijacked as spaces by extremists to attempt to radicalize children. At an international level, research has drawn particular attention to the potential role of madrassas in jihadist extremism. In the case of Pakistan, for example, the madrassa system has been blamed for contributing to radicalization in the region with some describing the madrassas as 'factories of jihad'.[29] While the jihadist extremists have a strategic religious aim, the religious backgrounds of the people who join the jihad are not always clear-cut. Sageman, for example, found that only 18 per cent of Islamist extremists had an Islamic religious primary or secondary education. In contrast, 82 per cent went to secular schools.[30] Overall, Sageman's early finding has been replicated by most subsequent studies on jihadist terrorists in the West which has found that relatively few grew up in particularly religious households and most were not regarded as religious as children. Increasing religiosity was something which occurred later in life.[31]

Even prior to the Haque case media coverage of UK madrassas has generally been negative, flagging issues around child welfare, the quality of education and the risk of radicalization.[32] Research into madrassas in the UK, however, suggests that fears about radicalization are typically exaggerated. For example, Cherti and Bradley conducted the most detailed survey to date on the operation of madrassas in England.[33] This research focused on 179 madrassas and involved interviews with staff, parents and pupils, as well as other stakeholders such as local authority representatives. The researchers found that madrassas played a significant role in developing a sense of identity for young people, but did not find evidence that they were havens for extremism.

Research, in general, suggests that a 'madrassa myth' has developed where madrassas have been singled out in the West as high-risk environments for radicalization. While there can sometimes be genuine concerns in terms of general child welfare issues and whether appropriate safeguards are in place, there is not evidence that madrassas are significant radicalizing spaces in the West. Actual cases of such radicalization are isolated, and studies suggest that students at madrassas have similar experiences and characteristics to students who attend Christian Bible study classes, or Jewish children who attend Hebrew school (and that similar concerns regarding standards and welfare apply).[34] Overall, Allan et al., in an evidence review of the drivers of radicalization, concluded that it was an error to regard madrassas as a significant driver of radicalization, arguing that 'the problem of madrassa-based radicalization has been significantly overstated'.[35]

Conclusion

Initially, policy-makers focused on community settings, such as mosques, as the locations where extremist ideology had to be blocked; later, they turned to prisons and universities; more recently, the focus has been on the circulation of extremist ideology through schools and social media. Even as the settings for policy implementation have changed, the arguments made for such policies have been constant.[36]

Ultimately, radicalization in both prison settings and madrassas and religious-education settings does occur or is attempted. The review has flagged a number of cases where this has clearly happened or has been seriously attempted. In a UK context, do these cases represent very isolated instances or evidence of a substantive and significant phenomenon? While other countries may have different experiences, the review finds that in the UK the evidence suggests that successful radicalization is rare in both settings. The evidence highlights that other factors play a role in the radicalization process and that physical setting alone appears to be a poor predictor for radicalization.

Nevertheless, it is also clear that both types of settings remain widely regarded by the media and within government as prominent centres of radicalization. This has led to policy being specifically directed to countering and preventing radicalization in such settings. There is no indication that this trend is about to change any time soon and we can continue to expect both prisons and madrassas being described as high-risk centres of radicalization in what is often a simplistic and poorly informed debate.

Notes

1 HM Government, *Prevent Strategy*, London: The Stationary Office, 2011.

2 T. Precht, 'Home Grown Terrorism and Islamist Radicalization in Europe: From Conversion to Terrorism', *Danish Ministry of Defence*, Research Report, 2007.

3 A. Kruglanski et al., 'The Psychology of Radicalization and Deradicalization: How Significance Quest Impacts Violent Extremism', *Political Psychology*, vol. 35, no. S1, 2014, pp. 69–93.

4 T. Helmus, 'Why and How Some People Become Terrorists', *Social Science for Counterterrorism*, vol. 74, no. 06-C, 2009, p. 71.

5 P. Neumann and B. Rodgers, *Recruitment and Mobilisation for the Islamist Militant Movement in Europe*, London: International Centre for the Study of Radicalisation and Political Violence, 2007.

6 S. Desmarais et al., 'The State of Scientific Knowledge Regarding Factors Associated with Terrorism', *Journal of Threat Assessment and Management*, vol. 4, no. 4, 2017, pp. 180–209.

7 M. Hamm, *The Spectacular Few: Prisoner Radicalization and Terrorism in the Post-9/11 Era*, New York: New York University Press, 2013; C. Jones, 'Are Prisons Really Schools for Terrorism? Challenging Rhetoric on Prisoner Radicalization', *Punishment & Society*, vol. 16, 2014, pp. 74–103; United Nations Office on Drugs and Crime, *Handbook on the Management of Violent Extremist Prisoners and the Prevention of Radicalization to Violence in Prisons*, Vienna: United Nations, 2016; R. Williams, *RAN P&P Practitioners' Working Paper Approaches to Violent Extremist Offenders and Countering Radicalisation In Prisons And Probation*, Amsterdam: Radicalisation Awareness Network, 2016; J. Brandon, *Unlocking al-Qaeda: Islamist extremism in British Prisons*, London: Quilliam Foundation, 2009; G. Hannah, L. Clutterbuck, and J. Rubin, *Radicalization or Rehabilitation: Understanding the Challenge of Extremist and Radicalized Prisoners*, Santa Barbara, CA: RAND Corporation, 2008; B. Useem and O. Clayton, 'Radicalization of US Prisoners', *Criminology & Public Policy*, vol. 8, no. 3, 2009, pp. 561–592.

8 D. Cameron, *Prison reform: Prime Minister's Speech*, London: Policy Exchange, 2016.

9 House of Commons, 'Extremism in Prison', *House of Commons Hansard*, vol. 624, 2017, available here: https://hansard.parliament.uk/Commons/2017-04-25/debates/3084EAEB-AEB6-47E8-892A-A9825431E2FE/ExtremismInPrisons.

10 G. Allen, L. Audickas and C. Watson, *Prisons Statistics, England and Wales. Briefing Paper Number CBP 8161*, London, UK: House of Commons Library, 2017.

11 A. Silke (ed.), *Prisons, Terrorism and Extremism: Critical Issues in Management, Radicalisation and Reform*, London: Routledge, 2014.

12 For a good review see: Hamm, *The spectacular few*.

13 United Nations Office on Drugs and Crime, *Handbook on the Management of Violent Extremist Prisoners and the Prevention of Radicalization to Violence in Prisons*.

14 For example, J. Brandon, *Unlocking al-Qaeda*; M. S. Hamm, 'Locking up Terrorists: Three Models for Controlling Prisoner Radicalization'. Working Paper, Indiana State University, 2011; E. Mulcahy, S. Merrington and P. J. Bell, 'The Radicalisation Of Prison Inmates: A Review Of The Literature On Recruitment, Religion And Prisoner Vulnerability', *Journal of Human Security*, vol. 9, no. 1, 2013, pp. 4–14.

15 M. Hamm, 'Prisoner Radicalization: Assessing the Threat in US Correctional Institutions', *NIJ Journal*, vol. 261, 2008, pp. 14–19; M. Hamm, 'Prison Islam in the Age of Sacred Terror', *The British Journal of Criminology*, vol. 49, no. 5, 2009, pp. 667–685; Hamm, *Locking up terrorists*; Hamm. *The spectacular few*.

16 A. Liebling, H. Arnold, and C. Straub, 'Staff-Prisoner Relationships at HMP Whitemoor: 12 years on', *Cambridge Institute of Criminology Prisons Research Centre*, Revised Final Report, 2011.

17 N. Thompson, 'Root Cause Approach to Prisoner Radicalisation', *Salus Journal*, vol. 4, no. 3, 2016, p. 18.

18 I. Acheson, *Summary of the Main Findings of the Review of Islamist Extremism in Prisons, Probation and Youth Justice*, London: Ministry of Justice, 2016.

19 House of Commons Justice Committee, *Oral Evidence: Radicalisation in Prisons and Other Prison Matters, HC 417*, 13 July 2016.

20 NOMS was renamed in 2017 and is now called Her Majesty's Prison and Probation Service.

21 Ministry of Justice, 'Dangerous Extremists to Be Separated from Mainstream Prison Population', Press Release, 21 April 2017, available here: https://www.gov.uk/government/news/dangerous-extremists-to-be-separated-from-mainstream-prison-population.

22 T. Hussein, 'Prison Radicalisation: Dealing with Muslim Inmates with Terror Convictions', Personal Website, 13 February 2017, available here: http://www.tamhussein.co.uk/2017/02/prison-radicalisation-dealing-muslim-inmates-terror-convictions/.

23 T. Veldhuis, 'Captivated by Fear. An Evaluation of Terrorism Detention Policy', PhD dissertation, University of Groningen, 2015; see also: T. Veldhuis, *Prisoner Radicalization and Terrorism Detention Policy. Institutionalized Fear or Evidence-Based Policy Making?*, London: Routledge, 2016.

24 See for example J. Bates-Gaston, 'Prisons and Detention: Reflections on the Northern Ireland Experience', in A. Silke (ed.), *Routledge Handbook of Terrorism and Counterterrorism*, Oxon, Routledge, (In Press).

25 M. Cherti and L. Bradley, *Inside Madrassas: Understanding and Engaging with British-Muslim Faith Supplementary Schools*, London: Institute for Public Policy Research, 2011.

26 N. Titheradge, 'Is There a Problem with Unregistered Schools?', *BBC News*, 27 February 2018, available here: http://www.bbc.co.uk/news/education-43170447.

27 J. Grierson, 'Isis Follower Tried to Create Jihadist Child Army in East London', *The Guardian*, 2 March 2018.

28 D. Casciani, 'How a Teacher Sought to Recruit a Terror "Death Squad"', *BBC News*, 2 March 2018, available here: http://www.bbc.co.uk/news/uk-43172379.

29 T. Andrabi et al., 'Religious School Enrolment in Pakistan: A Look at the Data', *Comparative Education Review*, vol 50, no. 3, 2006, pp. 446–477.

30 M. Sageman, *Understanding Terrorist Networks*, Philadelphia: University of Pennsylvania Press, 2004.

31 See, for example: A. Zammit, '*Who Becomes a Jihadist in Australia? A Comparative Analysis*', *Understanding Terrorism from an Australian Perspective: Radicalisation, De-Radicalisation and Counter Radicalisation*' Melbourne: Monash University Caulfield Campus, 2010, pp. 1–21; M. Danish Shakeel and P. J. Wolf, *Does Private Islamic Schooling Promote Terrorism? An Analysis of the Educational Background of Successful American Homegrown Terrorists*, EDRE Working Paper 2017–20, 2017.

32 M. Cherti, A. Glennie, and L. Bradle, *Madrassas in the British Media*, London: Institute for Public Policy Research (IPPR), 2011.

33 M. Cherti and L. Bradley, *Inside Madrassas: Understanding and Engaging with British-Muslim Faith Supplementary Schools*, London: Institute for Public Policy Research, 2011.

34 C. Fair. 'The Enduring Madrasa Myth', *Current History*, vol. 111, no. 744, 2012, pp. 135–140.

35 H. Allan et al., *Drivers of Violent Extremism: Hypotheses and Literature Review*, London: Royal United Services Institute, 2015.

36 Commission's Expert Group on European Violent Radicalisation, *Radicalisation Processes Leading to Acts of Terrorism*, Report Submitted to the European Commission, 2008.

Recommended Readings

Acheson, I., *Summary of the Main Findings of the Review of Islamist Extremism in Prisons, Probation and Youth Justice*, London: Ministry of Justice, 2016.

Allan, H., et al., *Drivers of Violent Extremism: Hypotheses and Literature Review*, London: Royal United Services Institute, 2015.

Allen, G., L. Audickas, and C. Watson, *Prisons Statistics, England and Wales. Briefing Paper Number CBP 8161*, London, UK: House of Commons Library, 2017.

Andrabi, T., et al., 'Religious School Enrolment in Pakistan: A Look at the Data', *Comparative Education Review*, vol. 50, no. 3, 2006, pp. 446–477.

Bates-Gaston, J., 'Prisons and detention: Reflections on the Northern Ireland Experience', in A. Silke (ed.), *Routledge Handbook of Terrorism and Counterterrorism*, Oxon: Routledge, (In Press).

Brandon, J., *Unlocking al-Qaeda: Islamist extremism in British Prisons*, London: Quilliam Foundation, 2009.

Cameron, D., *Prison Reform: Prime Minister's Speech*, London: Policy Exchange, 2016.

Casciani, D., 'How a Teacher Sought to Recruit a Terror "Death Squad"', *BBC News*, 2 March 2018, available here: http://www.bbc.co.uk/news/uk-43172379

Cherti, M. and L. Bradley, *Inside Madrassas: Understanding and Engaging with British-Muslim Faith Supplementary Schools*, London: Institute for Public Policy Research, 2011.

Cherti, M., A. Glennie, and L. Bradle, *Madrassas in the British Media*, London: Institute for Public Policy Research (IPPR), 2011.

Commission's Expert Group on European Violent Radicalisation, *Radicalisation Processes Leading to Acts of Terrorism*, Report Submitted to the European Commission, 2008.

Desmarais, S., et al., 'The State of Scientific Knowledge Regarding Factors Associated with Terrorism', *Journal of Threat Assessment and Management*, vol. 4, no. 4, 2017, pp. 180–209.

Fair, C., 'The Enduring Madrasa Myth', *Current History*, vol. 111, no. 744, 2012, pp. 135–140.

Grierson, J., 'Isis Follower Tried to Create Jihadist Child Army in East London', *The Guardian*, 2 March 2018.

Hamm, M., *The Spectacular Few: Prisoner Radicalization and Terrorism in the Post-9/11 Era*, New York: New York University Press, 2013.

Hamm, M., 'Prisoner Radicalization: Assessing the Threat in US Correctional Institutions', *NIJ Journal*, vol. 261, 2008, pp. 14–19.

Hamm, M., 'Prison Islam in the Age of Sacred Terror', *The British Journal of Criminology*, vol. 49, no. 5, 2009, pp. 667–685.

Hannah, G., L. Clutterbuck, and J. Rubin, *Radicalization or Rehabilitation: Understanding the Challenge of Extremist and Radicalized Prisoners*, Santa Barbara, CA: RAND Corporation, 2008.

Helmus, T., 'Why and How Some People Become Terrorists', *Social Science for Counterterrorism*, vol. 74, no. 06-C, 2009, p. 71.

HM Government, *Prevent Strategy*, London: The Stationary Office, 2011.

House of Commons, 'Extremism in Prison', *House of Commons Hansard*, vol. 624, 2017, available here: https://hansard.parliament.uk/Commons/2017-04-25/debates/3084EAEB-AEB6-47E8-892A-A9825431E2FE/ExtremismInPrisons

House of Commons Justice Committee, *Oral Evidence: Radicalisation in Prisons and Other Prison Matters, HC 417*, 13 July 2016.

Hussein, T., 'Prison Radicalisation: Dealing with Muslim Inmates with Terror Convictions', Personal Website, 13 February 2017, available here: http://www.tamhussein.co.uk/2017/02/prison-radicalisation-dealing-muslim-inmates-terror-convictions/

Jones, C., 'Are Prisons Really Schools for Terrorism? Challenging Rhetoric on Prisoner Radicalization', *Punishment & Society*, vol. 16, 2014, pp. 74–103.

Kruglanski, A., et al., 'The Psychology of Radicalization and Deradicalization: How Significance Quest Impacts Violent Extremism', *Political Psychology*, vol. 35, no. S1, 2014, pp. 69–93.

Liebling, A., H. Arnold, and C. Straub, *Staff-Prisoner Relationships at HMP Whitemoor*, London, UK: Cambridge Institute of Criminology Prisons Research Centre, 2011.

Ministry of Justice, 'Dangerous Extremists to Be Separated from Mainstream Prison Population', Press Release, 21 April 2017, available here: https://www.gov.uk/government/news/dangerous-extremists-to-be-separated-from-mainstream-prison-population.

Mulcahy, E., S. Merrington, and P. J. Bell, 'The Radicalisation of Prison Inmates: A Review of the Literature on Recruitment, Religion and Prisoner Vulnerability', *Journal of Human Security*, vol. 9, no. 1, 2013, pp. 4–14.

Neumann, P. R. and B. Rodgers, *Recruitment and Mobilisation for the Islamist Militant Movement in Europe*, London: International Centre for the Study of Radicalisation and Political Violence, 2007.

Precht, T., 'Home Grown Terrorism and Islamist Radicalization in Europe: From Conversion to Terrorism', *Danish Ministry of Defence*, Research Report, 2007.

Sageman, M., *Understanding Terrorist Networks*, Philadelphia: University of Pennsylvania Press, 2004.

Shakeel, D. M., and P. J. Wolf, *Does Private Islamic Schooling Promote Terrorism? An Analysis of the Educational Background of Successful American Homegrown Terrorists*, EDRE Working Paper 2017-20, 2017.

Silke, A., (ed.), *Prisons, Terrorism and Extremism: Critical Issues in Management, Radicalisation and Reform*, London: Routledge, 2014.

Thompson, N., 'Root Cause Approach to Prisoner Radicalisation', *Salus Journal*, vol. 4, no. 3, 2016, p. 18.

Titheradge, N., 'Is There a Problem with Unregistered Schools?', *BBC News*, 27 February 2018, available here: http://www.bbc.co.uk/news/education-43170447

United Nations Office on Drugs and Crime, *Handbook on the Management of Violent Extremist Prisoners and the Prevention of Radicalization to Violence in Prisons*, Vienna: United Nations, 2016.

Useem, B., and O. Clayton, 'Radicalization of US prisoners', *Criminology & Public Policy*, vol. 8, no. 3, 2009, pp. 561–592.

Veldhuis, T., 'Captivated by Fear. An Evaluation of Terrorism Detention Policy', PhD dissertation, University of Groningen, 2015.

Veldhuis, T., *Prisoner Radicalization and Terrorism Detention Policy. Institutionalized Fear or Evidence-Based Policy Making?*, London: Routledge, 2016.

Williams, R., *RAN P&P Practitioners' Working Paper Approaches to Violent Extremist Offenders and Countering Radicalisation in Prisons and Probation*, Amsterdam: Radicalisation Awareness Network, 2016.

Zammit, A., *Who Becomes a Jihadist in Australia? A Comparative Analysis', Understanding Terrorism from an Australian Perspective: Radicalisation, De-Radicalisation and Counter Radicalisation*, Melbourne: Monash University Caulfield Campus, 2010, pp. 1–21.

16 IMPROVED TERRORIST PRACTICAL LEARNING POTENTIALS FROM INTERNET-BASED PLATFORMS

Anne Stenersen

Introduction

With the recent fall of the Islamic State (IS) there has been speculation that IS will continue to survive online in the form of a 'virtual caliphate'.[1] In a sense, such a 'virtual caliphate' already exists. Ever since IS established the 'caliphate' in June 2014 it has had a formidable online presence, not least in the field of propaganda.[2] Now that IS has lost its physical territory in Iraq and Syria, it is surmised that the internet will become an even more important sanctuary for the group.

The questions addressed here are: will such a 'virtual caliphate' also involve 'virtual training camps'? What do we currently know about how jihadists use the internet for training and what are the major knowledge gaps? 'Training' in this context refers to the acquisition of skills relevant for planning or executing a terrorist attack – such as knowledge on how to build bombs or how to maintain operational security.

The author argues that jihadi 'online training' takes two forms. The first, and by far the most common form of training, is *self-study*: jihadists use the internet as a library from where they can access training materials, but they are themselves responsible for acquiring the knowledge they need to conduct a terrorist attack. The second form of training is *interactive*: jihadists acquire knowledge through participating in online discussions or colloquia with other jihadists. These sessions are often informal but occasionally they are led by an experienced jihadist who takes on the role as teacher.

Over the last ten years we know of at least two major developments regarding the online training of jihadists. First, the online training material produced by jihadists has become more pedagogical. Second, interactive forms of learning have become less common – at least on unencrypted platforms. Terrorist learning is likely taking place via encrypted communication apps, such as WhatsApp or Telegram, but in this field there is a huge gap in our knowledge. There is an urgent need for more research on how terrorists use encrypted apps for training purposes and on how social media influences online terrorist learning in general.

Learning through self-study

The most common form of 'online training' takes the form of self-study or self-training. This means that jihadists use the internet as a library, but they are completely responsible for their own learning.[3] Thus, they have to locate and select suitable training manuals, study their contents and implement the lessons in practice. The last step is to acquire the practical know-how needed to conduct a terrorist attack. This includes the ability to 'translate' a set of instructions to fit one's own local context: for example, a bomb that can easily be built in Iraq may not be built in Europe because Europe does not offer the same access to bomb-making chemicals as Iraq.[4]

Learning through self-study – in terrorism as in any other field – is demanding. It requires a certain level of cognitive skills, in addition to a number of personal qualities such as high motivation, patience and endurance. An extreme case of a 'self-learner' was the Norwegian right-wing terrorist Anders Breivik, who on 22 July 2011 set off a 2,000-pound fertilizer bomb in the centre of Oslo before killing sixty-nine in a shooting spree on Utøya Island. According to his diary he started reading bomb-making manuals ten months before the attack and to manufacture the actual bomb he spent 82 days – almost three months – in solitude.[5]

Jihadist groups and individuals have facilitated self-training ever since the 1990s, when the first training manuals were posted online.[6] There is today a large corpus of jihadist training material – mostly comprising documents but also audio-visual materials. Since 2001 the 'online library' that jihadists can use for self-study has gone through two notable developments. The first development was in the mid-2000s with the appearance of the first audio-visual learning aids – i.e. the instruction video. The development was pioneered by the Lebanese Hezbollah but was soon adopted by Sunni Muslim jihadists.[7]

The second development was the publication of training materials tailored towards Muslims living in the West. The first well-known example of such 'tailor-made' training material was *Inspire*, a magazine issued by Al-Qaeda on the Arabian Peninsula (AQAP). This was pioneered by a US citizen of Pakistani descent, Samir Khan, who moved to Yemen and joined AQAP in 2009.[8] *Inspire* contained pedagogical features that previously had only been seen sporadically in the jihadist literature. For one thing, it contained many very detailed colour pictures to accompany the bomb recipes. But more importantly the operative instructions found in the magazine were designed specifically to work in a

Western (rather than Middle Eastern or Asian) context. For example, in the margins of a page containing instructions on how to make the explosive TATP one could read the following tips: 'HINT: Acetone is also widely available in hardware stores. In the US for example, it could be found at places such as Home Depot, Sears and Wal-Mart.'[9] Authors of *Inspire* thus made bomb recipes somewhat easier to follow for inexperienced would-be terrorists living in Western countries.

Inspire contained other features that added to its popularity. In addition to the easy do-it-yourself 'recipes' the magazine contained theological justifications for attacks and a range of elements inspired by American pop or gangster culture. They included pictures of jihadists wearing hoodies, use of American slang and humoristic elements. None of *Inspire*'s features were entirely new. However, it was their combination into one and the same propaganda product – and the fact that the entire magazine was in English – that made it stand out from existing jihadi magazines at the time.[10]

While *Inspire* has continued to publish recipes on easy-to-make home-made explosives, IS has taken the strategy of 'the simpler the better' to the extreme. For example, in 2014 IS spokesman Abu Muhammad al-Adnani called for killing 'disbelievers' in any way possible: 'Smash his head with a rock, or slaughter him with a knife, or run him over with your car, or throw him down from a high place, or choke him, or poison him.'[11] Overall, IS learning materials seem to contain few innovative elements. They rather build on trends started by Al-Qaeda sympathizers in the 2000s, including the inclusion of audio-visual learning aids and the publication of tailor-made English-language magazines. The use of cars and knives as weapons had also been pioneered by Al-Qaeda and its affiliates. For example, the second issue of *Inspire* suggested welding steel blades to a truck and ramming it into a crowd of people.[12]

To sum up, the overall development within the online 'training literature' is that the material itself has become more pedagogical. This development means that it is now easier than ever for a dedicated terrorist to learn how to make bombs from self-study. However, there are still many challenges to the self-study method. One is that online training material is generally of varying quality, making it hard for an amateur to assess which information is technically accurate. In the case of bomb-making manuals for example, the consequences of a flawed bomb recipe can be fatal. Another challenge is that the material may be hacked, tampered with or taken down – but jihadists have generally found ways to circumvent some of these challenges.[13]

There are a few known examples of security services manipulating the content of jihadi training manuals.[14] Overall, such attempts do not seem to have had an impact on how jihadists view their reliability. The interference of security services on forums has, on the other hand, had a significant impact on jihadists' trust in forums as a suitable platform for peer-to-peer communication. This, in turn, has affected interactive forms of learning, which is discussed below.

Interactive learning forms

Another form of 'online training' is what the author refers to as 'interactive learning' – that is, when jihadists learn through online interaction with other jihadists. In the mid- to late 2000s such interaction could frequently be observed on jihadi discussion forums. The discussions could be informal or formal, or a mixture between the two.

Informal discussions were the most common, but also the most disorderly, as there was usually no 'expert' present to moderate the discussion. On the other hand, such discussions could be used for brainstorming new and creative ways to conduct terrorist attacks. Formal discussions were usually led by a self-appointed 'teacher' who posted 'lessons' and issued 'home assignments' to the students.[15]

In other words, the jihadi discussion forums created arenas where learning could take place through social interaction. According to some educational theorists this is a more effective way of learning. This is why group assignments and colloquia have found their way into Western learning institutions – as opposed to previously when students were expected to sit and listen passively to a teacher or professor. Theoretically, then, learning through discussion in online forums could be a powerful tool for the jihadists.

But the traditional discussion forums had drawbacks. The obvious disadvantage was that, over time, the forums became more and more penetrated by security services. This is one reason why jihadists today hardly use these platforms for discussing personal or incriminating information. Moreover, jihadists over time experienced the arrest and conviction of fellow forum members, as European countries adopted new and stricter terrorism legislation. In 2015 the administrators of a popular jihadi discussion forum explicitly warned participants against discussing explosives through personal messaging – as 'infiltrators' were known to use this method to identify terrorist suspects.[16] It seems safe to conclude that jihadists' trust in forums as a peer-to-peer communication platform is today severely reduced.

The distrust in online discussion forums constitutes a dilemma for the jihadists. On the one hand, jihadi organizations such as IS are presumably interested in recruiting and training as many new operatives as possible – this is the rationale for spreading explosives recipes and organizing interactive bomb-making courses on open platforms. The disadvantage is that such platforms are easily penetrated by security services, which in turn can lead to arrest of members. The compromise solution, for now, has been for the jihadists to move at least part of their online activity to applications with end-to-end encryption, such as WhatsApp and Telegram.[17] It means that the potential audience of the jihadists shrinks considerably. On the other hand, jihadi online communities using these platforms are harder to detect and disrupt. This creates a fertile ground for interactive learning.

Use of encrypted apps for learning

The proliferation of encrypted apps such as WhatsApp and Telegram has given the jihadists a competitive advantage vis-à-vis the security services. In a sense, the situation now resembles the situation in the early 2000s. At that time sensitive information was flowing more freely on jihadi discussion forums, as at the time they were perceived as relatively safe platforms for peer-to-peer interaction. This was before the security services had fully penetrated the forums. Towards the end of the 2000s jihadists gradually became more careful with what kind of information they exchanged online and administrators frequently encouraged the use of proxy servers and encryption tools.

To some extent the proliferation of encrypted communication apps has changed the way jihadists recruit and operate in Europe. This includes the emerging phenomenon of so-called 'remote-controlled attacks', in which the perpetrator(s) communicates with Islamic State handlers online without necessarily having met the handler in person. Attacks that were initially seen as lone-actor attacks have in fact turned out to involve an element of virtual instruction, direction and, in some cases, weapons facilitation.[18] The phenomenon may be more widespread than we currently know. Some observers have gone so far as arguing that virtual attacks represent a 'critical terrorist innovation' on the part of IS.[19] There is concern among security services that other groups may learn from IS and adopt the same modus operandi.

One of the challenges faced by security services today is the sheer number of free communication platforms available to the jihadists. Even if well-known applications like WhatsApp and Telegram were brought under stricter control jihadists could simply switch to other platforms. According to anecdotal evidence IS's virtual handlers have already used a wide variety of applications to communicate with potential attackers abroad.[20]

It is still too early to conclude where the phenomenon of remote-controlled attacks is heading. However, it seems safe to assume that encrypted apps are today used by IS not only to give operational orders, but also to share operational advice and instructions. Thus, we may already have entered a new era of online terrorist learning.

Conclusion

Online training may take one of two future directions. The optimistic view is that Western security services will find a way of monitoring or disrupting the encrypted apps that terrorists currently use for communication. If that happens we will probably revert to a situation similar to that at the end of the 2000s, when European security services had a competitive edge over the terrorists. This situation will last until the development of new communication technologies that may again give the terrorists an advantage.[21]

The pessimistic view is that security services will not find a way to control the spread of encrypted communication apps. In that case jihadists and other violent non-state actors will continue to use these apps for recruitment and operational planning. The author's hypothesis is that these apps will also be used for online training, including interactive forms of learning. This means that terrorists will have secure platforms on which they may organize brainstorming sessions and more formal colloquia - similar to those previously seen on the traditional discussion forums. This increases the risk of terrorists developing more innovative and dangerous attack methods, although the main trend will still be to share easy-to-do bomb recipes. In any case, such a scenario would probably lead to an increase in so-called 'remote-controlled attacks'. These attacks are challenging to detect for security services because the perpetrator does not need to seek out a real-life radical environment or to go abroad for training.

There is today a need for more research on how terrorists use encrypted apps for training purposes. There are a few academic studies addressing terrorist use of Telegram and similar applications, but they generally focus on the spread of propaganda material, not training manuals per se.[22] There is also a huge gap in our knowledge on whether, and to what extent, social learning processes take place on this new social media. Another suggestion for future research is to study the role of jihadi sub-culture in online learning. Some preliminary work has been carried out on terrorist learning in general,[23] as well as on the phenomenon of jihadi culture,[24] but the two fields are rarely combined. Such a study could contribute to more theoretical insight into the processes of terrorist learning and would thus be generalizable to other types of terrorists.

Notes

1 B. Farmer, 'UK Will Not Be Safe from Isil Until Their "Virtual Caliphate" Is Destroyed, Warns Theresa May's Security Adviser', *The Telegraph*, 23 November 2017, available here: http://www.telegraph.co.uk/news/2017/11/23/uk-will-not-safe-isil-virtual-caliphate-destroyed-warns-theresa/.

2 See, for example, C. Winter, *Documenting the Virtual 'Caliphate'*, London: Quilliam Foundation, 2015, available here: http://www.quilliaminternational.com/wp-content/uploads/2015/10/FINAL-documenting-the-virtual-caliphate.pdf.

3 A. Stenersen, 'The Internet: A Virtual Training Camp?' *Terrorism and Political Violence*, vol. 20, no. 2, 2008, pp. 215–233.

4 M. Kenney, '"Dumb" Yet Deadly: Local Knowledge and Poor Tradecraft among Islamist Militants in Britain and Spain', *Studies in Conflict & Terrorism*, vol. 33, no. 10, 2010, p. 922.

5 A. Berwick, '2083 – A European Declaration of Independence', 2011, pp. 1692–1693; 1730–1731.

6 H. Rogan, *Al-Qaeda's Online Media Strategies: From Abu Reuter to Irhabi 007*, Kjeller, FFI, 2007, p. 40, available here: https://www.ffi.no/no/Rapporter/07-02729.pdf (accessed 31 January 2018).

7 Stenersen, 'The Internet', p. 220.

8 A. F. Lemieux et al., 'Inspire Magazine: A Critical Analysis of Its Significance and Potential Impact through the Lens of the Information, Motivation, and Behavioral Skills Model', *Terrorism and Political Violence*, vol. 26, no. 2, 2014, pp. 356–357.

9 Dr. Khateer, 'Making Acetone Peroxide', *Inspire*, no. 6, Summer 2011, p. 41, available from Jihadi Document Repository, University of Oslo.

10 Lemieux, et al., 'Inspire Magazine', pp. 357–360.

11 Y. Bayoumy, 'Isis Urges More Attacks on Western "Disbelievers"', *The Independent*, 22 September 2014, available here: http://www.independent.co.uk/news/world/middle-east/isis-urges-more-attacks-on-western-disbelievers-9749512.html.

12 P. Nesser and A. Stenersen, 'The Modus Operandi of Jihadi Terrorists in Europe', *Perspectives on Terrorism*, vol. 8, no. 6, 2014, p. 19.

13 For more on this, see H. Rogan, *Al-Qaeda's Online Media Strategies: From Abu Reuter to Irhabi 007*, Kjeller, FFI, 2007.

14 D. Gardham, 'MI6 Attacks al-Qaeda in "Operation Cupcake"', *The Telegraph*, 2 June 2011, available here: http://www.telegraph.co.uk/news/uknews/terrorism-in-the-uk/8553366/MI6-attacks-al-Qaeda-in-Operation-Cupcake.html; E. Nakashima, 'U.S. disrupts al-Qaeda's online magazine', *The Washington Post*, 11 June 2013, available here: https://www.washingtonpost.com/world/national-security/officials-describe-how-us-disrupts-al-qaedas-online-magazine/2013/06/11/6a9196c6-ca07-11e2-9245-773c0123c027_story.html?utm_term=.7265d4c023c8.

15 A. Stenersen, '"Bomb-Making for Beginners"': Inside al Al-Qaeda E-Learning Course', *Perspectives on Terrorism*, vol. 7, no. 1, 2013, pp. 25–37.

16 'tahdhir wa tanbih… li-zuwwar mu'askar al-shumukh', *Al-Shumukh*, 25 April 2015, available here: https://shamukh.net/vb/showthread.php?t=236729.

17 See, for example, M. Bloom, H. Tiflati, and J. Horgan, 'Navigating ISIS's Preferred Platform: Telegram', *Terrorism and Political Violence*, 11 July 2017, DOI: 10.1080/09546553.2017.1339695; and N. Prucha, 'IS and the Jihadist Information Highway – Projecting Influence and Religious Identity via Telegram', *Perspectives on Terrorism*, vol. 10, no. 6, 2016, pp. 48–58.

18 S. Mullins, 'Lone-Actor vs. Remote-Controlled Jihadi Terrorism: Rethinking the Threat to the West', *War on the Rocks*, 20 April 2017, available here: https://warontherocks.com/2017/04/lone-actor-vs-remote-controlled-jihadi-terrorism-rethinking-the-threat-to-the-west/.

19 D. Gartenstein-Ross and M. Blackman, 'ISIL's Virtual Planners: A Critical Terrorist Innovation', *War on the Rocks*, 4 January 2017, available here: https://warontherocks.com/2017/01/isils-virtual-planners-a-critical-terrorist-innovation/.

20 R. Callimachi, 'Not "Lone Wolves" after All: How ISIS Guides World's Terror Plots from Afar', *New York Times*, 4 February 2017, available here: https://www.nytimes.com/2017/02/04/world/asia/isis-messaging-app-terror-plot.html.

21 T. Hegghammer, 'The Future of Jihadism in Europe: A Pessimistic View', *Perspectives on Terrorism*, vol. 10, no. 6, 2016, pp. 163–164.

22 A notable exception is B. Clifford, '"Trucks, Knives, Bombs, Whatever:" Exploring pro-Islamic State Instructional Material on Telegram', *CTC Sentinel*, vol. 11, no. 5, 2018, 23–29.

23 L. Kettle and A. Mumford, 'Terrorist Learning: A New Analytical Framework', *Studies in Conflict & Terrorism*, vol. 40, no. 7, 2017, pp. 523–538; J.J.F. Forest (ed.), *Teaching Terror: Strategic and Tactical Learning in the Terrorist World*, Lanham, MD: Rowman and Littlefield, 2006.

24 T. Hegghammer, *Jihadi Culture: The Art and Social Practices of Militant Islamists*, Cambridge: Cambridge Univeristy Press, 2017; and Gilbert Ramsay, *Jihadi Culture on the World Wide Web*, New York and London: Bloomsbury, 2015.

Recommended Readings

Bayoumy, Y., 'Isis Urges More Attacks on Western "Disbelievers"', *The Independent*, 22 September 2014, available here: http://www.independent.co.uk/news/world/middle-east/isis-urges-more-attacks-on-western-disbelievers-9749512.html.

Berwick, A., '2083 – A European Declaration of Independence', 2011, pp. 1692–1693; 1730–1731.

Bloom, M., H. Tiflati, and J. Horgan, 'Navigating ISIS's Preferred Platform: Telegram', *Terrorism and Political Violence*, 11 July 2017, DOI: 10.1080/09546553.2017.1339695.

Callimachi, R., 'Not "Lone Wolves" after All: How ISIS Guides World's Terror Plots from Afar', *New York Times*, 4 February 2017, available here: https://www.nytimes.com/2017/02/04/world/asia/isis-messaging-app-terror-plot.html.

Clifford, B., 'Trucks, Knives, Bombs, Whatever:" Exploring Pro-Islamic State Instructional Material on Telegram', *CTC Sentinel*, vol. 11, no. 5, 2018, 23–29.

Farmer, B., 'UK Will Not Be Safe from Isil until Their "Virtual Caliphate" Is Destroyed, Warns Theresa May's Security Adviser', *The Telegraph*, 23 November 2017, available here: http://www.telegraph.co.uk/news/2017/11/23/uk-will-not-safe-isil-virtual-caliphate-destroyed-warns-theresa/

Forest, J. J. F. (ed.), *Teaching Terror: Strategic and Tactical Learning in the Terrorist World*, Lanham, MD: Rowman and Littlefield, 2006.

Gardham, D., 'MI6 Attacks al-Qaeda in "Operation Cupcake"', *The Telegraph*, 2 June 2011, available here: http://www.telegraph.co.uk/news/uknews/terrorism-in-the-uk/8553366/MI6-attacks-al-Qaeda-in-Operation-Cupcake.html;

Gartenstein-Ross, D. and M. Blackman, 'ISIL's Virtual Planners: A Critical Terrorist Innovation', *War on the Rocks*, 4 January 2017, available here: https://warontherocks.com/2017/01/isils-virtual-planners-a-critical-terrorist-innovation/.

Hegghammer, T., *Jihadi Culture: The Art and Social Practices of Militant Islamists*, Cambridge: Cambridge University Press, 2017.

Hegghammer, T., 'The Future of Jihadism in Europe: A Pessimistic View', *Perspectives on Terrorism*, vol. 10, no. 6, 2016, 156–170.

Kenney, M., 'Beyond the Internet: Mētis, Techne, and the Limitations of Online Artifacts for Islamist Terrorists', *Terrorism and Political Violence*, vol. 22, no. 2, 2010, pp. 177–197.

Kenney, M., '"Dumb" Yet Deadly: Local Knowledge and Poor Tradecraft among Islamist Militants in Britain and Spain', *Studies in Conflict & Terrorism*, vol. 33, no. 10, 2010, pp. 911–932.

Kettle, L. and A. Mumford, 'Terrorist Learning: A New Analytical Framework', *Studies in Conflict & Terrorism*, vol. 40, no. 7, 2017, pp. 523–538.

Lemieux, A.F. et al., 'Inspire Magazine: A Critical Analysis of Its Significance and Potential Impact through the Lens of the Information, Motivation, and Behavioral Skills Model', *Terrorism and Political Violence*, vol. 26, no. 2, 2014, pp. 354–371.

Mullins, S., 'Lone-Actor vs. Remote-Controlled Jihadi Terrorism: Rethinking the Threat to the West', *War on the Rocks*, 20 April 2017, available here: https://warontherocks.com/2017/04/lone-actor-vs-remote-controlled-jihadi-terrorism-rethinking-the-threat-to-the-west/.

Nakashima, E., 'U.S. Disrupts al-Qaeda's Online Magazine', *The Washington Post*, 11 June 2013, available here: https://www.washingtonpost.com/world/national-security/officials-describe-how-us-disrupts-al-qaedas-online-magazine/2013/06/11/6a9196c6-ca07-11e2-9245-773c0123c027_story.html?utm_term=.7265d4c023c8.

Nesser, P. and A. Stenersen, 'The Modus Operandi of Jihadi Terrorists in Europe,' *Perspectives on Terrorism*, vol. 8, no. 6 (2014), pp. 2–24.

Nesser, P., A. Stenersen, and E. Oftedal, 'Jihadi Terrorism in Europe: The IS-Effect', *Perspectives on Terrorism*, vol. 10, no. 6, 2016, pp. 3–24.

Prucha, N., 'IS and the Jihadist Information Highway – Projecting Influence and Religious Identity via Telegram', *Perspectives on Terrorism*, vol. 10, no. 6, 2016, pp. 48–58.

Ramsay, G., *Jihadi Culture on the World Wide Web*, New York and London: Bloomsbury, 2015.

Rogan, H., *Al-Qaeda's Online Media Strategies: From Abu Reuter to Irhabi 007*, Kjeller, FFI, 2007, available from: https://www.ffi.no/no/Rapporter/07-02729.pdf (accessed 31 January 2018).

Stenersen, A., "Bomb-Making for Beginners': Inside al Al-Qaeda E-Learning Course', *Perspectives on Terrorism*, vol. 7, no. 1, 2013, pp. 25–37.

Stenersen, A., 'The Internet: A Virtual Training Camp?' *Terrorism and Political Violence*, vol. 20, no. 2, 2008, pp. 215–233.

Winter, C., *Documenting the Virtual 'Caliphate'*, Quilliam, 2015, available here: http://www.quilliaminternational.com/wp-content/uploads/2015/10/FINAL-documenting-the-virtual-caliphate.pdf.

17 LONE-ACTOR TERRORISM: THE NATURE OF THE THREAT AND RESPONSES

Paul Gill

Introduction

Lone-actor terrorism[1] provides the predominant terrorist threat in the West today. Such terrorists are idiosyncratic, capable of large-scale atrocities, inspire copycats, are difficult to detect and, when detected, are difficult to discern from keyboard warriors.[2] The problem is not a new one, however. Jensen characterizes the period from 1878 to 1934 as the 'classic age' of lone-actor terrorism dominated by lone anarchists.[3] The modern-day progenitor began within the extreme-right-wing movement in the United States in the early 1990s and quickly disseminated to the anti-abortion and pro-environmental violent groupings through the late 1990s, to Al-Qaeda in the 2000s and more recently to the Islamic State. Empirical research on the topic has involved both qualitative and quantitative research, open- and closed-source data and research on both the offenders and the offences themselves. The purpose of this chapter is to synthesize these findings.

Broadly speaking, the literature has come to eight key conclusions. First, there is no socio-demographic profile. Second, generally somebody knew something in the build-up about the individual's motivations, planning and intent. Third, motivation does not centre purely around ideology. Fourth, the attacks are rarely sudden and impulsive but things may be changing. Fifth, lone-actor terrorists look and behave a lot like mass murderers. Sixth, mental health problems are common and complex within the offender sample. Seventh, 'online radicalization' is a misnomer. Finally, managing the problem will entail interdisciplinary and multi-agency approaches. The chapter now elaborates upon each of these key findings.

There is no socio-demographic profile

Three separate data collection initiatives collected lone-actor socio-demographical data.[4] The studies differed in their inclusion criteria (e.g. temporal, geographical, definitional). They all, however, assert that there is no socio-demographic profile that characterizes their samples. For example, one dataset included teenagers and an individual who was eighty-eight years of age at the time of his attack.[5] Many lone actors were single but just as many were married or in a relationship. Some were PhD graduates, others high school drop-outs. Two-fifths had criminal convictions and the offences ranged from the very serious (e.g. homicide) to the very innocuous. Even if such a perfect profile were evident, however, an over-reliance on the use of such a profile would be unwarranted because it simply over-predicts who is likely to become a lone-actor and would generate an overwhelming number of false positives.

Generally somebody knew something

The traditional image of the lone-actor suggests he/she conducts every aspect of his/her radicalization, attack planning and preparation without any aid or interaction. This position is perhaps best characterized by the former US Homeland Security Secretary Janet Napolitano. She noted that lone-actor plots are the 'most challenging' to stop because 'by definition they're not conspiring. They're not using the phones, the computer networks, or any – they are not talking with others any other way that we might get some inkling about what is being planned'.[6] The empirical evidence suggests such traditional images are erroneous. The true loners have been few and far between. Although they have engaged in the violence by themselves, most lone actors have consumed and accepted a broad legitimating ideology and call to arms of others, were enabled by the provision of safe spaces to psychologically and physically prepare for engagement in violence, and a smaller number received some form of training or material support.[7] In the majority of cases, other individuals knew something concerning some aspect of the offender's grievance, intent, beliefs or extremist ideology prior to the event or planned event.

One study demonstrated that in 26.5 per cent of cases the offender produced letters or public statements prior to the event outlining his/her beliefs (but not necessarily his/her violent intent). This behaviour was largely confined to extremist forums. In 83.7 per cent of the cases other people were aware of the perpetrator's grievance that spurred the terrorist plot and in 87.8 per cent other individuals were aware of the perpetrator's commitment to a specific extremist ideology. In 59.2 per cent of the cases family and friends were aware of the perpetrator's intent to engage in terrorism-related activities because the offender verbally told them.[8] In a different study there was an identifiable bystander to the perpetrator's planning/preparation behaviours in 63.3 per cent of the cases. These are typically individuals who witnessed concerning behaviours (e.g. seeing the offender looking at bomb-making manuals at work) but were not privy to the perpetrator's specific plans. In 73.5 per cent of cases the offenders expressed a desire to hurt others. This desire was communicated through either verbal or written statements.[9] These findings suggest therefore that friends, family and concerned members of the public can play important roles in efforts that seek to prevent terrorist plots.

Motivation does not centre purely around ideology

On the surface, lone-actor terrorist attacks seem to defy explanation. The immediate aftermath of the phenomena is marked by drama, panic and an inevitable search for simple answers. In particular, there is an unerring tendency to reach for mono-causal master narrative explanations. The individual actor is either deranged, unbalanced, unhinged, disturbed, mad, crazy, nuts and unstable, or he/she is driven by a hateful ideology, radicalized, politically focused, inspired by some foreign 'entity', or determined to effect some social or political upheaval or policy change. In the days that follow an attack the framing of the individual's motivation usually takes on one of these two narratives. The chosen narrative depends upon the easy availability of information regarding their ideological position, mental health history or personal background details. Yet what we see from the literature is that such attacks are usually the culmination of a complex mix of personal, political and social drivers that crystalize at the same time to drive the individual down the path of violent action.[10] Whether the violence comes to fruition is usually a combination of the availability and vulnerability of suitable targets that suit the heady mix of personal and political grievances and the individual's capability to engage in an attack from both a psychological and technical capability standpoint.[11] Many individual cases share a mixture of unfortunate personal life circumstances coupled with an intensification of beliefs/grievances that later develop into the idea to engage in violence. What has differed is how these influences were sequenced. Sometimes personal problems have led to a susceptibility to ideological influences. Sometimes long-held ideological influences have become intensified after the experience of personal problems. This is why we should be wary of mono-causal master narratives (e.g. it was caused by mental illness). The development of these behaviours is usually far more labyrinthine and dynamic.[12]

The attacks are rarely sudden and impulsive but things may be changing

The available literature suggests preparatory conduct is typical though the degree to which individuals engage in it varies. The timeframe between deciding to conduct an attack and actually stepping out the door to conduct an attack has varied between three months and over two years.[13] Existing research is also generally in agreement that a low level of sophistication characterizes the weapons and methods utilized in lone-actor attacks. To a large extent case study approaches also reflect the large number of roadblocks and hurdles that lone actors encounter and must overcome in the successful commission of an attack. Often, this requires abandoning a more ambitious original plan for something less complicated.[14] Developing an understanding of these potential roadblocks, as well as how they function, may aid future investigations that seek to disrupt future potential lone-actor terrorist plots. In the absence of a group's cumulative human, financial, political and logistical capital, know-how and capability, lone-actor terrorist events are very difficult (albeit not impossible) to conduct using all but the most basic means. The literature suggests that in many cases the development of a lone-actor terrorist attack occurs over a long period of time, but that this time can be lessened dramatically when individuals choose to conduct more technically primitive attacks (e.g. vehicular assaults, stabbings) which appear to be the choice of many contemporary jihadi lone actors.[15]

Lone-actor terrorists look and behave a lot like mass murderers

Mass murderers look very similar to lone-actor terrorists, perhaps only differing in the ratio to which they are personally versus politically aggrieved. Many so-called 'lone-actor terrorists' display multiple distinct personal grievances. Many so-called 'mass murderers' display distinct political and social objectives underpinning their violence.[16] They display little to no discernible differences in terms of socio-demographic profile, their experience of risk factors, their leakage of intent and attack-planning behaviours.[17] Various analyses found that their 'radicalization' trajectory towards this act of violence was also similar.[18] Solely focusing upon those who conduct terrorist violence might improperly constrict our understanding of radicalization pathways. Answers may also be found in the scientific study of analogous violent actors such as the fixated and aggrieved, mass murderers and violent criminals.[19]

Mental health problems are common and complex

Four studies comparing lone- and group-terrorists demonstrated that the former are significantly more likely to have a mental disorder with one study placing it at just over 40 per cent.[20] Compared to the national base rate, schizophrenia, delusional disorder and autism spectrum disorders have exhibited a higher prevalence in the lone-actor sample than what would usually be expected. On the other hand, depression, sleep disorders and learning disabilities have exhibited a lower prevalence in the lone-actor sample than would be expected.[21] One study also found that those who were mentally disordered were just as (and in some cases more) likely to engage in a range of rational pre-attack behaviours as those who were not. Mentally disordered offenders were more likely to express violent desires, seek legitimization for their intended actions, stockpile weapons, train, carry out a successful attack, kill and injure, discriminate in their targeting, and claim responsibility. Most of these traits are typically viewed as rational behaviours and essential for success.[22] It should be reiterated though that these are purely correlational relationships. Just because a factor (such as mental disorder) was present does not make it causal. Nor does it necessarily make it facilitative. It may be completely irrelevant altogether. Mental health problems are undoubtedly important in some cases. Intuitively, we might see how in some cases it can make carrying out violence easier. In other cases, it may make the adoption of the ideology easier because of delusional thinking or fixated behaviours. However, it will only ever be one of many drivers in an individual's pathway to violence. In many cases it may be present but completely unrelated. The answer to causation remains elusive in the absence of first-hand clinical interview designs.

'Online radicalization' is a misnomer

The evidence suggests that the growth of the internet has not caused an increase in annual lone-actor terrorist activity but instead has altered the means of radicalization and learning.[23] The use of the internet has been largely for instrumental purposes whether it be pre-attack (e.g. surveillance, learning, practice, communication) or post-attack (e.g. disseminating propaganda). In criminological terms, these activities have been cyber-enabled rather than cyber-dependent.[24] There is little to no evidence to suggest that the internet has been the sole explanation that has led actors to the point of deciding to engage in a violent act. Instead, it has been just one factor amongst many that has helped crystallize motivation, intent and capability at the same time and place. A significant positive correlation has been found in a number of studies between those who virtually interact with co-ideologues and those who interact with co-ideologues face-to-face. Radicalization (at least for lone actors) is not a dichotomy of either offline or online, but rather an interaction with others versus no interaction with others dichotomy.[25] Not every potential user will make use of what the internet offers, nor will they use the internet in the same way. Of course, the degree to which different terrorists make use of the affordances offered by the internet is modulated based upon their goals, plans, values, beliefs and experiences. One study of over 200 UK-based terrorists highlighted that lone actors were over two times more likely to learn online than cell members. This potentially reflects that within a cell there is a likely pooling of human, social, technical and financial capital, the absence of which leads individuals to go online to learn how to conduct attacks and for other purposes.[26]

Managing the problem will entail interdisciplinary and multi-agency approaches

Approaches to countering lone-actor terrorism have centred around both mental health interventions and developing tools to discriminate 'real' leakages of intent and threats from noise. The former has seen prevention input from agencies outside the traditional counter-terrorism space. The latter has seen input from mathematical, linguistic and computer sciences. Starting with the former, analyses have accounted for the need for psychiatric input in the management of certain cases[27] and the development of joint police–mental health response units for potential grievance-fuelled lone offenders.[28] In terms of the latter, various studies have demonstrated the utility of computer science methods in detecting and fusing disparate digital traces of potential lone actors,[29] identifying linguistic markers[30] and identifying psychological and emotional states of lone actors based on a linguistic analysis of their manifestos.[31]

Conclusion

Despite the growth in knowledge on lone-actor terrorism, there are still a number of areas in need of additional examination. First, the bulk of the literature pertains to either descriptive secondary case study approaches that lack external validity or statistical approaches that offer correlation. Mixed-method approaches and other data sources may offer a more balanced middle ground. Second, validation of relevant risk assessment tools remains in its infancy and doubts persist over whether this will ever (or should) be achieved.[32]

Third and relatedly, the 'base rates' of how prevalent certain behaviours (said to be linked to lone-actor terrorism) within the general population remain, as yet, unquantified. Without a sense of base rate, it is difficult to pinpoint the importance of any one indicator, either in isolation or in combination with other indicators.[33]

Fourth, the sole focus of empirical studies has been on 'risk' factors with a resulting blind spot on 'protective' factors and inhibitors. Protective factors may come in many forms and include individual factors (e.g. attitudes, academic achievement, social orientation, self-control, personality factors), peer factors (e.g. close relationships with non-criminal peers, pro-social norms within peer group, number of affective relationships) and family factors (e.g. highly connected to family, involvement in social activities).

Fifth, evaluations of various interventions focused on lone actors remain unconducted or are not publicly available. Of course, when evaluating interventions in contexts where the base rate of terrorist attacks is low, estimating the impact of such interventions becomes very difficult. Similar problems are also apparent in clinical trials of treatments of rare conditions. Medical science suggests several options, including Bayesian probability distributions, the adoption of 'open trials' that analyse data as it accumulates, the development of biostatistical techniques that seek to maximize data from small subject numbers, the incorporation of 'historical' controls, case-control designs, cross-over and factorial designs, ranking designs and single-patient trials. Such approaches may help the field move away from 'predicting' lone-actor terrorists towards 'managing' concerning cases.

Sixth, little remains known about the ecology of lone-actor radicalization (e.g. where it happens). Similarly, the pathways through which lone actors gain exposure to radicalizing environments and the people in them, and whether these differ for group-based terrorists, remain largely unexplored.[34]

Finally, whilst great strides have been made in classifying scales of risk amongst samples of online extremists, these studies are largely limited by the fact that the 'outcome' (e.g. did they become a terrorist or not) of these participants remains unknown.

Notes

1 For the purpose of this chapter, the defining criterion of a lone-actor terrorist is whether they carried out or planned to carry out the terrorist attack alone. Lone-actor terrorists can operate with or without command and control links therefore. Some operate autonomously and independently of a group (in terms of training, preparation and target selection, etc.). Within this group, some may have radicalized towards violence within a wider group but left and engaged in illicit behaviours outside of a formal command and control structure. A violent plot carried out (or planned to be carried out) by the individual alone on behalf of some form of ideology is a second key inclusion criterion.

2 E. Bakker and B. De Graaf, 'Preventing Lone Wolf Terrorism: Some CT Approaches Addressed', *Perspectives on Terrorism*, vol. 5, no. 5–6, 2011.

3 R. B. Jensen, 'The Pre-1914 Anarchist "Lone Wolf" Terrorist and Governmental Responses', *Terrorism and Political Violence*, vol. 26, no. 1, 2014, pp. 86–94.

4 P. Gill, J. Horgan, and P. Deckert, 'Bombing Alone: Tracing the Motivations and Antecedent Behaviors of Lone-Actor Terrorists', *Journal of Forensic Sciences*, vol. 59, no. 2, 2014; M.S. Hamm and R. Spaaij, *Age of Lone Wolf Terrorism*, New York: Columbia University Press, 2017; C. Ellis et al., *Lone-Actor Terrorism. Final report*, London: Royal United Services Institute (RUSI), 2016.

5 P. Gill, *Lone-Actor Terrorists: A Behavioural Analysis*, London: Routledge, 2015.

6 D. Kerley, 'Homeland Security: More Lone Wolves Circulating in U.S.', *ABC News*, https://abcnews.go.com/WN/homeland-security-lone-wolves-circulating-us/story?id=10030050.

7 B. Schuurman et al., 'Lone-Actor Terrorist Attack Planning and Preparation: A Data-Driven Analysis', *Journal of Forensic Sciences*, vol. 63, no. 4, 2018, pp. 1191–1200.

8 Gill, Horgan and Deckert, 'Bombing Alone'.

9 P. Gill et al., 'What Do Closed Source Data Tell Us about Lone-Actor Terrorist Behaviour? The Preliminary Findings from Project Regulus', *Paper Under Review*.

10 Gill, *Lone-Actor*; L. Lindekilde, F. O'Connor, and B. Schuurman, 'Radicalization Patterns and Modes of Attack Planning and Preparation among Lone-Actor Terrorists: An Exploratory Analysis', *Behavioral Sciences of Terrorism and Political Aggression*, vol.11, no.2, 2019, pp. 113–133.

11 P. Gill and E. Corner, 'Lone-Actor Terrorist Target Choice', *Behavioral Sciences and the Law*, vol. 34, no. 5, 2016, pp. 693–705.

12 E. Corner, N. Bouhana, and P. Gill, 'The Multifinality of Vulnerability Indicators in Lone-Actor Terrorism', *Psychology, Crime and the Law*, vol.25, no.2, 2019, pp. 111–132.

13 Schuurman et al., 'Lone-Actor Terrorist Attack Planning and Preparation'.

14 J. R. Meloy, E. Habermeyer, and A. Guldimann, 'The Warning Behaviors of Anders Breivik', *Journal of Threat Assessment and Management*, vol. 2, no. 3–4, 2015, p. 164; N. Böckler, J. Hoffmann, and A. Zick, 'The Frankfurt Airport Attack: A Case Study on the Radicalization of a Lone-Actor Terrorist', *Journal of Threat Assessment and Management*, vol. 2, no. 3–4, 2015, p. 153; M. Tierney, 'Using Behavioral Analysis to Prevent Violent Extremism: Assessing the Cases of Michael Zehaf–Bibeau and Aaron Driver', *Journal of Threat Assessment and Management*, vol. 4, no. 2, 2017, p. 98.

15 Gill, *Lone-Actor.*

16 L. Malkki, 'Political Elements in Post-Columbine School Shootings in Europe and North America', *Terrorism and Political Violence*, vol. 26, no. 1, 2016, p. 182.

17 J. Horgan, et al., *Across the Universe? A Comparative Analysis of Violent Behavior and Radicalization across Three Offender Types with Implications for Criminal Justice Training and Education*, final report, National Criminal Justice Reference System, 2016; J. A. Capellan, 'Lone Wolf Terrorist or Deranged Shooter? A Study of Ideological Active Shooter Events in the United States, 1970–2014', *Studies in Conflict & Terrorism*, vol. 38, no. 6, 2015, pp. 395–413.; M. Liem et al., 'European Lone-Actor Terrorists versus "Common" Homicide Offenders: An Empirical Analysis', *Homicide Studies*, vol. 22, no. 1, 2018, pp. 45–69.

18 P. Gill et al., 'Shooting Alone: The Pre-Attack Experiences and Behaviors of US Solo Mass Murderers', *Journal of Forensic Sciences*, vol. 62, no. 3, 2017, pp. 710–714.

19 R. Borum, R. Fein, and B. Vossekuil, 'A Dimensional Approach to Analyzing Lone-Actor Terrorism', *Aggression and Violent Behavior*, vol. 17, 2012, pp. 389–396.

20 E. Corner and P. Gill, 'A False Dichotomy? Mental illness and Lone-Actor Terrorism', *Law and Human Behaviour*, vol. 39, no. 1, 2015, p. 23; E. Corner, P. Gill, and O. Mason, 'Mental Health Disorders and the Terrorist: A Research Note Probing Selection Effects and Disorder Prevalence', *Studies in Conflict & Terrorism*, vol. 39, no. 6, 2016, pp. 560–568.; J. Gruenewald, S. Chermak, and J. D. Freilich, 'Distinguishing "Loner" Attacks from Other Domestic Extremist Violence', *Criminology & Public Policy*, vol. 12, no. 1, 2013, pp. 65–91; C. Hewitt, *Understanding Terrorism in America: From the Klan to al Qaeda,* Psychology Press, London: Routledge, 2003.

21 Corner, Gill, and Mason, 'Mental Health Disorders and the Terrorist'.

22 Corner and Gill, 'A False Dichotomy?'.

23 P. Gill and E. Corner, 'Lone-Actor Terrorist Use of the Internet and Behavioural Correlates', in L. Jarvis, S. MacDonald, and T.M. Chen (eds), *Terrorism Online: Politics, Law and Technology*, London: Routledge, 2015, pp. 35–53.

24 P. Gill et al., 'Terrorist Use of the Internet by the Numbers: Quantifying Behaviors, Patterns & Processes', *Criminology and Public Policy*, vol. 16, no. 1, 2017, pp. 99–117.

25 Gill et al., 'Terrorist Use of the Internet by the Numbers'.

26 Gill et al., 'Terrorist Use of the Internet by the Numbers'.

27 J. Hurlow, S. Wilson, and D. James. 'Protesting loudly about Prevent Is Popular but Is It Informed and Sensible?', *BJPsych Bulletin*, vol. 40, no. 3, 2016, pp. 162–163.

28 M. T. Pathé, 'Establishing a Joint Agency Response to the Threat of Lone-Actor Grievance-Fuelled Violence', *The Journal of Forensic Psychiatry & Psychology*, vol. 29, no. 1, 2018, pp. 37–52; D. James, and F. Farnham, 'Outcome and Efficacy of Interventions by a Public Figure Threat Assessment and Management Unit: A Mirrored Study of Concerning Behaviors and Police Contacts before and after Intervention', *Behavioral Sciences & the Law*, vol. 34, no. 5, 2016, pp. 660–680.

29 J. Brynielsson et al., 'Harvesting and Analysis of Weak Signals for Detecting Lone Wolf Terrorists', *Security Informatics*, vol. 2, no. 5, 2013, pp. 1–15; K. Cohen et al., 'Detecting Linguistic Markers For Radical Violence in Social Media', *Terrorism and Political Violence*, vol. 26, no. 1, 2014, pp. 246–256.

30 F. Johansson, L. Kaati, and M. Sahlgren, 'Detecting Linguistic Markers of Violent Extremism in Online Environments', In *Combating Violent Extremism and Radicalization in the Digital Era*, Hershey, PA, USA: IGI Global, 2016, pp. 374–390.

31 L. Kaati, A. Shrestha and K. Cohen, 'Linguistic Analysis of Lone Offender Manifestos', in *2016 IEEE International Conference on Cybercrime and Computer Forensic (ICCCF)*, pp. 1–8. IEEE, 2016; S. J. Baele, 'Lone-Actor Terrorists' Emotions and Cognition: An Evaluation beyond Stereotypes', *Political Psychology*, vol. 38, no. 3, 2017, pp. 449–468.

32 K. M. Sarma, 'Risk Assessment and the Prevention of Radicalization from Nonviolence into Terrorism', *American Psychologist*, vol. 72, no. 3, 2017, p. 278.

33 P. Gill, 'Towards a Scientific Approach to Identifying and Understanding Indicators of Radicalization and Terrorist Intent: Eight Key Problems', *Journal of Threat Assessment and Management*, vol. 2, no. 3–4, 2015, pp. 187–191.

34 N. Bouhana et al. 'Lone-Actor Terrorism: Radicalisation, Attack Planning and Execution', in A. Silke (ed.), *Routledge Handbook of Terrorism and Counterterrorism*, London: Routledge, Forthcoming.

Recommended Readings

Baele, S.J., 'Lone-Actor Terrorists' Emotions and Cognition: An Evaluation beyond Stereotypes', *Political Psychology*, vol. 38, no. 3, 2017, pp. 449–468.

Böckler, N, J. Hoffmann, and A. Zick, 'The Frankfurt Airport Attack: A Case Study on the Radicalization of a Lone-Actor Terrorist', *Journal of Threat Assessment and Management*, vol. 2, no. 3-4, 2015, p. 153.

Borum, R., R. Fein, and B. Vossekuil, 'A Dimensional Approach to Analyzing Lone-Actor Terrorism', *Aggression and Violent Behavior*, vol. 17, 2012, pp. 389–396.

Capellan, J.A., 'Lone Wolf Terrorist or Deranged Shooter? A Study of Ideological Active Shooter Events in the United States, 1970–2014', *Studies in Conflict & Terrorism*, vol. 38, no. 6, 2015, pp. 395–413.

Corner, E., N. Bouhana, and P. Gill, 'The Multifinality of Vulnerability Indicators in Lone-Actor Terrorism', *Psychology, Crime and Law*. vol. 25, no. 2, 2019, pp. 111–132.

Corner, E. and P. Gill, 'A false dichotomy? Mental Illness and Lone-Actor Terrorism', *Law and Human Behaviour*, vol. 39, no. 1, 2015, p. 23.

Corner, E., P. Gill, and O. Mason, 'Mental Health Disorders and the Terrorist: A Research Note Probing Selection Effects and Disorder Prevalence', *Studies in Conflict & Terrorism*, vol. 39, no. 6, 2016, pp. 560–568.

Gill, P. and E. Corner, 'Lone-Actor Terrorist Use of the Internet and Behavioural Correlates', in L. Jarvis, S. MacDonald, and T. M. Chen (eds), *Terrorism Online: Politics, Law and Technology*, London: Routledge, 2015, pp. 35–53.

Gill, P. and E. Corner, 'Lone-Actor Terrorist Target Choice', *Behavioral Sciences and the Law*, vol. 34, no. 5, 2016, pp. 693–705.

Gill, P. et al., 'Shooting Alone: The Pre-Attack Experiences and Behaviors of US Solo Mass Murderers', *Journal of Forensic Sciences*, vol. 62, no. 3, 2017, pp. 710–714.

Gill, P. et al., 'Terrorist Use of the Internet by the Numbers: Quantifying Behaviors, Patterns & Processes', *Criminology and Public Policy*, vol. 16, no. 1, 2017, pp. 99–117.

Gill, P. et al., 'What Do Closed Source Data Tell Us about Lone-Actor Terrorist Behaviour? The Preliminary Findings from Project Regulus', *Paper Under Review*.

Gill, P., 'Towards a Scientific Approach to Identifying and Understanding Indicators of Radicalization and Terrorist Intent: Eight Key Problems', *Journal of Threat Assessment and Management*, vol. 2, no. 3-4, 2015, pp. 187–191.

Gill, P., J. Horgan, and P. Deckert, 'Bombing Alone: Tracing the Motivations and Antecedent Behaviors of Lone-Actor Terrorists', *Journal of Forensic Sciences*, vol. 59, no. 2, 2014.

Gill, P., *Lone-Actor Terrorists: A Behavioural Analysis*, London: Routledge, 2015.

Gruenewald, J., S. Chermak, and J. D. Freilich, 'Distinguishing "loner" Attacks from Other Domestic Extremist Violence', *Criminology & Public Policy*, vol. 12, no. 1, 2013, pp. 65–91.

Hamm, M.S. and R. Spaaij, *Age of Lone Wolf Terrorism*, New York: Columbia University Press, 2017.

Horgan, J., et al., *Across the Universe? A Comparative Analysis of Violent Behavior and Radicalization across Three Offender Types with Implications for Criminal Justice Training and Education*, final report, National Criminal Justice Reference System, 2016.

Jensen, R. B. 'The Pre-1914 Anarchist "Lone Wolf" Terrorist and Governmental Responses', *Terrorism and Political Violence*, vol. 26, no. 1, 2014, pp. 86–94.

Johansoon, F., L. Kaati, and M. Sahlgren, 'Detecting Linguistic Markers of Violent Extremism in Online Environments', in *Combating Violent Extremism and Radicalization in the Digital Era*, pp. 374–390, IGI Global, 2016.

Kaati, Lisa, Amendra Shrestha, and Katie Cohen. "Linguistic Analysis of Lone Offender Manifestos." In *Cybercrime and Computer Forensic (ICCCF), IEEE International Conference on*, pp. 1–8. IEEE, 2016.

Lindekilde, L., F. O'Connor, and B. Schuurman, 'Radicalization Patterns and Modes of Attack Planning and Preparation among Lone-Actor Terrorists: An Exploratory Analysis', *Behavioral Sciences of Terrorism and Political Aggression*, vol. 11, no. 2, 2019, pp. 113–133.

Malkki, L., 'Political Elements in Post-Columbine School Shootings in Europe and North America', *Terrorism and Political Violence*, vol. 26, no. 1, 2016, p. 182.

Meloy, J. R., E. Habermeyer, and A. Guldimann, 'The Warning Behaviors of Anders Breivik', *Journal of Threat Assessment and Management*, vol. 2, no. 3-4, 2015, p. 164.

Pathé, M. T., 'Establishing a Joint Agency Response to the Threat of Lone-Actor Grievance-Fuelled Violence', *The Journal of Forensic Psychiatry & Psychology*, vol. 29, no. 1, 2018, pp. 37–52.

Sarma, K.M., 'Risk Assessment and the Prevention of Radicalization from Nonviolence into Terrorism', *American Psychologist*, vol. 72, no. 3, 2017, p. 278.

Schuurman, B. et al., 'Lone-actor Terrorist Attack Planning and Preparation: A Data-Driven Analysis', *Journal of Forensic Sciences*, vol. 63, no. 4, 2018, pp. 1191–1200.

18 RETURNING FOREIGN FIGHTERS: THE EXTENT OF THE THREAT TO THE UK AND PROSPECTS FOR REINTEGRATION

Richard Barrett

The Threat

In its annual report for 2016–2017 the UK's Parliamentary Intelligence and Security Committee (ISC) quoted the Director General of the Security Service (DG) as saying that, by December 2016, more than 850 UK-based individuals of national security concern[1] were thought to have travelled to Syria, Iraq and the region[2] since the start of the uprising against President Bashar al-Assad in March 2011.[3] Of these, the Security Service believed around half had returned.[4] These figures have remained relatively unchanged since then,[5] even though the Islamic State (IS), which most of the travellers joined, had lost almost all its territorial holdings in Iraq and Syria by the end of 2017, forcing those remaining to leave the area or to go underground.

In a speech in October 2017 the DG said that there were 'well over 500' current counter-terrorist operations in the UK, focused on around 3,000 subjects of interest.[6] In a following interview he said that returnees, many of whom had come back to the UK 'several years ago', formed part of this pool of 3,000, with intelligence and police coverage allocated according to an assessment of the risk that each one posed.[7] The DG suggested that not many more would return for fear of arrest,[8] and other Western intelligence officials have confirmed that the flow of fighters both to and back from Syria/Iraq has been negligible since early 2017.[9]

Although there are British returnees from other international terrorist groups and from other conflict areas, notably Afghanistan/Pakistan, Somalia and Yemen, it is the returnees from Iraq and Syria, and in particular those who fought alongside IS, that give rise to the most concern. Although the threat is not determined by the number of returnees so much as their motivation, the degree of their engagement with whatever group they joined, and their intention and capability to continue to support its aims, the fact that so many people are back in the UK having been exposed to the ideology and brutality of IS places them in a category apart.

It is clearly wrong to assume that all returnees present the same risk and one of the key challenges for the security and law enforcement agencies, apart from identifying who the returnees are, is to determine which among them are the most immediately dangerous. This will always be difficult, but it has become easier as the amount of information about the motivation and activities of British foreign fighters has grown, along with the ability to analyse it. Nonetheless, noticing changes in motivation and behaviour sufficient to move a suspect from one priority to another requires close and almost constant scrutiny and, apart from the resource implications, there are legal and ethical reasons to limit such surveillance to as few cases as possible.

Those who went early and returned early are least likely to pose a threat;[10] their motives were generally humanitarian or to help the uprising against Assad, and even those attracted by IS propaganda appear more often to have been seeking a new beginning than to learn how to destroy what they had left behind.[11] In its early years, IS propaganda was dominated by the projection of an ideal state, offering opportunity and justice, and although these early recruits may have accepted some violence as necessary for self-defence, they most likely left when they became aware of the inherent brutality of IS.

Others who returned later may have been more disappointed with individual IS leaders than with the operation of the State. These returnees are not natural terrorists[12] but, even though IS failed to deliver their dream, they may come to believe that this was not the fault of IS so much as of its enemies, including the UK. By leaving for Syria/Iraq they turned their backs on their home state and, unless their identity with Britain is better established on return, they may seek revenge.[13]

Returnees who went with greater knowledge of the true nature of IS, or who came to believe in its apocalyptic vision of pre-ordained conflict, will present the greatest risk. Some, like the members of the external operations group of IS who carried out the Paris and Brussels attacks in November 2015 and March 2016, may return with the specific aim of mounting an attack. The longer that people stayed with IS, and the later they returned, the more likely they are to be among the most committed members of its foreign cohort and the least likely to reintegrate when back home.

By early 2018 no returnee from Syria or Iraq had engaged in a terrorist attack in the UK.[14] Of the seven perpetrators of the Islamist extremist attacks in Manchester and London in 2017,[15] only one (Salman Abedi – Manchester) had been abroad (Libya) and consorted with a violent jihadist group, while two (Khuram Butt and Youssef Zaghba – London Bridge) had talked of doing so.[16] Nonetheless, it is not surprising that the Security Service notes that 'UK nationals travelling overseas to serve with extremist groups as "foreign fighters" present a potential threat to the UK, both while they are overseas and when they return to the UK'.[17] It adds:

> foreign fighters can gain combat experience, access to training and a network of overseas extremist contacts. The skills, contacts and status acquired overseas can make these individuals a much greater threat when they return to the UK, even if they have not been tasked directly to carry out an attack on their return. Experience of fighting overseas with terrorist groups can also promote radicalisation.[18]

In all cases, the Security Service and the police will have to investigate why and when each returnee decided to go to Syria, what they did there and why and when they left, in order to assess the risk of their becoming domestic terrorists, or encouraging others to do so.[19]

Prospects for reintegration

Motivation is equally important when assessing the prospects for reintegration. People who went to Syria to escape disjointed lives and bad decisions will not easily fit back at home if the same conditions persist. A search for identity and belonging, and the hope for a new start, often prove key factors in the decision to join any sort of cult or gang, and the IS appeal is further strengthened by its religious overlay. In providing an alternative sense of belonging, reintegration programmes increasingly recognize the crucial role of the community, but even close-knit families may struggle to compete with the intensity of relationships formed in the excitement of battle or based on the shared beliefs of IS recruits. For those who felt most alienated from their environment when they set off for Syria, the challenge of return will have more to do with integration than reintegration. Furthermore, integration of returnees will also be a challenge for their home communities, which may regard them with high levels of suspicion and resentment.

A further problem in dealing with Western returnees is that neither those who go, nor those who return, fit a precise, standard profile. They are more often men than women (typically 80/20), most are in their twenties, many have a police record of petty crime, they often go in groups or from the same area, most have not shown much interest in religion up to the point of radicalization (though there is a higher percentage of converts than in the general population), they are preponderantly from immigrant families and ethnic minorities living in urban areas, but almost all were born or grew up in the West. In other words, they are not much different from hundreds of thousands of their compatriots who would never dream of becoming a foreign fighter. Their reasons for travelling to Syria were generally personal and specific and no general integration programme is likely to have much effect.

Given the challenges, it is not surprising that the problem of dealing with returning foreign fighters has so far attracted more discussion than action, even as it has become more pressing. A general reluctance by Western governments to repatriate fighters, or even women and small children, is ample evidence that no one has a good plan for dealing with them. The preference appears to be for them to stay where they are,[20] either in the hope that they may die,[21] or that someone else will deal with the complex issues of trial and punishment.[22] Small programmes exist, for example in various municipalities in Northern Europe,[23] but they are neither transferable nor scalable. More ambitious national programmes, such as the de-radicalization centres introduced briefly in France, have run into practical problems or faced insurmountable public opposition.[24] Nonetheless, practice is evolving and, rather than assuming that all returnees will go to prison, governments are encouraging local reintegration initiatives that they can support.

The UK is better placed than most because it deals with returnees within a broader and relatively well-established strategy to counter-extremism that has proved adaptable and pragmatic, and has overcome, to a certain extent, the initial community suspicion that all such programmes face – that they are discriminatory, stigmatizing and intrusive. Winning community trust is obviously essential for any government-supported reintegration programme, particularly in the marginalized parts of society from which many fighters emerge. Without community support, the task of identifying, assessing, reintegrating and subsequently monitoring returnees is simply impossible.

Returnees to the UK are subject to police and intelligence investigation on arrival to determine whether they should be charged with a crime, such as joining IS, but the evidence is hard to collect and harder still to verify. Nonetheless, the proper application of the law is an essential part of the process of winning community support. Returnees should not receive preferential treatment, nor should they receive disproportionate punishment, and the more that returnees and their families see the authorities as helping to deal with their problems, rather than perpetuating or compounding them, the more likely they are to cooperate, both with other investigations and with the task of reintegration.

Once investigation is sufficiently advanced for an assessment to be made, those who are of lowest risk will enter the Channel programme, part of the Prevent strand of the Government's CONTEST counter-terrorism strategy.[25] Channel is a referral programme largely for individuals considered to be at risk of being drawn into terrorism.[26] But as it has evolved Channel has moved further downstream to include returnees and prisoners convicted of terrorist crimes, especially just prior to release.[27] Channel is a partnership effort between local authorities and the relevant police service, and draws support from social welfare and associated agencies in designing and overseeing tailored programmes of assistance to meet common issues such as a desire for belonging and confusion over identity. If at the same time counsellors can promote a sense of purpose, and an understanding of why the world works as it does, this too can do much to undermine the sense of grievance that violent extremist groups such as IS hope to identify and exploit.

The imprisonment of higher-risk returnees may keep them off the streets, but it can lead to other problems and only delays the challenge of reintegration. Prison rehabilitation programmes may have some effect, but returnees can be good recruiters if left among the general prison population. However, if grouped together in a segregation unit, they can form stronger networks and become more fixed in their attitudes. The key objective in dealing with incarcerated returnees is to ensure that they disengage from violence, while keeping in view the longer-term objective of facilitating social integration post release. As with any reintegration programme, this requires an understanding of the factors that led the prisoner to become a foreign fighter in the first place, as well as well-trained prison staff.

Any reintegration programmes will be severely damaged if a beneficiary subsequently commits a terrorist crime. Unlike other crime, the public in most Western countries has zero tolerance of terrorism and is likely to see any recidivism as a sign of catastrophic failure by the authorities, rather than as inevitable. Reintegration programmes will work, however, only if the public at large accepts that they are 'works in progress' and can never promise total success. The prospects for the reintegration of returnees therefore rely on their own willingness to reject violence and re-join their community, their community's willingness to accept them back and the broader public's willingness to believe that not all returning foreign fighters are steeped in blood and thirsty for more.

It follows that a reintegration programme that demonstrates a returnee's rejection of violent extremism, perhaps by persuading others not to follow his path, is likely to be the most acceptable.[28] But few returnees have the capacity to act in this way, even if they have the desire. Such programmes also struggle to overcome suspicion that they target particular communities or even work as agents of government.

Conclusion

The greater the engagement of the community in any programme, the more likely that community leaders and officials will identify and direct resources towards common complaints that make recruitment to violent extremism attractive. Foreign fighters are not just part of a security problem; they are also indicators of social problems and, to have lasting effect, reintegration programmes should be as much about promoting social cohesion as helping an individual to feel part of the community.

Finally, one reintegration challenge that must be met is how to deal with the children of British fighters, whether born in the UK or in the 'Islamic State'. IS typically began to indoctrinate children at the age of five and from the age of nine gave them military training. These children, many of whom will be severely traumatized, will need supervision for many years to come, and probably psychiatric treatment. Their mothers and other returning women will also need supervision and treatment. It is quite wrong to think that women members of IS were all reluctantly there or lived apart from the violence. Many were as committed as the men and are quite capable of remaining active supporters once home.[29]

Notes

1 United Nations Security Council Resolution 2178 defines foreign (terrorist) fighters as:

> nationals who travel or attempt to travel to a State other than their States of residence or nationality, and other individuals who travel or attempt to travel from their territories to a State other than their States of residence or nationality, for the purpose of the perpetration, planning, or preparation of, or participation in, terrorist acts, or the providing or receiving of terrorist training. (United Nations Security Council Resolution 2178, 2014, p.8).

2 According to research by Aaron Zelin, thirty-six British nationals had joined violent extremist groups in Libya by the end of 2017. A. Y. Zelin, *The Others: Foreign Fighters in Libya*, Policy Notes, Washington DC: The Washington Institute for Near East Policy, Policy Notes 45, January 2018.

3 Intelligence and Security Committee of Parliament, *Intelligence and Security: Annual Report 2016–2017*, London: The Stationery Office, 2017.

4 Committee of Parliament, *Intelligence and Security.*

5 The Government's Counter-Terrorism Strategy (CONTEST), published in June 2018, quoted a figure of 'around 900 people of national security concern' who had gone to Syria from the UK, 20 per cent of whom were believed to have died. https://assets.publishing.service.gov.uk/government/uploads/system/uploads/attachment_data/file/714402/060618_CCS207_CCS0218929798-1_CONTEST_3.0_WEB.PDF.

6 Security Service MI5, 'DG MI5-Speech', *MI5 Video Transcripts*, 17 October 2017, available here: https://www.mi5.gov.uk/who-we-are-video-transcript.

7 Andrew Parker, interviewed by Frank Gardner, *BBC*, 17 October 2017, available here: http://www.bbc.co.uk/news/uk-41655488.

8 Andrew Parker, interviewed by Frank Gardner.

9 R. Barrett, *Beyond the Caliphate: Foreign Fighters and the Threat of Returnees*, The Soufan Group & The Global Strategy Network, [Online], October 2017; E. Schmitt, 'ISIS Fighters Are Not Flooding Home to Wreak Havoc as Feared', *The New York Times*, 22 October 2017, available here: https://www.nytimes.com/2017/10/22/us/politics/fewer-isis-fighters-returning-home.html.

10 This has so far proved true in all Western countries. T. Hegghammer and P. Nesser, 'Assessing the Islamic State's Commitment to Attacking the West', *Perspectives on Terrorism*, vol. 9, no. 4, 2015.

11 David Malet makes the same point: 'It Is Crucial to Distinguish between the Motivations of European Citizens Who Travel for Training with the Intent to Return Home, such as 7/7 London Bomber Mohammad Siddique Khan, and Those Who Travel to Fight on the Front Lines in Insurgencies in Foreign Lands'. T. Renard and

R. Coolsaet (eds.), *Returnees: Who Are They, Why Are They (Not) Coming Back and How Should We Deal With Them?*, Egmont – The Royal Institute for International Relations, Egmont Paper 101, [Online], 2018, p. 14.

12 'The Majority Who Long for an Islamic State Are Not Jihadist-Minded, Nor Do They Advocate the Murder of Civilians', A. Moaveni, 'The Lingering Dream of an Islamic State', *The New York Times*, 12 January 2018, available here: https://www.nytimes.com/2018/01/12/opinion/sunday/post-isis-muslim-homeland.html?_r=1.

13 Under the Immigration Act of 2014, the Home Secretary can revoke the citizenship of a dual national who has, for example, joined IS and is of a naturalized subject who has a reasonable expectation of gaining an alternative citizenship.

14 Some may have been involved in the twenty-two plots thwarted by the authorities between May 2013 and December 2017.

15 Westminster (March), London Bridge (June), and Parsons Green (September).

16 Report by David Anderson QC on the attacks in London and Manchester March to June 2017, and so not including the Parsons Green attack. D. Anderson, *Attacks in London and Manchester – March-June 2017*, Independent Assessment of MI5 and Police Internal Reviews, 2017.

17 'Foreign Fighters', *Security Service MI5* [Website], available here: https://www.mi5.gov.uk/foreign-fighters.

18 'Foreign Fighters'.

19 For a greater exploration of the various motives of foreign fighters see inter alia: H. el Said and R. Barrett, *Enhancing the Understanding of the Foreign Terrorist Fighters Phenomenon in Syria*, UN Office of Counter-Terrorism, July 2017; Barrett, *Beyond the Caliphate*.

20 E. Schmitt, 'Defeated in Syria, ISIS Fighters Held in Camps Still Pose a Threat', *The New York Times*, 24 January 2018, available here: https://www.nytimes.com/2018/01/24/world/middleeast/isis-syria-militants-kurds.html.

21 For example, UK Secretary of State for Defence, Gavin Williamson, in December 2017. L. Brown, 'Defence Secretary Is Accused of Dreaming up a Netflix-Style Plot by Threatening to "Eliminate" UK Jihadis before They Can Return to Britain', *The Daily Mail*, 6 December 2017, available here: http://www.dailymail.co.uk/news/article-5153613/Gavin-Williamson-Brits-fighting-be.htmlon. In at least two cases (Reyaad Khan and Ruhul Amin) the British Government appears to have ensured this was the case.

22 Exemplified by the varying attitudes towards Western foreign fighters captured by the Syrian Democratic Forces (SDF) in late 2017 and early 2018.

23 For example, Aarhus, Denmark and Vilvoorde, Belgium.

24 M. Crowell, 'What Went Wrong with France's Deradicalization Program', *The Atlantic*, 28 September 2017, available here: https://www.theatlantic.com/international/archive/2017/09/france-jihad-deradicalization-macron/540699/; France now offers psychological support services but has reached few of its 275 known returnees (as at February 2018).

25 Republished in June 2018. https://assets.publishing.service.gov.uk/government/uploads/system/uploads/attachment_data/file/714402/060618_CCS207_CCS0218929798-1_CONTEST_3.0_WEB.PDF.

26 HM Government, *Channel Duty Guidance: Protecting Vulnerable People from Being Drawn into Terrorism*, HM Government, [Online], 2015.

27 The release of extremist prisoners, including returnees, is likely to present a long-term problem without effective rehabilitation programmes. See for example, D. Kennedy, 'The Terrorist Who Terrorized French Prison Guards', *The Daily Beast* 29 January 2018, available here: https://www.thedailybeast.com/the-terrorist-who-terrorized-french-prison-guards.

28 For example, the Institute for Strategic Dialogue, and The Unity Initiative.

29 For example, in December 2017, Hans-Georg Maassen, the head of Germany's domestic intelligence service, the Office for the Protection of the Constitution (BfV), warned that many of the women repatriated to Germany from former IS bastions 'had become so radicalized and identify so deeply with IS ideology that, by all accounts, they must also be identified as jihadis'. D. Martin, 'German Intelligence part of Secret Anti-terror unit Targeting Returning IS Fighters – Report', *Deutsche Welle*, 3 February 2018, available here: http://www.dw.com/en/german-intelligence-part-of-secret-anti-terror-unit-targeting-returning-is-fighters-report/a-42441378.

Recommended Readings

Anderson, D., *Attacks in London and Manchester – March-June 2017*, Independent Assessment of MI5 and Police Internal Reviews, [Online], 2017.

Parker, A. interviewed by Frank Gardner, *BBC*, 17 October 2017, available here: http://www.bbc.co.uk/news/uk-41655488.

Barrett, R., *Beyond the Caliphate: Foreign Fighters and the Threat of Returnees*, The Soufan Group & The Global Strategy Network, [Online], October 2017.

Brown, L., 'Defence Secretary Is Accused of Dreaming up a Netflix-style plot by Threatening to "Eliminate" UK Jihadis before They Can Return to Britain', *The Daily Mail*, 6 December 2017, available here: http://www.dailymail.co.uk/news/article-5153613/Gavin-Williamson-Brits-fighting-be.htmlon.

Committee of Parliament, *Intelligence and Security: Annual Report 2016-2017*, 2017.

Corera, G. and F. Gardner, 'MI5 boss Andrew Parker Warns of "Intense" Terror Threat', *BBC*, 17 October 2017, available here: http://www.bbc.co.uk/news/uk-41655488.

Crowell, M., 'What Went Wrong with France's Deradicalization Program', *The Atlantic*, 28 September 2017, available here: https://www.theatlantic.com/international/archive/2017/09/france-jihad-deradicalization-macron/540699/

Cruickshank, P., 'A View from the CT Foxhole: Nicholas Rasmussen, Former Director National Counterterrorism Center', *CTC Sentinel*, vol. 11, no. 1, 2018, pp. 12–17.

El Said, H. and R. Barrett, *Enhancing the Understanding of the Foreign Terrorist Fighters Phenomenon in Syria*, New York: UN Office of Counter-Terrorism, [Online], July 2017.

'Foreign Fighters', *Security Service MI5* [Website], available here: https://www.mi5.gov.uk/foreign-fighters.

Gustafsson, L. and M., Ranstorp, *Swedish Foreign Fighters in Syria and Iraq: An Analysis of Open-Source Intelligence and Statistical Data*, Stockholm, Försvarshögskolan (FHS): Swedish Defence University, 2017.

Hegghammer, T. and P. Nesser, 'Assessing the Islamic State's Commitment to Attacking the West', *Perspectives on Terrorism*, vol. 9, no. 4, 2015.

HM Government, *Channel Duty Guidance: Protecting Vulnerable People from Being Drawn into Terrorism*, HM Government, [Online], 2015.

HM Government, *CONTEST: The United Kingdom's Strategy for Countering Terrorism*, 2018 available here: https://assets.publishing.service.gov.uk/government/uploads/

system/uploads/attachment_data/file/714402/060618_CCS207_CCS0218929798-1_CONTEST_3.0_WEB.PDF.
HM Government, *Immigration Act 2014*, London: The Stationery Office, 2014.
Kennedy, D., 'The Terrorist who Terrorized French Prison Guards', *The Daily Beast* 29 January 2018, available here: https://www.thedailybeast.com/the-terrorist-who-terrorized-french-prison-guards.
Khalil, J. and M. Zeuthen, *Countering Violent Extremism and Risk Reduction: A Guide to Programme Design and Evaluation*, London: Royal United Services Institute for Defence and Security Studies, 2016.
Martin, D., 'German Intelligence Part of Secret Anti-Terror Unit Targeting Returning IS Fighters – Report', *Deutsche Welle*, 3 February 2018, available here: http://www.dw.com/en/german-intelligence-part-of-secret-anti-terror-unit-targeting-returning-is-fighters-report/a-42441378.
Meleagrou-Hitchens, A., et al., *The Travelers: American Jihadists in Syria and Iraq*, Washington: Program on Extremism George Washington University, 2018.
Moaveni, A., 'The Lingering Dream of an Islamic State', *The New York Times*, 12 January 2018, available here: https://www.nytimes.com/2018/01/12/opinion/sunday/post-isis-muslim-homeland.html?_r=1.
Radicalisation Awareness Network, *Radicalisation RAN Manual: Responses to Returnees: Foreign Terrorist Fighters and Their Families European Union*, RAN Manual, Radicalisation Awareness Network, [Online], 2017.
Renard, T. and R. Coolsaet (ed.), *Returnees: Who Are They, Why Are They (Not) Coming Back and How Should We Deal With Them?*, Egmont Paper 101, 2018, p. 14.
Rosand, E., 'When It Comes to CVE, the United States Has a Lot to Learn from Others', *Lawfare*, 10 September 2017, available here: https://www.lawfareblog.com/when-it-comes-cve-united-states-stands-learn-lot-others-will-it.
Schmitt, E., 'Defeated in Syria, ISIS Fighters Held in Camps Still Pose a Threat', *The New York Times*, 24 January 2018, available here: https://www.nytimes.com/2018/01/24/world/middleeast/isis-syria-militants-kurds.html.
Schmitt, E., 'ISIS Fighters Are Not Flooding Home to Wreak Havoc as Feared', *The New York Times*, 22 October 2017, available here: https://www.nytimes.com/2017/10/22/us/politics/fewer-isis-fighters-returning-home.html.
Security Service MI5, 'DG MI5-Speech', *MI5 Video Transcripts*, 17 October 2017, available here: https://www.mi5.gov.uk/who-we-are-video-transcript.
United Nations Office on Drugs and Crime, *Handbook on Children Recruited and Exploited by Terrorist and Violent Extremist Groups: The Role of the Justice System*, Vienna: United Nations, 2017.
United Nations Security Council Counter-Terrorism Committee, *S/2015/975 – Implementation of Security Council Resolution 2178 (2014) by States Affected by Foreign Terrorist Fighters*, United Nations Security Council Counter-Terrorism Committee, [Online], 2014.
Van der Heide, L. and J., Greenen, *Children of the Caliphate: Young IS Returnees and the Reintegration Challenge*, The Hague, Netherlands: International Centre for Counter-Terrorism, 2017.
Van Ginkel, B. and E. Entenmann, *The Foreign Fighters Phenomenon in the European Union: Profiles, Threats & Policies*, The Hague, Netherlands: International Centre for Counter-Terrorism, 2016.
Zelin, A. Y., *The Others: Foreign Fighters in Libya*, Policy Notes, The Washington Institute for Near East Policy, Policy Notes 45, January 2018.

PART THREE

LEGISLATIVE AND INTELLIGENCE RESPONSES

19 RESPONDING TO TERRORISM THROUGH LEGISLATION

Max Hill, QC

Introduction

Before or after Brexit, the UK enjoys a criminal justice system which enshrines fundamental freedoms that we must all uphold even in the face of terrorism, one of those freedoms, of course, being freedom of speech, Article 10. The author has previously associated himself with the letter to the *Times* in October 2017 signed by the leaders of the legal professions as well as by Liberty and JUSTICE, which includes this: 'Suggestions made before the general election, that human rights prevented the police fighting terrorism, are misguided … Human rights exist to protect us all. Weakening human rights laws will not make us safer. Terrorists cannot take away our freedoms – and we must not do so ourselves.'

However, we should remember the words of Article 10(2) of the ECHR: 'The exercise of these freedoms, since it carries with it duties and responsibilities, may be subject to such formalities, conditions, restrictions or penalties as are prescribed by law and are necessary in a democratic society, in the interests of national security, territorial integrity or public safety, for the prevention of disorder or crime.' So, where should we stand, in the face of recent terrorist atrocities on our streets?

The UK, in fact England, has suffered the worst combination of terrorist attacks for many years. Since 22 March 2017 we have all lived through the pain of witnessing murderous attacks at Westminster Bridge, Manchester Arena and London Bridge followed by Borough Market. The attack outside Finsbury Park Mosque on 19th June marked the fourth in this series of major terrorism events, rounded off by the attempted attack at Parsons Green in September.

It came as no great surprise when the Prime Minister, speaking from outside Downing Street on 4 June 2017, the day after the London Bridge attack, declared that 'enough is enough', going on to announce her intention that Government should review the 'counter-extremism strategy', including a review of available legislation together with sentencing powers for terrorism offences.

After the General Election in early June the Government review swung into action. At the same time, commentators noted that the Queen's Speech at the opening of the new Parliament was largely devoid of intended new legislation, and in relation to 'terrorism' there appeared a reference to a 'commission for countering extremism' – which the author takes to be a reference to non-violent extremism, where our current legislation generally deals with violent extremism – but nothing further.

The author commenced work as Independent Reviewer on 1 March 2017, just in time to witness the horror that unfolded on Westminster Bridge exactly three weeks later. The task is to annually review our terrorism legislation, essentially the Terrorism Acts 2000 and 2006, together with the Terrorism Prevention and Investigation Measures (TPIM) Act 2011 and the Terrorist Asset Freezing Act 2010. The author is on record, from when he first came to post, as saying that in general we do not need more terrorism offences, and there may be examples of redundant terrorism offences which time has proved are not as necessary as Parliament thought.

Careful study of the relevant section of the Crown Prosecution Service website reveals that a wide range of statutory offences were deployed in charging recent terrorism cases, including preparation of terrorist acts (section 5, 2006 Act), encouraging terrorism (section 1, 2006), belonging to a proscribed organization, i.e. the Islamic State (section 11, 2000, together with inviting support for such an organization, section 12), funding terrorism (section 17, 2000), disseminating terrorist publications (section 2, 2006). Interestingly, training for terrorism under sections 6 and 8 of the 2006 Act was not charged at all in 2015 or 2016. Inciting terrorism overseas was charged once in the same two-year period. Possession of articles for terrorist purposes under section 57 of the 2000 Act was charged once in 2015 and not at all in 2016. Some revision and trimming of the current legislation may yet be possible, and that would be a good thing. In general, I would suggest that our legislators, i.e. Parliament, have provided for just about every descriptive action in relation to terrorism, so we should pause before rushing to add yet more offences to the already long list.

Having looked at recent charging activity, the author has suggested that careful consideration should be given in the near future to the existence of any ongoing need for the following offences:[1]

I. section 56, Terrorism Act 2000, directing terrorist organizations
II. section 57, Terrorism Act 2000, possession for terrorist purpose[2]
III. section 59, Terrorism Act 2000, inciting terrorism overseas
IV. sections 6–8, Terrorism Act 2006, training for terrorism[3]

But one cannot say with certainty whether or not fresh circumstances may emerge that will throw up an example or two that legislators have not yet covered.

Returning to past activity, let us spend a moment analysing one of the more significant recent trials, that of *R v Choudary and Rahman*,[4] which concluded in

2016. Both were convicted of inviting support for a proscribed organization for becoming signatories to an oath of allegiance document posted on the internet in 2014 as well as for things they said in specific lectures given in 2014. Mr Justice Holroyde said in his sentencing remarks that both had 'crossed the line between the legitimate expression of your own views and the criminal act of inviting support for an organisation which was at the time engaged in appalling acts of terrorism'. Each was sentenced to five years and six months imprisonment and made subject to notification requirements for a period of fifteen years. There was no evidence that anyone was inspired by their words to do any particular act which Mr Justice Holroyde cited as an important factor in limiting the sentences which they received.

I have highlighted the words of Mr Justice Holroyde, above, because they draw the very important distinction between the legitimate (i.e. lawful) expression of a view, and unlawfully inviting support for a proscribed organization. Thus, so-called 'hate preachers' can and should be prosecuted when they cross the line, as happened in this case.

Broadening our focus to the wider use of the terrorism legislation powers already in existence, the following headlines appeared in the author's Annual Report on the use of the legislation, published in January 2018:

- During 2016, the overall threat picture for the UK remained at Severe. The Islamic State continued to represent the most significant terrorist threat, but the UK faced a continuing threat of violence and terrorism from extremism, including the extreme right wing and far right. This was evidenced by the proscription of the extreme right-wing group National Action in December 2016 and the terrorism-related murder of Jo Cox MP in June 2016. (Chapter 2, Annual Report)

- Seventy-one organizations are proscribed under the Terrorism Act, and fourteen organizations in Northern Ireland. During autumn 2017, six people were subject to TPIM notices. (Chapter 3)

- The Terrorism Act stop and search powers were used 483 times in Great Britain with an arrest rate of 9 per cent. The powers were used 197 times in Northern Ireland. The power to stop and search without suspicion was once again not used. (Chapter 4)

- The frequency of use of Schedule 7 powers to examine people at ports and airports continued to decline, with 17,501 examinations in Great Britain in the year ending June 2017 compared to 23,719 examinations in the previous twelve months. (Chapter 5)

- The number of Terrorism Act arrests decreased compared to 2015, with Northern Ireland recording the lowest number of arrests in any year since 2001. The arrest power was once again used with far greater frequency in Northern Ireland than in Great Britain, but detention beyond forty-eight hours, common in Great Britain, is still rare in Northern Ireland. (Chapter 6)

- There were sixty-two trials for terrorism-related offences in 2016. Of these, fifty-four persons were convicted and eight acquitted. The concluded cases, including the cases of Thomas Mair and Anjem Choudary, are summarized in the report and a brief review of Terrorism Acts offences and maximum sentencing is included. (Chapter 7)

So where do we go next? It seems to me, thinking about the range of statutes in use by prosecutors as shown by recent cases, that we do not lack for legal powers to bring these cases to court. We do need to encourage investigators and prosecutors to use the full range of current powers at their disposal; which is not to say that they are ignorant of what Parliament has provided, but we do need to see the use of financial, identification, fraud, firearms, public order, offences against the person, and conspiracy offences being added to the indictment, in order to capture the full range of criminality represented by future cases. There should be no safe place for terrorists to hide. In fact, terrorism-related cases charged in the year ending December 2016 comprised the use of fifty-six Terrorism Act offences, and sixty-two non-Terrorism Act offences, in other words where other criminal statutes were used. More of this is the way forward.

We live in a modern, increasingly tech-savvy world. Can we legislate to rid ourselves of online terrorism? The author's answer is that Parliament has already done so in meaningful ways, including the dissemination offence noted above, section 2 of the 2006 Act. We lawyers should look hard into such areas, to see whether any amendments might hone these offences given recent technological advances. We should also look to see whether sentencing provisions in 2019 are apt for our world, for example where Parliament drew a line in 2000, and where nineteen years is a long time in tech terms. But apart from that, further legislation does not strike this author as the answer.

So, no, or very little new legislation, as it seems to the author. But legislation in this important area rarely stands still, so let's remind ourselves of changes which have been made during 2017:

(a) Schedule 8 of the TA 2000 was amended by Section 71 of the Policing and Crime Act 2017 to enable DNA profiles and fingerprints to be retained indefinitely where a person has convictions outside the UK.[5]
Section 68 of the 2017 Act (with more details in section 69) creates a new offence of breaching travel-related conditions of pre-charge bail (defined as 'travel restriction conditions') for those arrested on suspicion of committing a terrorist offence.

(b) The Criminal Justice Act 1988 (Reviews of Sentencing) (Amendment) Order 2017, SI 2017/1751, adds nineteen either way offences which trigger the terrorism notification requirements in Part 4 of the Counter-Terrorism Act 2008 to Schedule 1 of the original Review of Sentencing 2006 Order.

Part IV of the 2017 Order allows the Attorney General, with leave from the Court of Appeal, to refer certain cases to the Court of Appeal where he considers that a sentence imposed in the Crown Court was unduly lenient.

(c) Amendments were made to the TA 2000 and to Schedule 1 of the Anti-terrorism, Crime and Security Act (ATCSA) 2001 by Part 2 of the Criminal Finances Act 2017, including the introduction in Schedule 1 of the Act of a new power to administratively forfeit 'terrorist cash' in new Part 2A and new civil recovery powers in new Parts 4A and 4B to seize, detain and forfeit terrorist assets and terrorist money held in bank and building society accounts.[6]

(d) The Prison (Amendment) Rules 2017, SI 2017/560, which are linked to the special offences in the legislation, allow for a special separation regime for extremist prisoners as envisaged by the Acheson Report. By r.46A, there will be separation centres, with allocation on any of the following grounds:[7]

   i. the interests of national security;

   ii. to prevent the commission, preparation or instigation of an act of terrorism, a terrorism offence, or an offence with a terrorist connection, whether in a prison or otherwise;

   iii. to prevent the dissemination of views or beliefs that might encourage or induce others to commit any such act or offence, whether in a prison or otherwise, or to protect or safeguard others from such views or beliefs; or

   iv. to prevent any political, religious, racial or other views or beliefs being used to undermine good order and discipline in a prison.

It is clear that our terrorism legislation does not exist in a static state, but reacts to events and changes over time. Such amendments are necessary and welcome.

As for the mainframe, however, by which the author means the overarching structure of our main terrorism statutes, care must be taken to avoid legislating in haste or where it is unnecessary. Historical examples may be useful in this regard. The Explosive Substances Act 1883, passed by a late Victorian Parliament in record time, created criminal offences which are still in use today by prosecutors taking charging decisions in the twenty-first century. So, this is legislation which has stood the test of time. The Terrorism Act 2006, passed again in quick time by Parliament, is another good example which we all remember was in relation to the atrocity on 7/7 the previous year. Some of the new offences (e.g. under section 5, the preparation for terrorism offence; see below) are regularly used today, but the author has noted others which are not.

For now, we might agree that any debate about the need for bespoke terrorism legislation alongside general crime statutes springs from the fact that the UK attacks of 2017 were in many instances committed by individuals who moved from general criminality into terrorism. Sometimes this happens with alarming speed, partly at least because of the proliferation of online extremist propaganda. Because of this, anyone working in this area must think about precursor criminality and precursor offences. We have a good example of a precursor terrorism offence in section 5 of the 2006 Act already mentioned. Whilst not every incipient terrorist is a general criminal first, many are. Whether or not this is their route into terrorism, we need to consider whether our existing precursor offences are effective, and here that means ECHR-compliant too. As the regular hands in terrorism casework will confirm, Article 10 is the source of legal submissions in more current terrorism trials than not. Article 10 is not absolute; hence the legal submissions focus on Article 10(2). In the context of the dissemination offence, section 2 of the 2006 Act, Article 10(2) consideration seems to have been settled by *Brown*, the Anarchist Handbook case tried in Winchester by Blair J in 2011, and the author makes a bid for reference to his own case of *Faraz* in Kingston in the same year, where Calvert-Smith read down section 2 for Article 10 compliance in ways which the Court of Appeal found faultless.

So, with reference to Article 10 ECHR where this chapter started, we have come full circle. Whether on ECHR principles, or whether applying domestic jurisprudence alone and in light of our long experience of legislating against terrorism in all of its forms, any new consideration of precursor offending that may emerge from a review of the terrible events during 2017 will need to pass a stiff test, particularly if our legislators attempt to lower the bar for precursor criminality any further than at present.

Notes

1 These matters call for careful further exploration, including the fact that some of these offences are based on the ratification by the UK of international treaties, e.g. section 59 2000 Act and sections 6–8 2006 Act.

2 It may be thought that, in combination, the offences of collection of information, section 58 Terrorism Act 2000, and preparation for terrorism, section 5 Terrorism Act 2006, cover the territory formerly occupied by section 57.

3 Activity likely to be covered by section 5, Terrorism Act 2006.

4 Not included in the list of concluded cases in 2016 on the CTD-CPS website. See sentencing remarks here https://www.judiciary.gov.uk/wp-content/uploads/2016/09/r-v-choudary-sentencing.pdf.

5 Where the act constituting the offence would constitute a recordable offence under the law of England and Wales or Northern Ireland, or an imprisonable offence under the law of Scotland.

6 The full picture of relevance to terrorism financing: s.36 sharing of information; s.37 further information orders; s.41 extension of powers to financial investigators; s.42 offences in relation to financial investigators; s.43 cross jurisdiction enforcement; schedule 2 para.1 amends s.37/Sched 5 and s.37A/Sched.5A of the TA 2000; schedule

3 forfeiture – amends ATCSA 2001 sch.1 and sch.4A; schedule 4: forfeiture of money held in bank – amends ATCSA 2001 sch.1; Schedule 5 – minor amendments e.g. to TA 2000 s.21CA and 21G, s.115, 121 and Sched.14.

7 A direction must be reviewed every three months. The centres will be situated in three high-security prisons each holding up to twelve prisoners, most of whom will be Islamist extremists. One has already been established at HMP Frankland (Durham).

20 ASSESSING THE LEGISLATIVE RESPONSE TO TERRORISM: ADEQUACY, GAPS, WHAT'S UNNECESSARY OR COUNTERPRODUCTIVE

Lord David Anderson, KBE, QC

Point of departure

While it is entirely legitimate to discuss the legislative response to jihadist terrorism, there is a risk that such a narrow focus may obscure two broader truths.

The first of these truths is that terrorism is a form of violent crime – and, in Western countries at least, a relatively uncommon variety.[1] Established criminal laws and procedures are the starting point for the detection, investigation and prosecution of terrorism.[2] Special counter-terrorism laws exist, but they are supplemental to the general law, and must be rights-compliant and justified on the basis of operational need. Were it otherwise, the winners would be the terrorists who wish their crimes to be viewed as *sui generis* and who seek to characterize the state as oppressive and unfair.[3]

The second broad truth is that terrorism laws are ideology-blind.[4] Jihadists currently pose the main terrorist threat in Great Britain, and the particular nature of their activities has influenced the law (e.g. to allow prosecutions for acts committed abroad, as a response to the foreign fighter phenomenon). But every aspect of counter-terrorism law applies to all terrorism, irrespective of the ideology in whose name it is planned or committed. To prohibit conduct in the name of Islam that would be lawful if motivated by any other belief system would simply feed the grievance culture on which jihadist terrorism feeds.

Having made those two preliminary points, the author reviews some of the principal elements of the UK's terrorism-specific legislation, as it is used in relation to jihadist terrorism, and indicate some areas where it seems to him that further study might be particularly fruitful.[5]

The definition of terrorism

There is no internationally approved definition of terrorism. There are three cumulative ingredients to the UK's definition:

a. ***actions*** (taken or threatened): serious violence against a person, serious damage to property and actions which endanger life, create a serious risk to health and safety or are designed seriously to interfere with or to disrupt an electronic system;
b. ***target***: the actions described must be designed to *influence* a government or international organization, or to *intimidate* the public or a section of the public;
c. ***motive***: advancing a political, religious, racial or ideological cause.[6]

The breadth of the UK's definition is evident from the facts that terrorism can be directed against *any* government (however repellent); that it is enough for actions with the requisite motive to be designed to *influence* (rather than coerce) such a government; and that the target requirement need not be satisfied at all when firearms or explosives are used. The last two factors are unusual by international standards and mark the UK definition as one of the most extensive in the Western world.

There have been various attempts to reduce the scope of the definition, most recently by the Court of Appeal, which interpreted it so as to avoid the absurd consequence that, for example, an article written by someone opposed to vaccination on religious grounds would constitute terrorism.[7] The Supreme Court has commented that 'any legislative narrowing in the definition of "terrorism" ... is to be welcomed, provided that it is consistent with the public protection to which the legislation is directed'.[8]

But a legislative narrowing seems unlikely in the current threat climate; any over-breadth is not a major source of grievance; and most of those concerned with enforcing the law would subscribe to the verdict of Lord Carlile, my predecessor as Independent Reviewer, that the definition is 'useful and broadly fit for purpose'.[9]

Terrorist offences

It was fashionable to question, around the time of the 7/7 attacks, whether the traditional system of jury trial was adequate to prosecute terrorism in England and Wales.[10] The success since then of the Counter-Terrorism Division of the Crown Prosecution Service, together with better CPS–police cooperation and more active judicial case management, has banished such doubts. This is highly beneficial to the fight against terrorism, since the integrity and fairness of a jury trial are harder to question than the alternatives (notably, the executive orders), and because long sentences are the most effective disruption – subject to tackling prison radicalization, which is a topic for another paper.

The list of specialist offences in the Terrorism Act 2000, still the UK's principal counter-terrorism statute, was supplemented by the Terrorism Act 2006 following the 7/7 attacks and Tony Blair's declaration that 'the rules of the game have changed'.[11] These specialist crimes are for the most part 'precursor offences', designed to catch activity prior to the normal criminal thresholds of incitement, conspiracy and attempt. Examples include membership of proscribed organizations, encouragement to terrorism, dissemination of terrorist materials, preparing acts of terrorism, attendance at a training camp and the downloading of materials likely to be useful in terrorism. Some of these offences impinge to some extent on expressive and associative freedoms, and the current Independent Reviewer (at the time of writing) has rightly suggested that the need for each of them must be kept under review.[12] But carefully drawn precursor offences are usually considered to be justified, at least in principle, by the need to intervene in the interests of public protection before terrorist plots are fully ripe.

Recent years have seen extensions of extra-territorial jurisdiction and increased sentencing powers. The Sentencing Council is currently preparing sentencing guidelines, which will be a useful means of ensuring consistency in sentencing practice in England and Wales.

The perceived inadequacies of the criminal law are most evident in relation to the activities of 'hate preachers' such as Anjem Choudary, a former solicitor who was careful to stay within the bounds of legally protected free speech but whose various organizations have been instrumental in radicalizing many who have gone on to fight in Syria or to commit terrorist offences. As the then Independent Reviewer for Terrorism Legislation, the author reported in December 2016 that before his eventual conviction in 2016 for encouraging acts of terrorism, Choudary's activities were reported to the CPS on no fewer than ten occasions between 2002 and 2015, for offences ranging from proscription offences to incitement to religious hatred and to murder, without any prosecution resulting.[13] The author made some suggestions for possible legal improvements in that regard, and we may well see some tightening of the applicable laws in the Counter-Terrorism Bill that is expected later in 2018.

A further perceived lacuna is the difficulty in adducing specific evidence of terrorist activities overseas. Australia, which has even more counter-terrorism laws than the UK, has sought to address this difficulty by creating a 'declared area offence' of travelling to certain war zones save on very narrowly defined grounds. The operation of this offence was recently reviewed, and its retention recommended by Australia's equivalent of the Independent Reviewer of Terrorism Legislation.[14] Such an offence is something that the author has previously advised might be looked at in the UK.[15]

Police powers

The police power that was most resented by Muslims when the author began his stint as Independent Reviewer in 2011 was the former no-suspicion stop and search power in Terrorism Act 2000 s44. Used over 250,000 times in a single year (largely in London and on the national rail network), the exercise of that power caused considerable aggravation but did not result in a single conviction. Though it was repealed (following an adverse judgement of the European Court of Human Rights) not long before the London Olympics in 2012, the author has never spoken to a police officer who regrets its loss. The episode is a powerful reminder that measures which cannot be shown to be effective may easily be counter-productive, particularly when they are used selectively and yet are liable to impinge on the freedoms of large numbers of innocent people.

Far more useful, though still controversial, is the power under Schedule 7 to the Terrorism Act to detain (for up to six hours) and question travellers at ports and airports for the purpose of determining whether they are engaged in terrorism. The power is striking in its extent, requiring no suspicion for its exercise but allowing police to compel questions to be answered and to download and retain the entire contents of laptops and mobile phones. The number of examinations has fallen steadily from 87,200 in 2009/10 to 17,500 in 2017, 16,000 of which lasted less than an hour. Nonetheless, the power was criticized in some of its aspects by the Supreme Court in a recent case[16] and is still used as a campaigning tool by civil society groups, some of whose members may have jihadist sympathies.

The Schedule 7 power should on no account be repealed and it is difficult to see how it could be strengthened without running into difficulties in the courts. Suggestions for reform, including the author's own and those of his successor as Independent Reviewer, have been aimed at ensuring legal compliance while minimizing the impact on operational efficacy.[17] Further debate would, however, be possible in Phase 2 of the CoJiT initiative.

The law provides a special arrest power for use against suspected terrorists (Terrorism Act 2000 s41), which is, however, relatively little used.[18] Of more practical value is the possibility of questioning a terrorist suspect for up to fourteen days prior to charge (as against a maximum of four days under the normal PACE power). Though a lengthy period by the standards of most other common law countries, this compares with a twenty-eight-day maximum prior to 2011 and with aspirations by the Blair and Brown governments to legislate for periods of, respectively, ninety and forty-two days. The fourteen-day period has survived repeated legal challenge, though only because warrants for further detention must be obtained (initially after forty-eight hours) from a court.

Having observed the volume of evidence that needs to be assimilated and the pace at which these investigations proceed, particularly in the case of complex plots where encrypted communications and language difficulties may be in play, the author would be sympathetic to a modest extension of the fourteen-day period, should the police succeed in establishing a strong operational case for it.[19] A draft Bill to that effect already exists, in case a series of major arrests should necessitate its immediate passage. But to date, admirably, the police have resisted the temptation to press for an extension.

Executive orders

The courts struck down in 2004 a scheme, introduced after the 9/11 attacks, for the indefinite detention of undeportable foreign nationals. The 2005 replacement scheme of control orders (applicable also to British citizens) allowed the Home Secretary, subject to review by the courts, to impose restrictions on a subject's place of residence, permitted travel, associations and use of communications. When the Coalition Government in 2011 replaced control orders with the looser Terrorist Prevention and Investigation Measures, or TPIMs, they were responding not to any legal direction but to the excesses of control orders as they were perceived in some quarters. When TPIM subjects started to abscond, political criticism ensued and the result in 2015 was a TPIM Mk II regime, restoring the power that existed under control orders to relocate subjects away from their home cities (but retaining the two-year maximum duration of the TPIM, in contrast to control orders which could be renewed indefinitely).

TPIMs Mk II (the main features of which were introduced on the author's recommendation) is certainly more workable than Mk I. It remains the case, however, that only a handful of TPIMs are in force at any one time, which some have found curious given that many foreign fighters have returned to the UK and yet not been prosecuted. The author has never been particularly troubled by this, given that TPIMs to his mind should be used only as a last resort. Their existence informs subjects that they are being watched; their onerous constraints may be imposed without proof of guilt; and subjects are required to challenge them without access to the so-called '*secret evidence*' against them (though with the assistance of a security-cleared special advocate). The last two factors could make TPIMs a powerful jihadist recruiting sergeant were they to be used on a significantly larger scale, as would the fact that they have only ever been used on so-called Islamist terrorists.

The author does not sense any current strong wish on the part of MI5 or Counter-Terrorism police to make significantly expanded use of these resource-intensive measures. Nonetheless, the issue of executive orders (including asset-freezing orders) and how their utility should be maximized is one to which it may be wished to give more consideration in Phase 2 of the CoJiT initiative. Any such discussion could take account of the proscription powers under the Terrorism Act 2000,[20] Terrorist Exclusion Orders (introduced in 2015 and not yet reported on by an Independent Reviewer) and the asset-freezing powers to be included in the Sanctions and Anti-Money Laundering Bill 2017–19, currently before Parliament (at the time of writing).[21]

Immigration and nationality

Increasingly, terrorism in the UK is committed by British citizens who enjoy the right of abode and in respect of whom immigration and deportation powers have no application.

Where foreign or dual nationals are concerned, there is no doubt that such powers (e.g. of deportation, refusal of entry, citizenship deprivation and withdrawal of passport facilities) are used by the Home Secretary – vigorously in some cases – as counter-terrorism measures. During the author's term of office, the Government resisted calls for the jurisdiction of the Independent Reviewer to be extended to these powers.[22] It will be for CoJiT to decide whether these are aspects of the law which they consider it appropriate to investigate further in Phase 2, and if so – in the light of the limited public information available – how best to do so.

Investigatory powers

The subject of counter-terrorism is frequently linked with the law governing investigatory powers (recently reviewed and reformed in the Investigatory Powers Act 2016, which is itself currently the subject of legal challenge). None of those powers is unique to counter-terrorism, though some (e.g. the collection of bulk content and metadata by MI5, MI6 and GCHQ, and the use by them of bulk personal datasets) are reserved to security and intelligence agencies which devote a significant part of their resources to the fight against jihadist terrorism.

The author made two detailed examinations of the nature and function of these powers in 2014–16,[23] and could elaborate further, but in view of the fact that they are not terrorism-specific, assumes that they are unlikely to feature in Phase 2.

Counter-extremism

A final legal element at least indirectly related to terrorism is the notion of counter-extremism – an inherently controversial subject, given that the expression of non-violent opinions is heavily protected under the European Convention of Human Rights and under the common law.[24] The concept of extremism (as variously defined) extends well beyond terrorism but has been seen by some as an alternative vehicle for countering the activities of hate preachers, discussed in the context of criminal offences at paragraph 12 above.

In particular:

a. The Prevent strategy was put on a statutory footing in 2015, and at the time of writing remains under review as part of the CONTEST refresh.

b. Controversial plans announced in 2015 and 2016 for a Counter-Extremism Bill[25] appear not to have borne fruit, but have been superseded by the establishment of a Counter-Extremism Commission.

No doubt counter-extremism and the allied (though, the Government insists, distinct) subject of Prevent will feature in Phase 2.

Conclusion

In this far from comprehensive account of the legislative response to jihadist terrorism, the author has sought to draw attention to some areas which might merit further investigation in Phase 2.

In general, and despite (or perhaps because of) a number of wrong turnings both in twentieth-century Northern Ireland and in the UK's response to terrorism since 9/11, the author would characterize the existing legislative response to terrorism as in most respects satisfactory.[26] Strong by the standards of other Western democracies, it is nonetheless generally rights-compliant and well calibrated both to current threat levels and to community sensitivities. That is not to be complacent about the current terrorist threat, but rather to acknowledge the limits on the capacity of the laws to reduce it.

The author's relatively positive assessment of the legislation may, of course, reflect the fact that he has lived closely with it for almost seven years now. Changed circumstances are always liable to require changed laws, and fresher pairs of eyes than the author's may be better placed to suggest them. On the other hand, the value and persuasiveness of research in this area (particularly into the operation of the executive orders, and in the largely unreviewed areas of immigration and nationality law) will be reduced to the extent that access to classified material is not available in Phase 2.

Notes

1 An average of some five persons per year have been killed since 2001 by terrorist attacks in Great Britain (nearly all of them in the 7/7 attacks of 2005 and in the four successful attacks of 2017). This is a small fraction of the numbers killed in gang fights or incidents of domestic violence.

2 Thus, the most serious terrorist offenders – for example the Canary Wharf bomber of 1996, the failed 21/7 bombers of 2005 and the killers of Lee Rigby in 2013 – are invariably charged not with any specialist offences but with murder or attempted murder.

3 The author observed during his tenure as Independent Reviewer of Terrorism Legislation (2011–17) that references to internment, last used in 1975, are still used to radicalize young republicans in Northern Ireland.

4 The dramatic jihadist attacks on the Twin Towers in 2001, which killed almost 3,000, have forged Western perceptions of terrorism since 2001. But 3,500 deaths in the Northern Irish Troubles of 1968–1998, and the 77 victims of Anders Breivik in 2011, remind us that mass casualty attacks – as well as smaller terrorist attacks such as the murders of Jo Cox (Birstall, 2016) and Makram Ali (Finsbury Park, 2017) – may be inspired by a variety of ideologies.

5 For further reading see, among much else, K. Roach, *The 9/11 Effect: Comparative Counter-Terrorism*, Cambridge University Press, 2011; C. Walker and G. Lennon, *Routledge Handbook of Law and Terrorism*, London: Routledge, 2015.

6 *Terrorism Act* 2000 s1.

7 *R(Miranda) v Home Secretary* [2016] EWHC 6.

8 *R v Gül* [2013] UKSC 64, §62.

9 A. Carlile QC, *The Definition of Terrorism*, Cm 7052, 2007.

10 The non-jury courts still made available for terrorism cases in Northern Ireland have not been replicated in Great Britain, where terrorist cases remain subject to jury trial.

11 PM's Press Conference, 5 August 2005 http://webarchive.nationalarchives.gov.uk/20080909054553/http://www.number10.gov.uk/Page8041.

12 M. Hill QC, *The Terrorism Acts in 2016*, January 2018, pp. 7.10–7.12. Some amendments to the existing precursor offences were put forward in the Counter-Terrorism and Border Security Bill of June 2018.

13 D. Anderson QC, *The Terrorism Acts in 2015*, December 2016, pp. 9.43–9.51.

14 Independent National Security Legislation Monitor, *Sections 119.2 and 119.3 of the Criminal Code: Declared areas*, September 2017.

15 D. Anderson QC, *The Terrorism Acts in* 2013, July 2014, 10.69–10.70; The *Terrorism Acts in 2014*, September 2015, 8.21.

16 *Beghal v DPP* [2015] UKSC 49.

17 Anderson QC, *The Terrorism Acts in 2015*, chapter 7; Hill QC, *The Terrorism Acts in 2016*, chapter 5.

18 Of the terrorist-related arrests recorded in 2016, 260 were under PACE and only 37 under s41.

19 Anderson QC, *The Terrorism Acts in 2015*, 8.7–8.10.

20 Anderson QC, *The Terrorism Acts in 2015*, chapter 5.

21 Replacing, in part, the *Terrorist Asset-Freezing &c. Act 2010* on which the author reported regularly as Independent Reviewer between 2011 and 2015.

22 Though at the request of Ministers the author did produce one-off reports in 2015–2016 on citizenship deprivation and deportation with assurances.

23 D. Anderson QC, *A Question of Trust: Report of the Investigatory Powers Review*, London: Home Office, June 2015; D. Anderson QC, *Report of Bulk Powers Review*, London: Home Office, August 2016.

24 Though the protection is not absolute, as may be seen from the existence of certain hate speech and public order offences.

25 D. Anderson QC, *The Terrorism Acts in 2014*, chapter 9.

26 The author's outstanding recommendations, in relation to the parts of the law that the author had responsibility for reviewing, were set out in his last report as Independent Reviewer: Anderson QC, *The Terrorism Acts in 2015*, chapter 10.

Recommended Readings

Anderson QC, D., *The Terrorism Acts in* 2013, July 2014.

Anderson QC, D., *The Terrorism Acts in 2015*, December 2016.

Anderson QC, D., *A Question of Trust*, 2015.

Anderson QC, D., *Report of Bulk Powers Review*, 2016.

Beghal v DPP [2015] UKSC 49.

Hill QC, M., *The Terrorism Acts in 2016*, January 2018.

Independent National Security Legislation Monitor, *Sections 119.2 and 119.3 of the Criminal Code: Declared areas*, September 2017.

Lord Carlile QC, *The Definition of Terrorism*, Cm 7052, 2007.

R(Miranda) v Home Secretary [2016] EWHC 6.

R v Gül [2013] UKSC 64, §62.

Roach, K., *The 9/11 Effect: Comparative Counter-Terrorism*, New York: Cambridge University Press, 2011.

The Terrorism Acts in 2014, September 2015.

Terrorism Act 2000 s1.

Terrorist Asset-Freezing &c. Act 2010.

Walker, C. and G. Lennon, *Routledge Handbook of Law and Terrorism*, London: Routledge, 2015.

21 INDEPENDENT ASSESSMENT OF THE CURRENT BALANCE BETWEEN COUNTER-TERRORISM LEGISLATION AND CIVIL LIBERTIES: THE ROLE OF THE INDEPENDENT REVIEWER OF TERRORISM LEGISLATION

Jessie Blackbourn and Clive Walker*

Introduction

It has become axiomatic that every nation should gird itself with strong counter-terrorism legislation. That is now the dictate of international and regional laws, which have proliferated since 11 September 2001.[1] Rather less certain is the relationship between this stipulation and the safeguarding of civil liberties. Much has been written about this issue, especially since the pursuit of counter-terrorism has in law given rise to substantial human rights restraints, ranging from detention without trial to pervasive physical policing and electronic surveillance.[2] Furthermore, counter-terrorism practices have sometimes even exceeded the indulgent bounds set by laws and have sustained egregious abuses, whether in the 1970s in Northern Ireland,[3] or during the new millennium in Iraq.[4] In these ways, the issue of 'balance' remains unresolved and contentious. For the purpose of this chapter, two further limits to the terms of debate should be noted.

---

* The latter author discloses that he has acted as senior special adviser to the Independent Reviewer of Terrorism Legislation since 2011.

The first limit is philosophical and concerns the framing reference in the title to 'current balance'. For several reasons, no blanket or mechanical balance can be set between counter-terrorism and civil liberties, and one may even dispute whether 'balance' is the suitable basis for debate. Amongst the irresolvable problems are those of measurement and causation – how much change to civil liberties (and which liberties) is needed for the sake of counter-terrorism, and how can we be sure that the two are causally related? Measurement is difficult when so many other factors are in play,[5] when some factors and the calculation of them may be emotive rather than rational,[6] and when issues of liberties can affect both sides since protection of the right to life is a key objective of counter-terrorism.[7] The position is further complicated by the fact that some civil liberties should not be balanced at all because they are absolute – rights against torture being the prime example – while others (such as liberty and due process) may be balanced only against specified values involving other rights and not against broader societal goods (including national security).[8]

The second limit arises from the potential range of mechanisms relevant to 'independent assessment'. Because of the overall focus of the 'Combating Jihadist Terrorism in the UK' project, one might discount consideration in this chapter of international mechanisms.[9] However, within the UK jurisdiction alone, multiple bodies view themselves as fulfilling the function of 'independent assessment'. That catalogue might include Parliament, especially through its specialist committees.[10] Emboldened by the Human Rights Act 1998, the UK courts have also revealed themselves to be increasingly willing to engage in the judicialization of security disputes.[11] Civil society organizations can also claim a fine heritage of appraisal, with groups such as Liberty[12] and the Committee for the Administration of Justice[13] long prominent in the field. All would be worthy subjects of further assessment. However, given constraints of space, this chapter instead concentrates only on the office of the Independent Reviewer of Terrorism Legislation ('IRTL'). The reason is that the IRTL is the prime purpose-designed independent assessor within the UK constitution and has a longer and more intense record than most of the other mechanisms. Therefore, the remainder of this chapter will conduct an analysis based on, first, the details and history of the office of the IRTL. A sense of its performance in terms of outputs and impacts will then be given, followed by some conclusions.

Independent Reviewer of Terrorism Legislation: Nature and history of the office

When the Prevention of Terrorism (Temporary Provisions) Act ('PTA') was passed in November 1974 in response to the horrific Birmingham pub bombings, the Home Secretary of the day, Roy Jenkins, depicted the legislation as 'Draconian'.[14] Thus, it was recognized at the outset that the potential incursion upon civil liberties required special safeguards. One built-in safeguard was the requirement of parliamentary approval for extension of its lifespan.[15] The additional need for an independent assessor, not only to inform these periodic reviews but also to conduct more continuous oversight, was soon realized. At first, the independent assessment was rather disjointed and appointees were confined to episodic exercises. Some individual assessors, Lord Shackleton,[16] Earl Jellicoe,[17] Viscount Colville,[18] reported on the PTA, while Lord Gardiner,[19] Sir George Baker[20] and John Rowe[21] covered the equivalent legislation in Northern Ireland, the Northern Ireland (Emergency Provisions) Acts 1973–1998 ('EPA').[22] After 1983,[23] an annual non-statutory review was instituted for the PTA, with a corresponding system for the EPA from 1987.[24] As set out in 1984, and not significantly altered since, the Independent Reviewer's function was 'To consider, for example, whether he saw emerging any change in the pattern of their use which required to be drawn to the attention of Parliament. … his task would not be to judge individual cases but to examine the overall use made of the powers'.[25]

This phase of independent assessors culminated in Lord Lloyd's review of both codes in 1996, which presaged the current Terrorism Act 2000 ('TA 2000').[26] Lord Lloyd suggested that the new legislation should be permanent; thus there was no requirement for periodic renewal and so no need for a reviewer.[27] Yet, this finding did not tally with his principle that 'The need for additional safeguards should be considered alongside any additional powers'.[28] Parliament preferred the latter edict. Since then, specific assessors have reappeared sporadically to respond to acute problems, such as the replacement of detention without trial[29] or control orders,[30] but the model of review, especially after the dropping of periodic renewal requirements in the TA 2000,[31] has prioritized permanent and continuous review by the IRTL.[32]

As for the current IRTL office, the TA 2000 places on the Home Secretary a bare duty to 'lay before both Houses of Parliament at least once in every 12 months a report on the working of this Act'[33] but without explanation of its provenance.[34] Subsequently, the office of the IRTL was explicitly recognized by the Terrorism Act 2006,[35] but the production of reviews is left unelaborated.[36]

It follows that the remit of the IRTL is left opaque, reflecting at best 'pragmatic incrementalism'.[37] The TA 2000 is fully reviewed, as well as Part I (only) of the Terrorism Act 2006. The Terrorism Prevention and Investigation Measures Act 2011 ('TPIMs Act') is distinctly reviewed (but by the same IRTL),[38] but just one out of several asset-freezing regimes is reviewed (under the Terrorist Asset Freezing etc. Act 2010)[39] and this commission is to be ended by the Sanctions and International Money Laundering Bill 2017–19.[40] Following the Coroners and Justice Act 2009,[41] the arrangements for the detention of suspected terrorists must be reviewed;[42] any detention extended beyond fourteen days must also be reviewed under the Protection of Freedoms Act 2012,[43] as must any invocation of the Draft Enhanced Terrorism Prevention and Investigation Measures Bill.[44] The review of the Justice and Security (Northern Ireland) Act 2007 remains allocated to a separate reviewer.[45]

This increasingly haphazard list was eventually reformulated by the Counter-Terrorism and Security Act 2015.[46] Reflecting earlier informal concessions,[47] the remit was extended to encompass the Anti-Terrorism, Crime and Security Act 2001 (but only Part I and Part II), the Counter-Terrorism Act 2008 and Part 1 of the 2015 Act. Reflecting this heavier workload, the IRTL must notify the Secretary of State at the beginning of each calendar year of those matters which are intended to be reviewed in the following twelve months,[48] the implication being that a full annual review of every topic is not only unsustainable on the basis of allocated resources but also perhaps unnecessary. The IRTL had also argued for more flexible arrangements,[49] though reviews of the TA 2000 and of extended detentions beyond fourteen days remain obligatory.

The result is that most of the special counter-terrorism legislation is now subject to review, but this scrutiny does not apply to the application of 'normal' laws to terrorism, no matter how specialized or significant.[50] One potential retort is that the IRTL can also be commissioned to undertake thematic reviews[51] or can take the initiative to conduct an inquiry (subject to funding). This possibility has frequently occurred. Thus, the IRTL has engaged in parliamentary debates about specific legislative proposals,[52] or committee inquiries. Formal assignments have related to the definition of terrorism in 2007,[53] specific policing operations in 2009 and 2011,[54] the 2011 review of the *Prevent Strategy*,[55] and the audit of the handling of the 2017 attacks.[56] Major studies of proposed legislation or legislative operations in areas closely linked to counter-terrorism, such as surveillance powers,[57] deportation[58] and statelessness,[59] have also been commissioned.

This inevitably *ad hoc* approach is also reflected in the resourcing of the IRTL. Until 2011, the IRTL was a one-man band – in every case a full-time barrister and part-time reviewer.[60] In 2011, a special adviser was appointed by the Home Office. However, the continued accrual of functions, especially as sanctioned by the Counter-Terrorism and Security Act 2015, called for new arrangements. The IRTL had recommended the appointment of further advisory staff.[61] However, the 2015 Act opted for a more ambitious scheme. It allows the Secretary of State to create a Privacy and Civil Liberties Board which would act in support of the IRTL.[62] This model was supposedly influenced by the Liberal Democrat members of the then Coalition Government, impressed by the US Privacy and Civil Liberties Oversight Board.[63] However, after the general election of 2015, the policy was peremptorily dropped in favour of adding three extra staff to the office of the IRTL.[64]

The other aspect of resourcing which remains somewhat ramshackle concerns the powers of the IRTL. In short, no formal powers are granted. In practice, the IRTL is supported by the Home Office, has a high level of security clearance and is undoubtedly respected by respondent police and security authorities. Nevertheless, the IRTL has called for 'express statutory provision for: a) access to classified information; b) information gathering powers; c) the exclusion of sensitive information from reports'.[65] Invidious comparisons can be made in these respects with the Independent National Security Legislation Monitor Act 2010 in Australia, sections 21 to 28 of which grant express powers for the equivalent office-holder in that jurisdiction to hold hearings, to summon persons, to take evidence on oath or by affirmation, or to request production of a document or other evidence, and all these powers are backed by criminal penalties. However, these powers have in practice been held mainly in reserve[66] and so this formal grant of strength has not evidently been translated into greater impact or effectiveness for the Australian model compared to the UK.[67] Indeed, the life of the Australian office has been much more precarious than the UK counterpart, with three appointments since 2011[68] and even a proposal for repeal in 2014.[69] One may perhaps conclude that a reviewer's abilities to express expertise and insights in an accessible and actionable way together with their political acumen may represent more significant augurs of success than formal powers.

Overall, the IRTL structure works despite the gaps, but more could be achieved by a Privacy and Civil Liberties Board, which relied less upon the capacity of just one person, no matter how able and energetic.[70] The security landscape is now so large and diffuse and some important aspects, such as 'Prevent' and 'Protect',[71] are not covered at all by the IRTL or any other reviewer. A review board would also allow for the consolidation of the TA 2000 reviews with the Justice and Security (Northern Ireland) Act 2007 reviews. In addition, a board could address different audiences. Parliament and government are the prime audiences but the communities most affected by the legislation, the lawyers who work with it and the general public, all have legitimate interests in greater knowledge about the legislation which can then be further debated and challenged.

Independent Reviewer of Terrorism Legislation: Performance of the office

Overall, the outputs of the IRTL have achieved to a high degree the key performance indicators, namely, effective and independent scrutiny. As for effective scrutiny, the review reports are unfailingly accurate, informative and increasingly detailed. Hence, the average length of TA 2000 reviews has risen from 79 pages in 2004 to 2006 to 118 pages in 2014 to 2016. Particular strengths of the IRTL reside in the accumulation and analysis of detailed information (including information based on privileged access such as sensitive security information and ministerial correspondence), openness to representations not only from state agencies but also from civil society,[72] a willingness to reveal briefings, observations and assessments of the working of the legislation, and the ability to act as catalysts for public and parliamentary debates. The systems show no signs of being hampered by lack of information,[73] though, as already discussed, this is achieved more in practice through good working relationships than through the mechanics of the office. On this point, it might be argued that constituting the IRTL as a single point of contact (rather than a board) helps to cement good relations. However, the demarcation of jobs (and thereby specific relationships) would still be possible within a panel. A possible model is the appointment of the Investigatory Powers Commissioner plus other Judicial Commissioners under the Investigatory Powers Act 2016,[74] who together carry out highly sensitive oversight functions, albeit armed with investigation powers.[75]

As for independence, the IRTL structures lack the formal assurance of independence, despite the importance of that attribute.[76] The office has only recently been advertised with clear job specifications.[77] Appointees have all reflected distinctly partial prior experiences: Lord Carlile was a Liberal Democrat politician (and QC), David Anderson was a leading European law QC and Max Hill was a QC known as a leading terrorism prosecutor. These background experiences can, of course, offer deep understanding and springboards to a fresh look at existing legislation and its shortcomings. Certainly, few criticisms have arisen of undue tendencies by the IRTLs towards favouring their prior preoccupations. Quite the reverse has been true – for instance, Max Hill was criticized in 2017 for advocating social reintegration rather than blanket prosecution of returning foreign terrorism fighters.[78]

A comprehensive survey of specific deliverables and impacts would require a much longer chapter than is possible here. Furthermore, the constitutional position is that the IRTL has the status of an independent adviser and so the duly appointed government, elected legislators and appointed judges should be responsive but should still be accorded precedence over an unelected expert. Therefore, just a few selective illustrations will be given of where change has, or has not, been secured.

On the positive side, one can first point to the improvement of practices during police detention. Thus, lessons from the *Operation Pathway* review by Lord Carlile related to the rigour of interrogation practices and detention reviews under schedule 8 of the TA 2000 and the need to involve the Crown Prosecution Service.[79] Subsequently, it was revealed in *Sher v Chief Constable of Greater Manchester Police*[80] that it is the practice of the police to produce a 'Pre-Interview Briefing Document' for each session, an excellent device to encourage professionalism and transparency. In addition, Crown Prosecution Service involvement has been encouraged,[81] as has the need for reviews to extend to substance as well as to the efficiency of the process.[82] These practices have been crucial in avoiding the need for detention even longer than fourteen days, in achieving a high conviction rate, and in avoiding breaches of human rights.[83]

A second significant improvement was secured in regard to port and border controls under schedule 7 of the TA 2000. After a succession of critical reports and recommendations for tighter restraints by David Anderson,[84] important reforms were instituted by the Anti-Social Behaviour, Crime and Police Act 2014.[85] The changes have encouraged a dramatic reduction in usage; 16,919 examinations were carried out under Schedule 7 in the year ending September 2017, a fall of 73 per cent since the data were first collected in the year ending September 2012 (61,711 examinations).[86]

A third example of important change as a result of the IRTL's intervention concerns the availability of relocation as a measure under the TPIMs Act. Relocation had been available for the predecessor control orders, but was dropped in 2011 as one of several 'liberalising' measures.[87] However, an alleged effect of the change was that the administrative measure had been grievously weakened so that it was no longer worthwhile to issue any more orders. Thus, reporting in early 2014, when only two TPIMs were in force, and no new TPIMs had been imposed since October 2012, the Joint Committee on Human Rights assessed that 'TPIMs may be withering on the vine as a counter-terrorism tool of practical utility.'[88] The IRTL was invited to take a special look at the files and recommended the restoration of relocation, albeit in a setting which applied more searching judicial scrutiny.[89] These changes were duly made by the Counter-Terrorism and Security Act 2015,[90] and new TPIMs have begun to be issued.

These examples of successes are more than 'negligible'[91] but do not represent the balance sheet as a whole. Rather, most recommendations are not implemented in the government's reply papers,[92] and some proposals have been rejected repeatedly and rather summarily. Three such instances might again be cited. One concerns the definition of terrorism, as set out in the TA 2000,[93] the breadth of which has long been highly controversial.[94] A review by Lord Carlile in 2007[95] did result in some minor changes in the Counter-Terrorism Act 2008,[96] but most of the further reforms suggested by David Anderson have not been endorsed.[97] The cherry-picking of ideas which correspond to those of the government is perhaps to be expected, but should be explained rather more than is the current practice. The second impasse has concerned the argument that the police should have powers to release on bail detainees held under section 41 of the TA 2000.[98] In its absence, detention is arguably longer than necessary and the police are resorting to alternative powers (under the Police and Criminal Evidence Act 1984) where police bail is available but where the special safeguards for the treatment of terrorist suspects are not applied.[99] A third instance of an impasse concerns the IRTL's repeated proposals for reform of the processes relating to the proscription of terrorist organizations, especially the need for formal regular review.[100] The government retort that it wishes to maintain a 'cautious' approach is not based on any detailed arguments.[101]

The foregoing illustrations, whether positive or negative, primarily relate to the reactions to the IRTL by the executive branch of the state. To complete the survey, the operation of the IRTL should be spied through the prism of both the courts and Parliament.

Regarding the courts, around three dozen cases have cited work by the IRTL, always with approbation. Three important examples which were heard in the UK Supreme Court were: *R (Gillan) v Commissioner of Police for the Metropolis* (stop and search powers),[102] *R v Gul* (definition of terrorism)[103] and *Beghal v Director of Public Prosecutions* (port controls).[104]

Parliament has a more uneven relationship with the IRTL. On the one hand, reports are often cited as authoritative sources in debates, and personal testimony before select and standing legislative committees is frequently invited and prominently cited. On the other hand, routine statutory-based review has been reduced, with no annual debate under the TA 2000 or the TPIM Act 2011,[105] and so the influence has arguably declined.[106] Parliament can be more easily persuaded to follow eye-catching issues rather than engage in more painstaking scrutiny. An example might be the failure to engage with the foregoing three negative responses to long-standing IRTL recommendations, including the review of proscription processes, whereas the extension of the proscription of Hezbollah can trigger a forlorn debate.[107] This example illustrates that, in a parliamentary system, much depends on content and timing. The parliamentary response could be strengthened if one of the specialist select committees in Parliament were designated to act as default chief correspondent to the IRTL.[108] However, the critics of government, whether independent reviewers or parliamentary committees, must not expect to be dealt trump cards, but must maximize policy engagement as a value in itself even if uncertain in terms of ultimate outcome. That most reports have been at most times supportive of the legislation and its implementation should not alone be a reason for denunciation provided worthwhile information and explanations are furnished and opportunities for further debate and challenge then arise.

Conclusion

The IRTL represents a strong model which has won admirers elsewhere, especially in Australia and Canada.[109] Thus, the notion of an independent expert assessor adds value to the other devices of accountability. The IRTL can counter the self-serving partiality and secrecy of the executive, the politically driven partisanship, short attention span and limited investigative powers of the legislature, and the reactive and individualistic remit of the courts. In this way, independent assessment has been enhanced by the IRTL. Less clear is whether balancing of civil liberties has been so successfully handled. Perhaps it is more productive to view the task as ultimately one of good governance in which the wider values to be secured are the rule of law, through clarity and accountability, and effectiveness, through strategic clarity, innovation and good design, as well as rights observance. This richer diet of objectives might help to secure a wider form of policy balance and to detoxify some of the arguments, beloved of tabloid newspapers, based on a perception of undue attention to liberties. In so far as the IRTL can present to government a more expert resolution to problems involving liberties, then the office will represent a valuable adjunct to the legitimacy of counter-terrorism in the UK.

Notes

1 See especially UNSCR 1373 of 28 September 2001, 1624 of 14 September 2005, 2178 of 24 September 2014; Council of Europe Convention on the Prevention of Terrorism (CETS 196, 2005) and Additional Protocol (CETS 217, 2015); European Union Framework Directive on Combating Terrorism (2002/475/JHA) and amending decision (2008/919/JHA), as replaced by Directive (EU) 2017/541 of the European Parliament and of the Council of 15 March 2017 on combating terrorism.

2 See J. Waldron., 'Security and Liberty: The Image of Balance', *Journal of Political Philosophy*, vol. 11, no. 2, 2003, p. 191; L. Zedner, 'Securing Liberty in the Face of Terror', *Journal of Law & Society*, vol. 32, no. 4, 2005, p. 507; K. Roach, 'Must We Trade Rights for Security?', *Cardozo Law Review*, vol. 27, 2006, p. 2157; R. A. Posner, *Not a Suicide Pact*, New York: Oxford University Press, 2006; L. K. Donohue, *The Cost of Counterterrorism*, Cambridge: Cambridge University Press, 2007; T. Meisels, *The Trouble with Terror*, Cambridge: Cambridge University Press, 2008; C. Gearty, *Liberty and Security*, Cambridge: Polity, 2013; H. Duffy, *The 'War on Terror' and the Framework of International Law*, 2nd edn., Cambridge: Cambridge University Press, 2015; P. Sands, *Lawless World: Making and Breaking Global Rules*, 3rd edn., Harmondsworth: Penguin, 2016.

3 See HMSO, *Report of an Enquiry into Allegations against the Security Forces of Physical Brutality in Northern Ireland Arising out of Arrests on the 9 August 1971*, London, Cmnd.4828, 1972; HMSO, *Report of the Committee of Privy Counsellors Appointed to Consider Authorised Procedures for the Interrogation of Persons Suspected of Terrorism*, London, Cmnd.4901, 1972; HMSO, *Report of the Committee of Inquiry into Police Interrogation Procedures in Northern Ireland*, London, Cmnd.7497, 1979; *Ireland v United Kingdom* App no 5310/71, Ser A 25, 1978.

4 Sir W. Gage, *Report of the Baha Mousa Inquiry*, 2010–2012 HC, p. 1452; United States Senate Select Committee on Intelligence, *Committee Study of the Central Intelligence Agency's Detention and Interrogation Program*, Washington DC, 2014.

5 See A. Ashworth, 'Security, Terrorism and the Value of Human Rights', in B. Goold and L. Lazarus (eds.), *Security and Human Rights*, Oxford: Hart, 2007, pp. 209–210; J. Mueller, and M. G. Stewart, *Terror, Security, and Money: Balancing the Risks, Benefits, and Costs of Homeland Security*, New York: Oxford University Press, 2011.

6 See E. A. Posner and A. Vermeule, *Terror in the Balance*, New York: Oxford University Press, 2007; J. H. Marks, '9/11 + 3/11 + 7/7 =? What Counts in Counterterrorism?', *Columbia Human Rights Law Review*, vol. 37, no. 3, 2006, p. 559; C.R. Sunstein, *Worst-Case Scenarios*, Cambridge: Harvard University Press, 2007.

7 See *McCann v United Kingdom*, App. no.18984/91, Ser.A vol.324, 1995; *Tagayeva v. Russia*, App. no.26562/07, 13 April 2017.

8 See European Convention on Human Rights 1950 (CETS 4) arts 3, 5, 6, 8–10.

9 See UN Special Rapporteur on the promotion and protection of human rights and fundamental freedoms while countering terrorism (UN Commission on Human Rights, Resolution 2005/80).

10 See A. Horne and C. Walker, 'Parliament and National Security' in A. Horne and A. Le Sueur, (eds.), *Parliament: Legislation and Accountability*, Oxford: Hart, 2016.

11 See C. Walker, 'Counter-Terrorism and Human Rights in the UK', in M. Breen-Smyth, (eds.), *Ashgate Companion to Political Violence*, Abingdon: Ashgate, 2012.

12 Formerly the National Council for Civil Liberties. Output began with the National Council for Civil Liberties, *Special Powers Acts of Northern Ireland: A Review of the 1936 N.C.C.L. Commission of Inquiry in the Light of Subsequent Events*, London: National Council for Civil Liberties, 1972. See also https://www.liberty-human-rights.org.uk/human-rights/countering-terrorism.

13 See https://caj.org.uk/about/.

14 Hansard (House of Commons) vol.882 col.743 25 November 1974, Roy Jenkins.

15 The original period was six months (PTA 1974, s.12), but it became twelve months under the PTA 1976, s.17.

16 Baron Edward Shackleton, *Review of the Operation of the Prevention of Terrorism (Temporary Provisions) Acts 1974 and 1976*, Cmnd 7324, London: HM Stationery Office, 1978.

17 Earl Jellicoe, *Report of the Operation of the Prevention of Terrorism (Temporary Provisions) Acts 1976*, Cmnd 8803, London: HM Stationery Office, 1983.

18 *Review of the Operation of the Prevention of Terrorism (Temporary Provisions) Act 1984*, Cm 264, London: 1987.

19 *Report of a Committee to Consider, in the Context of Civil Liberties and Human Rights, Measures to Deal with Terrorism in Northern Ireland,* Cmnd.5847, London, 1975.

20 *Review of the Operation of the Northern Ireland (Emergency Provisions) Act 1978,* Cmnd.9222, London, 1984.

21 *Review of the Northern Ireland (Emergency Provisions) Act 1991*, Cm.2706, London, 1995.

22 Though it has no specific remit, review was also undertaken by the Standing Advisory Commission on Human Rights (see *Northern Ireland Constitution Act 1973*, s.20). The Northern Ireland Human Rights Commission (*Northern Ireland Act 1998*, s.68) now performs this role.

23 *Report of the Operation of the Prevention of Terrorism (Temporary Provisions) Act 1976*, para.14. See further para.17.

24 The reviewers were Sir Cyril Philips (1984–85), Viscount Colville (1986–1992), and John Rowe (1993–2000).

25 Hansard (House of Lords) vol.449 on 8 March 1984, Lord Elton.

26 *Inquiry into Legislation against Terrorism*, Cm.3420, London, 1996; Home Office and Northern Ireland Office, *Legislation against Terrorism*, Cm.4178, London, 1998.

27 *Inquiry into Legislation against Terrorism*, Cm.3420, London, 1996. Para. 1.20, 17.6.

28 *Inquiry into Legislation against Terrorism*, para.3.1.

29 *Privy Counsellor Review Committee, Anti-Terrorism, Crime and Security Act 2001 Review Report*, 2003–04 HC 100; Home Office, *Counter-Terrorism Powers: Reconciling Security and Liberty in an Open Society*, Cm.6147, London, 2004.

30 K. Macdonald, *Review of Counter-Terrorism and Security Powers*, Cm.8003, London, 2011; Home Office, *Review of Counter-Terrorism and Security Powers: Review Findings and Recommendations*, Cm.8004, London, 2011.

31 Pt.VII of the Act, relating to Northern Ireland, was not permanent and so required special review which was undertaken by Lord Carlile. Pt.VII was replaced by the Justice and Security (Northern Ireland) Act 2007, and has in turn been reviewed by Robert Whalley (2007–2013) and David Seymour (2013-).

32 See further J. Blackbourn, 'Evaluating the Independent Reviewer of Terrorism Legislation', *Parliamentary Affairs*, vol. 65, 2012, p. 1; C. Walker, *The Anti-Terrorism Legislation*, 3rd edn, Oxford: Oxford University Press, 2014, chap. 10; J. Blackbourn, 'Evaluating the Independent Reviewer of Terrorism Legislation', *Parliamentary Affairs*, vol. 67, no. 4, 2014, p. 955; J. Blackbourn, 'Anti-Terrorism Review Reform', *Oxford Human Rights Hub*, 8 August 2014; D. Anderson, 'The Independent Review of Terrorism Laws', *Public Law*, 2014, p. 403; D. Anderson, 'The Independent Review of UK Terrorism Law', *New Journal of European Criminal Law*, vol. 5, 2014, p. 432; See also https://terrorismlegislationreviewer.independent.gov.uk/history/.

33 *Terrorism Act 2000*, s.126.

34 Hansard (HC) Standing Committee D, col 312 (8 February 2000), Charles Clarke.

35 *Terrorism Act 2006*, s.36.

36 But see *Protection of Freedoms Act 2012*, s.115(1), Sch.9, para.32(b).

37 A. Carlile, Conference on the Regulation of Criminal Justice, Manchester, 9 April 2008.

38 *Terrorism Prevention and Investigation Measures Act 2011*, s.20.

39 *Terrorist Asset Freezing etc Act 2010*, s.31.

40 HL 78.

41 *Coroners and Justice Act 2009*, s.117.

42 See SI 2012/1810.

43 *Protection of Freedoms Act 2012*, s.58(3).

44 See C. Walker, 'The Governance Of Emergency Arrangements', *International Journal of Human Rights*, vol. 18, no. 2, 2014, p. 211.

45 *Justice and Security (Northern Ireland) Act 2007*, s.40.

46 Home Office, *Counter-Terrorism and Security Act 2015*, s.44.

47 See D. Anderson, *Report on the Operation in 2011 of the Terrorism Act 2000 and Part I of the Terrorism Act 2006*, London: Home Office, 2012, para.1.34 and Home Office, Letter of 12 March 2013 p. 1.

48 Home Office, *Counter-Terrorism and Security Act 2015* ss.44–45.

49 D. Anderson, *Report on the Operation in 2014 of the Terrorism Act 2000 and Part I of the Terrorism Act 2006*, London: Home Office, 2015, para.11.28.

50 In his final report on the Terrorism Acts in 2015, Anderson recalled his 'past suggestion that the Independent Reviewer (like the Reviewer's Australian counterpart, the Independent National Security Legislation Monitor) should be empowered to review not only laws directed specifically to terrorism but to "*any other law to the extent that it relates to counter-terrorism*"' (emphasis in original). D. Anderson, *Report on the Operation in 2015 of the Terrorism Act 2000 and Part I of the Terrorism Act 2006*, London: Home Office, 2016, para.1.14.

51 This possibility is expressly recognized under the *Justice and Security (Northern Ireland) Act 2007*, s.40(3).

52 See A. Carlile, *Proposals by Her Majesty's Government for Changes to the Laws against Terrorism*, London: Home Office, 2005; A. Carlile, *Report on Proposed Measures for Inclusion in a Counter-Terrorism Bill*, London, Cm 7262, 2007; Supplementary Memorandum to the Joint Committee on Human Rights, *The Justice and Security Green Paper*, 2010–12 HL 286/HC 1777, JS12A.

53 A. Carlile, *The Definition of Terrorism*, London, Cm.7052, 2007 and Government Reply, Cm.7058, London, 2007.

54 A. Carlile, *Operation Pathway*, London: Home Office, 2009; D. Anderson, *Operation Gird*, London: Home Office, 2011.

55 A. Carlile, *Report to the Home Secretary of Independent Oversight of Prevent Review and Strategy*, London: Home Office, 2011.

56 D. Anderson, *Attacks in London and Manchester, March–June 2017: Independent Assessment of MI5 and Police Internal Reviews*, London: Home Office, 2017.

57 D. Anderson, *A Question of Trust: Report of the Investigatory Powers Review*, London: Home Office, 2015 (commissioned under the *Data Retention and Investigatory Powers Act 2014*, s.7); *Report of the Bulk Powers Review*, Cm.9326, London, 2016.

58 D. Anderson and C. Walker, *Deportation with Assurances*, Cm.9462, London, 2017.

59 D. Anderson, *Citizenship Removal Resulting in Statelessness*, London: Home Office, 2016.

60 Lord Alex Carlile QC (2001–2011); David Anderson QC (2011–2017); Max Hill QC (2017–2018); Jonathan Hall QC (2019–). The Northern Ireland reviewers have been retired civil servants: Robert Whalley (2007–13); David Seymour (2013-).

61 Anderson, *Report on the Operation in 2014 of the Terrorism Act 2000 and Part I of the Terrorism Act 2006*, paras.10.2–5, 11.32; Anderson, *Report on the Operation in 2015 of the Terrorism Act 2000 and Part I of the Terrorism Act 2006*, para.1.7.

62 Home Office, *Counter-Terrorism and Security Act 2015*, s.46.

63 *Intelligence Reform and Terrorism Prevention Act of 2004* (PL 108–408). See G. Hatch, *Privacy and Civil Liberties Oversight Board: New Independent Agency Status*, RL34385 7–5700, Congressional Research Service, Washington DC, 2012); M. Schlanger, 'Intelligence legalism and the National Security Agency's Civil Liberties Gap', *Harvard National Security Journal*, vol. 6, 2015, p. 112. See also Joint Committee on Human Rights, *Counter–Terrorism Policy and Human Rights (Seventeenth Report): Bringing Human Rights Back In*, 2009–10 HL 86/HC 111, para. 116, 117.

64 Anderson, *Report on the Operation in 2014 of the Terrorism Act 2000 and Part I of the Terrorism Act 2006*, para.10.13.

65 Anderson, *Report on the Operation in 2014 of the Terrorism Act 2000 and Part I of the Terrorism Act 2006*, para.11.34.

66 One notice was issued in 2013 to the Secretary of the Department of Foreign Affairs and Trade regarding applications for revocations of sanctions listings under the *Charter of the United Nations Act 1945* (Cth): Independent National Security Legislation Monitor, *Annual Report 7th November 2013* (Canberra, 2013) p.30.

67 See A. Lynch and N. McGarrity, 'A "watchdog" of Australia's Counter-Terrorism Laws', *Flinders Journal of Law Reform*, vol. 12, 2010, p. 83; J. Blackbourn, 'The Independent National Security Legislation Monitor's first term: an appraisal', *University of New South Wales Law Journal*, vol. 39, 2016, p. 975; B. Walker, 'Reflections of a former Independent National Security Legislation Monitor', *AIAL Forum*, no. 84, 2016, p. 74.

68 Bret Walker SC (21 April 2011 to 20 April 2014); Hon Roger Gyles AO QC (20 August 2015 to 31 October 2016); Dr James Renwick SC (24 February 2017-present). For their outputs, see https://www.law.ox.ac.uk/research-and-subject-groups/counter-terrorism-review/australian-counter-terrorism-review.

69 See Independent National Security Legislation Monitor Repeal Bill 2014 (https://www.aph.gov.au/Parliamentary_Business/Bills_Legislation/Bills_Search_Results/Result?bId=r5189).

70 For other views, see Home Office, *Consultation on establishing a UK Privacy and Civil Liberties Board*, London: Home Office, 2014; House of Lords Select Committee on the Constitution, Counter-Terrorism and Security Bill, 2014–15 HL 92, paras.1–6; Joint Committee on Human Rights, *Legislative Scrutiny: Counter-Terrorism and Security Bill*, 2014–15 HL 86/HC 859, Pt.7; Home Office, *Counter-Terrorism and Security Act 2015 – Privacy and Civil Liberties Board – Royal Assent: Impact Assessment*, IA No: HO0149, London, 2015.

71 See Home Office, *Countering International Terrorism*, Cm.6888, London, 2006.

72 Critics have exploited this necessary aspect of the office: T. Shipman and R. Kerbaj, 'Watchdog offers to meet Islamists; Reviewer contacts group that called "Jihadi John" beautiful', *Sunday Times*, 3 September 2017, p. 2.

73 D. Anderson, 'The Independent Review of Terrorism Legislation', *European Human Rights Law Review*, vol. 5, 2011, p. 547.

74 *Investigatory Powers Act 2016*, s.227.

75 *Investigatory Powers Act 2016*, s.235.

76 Cabinet Office Public Bodies Reform Team, *Functional Review of Bodies Providing Expert Advice to Government*, London, 2017: 'Independence is key to delivering the value that departments derive from their advisory bodies'. (para.2.4).

77 Home Office, *Independent Reviewer of Terrorism Legislation Recruitment Information Pack*, August 2016. Anderson described his method of appointment 'intriguing, if indefensible'. D. Anderson, 'The independent review of UK terrorism law', *New Journal of European Criminal Law*, vol. 5, no. 432, 2014, pp. 434–435.

78 See H. Cole, 'Let Teen Jihadis Go Free; QC: Brits Naive; Shock Call by Watchdog', *The Sun*, 20 October 2017 p. 12. The journalists do not cite the detailed arguments in Anderson, *Report on the Operation in 2015 of the Terrorism Act 2000 and Part I of the Terrorism Act 2006*, Annex 2.

79 A. Carlile, *Operation Pathway*, London: Home Office, 2009, paras 48–51, 76, 91.

80 [2010] EWHC 1859 (Admin).

81 Anderson, *Report on the Operation in 2011 of the Terrorism Act 2000 and Part I of the Terrorism Act 2006*, para.7.56; Lord Advocate's Guidelines on: The extension of detention of persons arrested under section 41 and Schedule 8 of the Terrorism Act 2000 and post-charge questioning under section 23 of the Counter-Terrorism Act 2008 (2012).

82 *Re Duffy* [2009] NIQB 31, para.26.

83 See *Magee v UK*, App. no.26289/12, 12 October 2015; *Sher v UK*, App. no.5201/11, 20 October 2015.

84 See Anderson, *Report on the Operation in 2011 of the Terrorism Act 2000 and Part I of the Terrorism Act 2006*, chap. 9; D. Anderson, *Report on the Operation in 2012 of the Terrorism Act 2000 and Part I of the Terrorism Act 2006*, London: Home Office, 2013, chap. 10.

85 *Anti-Social Behaviour, Crime and Police Act 2014*, s.148 and Sch.9.

86 Home Office, *Operation of Police Powers under the Terrorism Act 2000 and Subsequent Legislation: Arrests, Outcomes, and Stop and Search, Great Britain, Quarterly Update to September 2017*, Statistical Bulletin 24/17, 2017, p. 20.

87 See Walker, *The Anti-Terrorism Legislation*, chap. 7.

88 Joint Committee on Human Rights, *Post-Legislative Scrutiny: Terrorism Prevention and Investigation Measures Act 2011* (2013–14 HL113\HC 1014), p. 25.

89 D. Anderson, *Terrorism Prevention and Investigation Measures in 2014: Third Report of the Independent Reviewer on the Operation of the Terrorism Prevention and Investigation Measures 2011*, London: HM Stationery Office, 2015, para.3.15.

90 Home Office, *Counter-Terrorism and Security Act 2015*, s.16,

91 Blackbourn, 'Evaluating the Independent Reviewer of Terrorism Legislation', p. 10.

92 For the most recent, see Home Office, *The Government Response to the Report by David Anderson on Terrorism Prevention and Investigation Measures in 2014*, Cm.9041, London, 2015; HM Treasury, *Operation of the Terrorist Asset-Freezing Etc. Act 2010: Response to the Independent Reviewer's Fourth Report* Cm.9118, London, 2015; Home Office, *The Government Response to the Annual Report on the Operation of the Terrorism Acts in 2015 by* the Independent Reviewer of Terrorism Legislation, Cm.9489, London, 2017.

93 *Terrorism Act 2000*, s.1.

94 See Walker, *The Anti-Terrorism Legislation*, chap. 1.

95 Carlile, *The Definition of Terrorism.*

96 *Counter-Terrorism Act 2008*, s.75.

97 Anderson, *Report on the Operation in 2015 of the Terrorism Act 2000 and Part I of the Terrorism Act 2006*, para.4.2. The exception is the *Counter-Terrorism and Security Act 2015*, s.20(2).

98 Anderson, *Report on the Operation in 2011 of the Terrorism Act 2000 and Part I of the Terrorism Act 2006*, paras.7.71–7.73 and 12.15; D. Anderson, *Report on the Operation in 2013 of the Terrorism Act 2000 and Part I of the Terrorism Act 2006*, paras.8.31–8.32; Anderson, *Report on the Operation in 2015 of the Terrorism Act 2000 and Part I of the Terrorism Act 2006*, paras.8.52–8.55.

99 See PACE Code H in connection with the Detention, Treatment and Questioning by Police Officers of Persons under Section 41 of, and Schedule 8 to, the Terrorism Act 2000, available here:

https://www.gov.uk/guidance/police-and-criminal-evidence-act-1984-pace-codes-of-practice.

100 See M. Wall, *Report on the Operation in 2016 of the Terrorism Act 2000 and Part I of the Terrorism Act 2006*, London: Home Office, 2018, Annex 2.

101 See *Government's Response to the Annual Report on the Operation of the Terrorism Acts in 2014 by the Independent Reviewer of Terrorism Legislation*, Cm.9357, London, 2016, p. 3; Home office, *Government Response to the Annual Report on the Operation of the Terrorism Acts in 2015 by the Independent Reviewer of Terrorism Legislation*, p. 3.

102 [2006] UKHL 12, para.79. The IRTL was also referred to by the European Court of Human Rights: *Gillan and Quinton v United Kingdom*, App no 4158/05, 12 January 2010, para.37.

103 [2013] UKSC 64, paras.31–35.

104 [2015] UKSC 49 paras.19–26.

105 But the Independent Reviewer's negotiations with the Joint Committee on Human Rights helped to prompt a review of TPIMs in 2013: *Post-Legislative Scrutiny: Terrorism Prevention and Investigation Measures Act 2011* (2013–14 HL113\HC 1014).

106 See A. Horne and C. Walker, 'Lessons Learned From Political Constitutionalism? Comparing the Enactment of Control Orders and Terrorism Prevention And Investigation Measures by the Uk Parliament', *Public Law*, 2014, p. 267.

107 See Hansard (House of Commons) vol. 635 col.478 25 January 2018.

108 See Joint Committee on Human Rights, *Terrorism Policy and Human Rights: Annual Review of Control Orders Legislation 2008*, 2007–08 HL 57/HC 356, para 33;

A. Carlile, *Report on the Operation in 2009 of the Terrorism Act 2000 and Part I of the Terrorism Act 2006*, London: Home Office, 2010, para 13.

109 See (Australia) *Independent National Security Legislation Monitor Act 2010*; (Canada) C. Forcese and K. Roach, *False Security*, Toronto: Irwin, 2015, p. 417.

Recommended Readings

Anderson, D., 'The Independent Review of Terrorism Legislation', *European Human Rights Law Review*, vol.5, 2011 p. 547.

Anderson, D., *Operation Gird*, London: Home Office, 2011.

Anderson, D., 'The Independent Review of UK Terrorism Law', *New Journal of European Criminal Law*, vol. 5, 2014 p. 432.

Anderson, D., 'The Independent Review of Terrorism Laws', *Public Law*, 2014 p. 403.

Anderson, D., *A Question of Trust: Report of the Investigatory Powers Review*, London: Home Office, 2015.

Anderson, D., *Citizenship Removal Resulting in Statelessness*, London: Home Office, 2016.

Anderson, D., *Attacks in London and Manchester, March–June 2017: independent assessment of MI5 and police internal reviews*, London: Home Office, 2017.

Anderson, D. and Walker, C., *Deportation with Assurances*, Cm.9462, London: Home Office, 2017.

Baker Report, *Review of the Operation of the Northern Ireland (Emergency Provisions) Act 1978*, Cmnd.9222, London: HM Stationery Office, 1984.

Bennett Report, *Report of the Committee of Inquiry into Police Interrogation Procedures in Northern Ireland*, Cmnd.7497, London: HM Stationery Office, 1979.

Blackbourn, J., 'Evaluating the Independent Reviewer of Terrorism Legislation', *Parliamentary Affairs*, vol. 65, 2012 p. 1.

Blackbourn, J., 'Evaluating the Independent Reviewer of Terrorism Legislation', *Parliamentary Affairs*, vol. 67, 2014, p. 995.

Blackbourn, J., 'The Independent National Security Legislation Monitor's First Term: An Appraisal', *University of New South Wales Law Journal*, vol. 39, 2016 p. 975.

Carlile, A., *Proposals by Her Majesty's Government for Changes to the Laws against Terrorism*, London: Home Office, 2005.

Carlile, A., *Report on Proposed Measures for Inclusion in a Counter-Terrorism Bill*, Cm. 7262, London: Home Office, 2007.

Carlile, A., *The Definition of Terrorism*, Cm.7052, London, 2007; and Government Reply, Cm.7058, London, 2007.

Carlile, A., *Operation Pathway*, London: Home Office, 2009.

Carlile, A., *Report to the Home Secretary of Independent Oversight of Prevent Review and Strategy*, London: Home Office, 2011.

Colville Report, *Review of the Operation of the Prevention of Terrorism (Temporary Provisions) Act 1984*, Cm 264, London, 1987.

Coroners and Justice Act 2009, section 117.

Counter-Terrorism and Security Act, 2015, sections 44–45, https://terrorismlegislationreviewer.independent.gov.uk/(IRTL website and reports).

Gardiner Report, *Report of a Committee to Consider, in the Context of Civil liberties and Human Rights, Measures to Deal with Terrorism in Northern Ireland*, Cmnd.5847, London, 1975.

Hatch, G., *Privacy and Civil Liberties Oversight Board: New Independent Agency Status*, RL34385 7-5700, Washington DC: Congressional Research Service, 2012.

that emphasized partnering by government with Muslim communities and local capacity-building to tackle the causes of violent extremism. It was based on four key strands: 'promoting shared values, supporting local solutions, building civic capacity and leadership and strengthening the role of faith institutions and leaders'.[7] To achieve these objectives, the 2007 policy placed particular emphasis on the role of local authorities in implementing Prevent.

That approach was much criticized. In particular, many were critical of the model of community engagement that was developed under Prevent: some feared its purpose was to enable the surveillance of Muslim communities due to perceived overlaps between Prevent and Pursue,[8] whilst others were concerned that engagement with Muslim communities through Prevent meant that when government did engage with Muslims it was as suspects rather than as citizens.[9]

Despite these criticisms and notwithstanding the limitations of conducting community engagement through a counter-terrorism rubric, in some places innovative and sometimes effective forms of engagement with Muslim communities were put in place by local authorities.[10] This was due in large part to the relative autonomy that local authorities had in that period to determine how they implemented Prevent in their areas.

Prevent 2011–2018: Centralization and conceptual and operational expansion

When the Coalition government came into power in 2010 it announced a review of Prevent. The revised strategy that was published in 2011[11] marked some significant changes, including a more centralized approach – to address what government saw as inconsistencies in the local implementation of Prevent (inconsistencies that had also generated some positive initiatives that were sensitive to local contexts) and with less and more tightly and centrally controlled funding (which also reduced the leeway for local authorities to shape the implementation of Prevent). The revised strategy saw a shift away from an emphasis on Muslim community engagement to a focus on seeking to mobilize front-line personnel in public sector institutions to spot and report on signs of radicalization – such that, in the words of the Prevent strategy: 'there should be no ungoverned spaces'.[12] Significantly, the 2011 strategy set out an explicit aim to tackle *all* forms of extremism – to include not just Islamist, but also right-wing, extremism. More controversially, the new approach shifted the focus of Prevent from preventing violent extremism to countering extremism more broadly defined as opposition to 'fundamental British values', which the 2011 Prevent strategy specified as 'democracy, the rule of law, individual liberty and mutual respect and tolerance of different faiths and beliefs'.[13] The 2011 Prevent strategy also included in the definition of extremism 'calls for the death of members of our armed forces, whether in this country or overseas'.

remit of the Counter-Extremism Community Coordinators from that of Prevent Coordinators, although both are managed by the Home Office.

In June 2018, a new CONTEST strategy document was released, setting out some critical updates to Prevent. Significantly, in the 2018 document there is a more explicit account of the overlap between Prevent and Pursue: thus, it states the 'links between the Prevent and Pursue work strands are particularly important'[25] (marking a shift from previous attempts to maintain that Prevent and Pursue are entirely separate[26]). This overlap is signalled particularly by the introduction to Prevent of work to rehabilitate and reintegrate those who have already been involved in terrorism (the Desist and Disengage Programme) – which moves Prevent from its previously largely pre-emptive, 'pre-crime' focus. The 2018 strategy iterated the claim that Counter-Extremism work is distinct and separate from Prevent and expressed government's wish to 'Build stronger partnerships with communities, civil society groups, public sector institutions and industry to improve Prevent delivery'.[27] The latter aim may have been influenced by charges that Prevent has since 2011 become too centralized and disconnected from local communities.[28] The Contest strategy also sought to defend Prevent from its many critics, claiming government's approach to Prevent is not based on assumptions that there is a conveyor belt to radicalization or that there are any necessary links between mental health and terrorism, and that the Prevent Duty in Higher Education does not undermine the statutory duty on universities to ensure freedom of speech.[29] The strategy continued to advance the view that referrals to Prevent from public agencies should be seen as a form of 'safeguarding'.

...nt challenges for Prevent

...various changes to Prevent that have taken place since 2011, a number ... remain. Prevent and the Counter-Extremism agenda continue to ...gh levels of criticism, particularly in relation to the shift to a more ...s on countering non-violent extremism, the imposition of Prevent ...uty across the public sector and the implications of Prevent and ...ism for Muslim community and civic engagement.

...extremism'

...kling violent extremism to countering extremism, defined as ...mental British values', accompanied by the development of ...owers, and their inclusion as a requirement in the statutory ...ce issued to public sector institutions, has raised concerns ... for civil liberties, given that this definition of extremism ...very wide range of political positions and social beliefs.[30]

The 2011 strategy sought to separate Prevent from integration policies, asserti that – learning from past mistakes – 'Government will not securitize its integra strategy': a separation that has proven harder to implement on the ground.[14] asserted that 'Policy and programmes to deal with extremism and with ex organizations more widely are not part of Prevent and will be coordina the Department for Communities and Local Government (DCLG)'.[15] Home Office does manage both Prevent and Counter-Extremism (and in a more centralized way since 2011[16]). It is difficult to se conceptually, strategically or operationally these agendas do not ov

The 2011 strategy did not seek to make compliance with requirement. That position began to change in the aftermath of t attack and with the establishment of the Task Force on Tack and Extremism (TERFOR), whose recommendations signa of implementation at the local level, with the recommend should introduce legal requirements for local authorities ir Prevent and the Channel programme.[17]

Following the passing of the Counter-Terrorism Prevent was placed on a statutory footing with the Duty across public sector institutions requiring due regard to the need to prevent people from bei was accompanied by the release of statutory and implementation of the Prevent Duty and the training for front-line personnel. Accordin training has been completed over 1 million the Home Office put in place Prevent coord to 50',[20] local Prevent priority areas.

In the same year, government releas It has yet, however, to introduce the C that was announced in the 2015 Extremism Community Coordinat funding aimed at mobilizing com objectives, such as the *Buildin* recently, in March 2018, with Khan, government launched is charged with supporting extremism'. Subsequently, is currently gathering ev government.[23] Govern Counter-Extremism a harms caused by ex radicalized or terr Charter states: 'T including Preve

This is underscored by the difficulties government has encountered in arriving at a legally defensible definition of extremism as a basis for further legislation (and presumably why the legislation promised in 2015 has yet to be introduced). The parliamentary Joint Committee on Human Rights argued in 2016 that the government's definitions of extremism:

> are couched in such general terms that they would be likely to prove unworkable as a legislative definition … It is difficult to arrive at a more focused definition of extremism and it does not appear that the Government so far has been successful in arriving at one. It is far from clear that there is an accepted definition of what constitutes extremism, let alone what legal powers there should be, if any, to combat it.[31]

Consequently, it recommended: 'The Government should not legislate, least of all in areas which impinge on human rights, unless there is a clear gap in the existing legal framework.'[32]

Operational expansion of Prevent and Counter-Extremism

There are ongoing concerns that the requirements of the Prevent Duty are having discriminatory effects[33] and are creating a climate of suspicion around Muslim pupils, students, patients and public sector employees. For instance, a report by Just Yorkshire, *Rethinking Prevent*,[34] argued that the Prevent Duty has created a hostile climate towards Muslims in public sector institutions, whilst a report by the Open Society Justice Initiative, *Eroding Trust*,[35] argued that its application in schools,[36] colleges and healthcare institutions was damaging trust in those institutions and risked violating human rights. Research by Heath-Kelly and Strausz [37] on the operation of Prevent in healthcare found that staff were interpreting signs of radicalization in ways that went beyond the guidance of the Prevent training, to include hate speech, the possession of radical Islamic/Anarchist philosophy and anger at foreign policy – raising concerns that the Prevent Duty is being implemented in ways that are discriminatory or in conflict with civil liberties. In part, this relates to the quality of Prevent training, which has faced ongoing criticisms that it is too superficial, inconsistent, based on a decontextualized reading of radicalization and a check-list approach to vulnerabilities that closes down debate, and that there are insufficient mechanisms for quality control.[38]

The parliamentary Joint Committee on Human Rights noted that creating further legal powers to counter-extremism would likely involve public sector institutions in managing conflicting obligations to uphold rights and freedoms. Indeed, the placing of Prevent on a statutory footing in public sector institutions has given rise to a series of tensions with other sets of professional values in those institutions. The characterization of Prevent as an extension of schools' existing safeguarding duties has been challenged by teaching professionals. The National Union of Teachers (NUT) passed a motion at its annual conference in 2016 calling for the reform of Prevent, arguing that Prevent was not compatible with the understanding of safeguarding among teaching professionals, which emphasizes the need to create safe spaces for children to express views or discuss difficult issues.[39]

The Open Society Justice Initiative report on Prevent was similarly concerned with the ways in which the safeguarding duty in schools is in tension with the requirements of the Prevent duty: 'Although the government describes Prevent as a form of "safeguarding" (…), the two sets of obligations have materially different aims, particularly with respect to children. In contrast to the Prevent strategy, for which the primary objective is preventing terrorism, the primary objective of the duty to safeguard children under domestic legislation is the welfare of the child.'[40] Similarly, Heath-Kelly and Strausz's research found that, in relation to health, the 'positioning of the Prevent Duty as a safeguarding measure is ambiguous. Safeguarding professionals alerted us that they are operating in a "grey area" with Prevent, and that significant differences exist between Prevent Duty safeguarding and normal safeguarding'.[41]

In Higher Education, there has been ongoing debate about the tensions between the Prevent Duty and the requirement that universities protect freedom of speech – which the Prevent Duty is seen to jeopardize.[42] A case heard by the High Court (*Salman Butt v Secretary of State for the Home Department* 2016) sought to challenge the requirement on universities to counter-extremism and resulted in a ruling that countering non-violent extremism does fall within the terms of the Prevent Duty, but only where it is deemed to create 'a risk of being drawn into terrorism'. Thus, the judge ruled: 'The active opposition to fundamental British values must in some respect risk drawing others into terrorism before the guidance applies to it.'[43] Whilst that ruling appears to limit the scope of counter-extremism in universities, this distinction nonetheless is likely to be difficult to maintain in practice.

A further challenge to the more conceptually and operationally expansive nature of Prevent relates to the scale of Prevent referrals. Government has responded to calls for more transparency over Prevent referrals and released annual figures on referrals to Prevent and Channel. These revealed that 6,093 individuals were referred to Prevent in 2016/17. Of these, 36 per cent 'left the process requiring no further action', 45 per cent 'were signposted to alternative services' and 19 per cent 'were deemed suitable, through preliminary assessment, to be discussed at a Channel panel'. This means that the majority (81 per cent) of Prevent referrals do not result in Channel referrals (and of these even fewer referrals go through to 'receive Channel support', which is voluntary).[44] There is a risk in this process that Prevent police are becoming a front-line service for dealing with a range of issues relating to mental ill-health, family breakdown, substance abuse and so on – issues which ought not to be securitized.

Implications for Muslim civic engagement

A significant aspect of the recent revisions to Prevent has been the shift away from the 'hearts and minds' approach of the 2007 policy, which enabled some, especially local-level, engagement between government and Muslims on issues relating to Prevent. More broadly, according to Baroness Sayeeda Warsi, over the last decade, successive governments have been engaged in an 'impractical' and 'counter-productive' 'policy of disengagement' from Muslim communities.[45] Although government has stated its intention to engage with Muslim (and other) communities in relation to Prevent, it has in recent years tended to engage with a narrow range of groups (often counter-extremism ones rather than Muslim civil society organizations), and typically with those that agree with its stance, rather than those that offer critical feedback to it. Consequently, the House of Commons Home Affairs Committee commented that: 'Rather than being seen as the community-led approach Prevent was supposed to be, it is perceived to be a top-down "Big Brother" security operation.'[46] It went on to argue that 'Allaying these concerns and building trust will require full and wide engagement with all sections of the Muslim community, including at grassroots level – and not just with groups which already agree with the Government'. It advocated that 'The focus of the strategy should be around building a real partnership between community groups and the state'. Noting that Muslim communities have shared concerns about radicalization, it suggested that 'If stakeholders buy into such a strategy it can be successful, but unfortunately that is not what is currently happening'.[47]

Perhaps responding to these concerns, the 2018 CONTEST Strategy signalled the aim to 'Build stronger partnerships with communities, civil society groups, public sector institutions and industry to improve Prevent delivery'.[48] However, the emphasis remains on mobilizing such actors for the purpose of delivery rather than creating opportunities for them to shape responses to extremism or radicalization.

Interestingly, the Mayor of Greater Manchester, Andy Burnham, following the Manchester arena attack, and responding to the view that Prevent has become too 'top-down', is pursuing an alternative, regionally led approach that 'commands the confidence of the region's Muslim communities'.[49] To this end he established the Preventing Hateful Extremism and Promoting Social Cohesion Commission in September 2017, which reported in 2018.[50]

Issues to address

Despite various reforms since 2011, Prevent continues to attract controversy. Criticisms of Prevent and Counter-Extremism emanate from a wide range of commentators – and not just from an 'anti-Prevent movement' with a single ideological perspective. Nor are the criticisms of Prevent due to a lack of clarity about its aims – rather they are directed at both the rationale and implementation of Prevent itself. Steps that could address these issues include:

- Establishing an independent review of Prevent and the Counter-Extremism agenda that addresses:
    - the definition of extremism that underpins government's approach to counter-terrorism;
    - the impact of Prevent and Counter-Extremism policies on equalities and civil liberties;
    - the remit of Prevent and Counter-Extremism policies, paying attention to the implications of overlap between these and other policy areas (such as integration);
    - the implications of Prevent and Counter-Extremism policies on Muslim civic engagement.
- Addressing the centralization of Prevent by developing more locally driven and sensitive approaches, which permit local actors to feed into the development of, and give critical feedback to, counter-radicalization policy. This would need to go beyond simply mobilizing local and civil society actors for the purposes of implementation.
- Developing mechanisms for state engagement with Muslim communities at national and local levels, and with a wide range of (including critical) groups and voices. Such engagement, furthermore, should go beyond a narrow focus on the needs of the Prevent agenda: a broader approach to engagement is likely to be beneficial to counter-radicalization, but will achieve more by not being subsumed by Prevent.

Notes

1 See for example: K. Khan, *Preventing Violent Extremism (PVE) & Prevent: A Response from the Muslim Community*, Brent: An-Nisa Society, 2009; MCB, *The Impact of Prevent on Muslim Communities*, London: Muslim Council of Britain, 2016.

2 See for example: C. Heath-Kelly, 'The Geography of Pre-Criminal Space: Epidemiological Imaginations of Radicalisation Risk in the UK Prevent Strategy, 2007–2017', *Critical Studies on Terrorism*, vol. 10, no. 2, 2017, pp. 297–319; P. Thomas, 'Youth, Terrorism and Education: Britain's Prevent Programme'. *International Journal of Lifelong Education*, vol. 35, no. 2, 2016, pp. 171–187; C. Husband and Y. Alam, *Social Cohesion and Counter-Terrorism: A Policy Contradiction?* Bristol: Policy Press, 2011.

3 See for example: A. Kundnani, *Spooked! How Not to Prevent Violent Extremism*, London: Institute of Race Relations, 2009; Rights Watch, *Preventing Education? Human Rights and UK Counter-Terrorism Policy in Schools*, London: Rights Watch UK, 2016.

4 See for example: *UCU and NASUWT Statement on the Counter-Terrorism and Security Act 2015*: https://www.ucu.org.uk/counterterrorismact.

5 A former senior metropolitan police officer, Dal Babu, described Prevent as a 'toxic brand' that is widely mistrusted: *The Independent*, 9 March 2015. The former independent reviewer of the government's counter-terrorism legislation, David Anderson QC, argued that 'Prevent is controversial, to the point where reputable community organisations refuse to engage with it' and that it needs significant reform – including more engagement with Muslim communities and independent oversight: *Evening Standard*, 15 February 2017. Following the terrorist attack in Manchester in May 2017, the Greater Manchester Mayor, Andy Burnham, announced his intention to explore an alternative approach to Prevent in Manchester that would address the problem of the lack of 'buy-in at a community grassroots level': *The Guardian*, 22nd June 2017.

6 DCLG, *Preventing Violent Extremism: Winning Hearts and Minds*, London: Department for Communities and Local Government, 2007.

7 DCLG, *Preventing Violent Extremism: Winning Hearts and Minds*, p. 5.

8 A. Kundnani, *Spooked: How Not to Prevent Violent Extremism*, London: Institute of Race Relations, 2009.

9 Y. Birt, 'Promoting Virulent Envy?', *The RUSI Journal*, vol. 154, no. 4, 2009, pp. 52–58; C. Pantazi and S. Pemberton, 'From the "Old" to the "New" Suspect Community: Examining the Impacts of Recent UK Counter-Terrorist Legislation', *British Journal of Criminology*, vol. 49, 2009, pp. 646–666.

10 T. O'Toole, D. Nilsson DeHanas, T. Modood, N. Meer, and S. H. Jones, *Taking Part: Muslim Participation in Contemporary Governance*, Bristol: University of Bristol, 2013; A. Lewicki, T. O'Toole and T. Modood, *Building the Bridge: Muslim Community Engagement in Bristol*, Bristol: University of Bristol, 2014.

11 Home Office, *Prevent Strategy*, London: Home Office, 2011.

12 Home Office, *Prevent Strategy*, p. 9, para 3.39.

13 Home Office, *Prevent Strategy*, p. 107. This definition was then incorporated by the DfE into teaching standards in schools in 2014, although the definition shifted from 'tolerance of different faiths and beliefs' to: 'tolerance of those with different faiths and beliefs'; see DfE, *Promoting fundamental British values as part of SMSC in schools: Departmental advice for maintained schools*, London: Department for Education, 2014, p. 5.

14 T. O'Toole, D. Nilsson DeHanas, and T. Modood, 'Balancing Tolerance, Security and Muslim Engagement in the United Kingdom: The Impact of the Prevent Agenda', *Critical Studies on Terrorism*, vol. 5, no. 3, 2012, 373–389.

15 Home Office, *Prevent Strategy*, p. 6.

16 B. Ganesh, 2015, *Implementing Prevent: From a Community-Led to a Government-Centred Approach: A Consultation for London Assembly and MOPAC*, London: Faith Matters, available here: www.faith-matters.org.

17 See HM Government, *Tackling extremism in the UK December 2013 Report from the Prime Minister's Task Force on Tackling Radicalisation and Extremism*, London: Cabinet Office, 2013.

18 Counter-Terrorism and Security Act (2015) 26:1. The duty was imposed on 'specified authorities' set out in Schedule 6 of the CTSA, which included: local government, criminal justice, education, childcare etc., health and social care and police: http://www.legislation.gov.uk/ukpga/2015/6/contents/enacted.

19 Home Office, *CONTEST: The United Kingdom's Strategy for Countering Terrorism*, London: HM Government, 2018, p. 31. This is not to say necessarily that over 1 million employees have completed the training – rather the training has been completed over 1 million times.

20 HM Government, *Revised Prevent Duty Guidance*, London: HM Government, 2015, p. 5.

21 Cabinet Office, *Queen's Speech 2015,* HM Government, [Transcript], 27 May 2015, available here: https://www.gov.uk/government/speeches/queens-speech-2015.

22 See Home Office: https://www.gov.uk/guidance/building-a-stronger-britain-together.

23 See Home Office, *Commission for Countering Extremism Launches Evidence Drive*, 11 July 2018, available here: https://www.gov.uk/government/news/commission-for-countering-extremism-launches-evidence-drive.

24 Home Office, *Charter for the Commission for Countering Extremism*, London: Home Office, 2018, available here: https://www.gov.uk/government/publications/charter-for-the-commission-for-countering-extremism/charter-for-the-commission-for-countering-extremism.

25 Home Office, *CONTEST*, p. 29.

26 See T. O'Toole, N. Meer, D. Nilsson DeHanas, S.H. Jones, and T. Modood, 'Governing through Prevent? Regulation and Contested Practice in State–Muslim Engagement', *Sociology*, vol. 50, no. 1, 2016, 160–177.

27 Home Office, *CONTEST*, p. 33.

28 See: Home Affairs Committee, *Radicalisation: The Counter-Narrative And Identifying The Tipping Point*, London: House of Commons, 2016, p. 26., para. 11.

29 This is a requirement of universities under Section 43 the Education (No.2) Act 1986.

30 See Home Affairs Committee, *Radicalisation*. And, see Julian Rivers, 'How (not) to Counter Extremism', *University of Bristol Law School Blog*, [Online], 2 July 2018, available here: https://legalresearch.blogs.bris.ac.uk/2018/07/how-not-to-counter-extremism/#more–1156.

31 Joint Committee on Human Rights, *Counter-Extremism: Second Report of Session 2016–17*, London: House of Lords and House of Commons, 2016, pp. 3–4.

32 Joint Committee on Human Rights, *Counter-Extremism*. pp. 3–5.

33 See: Liberty (2017) 'Prevent Duty Must Be Scrapped: LEA Admits Discrimination after Teachers Call Police over Seven-Year-Old Boy's Toy Gun': https://www.libertyhumanrights.org.uk/news/press-releases-and-statements/prevent-duty-must-be-scrapped-lea-admits-discrimination-after.

34 B. Murtuja and W. Tufail, *Rethinking Prevent: A Case for an Alternative Approach*, Rotherham: Just Yorkshire, 2017, available here: http://rethinkingprevent.org.uk/wp-content/uploads/2017/09/Rethinking-Prevent-A-Case-for-an-Alternative-Approach-v1.04.pdf.

35 Open Society Justice Initiative, *Eroding Trust: The UK's Prevent Counter-Extremism Strategy in Health and Education*, New York: Open Society Foundations, 2016, available here: https://www.opensocietyfoundations.org/sites/default/files/eroding-trust-20161017_0.pdf.

36 See also S. Weale, 'Prevent Strategy Stigmatising Muslim pupils, Say Teachers', *The Guardian*, 3rd July 2017, available here: https://www.theguardian.com/uk-news/2017/jul/03/prevent-strategy-anti-radicalisation-stigmatising-muslim-pupils-teachers.

37 C. Heath-Kelly and E. Strausz, 'The Banality of Counterterrorism "after, after 9/11"? : Perspectives on the Prevent Duty from the UK Healthcare Sector', *Critical Studies on Terrorism*, vol. 12, no. 1, 2019, pp. 89–109.

38 See Home Affairs Select Committee, *Radicalisation*, pp. 20–22.

39 Thus, the conference noted that 'The statutory duty placed on schools, colleges and local authorities sits alongside a responsibility to ensure a safe space for children and young people to explore their relationship with the world around them'. NUT Prevent motion 2016: http://schoolsweek.co.uk/nut-prevent-strategy-motion-what-it-actually-says/.

40 Open Society Justice Initiative, *Eroding Trust*, p. 17.

41 Heath-Kelly and Strausz, 'The Banality of Counterterrorism "after, after 9/11"?', pp. 89–109.

42 A. Scott-Baumann, 'Ideology, Utopia and Islam on Campus: How to Free Speech a Little from Its Own Terrors', *Education, Citizenship and Social Justice*, vol. 12, no. 2, 2017, pp. 159–176.

43 Salman Butt v Secretary of State, [2017] EWHC 1930 (Admin) para 30.

44 See Home Office, *Individuals Referred to and Supported through the Prevent Programme, April 2016 to March 2017*, London: Home Office, 2018, available here: file://ads/filestore/SocSci/spais/somtot/Research/Prevent/individuals-referred-supported-prevent-programme-apr2016-mar2017.pdf.

45 S. Warsi, *The Enemy Within: A Tale of Muslim Britain*, Allen Lane, 2017.

46 Home Affairs Select Committee, *Radicalisation*, p. 36, para 11.

47 Home Affairs Select Committee, *Radicalisation*, p. 36, para. 11. And see: Press Association, 'Prevent Programme Lacking Referrals from Muslim Community'. *The Guardian*, [Online], 25 December 2015: https://www.theguardian.com/uk-news/2015/dec/25/prevent-programme-lacking-referrals-from-muslim-community.

48 HM Government, CONTEST, p. 33.

49 See: J. Halliday, 'Andy Burnham Pledges to Replace Prevent Strategy in Manchester', *The Guardian*, [Online], 22 June 2017: https://www.theguardian.com/uk-news/2017/jun/22/prevent-andy-burnham-greater-manchester-muslim-communities.

50 See Greater Manchester Preventing Hateful Extremism and Promoting Social Cohesion Commission, *A Shared Future: A Report of the Greater Manchester Preventing Hateful Extremism and Promoting Social Cohesion Commission*, Greater Manchester Combined Authority, [Online], July 2018, available here: https://www.greatermanchester-ca.gov.uk/media/1170/preventing-hateful-extremism-and-promoting-social-cohesion-report.pdf.

Recommended Readings

Birt, Y., 'Promoting Virulent Envy?', *The RUSI Journal*, vol. 154, no. 4, 2009.

DCLG, *Preventing Violent Extremism: Winning Hearts and Minds*, London: Department for Communities and Local Government, 2007.

DfE, *Promoting Fundamental British Values as Part of SMSC in Schools: Departmental advice for Maintained Schools*, London: Department for Education, 2014.

Ganesh, B., *Implementing Prevent: From a Community-Led to a Government-Centred Approach: A Consultation for London Assembly and MOPAC*, London: Faith Matters, 2015.

Heath-Kelly, C., 'The Geography of Pre-Criminal Space: Epidemiological Imaginations of Radicalisation Risk in the UK Prevent Strategy, 2007–2017', *Critical Studies on Terrorism*, vol. 10, no. 2, 2017, pp. 297–319.

HM Government, *Counter-Terrorism and Security Act*, London: HM Stationary Office, 2015.

HM Government, *Revised Prevent Duty Guidance*, London: HM Government, 2015.

HM Government, *Tackling Extremism in the UK December 2013 Report from the Prime Minister's Task Force on Tackling Radicalisation and Extremism*, London: Cabinet Office, 2013.

Home Affairs Committee, *Radicalisation: The Counter-Narrative and Identifying the Tipping Point*, London: House of Commons, 2016.

Home Office, *Charter for the Commission for Countering Extremism*, London: Home Office, 2018.

Home Office, *CONTEST: The United Kingdom's Strategy for Countering Terrorism*, London: HM Government, 2018.

Home Office, *Individuals Referred to and Supported through the Prevent Programme, April 2016 to March 2017*, London: Home Office, 2018.

Home Office, *Prevent Strategy*, London: Home Office, 2011.

Husband, C. and Y. Alam, *Social Cohesion and Counter-Terrorism: A Policy Contradiction?*, Bristol: Policy Press, 2011.

Joint Committee on Human Rights, *Counter-Extremism: Second Report of Session 2016–17*, London: House of Lords and House of Commons, 2016.

Khan, K., *Preventing Violent Extremism (PVE) & Prevent: A Response from the Muslim Community*, Brent: An-Nisa Society, 2009.

Kundnani, A., *Spooked! How Not to Prevent Violent Extremism*, London: Institute of Race Relations, 2009.

Lewicki, A., T. O'Toole, and T. Modood, *Building the Bridge: Muslim Community Engagement in Bristol*, Bristol: University of Bristol, 2014.

Liberty, 'Prevent Duty Must Be Scrapped: Lea Admits Discrimination after Teachers Call Police over Seven-Year-Old Boy's Toy Gun', Liberty, [online], 27 January 2017.

MCB, *The Impact of Prevent on Muslim Communities*, London: Muslim Council of Britain, 2016.

Murtuja, B. and W. Tufail, *Rethinking Prevent: A Case for an Alternative Approach*, Rotherham: Just Yorkshire, 2017.

Open Society Justice Initiative, *Eroding Trust: The UK's Prevent Counter-Extremism Strategy in Health and Education*, New York: Open Society Foundations, 2016.

O'Toole, T., D. Nilsson DeHanas, T. Modood, N. Meer, and S.H. Jones, *Taking Part: Muslim Participation in Contemporary Governance*, Bristol: University of Bristol, 2013.

O'Toole, T., N. Meer, D. Nilsson DeHanas, S.H. Jones, and T. Modood, 'Governing through Prevent? Regulation and Contested Practice in State–Muslim Engagement', *Sociology*, vol. 50, no. 1, 2016, pp. 160–177.

O'Toole, T., D. Nilsson DeHanas and Tariq Modood, 'Balancing Tolerance, Security and Muslim Engagement in the United Kingdom: The Impact of the Prevent Agenda', *Critical Studies on Terrorism*, vol. 5, no. 3, 2012, pp. 373–389.

Pantazis, C. and S. Pemberton, 'From the 'Old 'to the 'New' Suspect Community: Examining the Impacts of Recent UK Counter-Terrorist Legislation', *British Journal of Criminology*, vol. 49, 2009, pp. 646–666.

Rights Watch, *Preventing Education? Human Rights and UK Counter-Terrorism Policy in Schools*, London: Rights Watch UK, 2016.
Rivers, J., 'How (Not) to Counter Extremism', *University of Bristol Law School Blog*, [Online], 2 July 2018.
Salman Butt v Secretary of State, [2017] EWHC 1930 (Admin) para 30.
Scott-Baumann, A., 'Ideology, Utopia and Islam on Campus: How to Free Speech a Little from Its Own Terrors', *Education, Citizenship and Social Justice*, vol. 12, no. 2, 2017, pp. 159–176.
The Guardian, 'Andy Burnham Pledges to Replace Prevent Strategy in Manchester', *The Guardian*, 22 June 2017.
The Guardian, 'Prevent Programme Lacking Referrals from Muslim Community', *The Guardian*, 25 December 2015.
Thomas, P., 'Youth, Terrorism and Education: Britain's Prevent Programme', *International Journal of Lifelong Education*, vol. 35, no. 2, 2016, pp. 171–187.
Warsi, S., *The Enemy Within: A Tale of Muslim Britain*, London: Allen Lane, 2017.
Weale, S., 'Prevent Strategy Stigmatising Muslim Pupils, Say Teachers', *The Guardian*, 3 July 2017.

23 INTELLIGENCE-LED POLICING AND COUNTER-TERRORISM

Michael Clarke

Introduction

Intelligence-led policing (ILP) is not merely to be judged by its operational effectiveness and its role in helping to prevent and disrupt terrorism. This, to be sure, may be regarded as its primary purpose. But ILP also has to be measured against different objectives that seek to insulate jihadist extremists from their potential bases of support within their own domestic communities. Over the longer run this is a necessary component of operational effectiveness. If the 'Prevent' agenda is primarily intended to address the phenomenon of extremism inside communities directly, intelligence-led policing is also intended to address it indirectly as an associated objective. In this respect it is intended to help build a base for two-way intelligence and information flows between police and community and to help offer individuals and groups within communities some reassurance that they are not isolated, misunderstood or distrusted when they try to put their own weight against violent radicalization. Committed jihadist terrorists and hard-line radicals are unlikely to be persuaded by anything the UK government or the wider British establishment says to them. But they can be contained in the longer term and effectively isolated from their nascent sources of support. This is the most realistic mid-term objective that good intelligence-led policing, in conjunction with a well-developed Prevent agenda – if it is successful, can achieve.

In this respect, certain fundamentals emerge from the present picture. One is that intelligence-led policing is generally well understood in the UK and that the police and security services have become quite well coordinated to pursue this approach over the last quarter of a century, certainly in relation to terrorism. Another, however, is that good coordination is not, in itself, sufficient to ensure that intelligence leads are all well handled as the current jihadist terror challenge evolves to mobilize individuals whose intelligence signature may be very faint or non-existent. And thirdly, there is always the danger that at the community level, where intelligence-led policing either succeeds or fails, the approach may not be as successful as it appears to be at the top – policy – level; or even that it can have negative effects on community relations that have to be set against any operational successes attributed to it. On the first two questions, available evidence is reasonably plentiful and reflects a secure consensus among analysts. On the last question, however, there is little hard evidence and a number of contradictory indicators.

The adoption and organization of intelligence-led policing

Though the UK has always adopted the principle of ILP responses to terrorist campaigns in this country, the process across the UK in relation to policing as a whole, with the notable exception of Northern Ireland, was generally uneven until the mid-1990s. A spike in crimes against property and automobiles in the late 1980s, and the need for greater economy in policing, led the Audit Commission in 1993 to recommend much greater emphasis on the use of intelligence resources in policing.[1] It was echoing similar thinking in the United States and it represented something of a shift from the previous emphasis on community policing where events were dealt with more discretely as and where they happened. ILP would make far greater use of information and analytics to identify patterns, incentives and motives; explicitly gather intelligence from all sources within a community, including informers; and it would command policing resources more proactively to disrupt and prevent crime as well as to pursue it after its commission.[2] ILP was not intended to be a clear alternative to 'problem orientated policing' or community policing but rather to supplement them with both a fresh emphasis on gathering and using information, and therefore resources, more efficiently.[3]

The UK had instinctively adopted intelligence-led policing approaches to the terrorist campaigns that had affected the country over many years, from the troubles in Northern Ireland, to Palestinian or Iranian separatist terrorism perpetrated in the UK during the 1970s and 1980s. Nevertheless, this new emphasis in policing had particular relevance to the jihadist terrorism that became evident in the UK from around 1998. This became even more relevant in the digital age and in the light of the fact that all modern terrorist groups have sought to use cyber-weapons, information and social media as part of their various modus operandi. ILP also became the most explicitly institutionalized aspect of operational practice within the police and security services. The National Intelligence Model (NIM) still stands as the essential framework for the policing intelligence process, having a statutory footing through the Police Reform Act 2000.[4] NIM has been referred to as a 'business model for law enforcement' and specifies the various stages of the 'intelligence cycle', from identifying the resources for information gathering ('assets'), the sources of information (e.g. witnesses, undercover operatives), the recording and analysis of intelligence, through tactical and action planning (e.g. targeted patrol) to operational review. NIM acts as formal direction to police forces and to units within police forces on the processes of ILP and is an established part of the police mindset in the field of police investigation and operational command.[5]

Jihadist terrorism has, however, posed new challenges to ILP approaches, which continue to evolve as jihadist extremism persists within British society. Its presence and social impact have required that UK intelligence services, as well as the police, have to collaborate at far deeper and more integrated levels than was ever previously the case, domestically and also in relation to international partners. This has taken place rapidly since the early 2000s within the intelligence community itself and in the way that police intelligence operates alongside it. The College of Policing promotes the use of a common intelligence framework so that information can be easily exchanged between forces and shared more easily with other agencies as and when necessary.[6] The same police and intelligence services are also more effectively coordinated at the centre – the cabinet office level – than was ever previously the case: through the Office of Security and Counter-Terrorism, the Joint Terrorism Analysis Centre, the Joint Intelligence Committee and the National Security Council. In this respect, the UK compares very well with many of its partner countries in its ability to evaluate, share and act on relevant information as and when it comes into the country from foreign sources, or else as it arises from its own policing and community engagement activities.

Intelligence-led policing attempts to work both from the top down and from the bottom up, assessing information 'from the top' in a centralized way so as to deploy resources in a timely and efficient manner; and from the 'bottom up' by creating channels of two-way communication among the sectors and communities from which terrorist activities might arise, in an effort also to help mobilize a community against criminality and terrorist activities. Both top-down and bottom-up approaches can claim quite high levels of operational success but there are also significant new challenges in both spheres.

Top-down challenges for intelligence-led counter-terrorism policing

While UK intelligence agencies and their policing counterparts have a genuinely high reputation for their ability to gather and process intelligence at national and international levels, the challenges are increasing in both scope and diversity.

The modalities of jihadist terrorism look for novel ways of mounting attacks, so significantly more communication and planning techniques now have to be monitored. In particular, jihadist terrorism has moved from highly centralized planning of the sort that Al-Qaeda carried out when it had a secure base across parts of south Asia, to something far more laissez-faire as Al-Qaeda has dispersed and so-called 'Islamic State' has adopted a quite different approach to recruitment and operations. Individuals with little training or experience, and individuals who have not visited any of the jihadist heartlands for instruction and training, are simply encouraged to commit whatever acts of violence within the UK and other Western countries that may be within their power. This does not mean that such individuals are not connected within their own informal networks – from most recent cases it is clear that they are. But it may mean that their visibility to the security services or local police forces may be very low – fitful connections to known jihadists but nothing highly specific, or petty crime and a pattern of personal alienation but little to suggest a jihadist terror response. And indeed, many would-be perpetrators have not fallen into either of these categories at all. In the current climate, one of the new realities is that would-be perpetrators of such individualistic and laissez-faire terrorist violence can go from being invisible to intelligence, or firmly in a 'low-risk' category, to a 'high risk' or 'activated' category remarkably quickly, and certainly more quickly than can easily be tracked by present ILP procedures.

A further challenge is that the day-to-day electronic communication between individuals who may be of some interest to counter-terrorism police and security services is not as accessible to warranted procedures as was the case even five years ago. The Investigatory Powers Act 2016 provides a legal basis for the authorities to access, with appropriate written warrants, the electronic and telephonic communications data between individuals and also, in some selected cases, the detailed content of those communications. The legal authority, however, is not the same as the technical capability to do this. For the police and security agencies, the internet goes progressively 'dark' as end-to-end encryption and the changing business models of the internet giants have the effect of freezing the access of the agencies to important areas of communication for intelligence purposes. Internet companies as well as their customers now demand greater levels of encryption, as data security becomes ever more necessary and desirable. Well-documented system-hacking in many spheres, alongside the furore created within the industry by the revelations of Edward Snowden in 2013 regarding US government surveillance activities, had the effect of increasing the push towards end-to-end encryption. It also encouraged the internet companies to make encryption user-controlled, so that even the service providers could not crack the encryption codes they used to transmit data on behalf of their customers.

Alongside the increasing 'darkness' (some describe it as 'balkanization') of the internet the phenomenon of the internet app adds a further dimension to ILP. In 2000 apps using internet services barely existed: the earliest performing and recognizably internet-based app functions can be dated to around 1997.[7] But by March 2017 the five market leaders were responsible for supplying more than 6.5 million different apps, a high proportion of them capable of being misused for criminal purposes. Since apps for mobile devices – smartphones, tablet computers and wearables – are generally easier and cheaper to produce than for static computers their growth has been exponential. Apple estimated that by September 2016 its 2.2 million apps had been cumulatively downloaded around 140 billion times.[8]

In addition to the downloading of vast amounts of data through these technologies, social networks distribute and proliferate material of all kinds – text, images, interactive functions – to an unprecedented degree. Facebook has over 2 billion users, WhatsApp around 500 million, Instagram around 600,000 and Twitter over 330 million. Facebook estimates that, on average, written material or images are distributed by its users (i.e. 'liked' or 'shared') almost 10 million times every day.[9] The scope for criminal and terrorist communication through the use and misuse of social networks and apps, in addition to more conventional sources of electronic and telephonic communication, is simply vast and appears, at present, to be without any obvious technical limits. Intelligence-led policing plays a continual game of catch-up in attempts to bring modern data analytics to bear on it in ways that can isolate patterns of behaviour among groups or individuals to give warning of a nascent terrorist conspiracy or an intention to commit a particular act of terror.

Not the least challenge to ILP at the macro level is that of working with less democratic, or simply undemocratic, countries to share intelligence on terrorist organizations and emerging plots. This has become increasingly difficult in recent years. This is partly because democracy and the rule of law are in retreat around the world and the growth of international terrorism has provoked many brutal reactions that would be clearly illegal under UK law on the part of many foreign governments. The UK has intelligence relations of some sort with around sixty other countries in the world, and it has progressively tightened its own intelligence and counter-terrorism policing protocols and oversight arrangements in recent years – in particular through the Investigatory Powers Act 2016, the enduring use of the Human Rights Act 1998 and the new Data Protection Act 2018. Intelligence professionals will not willingly give up access to relevant information from any source if they think it will help in their own work, but top-level intelligence-sharing is a two-way process and, since UK officials are increasingly constrained in how they may cooperate and in what they can give to other governments who behave in dubious ways, there is a reciprocal reluctance from those authorities to share and cooperate to an extent that would have seemed reasonable only a few years ago.

ILP and the mobilization of communities in countering extremism and terrorism

At the other end of the ILP spectrum is the work done on the ground and in ways that can link policing directly to citizens. Intelligence-led policing is concerned as much with gaining local intelligence about crime and criminal groups as it is about integrating all-source information from the centre and crunching numbers. All policing in democratic societies relies fundamentally on public consent, and the cooperation and intelligence derived from engagement at the community level are a natural part of effective policing – all the more so in the case of counter-terrorism policing. So, too, the collection of intelligence at the ground level should be conducted in such a way as to reinforce the commitment of citizens and community groups to support the work of the police in countering crime in general and terrorist crime in particular.

In 2006 when the Prevent programme was first publicly launched, ILP appeared to fit naturally with its general objectives, which were defined as the promotion of 'shared values, supporting local solutions, building civic capacity and leadership and strengthening the role of faith institutions and leaders'.[10] It was conceived as operating primarily through the local authorities, since it would be a community-based series of initiatives. But it was immediately dogged by suspicions that as one of the four elements of the government's CONTEST counter-terrorism strategy Prevent would be difficult to disentangle from the other three and that it would be as much about gaining operational intelligence as about affecting the sources of radicalization within a community. Even more, it seemed to imply that Muslims could be regarded by it as suspects more than citizens. Indeed, long-standing, more general crime prevention strategies within many communities had already grappled with this sort of inherent suspicion and many had used deep local knowledge and contacts to overcome them. But as a Whitehall-driven initiative, and lauded as part of an overall national counter-terror strategy, the first iteration of Prevent did not look, and did not perform, as it had been intended, namely as a more specialized and rather particular crime prevention initiative.[11]

The work of the Prevent programme is assessed directly in other contributions to this volume. It has been subject to regular reviews in the face of consistent criticisms since 2006. The most recent review of Prevent (alongside the other three aspects of the overall CONTEST strategy) took place in 2016 but did not appear until the summer of 2018, where it suggested a much wider remit for future work under the Prevent programme. From a policy perspective a number of trends are becoming clear, even though Prevent is evidently in the midst of a significant evolution.[12]

Proving a negative is logically impossible but senior police officers and officials responsible for operating Prevent at the local level are in no doubt that the initiative has proved successful in contributing to ILP and that it has both headed off likely incidents and provided valuable channels of information from the community to the authorities that has in turn relayed important information contributing to operational policing.[13] As in any crime prevention scheme – of which there are many – there is a thin definitional line between community-based organizations, schools, local authority groups, neighbourhood organizations and so on 'spying' or 'snooping' on individuals, as opposed to providing important contextual information to police forces that allow then to intervene, disrupt or anticipate criminal acts before they take place. But for the police and security services Prevent has provided direct operational advantages, even as they acknowledge that it may also have had some dysfunctional effects on local community relations. It is accepted that, at the very least, Prevent offers an easy target for jihadist conspiracy theorists, among others, who choose to argue that the government is demonizing British Muslim communities and creating a framework for continual surveillance. Nevertheless, from a police perspective, the most significant failures of the Prevent programme have been in those cases – some of them very well publicized after a successful attack – where the programme appears to have failed to transmit community concerns about an individual's behaviour or attitudes and therefore to have missed what subsequently turned out to be a significant intelligence source.

Statistical evidence, in this respect, can only be a matter of inference. ILP in relation to counter-terrorism is far wider than the activities of the Prevent programme. A great deal of vital information, for example, derives from informers within or close to any nascent terrorist group; and the security services are believed to have been assiduous, and generally successful, in getting trained agents into useful positions in and around UK terrorist networks. Nevertheless, the Prevent programme is the flagship initiative to help mobilize individuals and organizations in local communities to support the work of the authorities, and the statistical information offers a number of potential performance metrics. In 2017, for example, the Home Secretary revealed that some 150 people (50 of them children) had been dissuaded by the programme from travelling to Syria to join the Islamic State organization during the time it still existed.[14] Or again, under the Prevent scheme the Police Counter-Terrorism Internet Referral Unit (CTIRU) claimed to have worked with internet companies to remove over 300,000 pieces of terrorist internet content[15] and in 2016–2017 some 6,093 individuals were referred to the Prevent programme through community engagement. Of these people, no action was taken in 2,193 cases (36 per cent of the total). In 2,741 cases (45 per cent of the total) individuals were given advice and 'referred' to alternative sources of knowledge, and some 1,157 individuals were taken on by one of the 'channel' programme panels which actively try to run a process to turn away from violence any given individual referred to them.

The channel process is entirely voluntary for the individual concerned and during 2016–2017 a total of 332 of the 1,157 individuals discussed by the panels voluntarily underwent a channel intervention. Of these, 262 of them were assessed as no longer at risk of further radicalization following the process, with seventy cases judged indeterminate.[16] This may be regarded as definable policy outputs from Prevent but we can only infer what the policy *impact* of these actions might have been. The absolute numbers are impressive and show how active Prevent initiatives have been in recent years. But the number of those identified who were merely referred and advised is high, while the number of those judged at risk of radicalization and who were judged, eventually, to have been successfully deradicalized, is low. If there were only 262 evident 'successes' from some 1,157 cases thought worthy of a channel intervention, a success rate of 22.6 per cent is not, in itself, impressive. And less than 29 per cent of all those originally identified as at risk agreed to be part of the process at all.

Any policy judgement must give some weight to these figures alongside the (sometimes conflicting) anecdotal information and professional instincts of senior police officers, community workers, local officials and social security professionals.[17] On this basis, a preliminary judgement would be that Prevent is certainly not irrelevant, and that any such crime prevention initiative that has enjoyed as much funding will have made a difference to counter-terrorism policing. But it may well be missing engagement with the essence of the collective problem – dealing usefully on the periphery of the phenomenon but still not able to engage with the numerical or ideological core of it. There is ample anecdotal evidence, on the other hand, that it has helped intelligence-led policing, even as it has certainly focused on – and partly created – dysfunctional responses within some sectors of some communities, Muslim and otherwise.[18] There is little general agreement among analysts, however, as to how these contradictory aspects should be weighed up or traded off against each other.

Conclusion

Ultimately, there is no feasible alternative to tackling terrorism, of any variety, other than through intelligence-led policing, whatever the difficulties of implementing that approach may be. Declaring either domestic or international 'wars' on terrorism has a record in world history of almost total failure. Terrorism is a particular form of criminality and reaches into gang warfare, serious organized crime and mafia-style behaviour as well as being intrinsic to overtly terrorist religious/ideological campaigns. In the long run it is vital that the state countering all of these manifestations of terrorism maintains the legal and moral high ground. It must treat terrorism as a type of crime and fight it essentially through policing, not warfare. As such, operating policing through an intelligence lens is a matter of ethical commitment just as much as it is common sense.

Notes

1 Audit Commission, *Helping with Enquiries: Tackling Crime Effectively*, vol. 1, London: HMSO, 1993.

2 E. F. McGarrell, et al., 'Intelligence-Led Policing as a Framework for Responding to Terrorism', *Journal of Contemporary Criminal Justice*, vol. 23, no. 2, 2007, pp. 142–158.

3 R. Anderson, 'Intelligence Led Policing: A British Perspective', in A. Smith (ed.), *Intelligence Led Policing: International Perspectives on Policing in the 21st Century*, Lawrenceville, NJ: International Association of Law Enforcement Intelligence Analysts, 1994, pp. 5–8.

4 A. James, *Examining Intelligence-Led Policing: Developments in Research, Policy and Practice*, Basingstoke: Palgrave Macmillan, 2013, pp. 2–7.

5 Association of Chief Police Officers, Centrex, 2005, p. 8, at: https://www.norfolk.police.uk/sites/norfolk/files/investigations_-_fpd_r4_1.pdf;

See also ACPO, *Practice Advice on Core Investigative Doctrine*, Centrex, 2005.

6 See, http://www.college.police.uk/What-we-do/Learning/Professional-Training/Intelligence/Pages/Intelligence.aspx.

7 AVG Technologies, A History of Mobile Apps: 1983 and Beyond, 4 February 2015, available at: https://prezi.com/rwc6qmvqkrt-/a-history-of-mobile-apps/. 'Apps' is not a precise description and some mobile devices that contained early applications, such as *Psion* personal organizers or *Newton Message Pads*, were available in the late 1980s, though not using the internet for their essential functionality. 'Apps' in the way they are now commonly understood can be traced to the Palm OS of 1996 and especially the Nokia 6110 mobile phone, launched in 1997, which had the *Snake* game pre-loaded on it.

8 'Number of Apps Available in Leading App Stores as of 3rd quarter 2018', *Statistica: the Statistical Portal*, [Website]. No author and undated. available here: https://www.statista.com/statistics/276623/number-of-apps-available-in-leading-app-stores/.

9 'The Top 20 Valuable Facebook Statistics – Updated January 2018', *Zephoria: Digital Marketing*, [Website]. No author and undated, updated 4 January 2018, available here: https://zephoria.com/top-15-valuable-facebook-statistics/. see also: https://zephoria.com/twitter-statistics-top-ten/.

10 DCLG, *Preventing Violent Extremism: Winning Hearts and Minds* London: Department for Communities and Local Government, 2007, p. 5.

11 Y. Birt, 'Promoting Virulent Envy?', *RUSI Journal*, vol. 154, no. 4, 2009, pp. 52–58.

12 HM Government, *CONTEST: The United Kingdom's Strategy for Countering Terrorism*, Cm 9608, June 2018.

13 Personal interviews, July 2018.

14 C. Graham, 'What Is the Anti-Terror Prevent Programme and Why Is It Controversial?' *Daily Telegraph*, 26 May 2017.

15 Though the government does not say over how many years this figure has been achieved. HM Government, *CONTEST*, p. 35.

16 HM Government, *CONTEST*, p. 39.

17 See, for example, R. Minhas, et al., 'An Exploration of Perceptions of Real-Life Suspects from an Asian Muslim Community Relating to Police Interviewing Practices in England', *Journal of Policing, Intelligence and Counter-Terrorism*, vol. 12, no. 2, 2017, pp. 158–174.

18 A good summary of the range of anecdotal evidence is provided by Graham, *op. cit.*

Recommended Readings

Adrian James, *Examining Intelligence-Led Policing: Developments in Research, Policy and Practice*, Basingstoke: Palgrave Macmillan, 2013.

Adrian James, *Understanding Police Intelligence Work*, Key Themes in Policing Series, Bristol: Polity Press, 2016.

College of Policing, *Intelligence Management*, London: College of Policing, 2015.

Phythian, Mark (ed.), *Understanding the Intelligence Cycle*, London: Routledge, 2013.

PART FOUR

GENERAL PERSPECTIVES ON THE JIHADIST TERRORIST THREAT AND RESPONSES

24 PERSONAL AND ORGANIZATIONAL PATTERNS OF KNOWN TERRORISTS AND RELATED GROUPS IN THE UK SINCE 1998

Raffaello Pantucci

Introduction

The aim of this chapter is to sketch out the waves of jihadist terrorism in the United Kingdom since 1998. Given the relatively constrained space available, the chapter will focus on four periods of time which mark out the violent Islamist threat to the UK during the last two decades (though the traces of the UK's jihadist threat go back as far as 1979 and the conflict in Afghanistan), and then focus on the personal and organizational traits of terrorist plots during each period using a similar structure in an attempt to provide an easily analysable overview. The focus will be terrorist plots conducted in the UK or abroad by individuals with a deep footprint in the UK. This will provide a helpful structure to what is otherwise a huge and disparate dataset that can be difficult to define. In concluding, the chapter will sketch out some broad patterns which are discernible and capture the changing nature of jihadist terrorist activity in the UK since 1998. This will hopefully provide an adequate synthesis answer to the question at hand.

The four time periods used in this chapter are defined by the nature of the external jihadist terrorist threat to the United Kingdom:

A. 1998–2004 – defined as the period when Al-Qaeda was prominent and seeking to hit the United States. Seven plots are used for this period;
B. 2004–2009 – defined as the period when the Al-Qaeda threat directly to the UK matured. Fifteen plots are used for this period;

of plots including the July 7, July 21 and Airlines plot all linked back to British jihadist Rashid Rauf, who rose up to a senior role within Al-Qaeda core.[12] Outside this chain of plots an additional three plots show evidence of links to the network from which the Al-Qaeda-directed plots emanated, with further evidence of links to senior Al-Qaeda figures.

In almost all plots there was evidence of bomb-making, with individuals in around half of cases receiving training to build bombs abroad. Beyond this, one beheading plot was disrupted (Parviz Khan in Birmingham[13]), one mass shooting was prevented (Kazi Rahman[14]) and there was an attempted firebombing of a publisher's house (Ali Beheshti).[15] Plotting was largely in London when directed through, or linked to, large networks, but the lone actors showed up at random around the country.

This was also a period in which self-starting plots started to emerge in numerous different forms. There were at least four isolated bombmakers. In every case they had had contact with others with whom they had discussed their plans either online or in person, but they were seeking to launch attacks with no clear direction from any known organization. There was also the attempted bombing of the Tiger, Tiger nightclub in London and the Glasgow International Airport attack by a cell that had received training but with no clear evidence of direction from Al-Qaeda in Iraq.[16] Similarly, Parviz Khan's beheading plot, Aabid Khan's network[17] and Ali Beheshti showed links to groups in South Asia but with no evidence of clear direction. Most worrying was the rise of the lone-actor threat from individuals who appeared to suffer from some form of mental health issues – Nicky Reilly,[18] Andrew Ibrahim[19] and Krenar Lusha all appear to have decided to seek to launch attacks in the UK (though in Lusha's case, his plot appears very unclear: he was arrested with substantial volumes of potential terrorist bomb-making material but little evidence of what his specific target was[20]) – in the name of an ideology which they little understood and was very far from their ordinary lives.

Women are again absent from these attack networks, though they continued to feature in the background community of extremists. In a few cases the women were even arrested and charged – such as the wives, sisters and female friends of the 21/7 bombers.[21] In one particularly dramatic case the wife of one of the 7/7 bombers, Samantha Lewthwaite, departed to East Africa where she later emerged as a significant figure in the al Shabaab networks.[22]

The average age of perpetrators started to shift downwards, with very young men (late teenagers) involved in attack planning directed by Al-Qaeda. Additionally, the network around Aabid Khan (which sought to launch attacks in the UK, had links to cells across Europe and North America and involved the then-youngest convicted terrorist in the UK, sixteen-year-old Hammad Munshi[23]) showed the growing complexity of the threat faced and the importance of the Internet in terrorist plotting and network formation. That network was noticeable in tying together cells in at least five different countries (UK, USA, Canada, Denmark and Bosnia) and included one of the earliest identifiable digital natives, Younes Tsouli, who played a hugely influential role in Al-Qaeda in Iraq. Going by the online handle Irhabi007 (terrorist 007), he was able to build websites, post videos and disseminate material being put out by Al-Qaeda in Iraq at the time.[24]

Foreign fighting remained of interest during this period, though the flow to South Asia slowed as time went on in the face of an aggressive drone campaign in Pakistan, which made joining and training with Al-Qaeda core increasingly difficult. In addition, the battlefield in Somalia grew in interest to UK groups, while Anwar al Awlaki moved from the UK to Yemen, creating a growing attraction for British jihadists to head there. As the narrative of conflict in Somalia developed, with the Islamic Courts Union projecting an image of being an East African version of the Taliban, and with the later emergence of al Shabaab, the Horn became a place of growing attraction for UK jihadists. The community heading to Somalia was closely linked to those going to Yemen.

2009–2013

Terrorist plots and attacks during this period are marked by the growth in threat to the UK or through the UK from Yemen and Al-Qaeda in the Arabian Peninsula in particular. The community from which the threat picture is drawn broadens out beyond known networks around the radical preachers, though they remain the core of the threat. By this point the big three radical preachers had all been ejected from the country and a new generation of al Muhajiroun preachers in particular rose up and became the core of the group and became a problem for the UK. There was also a growth in plots within the UK by individuals who were long-term features of the radical community in the UK and who seemed to activate themselves to try to launch terrorist attacks at home.

The rise in plots emanating from Yemen and Al-Qaeda in the Arabian Peninsula (AQAP) is particularly noticeable during the first years of this period – though the priority target of the plots disrupted or linked to the UK seemed to have been the United States. Umar Farouk Abdulmutallab was a student in the UK, who was drawn to Awlaki in Yemen and was then despatched by the group to blow himself up over the United States.[25] The printer cartridge bomb intercepted in the UK in November 2010 was one of a pair heading towards the United States. In intercepted messages to Rajib Karim, Anwar al Awlaki stated how 'anything' that might hit the United States would be better than something in the UK. They planned to use British Airways, the company Karim worked for, as a vector to launch an attack.[26] The possible exception to this was the plot around Minh Quang Pham, who was supposedly intended to be a suicide bomber in the UK (though it is possible that his goal was to attack the United States. He currently resides in an American high-security prison).[27] At the same time, the threat from Al-Qaeda core persisted, with two plots demonstrating evidence of direction by the group in Pakistan, including individuals who had been to training camps and had been taught how to make bombs. Both of these plots targeted the UK directly (a plot to attack Northern UK cities,[28] and a planned bombing campaign by Birmingham extremist Irfan Naseer[29]).

The threat from AQAP in the UK also matured in new ways. The case of Roshonara Choudhry, a terrorist who attempted to murder MP Stephen Timms after watching Anwar al Awlaki videos, showed the power of his messaging.[30] While the murder of Lee Rigby in Woolwich by Michael Adebolajo and Michael Adebowale showed the wide network of links that AQAP had into the UK. It also highlighted the multifaceted threat that AQAP and Anwar al Awlaki were able to pose through a community that brought together born Muslims and converts from a variety of communities. Awlaki's global reach was a broad one and the specific group in the UK that was drawn to him in Yemen very much reflected this.[31]

The personal profile of the cohort during this period appears to revert to earlier forms in that the majority were young men (in their 20s or 30s), though the UK also saw its first female attacker during this period (Roshonara Choudhry). The group was again very diverse in terms of personal profiles (almost every plot involved multiple individuals, including at least one convert), though it is observable that almost all of the cells disrupted (seeking attacks in the UK) were drawn from the community around Al-Muhajiroun in London and a similar network in Birmingham.

There was also a persistent level of activity by individuals who were not directly linked to known networks and appeared to be operating in the name of ideologies with which they had had little interaction or connection. For example, the Khans in Manchester were planning a terror campaign against the Jewish community and, while they appear to have sought links to the Al-Muhajiroun community, they do not appear to have been connected with it.[32] Similarly, while Taimour Abdulwahab al Abdaly told others of what he was going to do, and appears to have moved in radical circles in Luton, there is no evidence he was steered by them to launch his attack in Stockholm.[33] Finally, in the cases of Mark Townley (a converted former soldier who was reportedly planning to murder Prince Harry)[34] and the attempted murder of a prison warden in the wake of the murder of Lee Rigby in Woolwich,[35] the individuals involved were more inspired by extremist methodologies rather than ideologies.

Foreign fighting also remained interesting to networks during this period, with people seeking to go to a number of different locations. Authorities had, however, started to be more attentive to the phenomenon and worked with foreign partners to prevent travel, making it increasingly difficult. Measures like Terrorism Prevention and Investigation Measures (TPIMs) were deployed to prevent a specific (mostly London-based) community of young men going to Somalia, while travelling to Pakistan remained difficult. Yemen remained of interest, though, as time went on, it became harder to travel there as well. The result, however, was an increase in plots linked to 'blocked traveller' individuals who were seeking to get to jihad, were frustrated in their inability to do so and who instead sought to launch attacks in the United Kingdom.

2013–2018

The most noticeable change in the final period covered is the rise of the threat from Syria and the Islamic State. The starting point for this cohort of thirty plots is the case of Erol Incedal, who was linked to the first and only plot identifiable in the UK as an example of someone being sent and directed to launch some sort of attack in the UK from the Levant (and there is even some dispute around this),[36] while almost all of the others show evidence of some links either through online communications or ideologically to the conflict in Syria and Iraq. The threat from Al-Qaeda during this period seems to have almost completely evaporated, though there remained links to historical extremist communities who had links to Al-Qaeda.

Of the thirty plots highlighted during this period, fourteen consisted of isolated individuals who in some cases were talking to extremists online but were largely advancing their terrorist plots by themselves. Of the rest, three consisted of couples and the others were made up of cells of varying magnitude. Of the isolated individuals, four had issues relating to social disorders and mental health, with two ultimately sectioned under the Mental Health Act.[37]

The profiles of the individuals involved also broadened out considerably, with an all-female cell detained in mid-2017[38] and a number of very young people detained as part of attack plots. An anonymous fourteen-year-old from Blackburn was arrested in 2015 while trying to direct a teenager in Australia to launch an attack on an ANZAC Day parade;[39] a seventeen-year-old girl was captured trying to source guns and grenades off the internet after her jihadi husband in Syria was killed (she had married him over Skype);[40] and in June 2017, Lloyd Gunton was arrested after his Instagram posts were noticed by authorities and he was discovered to be planning an attack of some sort at a Justin Bieber concert.[41]

Active radicalization of children was also uncovered as a more common feature. Umar Haque was an Islamic school teacher who was indoctrinating children into IS ideas and trying to prepare some of them to join him in jihad.[42] A number of extremist families were disrupted, with the parents arrested and detained or the children taken away from them and put into care. Usually, these parents had tried to take them to Syria with them or were committed extremists who were radicalizing their children.[43] In some cases children were being brought back from Syria and Iraq having spent time in the IS Caliphate.[44]

The nature of terrorist plotting also transformed – from plots which were involving explosives the threat picture shifted to an overwhelming majority of plots that focused on using knives or cars to launch attacks. At least half of the plots discussed prepared or used knives in advance of their attacks. A further four spoke of using guns, with only one managing to obtain one. Ten spoke of using bombs, with only a few making moves towards actually making them and with two actually building viable devices. In addition, at least eight plots were able to advance to the point of actually conducting some sort of attack, though in three cases (Ahmed Hassan, the Parsons Green bomber,[45] Muhaydin Mire, the Leytonstone underground knifeman[46] and an individual who sought to attack police at Buckingham Palace[47]) they were only able to injure people.

The scattered nature of the attacks and individuals involved is further reflected in the locations from where foreign fighters come from. Whereas previously extremist networks tended to come from certain prominent places, and networks were largely clustered around specific radical preachers, there was a shift towards more disparate networks around the UK. Each of these networks included the aspect of a mini-radical-preacher-led cell, with a prominent leader among them who often acted as the pathfinder foreign fighter that the others would follow. What is, however, fairly constant was their end goal of reaching Syria. There has been some evidence of transit to other locations, such as Libya or other parts of Africa, but the dawn of the conflict in Syria was the main magnet for UK extremists.

Conclusion

Looking across the two decades covered by this chapter, it is possible to observe some broad changes in patterns over time. In the first place, the threat picture has evolved in terms of the UK going from being a launching pad for terrorist attacks elsewhere, to becoming the heart of the threat from Al-Qaeda core, to shifting once again to being a conduit for the threat elsewhere, to then once more becoming a direct target in itself.

There are some issues which remain broadly constant over the two decades. For example, fundraising by terrorist cells has remained a fairly creative activity which has evolved to reflect the changing nature of society and how money flows more generally – for example, the use by terrorists of bitcoin or new methods of fraud to take advantage of fissures in our financial systems as they emerge (e.g. an early North African cell in Leicestershire was using credit card fraud in the late 1990s[48] and early 2000s; the July 7 bombers took out fraudulent loans;[49] and more recently, in 2015, a group of telephone scammers was uncovered stealing from the elderly to send money to fighters in Syria[50]). Classic fundraising through obtaining money from relations, or community fundraising, has continued, as has the deployment of petty criminality, fraud or other methods to make money to advance terrorist causes.

A similar narrative can be drawn for communications, where terrorists' use of these has also largely evolved as societal norms have. In other words, terrorists simply use the same methods of communication as the rest of society, but they use them for nefarious purposes. Terrorist cells have tended to be early adopters of new communications technology, but this is something that largely evolves, as it develops in broader society. Finally, terrorist use of training camps at home has largely stayed the same, though over time people have stopped congregating to train or camp in public locations, fearful of detection. Gyms have remained a place of congregation throughout.

Looking at the biographical data of the community of terrorists in the UK over the period covered in this chapter, it has stayed fairly constant over time. Young men make up the biggest proportion, drawing from across the UK's Muslim community. Over time, what has noticeably changed is the number of people with mental health issues emerging in attack plans, as well as a more prominent role from very recent converts. More very young plotters have emerged, with some teenagers showing up as being involved in attack planning, and a growing number of women have started to emerge as participating directly in attacks rather than simply acting in a support role for men. According to the useful analysis of conviction rates by Hannah Stuart at the Henry Jackson Society, 'Women's involvement in Islamism-inspired terrorism, while small in actual numbers, has nearly tripled in the last five years from the previous 13 years' – between 1998 and 2010, 4 per cent of convictions were of women, whereas between 2011 and 2015 they made up 11 per cent.[51] In the same dataset Ms Stuart observes a very limited change over time in the age range of convicted terrorists.

Ancillary to this, there has been a growth of children being brought up in radical families, children being taken by their parents to conflict zones in Syria and Iraq and people specifically seeking to radicalize children in schools. While aspects of this have all emerged previously, this has been something that has been particularly pronounced since the emergence of the Islamic State. One phenomenon which has been much commented upon is the emergence of more individuals with criminal profiles among the cohort of terrorists – and while absolute numbers are hard to calculate, it is not clear whether this represents, in the UK context, a huge divergence from the past. According to Ms Stuart's dataset, from 1998 to 2015, overall 38 per cent of the individuals included had a previous conviction for a variety of offences.[52]

Looking instead at the organizational aspect of terrorism and terrorist networks during this period, they have also been marked by a gradual shift away from groups based around specific radical preachers to a more diffuse and disparate form, which is characterized as being scattered and isolated individuals around the country. From a concentration of people in a few locations, increasingly, the story of radicalization and jihadist extremism is one that can be found across the UK. What becomes novel about this as time goes on, and is particularly pronounced in the Islamic State era, is that it is not always clear if there is a connection to traditional networks in some of these new locations. While previously it was possible to find small pockets of individuals around the country, there was usually also evidence of some connection to the broader network that was concentrated in the cities. Over time, this has changed to more isolated individuals adopting the ideology and choosing terrorist methodologies through connections and ideas that they have found through online contact. Traditional networks still exist, but they are more diffuse and have developed more local cellular structures (something reflected in the clusters of foreign fighters from around the UK who went to fight in Libya, Syria and Iraq).

Turning to attack methodologies – these have also shifted from fairly conventional to increasingly low-tech and ever more random soft targets. The early years are characterized by bombs, usually ones which people have been trained abroad to make, while the later years are characterized by attempts to make bombs at home with limited training or experience and people seeking to use knives. The targets chosen also go from targeting public infrastructure and institutions to the general public at random.

None of these changes are abrupt, and shades of previous structures and models of behaviour still exist in the current context. But the overall pattern of distant forces stirring homegrown groups through networks they were able to control and link up with has now shifted more to homegrown groups connecting with foreign ideologies. At the same time, the profile of those becoming involved, in terms of either connecting with ideologies at home or seeking to travel, has been transformed by what was the relative ease of access to the battlefield in Syria and Iraq, and the very broad appeal and accessibility of the ISIS ideology, in particular, and their easy online connectivity.

Notes

1 R. Carroll and I. Black, 'Three More Britons Held in Yemen', *Guardian*, 28 January 1999.

2 'Bomb Suspect "Part of Network"', *BBC News*, 26 December 2001.

3 E. Brockes, 'British Man Named as Bomber Who Killed 10', *Guardian*, 28 December 2000.

4 'Bomb Britons Appear on Hamas Tape', *BBC News*, 8 March 2004.

5 S. Morris, 'Bomb Factor Muslim Jailed for 20 Years', *Guardian*, 28 February 2002.

6 N. Bunyan, 'The Bungled Raid That Left a Policeman Face to Face with an Al-Qa'eda Assassin', *Telegraph*, 14 April 2005.

7 'Killer Jailed over Poison Plot', *BBC News*, 13 April 2005.

8 *USA vs. Zacarias Moussaoui*, statement of facts, filed in open court 22 April 2005.

9 *USA vs Mostafa Kamel Mostafa*, Saajid Badat testimony in open court, 30 April 2014.

10 A. Levy and C. Scott-Clark, *The Meadow: Kashmir 1995 – Where the Terror Began*, UK: HarperPress, March 2012.

11 V. Dodd and O. Bowcott, 'Police Accused after Brother And Sister Are Cleared of Failing to Tell of Bombing Plan', *Guardian*, 29 November 2005.

12 R. Pantucci, 'A Biography of Rashid Rauf: Al-Qa'ida's British Operative', *CTC Sentinel*, vol. 5, no. 7, July 2012.

13 *Regina vs. Parviz Khan*, appeal before Lord Justice Hughes, Justice Holroyd and Sir Christopher Holland, Royal Courts of Justice, 20 May 2009.

14 'Missile Plot Briton Sent to Jail', *BBC News*, 30 April 2007.

15 'Three Jailed for Published Arson', *BBC News*, 7 July 2009.

16 C. Greenwood, 'Terror Suspect Supports Iraqi Insurgency, Court Told', *Press Association*, 11 November 2008.

17 E. Kohlmann, 'Anatomy of a Modern Homegrown Terror Cell: Aabid Khan et al, (Operation Praline)', *NEFA Foundation*, September 2008.

18 R. Preston-Ellis, '10 Years On: How Nicky Reilly Brought Terror to the Streets of Exeter', *Devon Live*, 22 May 2018.

19 R. Pantucci, 'Britain Jails "Lone Wolf" Terrorist Isa Ibrahim,' *Jamestown Foundation Terrorism Monitor*, vol. 7, no. 23, 30 July 2009.

20 *Regina vs Krenar Lusha*, appeal before Lord Justice Thomas, Mr Justice Bean and Mrs Justice Sharpe DBE, Royal Courts of Justice, 6 July 2010.

21 *Regina vs. Yeshiembert Girma, Esayas Girma, Mulumebet Girma and Mohammed Kabashi*, 15 May 2009; *Regina vs. Abdul Sherif, Siraj Ali, Muhedin Ali, Wahbi Mohamed, Islmail Abdurahman, Fardosa Abdullahi.*

22 A. Wishart, 'The White Widow: Searching for Samantha', *BBC Documentary*, June 2014.

23 E. Kohlmann, 'Anatomy of a Modern Homegrown Terror Cell: Aabid Khan et al, (Operation Praline),' *NEFA Foundation*, September 2008.

24 Kohlmann, Anatomy of a Modern Homegrown Terror Cell.

25 *USA vs Umar Farouk Abdulmutallab,* superseding indictment, filed 15 December 2010.

26 S. Swann, 'Rajib Kraim: The Terrorist inside British Airways,' *BBC News*, 28 February 2011.

27 *USA vs Minh Quang Pham*, sealed indictment, 2012.

28 D. Casciani, 'Operation Pathway: What Happened', *BBC News*, 18 May 2010.

29 *Regina vs Irfan Naseer, Irfan Khalid & Ashik Ali*, 19 October 2012.

30 V. Dodd, 'Roshonara Choudhry: Police Interview Extracts', *Guardian*, 3 November 2010.

31 'Report on the Intelligence Relating to the Murder of Fusilier Lee Rigby', report by the Intelligence and Security Committee of Parliament, chaired by the Rt. Hon. Sir Malcolm Rifkind, MP, 25 November 2014.

32 *Regina vs. Mohammed Sajid Khan*, 5 June 2013.

33 M. Storm, P. Cruickshank and T. Lister, *Agent Storm: My Life inside al-Qaeda*, UK: Viking, July 2014.

34 T. Allen, 'Prince Harry Death Plot Man Was Kicked out of British Army', *Belfast Telegraph*, 17 February 2014.

35 R. Silverman and T. Whitehead, 'Terror Police Called in after Prison Warden Stabbed in Attack "Inspired by Woolwich Murder"', *Telegraph*, 28 May 2013.

36 S. Castle, 'A Terrorism Case in Britain Ends in Acquittal, but No One Can Say Why', *New York Times*, 25 July 2015.

37 The two who were detained on mental health grounds were 'Nicholas Salvador Detained over Woman's Beheading', *BBC News*, 23 June 2015, and Jamie Grierson, 'Leytonstone Knife Attacker Sentenced to Life', *Guardian*, 1 August 2016. Whilst the other cases were 'Fairy Lights Bomb Plotter Zahid Hussain Jailed for Life', *BBC News*, 9 October 2017 and 'Lloyd Gunton Locked up for Bieber Terror Plot', *BBC News*, 2 March 2018. There are additional cases which may also fit this profile, but

information has been difficult to obtain due to sensitivities. Also, since the delivery of the draft of this paper, additional cases have emerged, but again information around them has not been released.

38 D. Casciani, 'Teenage Safaa Boular Jailed for Life over IS Terror Plot', *BBC News* (online), 3 August 2018.

39 'Blackburn Boy's ANZAC Day Terror Plot, "Likely to Have Resulted in Deaths", Court Told,' *Lancashire Telegraph*, 1 October 2015.

40 *Regina vs Safaa Boular*, May 2018.

41 *Regina vs. Lloyd Gunton*, 2 November 2017.

42 *Regina vs. Umar Ahmed Haque, Abuthaher Mamun, Muhammad Abid & Nadeem Ilyas Patel*, 15 January 2018.

43 For example, X (Children) (No 3) [2015] EWHC 3651 (Fam), before Sir James Munby, President of the Family Division, Liverpool, 16 December 2015.

44 'Child Returnees from Conflict Zones,' RAN Issue paper, November 2016.

45 *Regina vs. Ahmed Hassan*, 2 March 2018.

46 T. Kirk 'Leytonstone Tube Attack: ISIS-Inspired Former Uber Driver Muhaydin Mire Guilty of Attempting to Behead Stranger at Tube Station,' *Evening Standard*, 8 June 2016.

47 *Regina vs. Mohiussunnath Chowdhury*, 1 May 2018. It is important to note that ultimately Chowdhury was cleared of his charges after two trials, even though police on the stand reported that he had reached for a 42-inch sword that he had in his vehicle with him (after he crashed his car into police outside Buckingham Palace). The *Independent* reported that 'Prosecutors said Sgt Gavin Hutt and PC Ian Midgley attempted to stop the driver slashing or stabbing them in what a "desperate struggle"[sic]. The court heard that Mr Chowdhury shouted "Allahu akbar" repeatedly during the fight, which ended when he was overpowered using CS spray and detained', Lizzie Dearden, 'Man Who Attacked Police with Lord of Rings Sword outside Buckingham Palace Found Not Guilty of Terrorism,' *Independent*, 19 December 2018. Chowdhury claimed that his intent was to be killed by the police as he was depressed rather than having any terrorist intent.

48 'Al-Qaida Terrorists Jailed for 11 years', *Guardian*, 1 April 2003.

49 'Could 7/7 Have Been Prevented? Review of the Intelligence on the London Terrorist Attacks on 7 July 2005', Intelligence and Security Committee, chaired by the Rt Hon Dr Kim Howells, MP, May 2009.

50 'Courier Fraud Conviction,' Metropolitan Police press release, December 10, 2015

51 H. Stuart, *Islamist Terrorism: Analysis of Offences and Attacks in the UK (1998–2015)*, London: Henry Jackson Society, 2017, available here: http://henryjacksonsociety.org/wp-content/uploads/2017/03/Islamist-Terrorism-preview-1.pdf – the important caveat to add here, of course, is the fact that Ms Stuart's report is only of offenders convicted of terrorism which unfortunately does not cover the entire gamut of extremists within the UK.

52 Stuart, *Islamist Terrorism*.

Recommended Readings

Bowen, I., *Medina in Birmingham, Najaf in Brent: Inside British Islam*, London: Hurst, 2014.

Gill, P., *Lone Actor Terrorists: A Behavioural Analysis*, London: Routledge, 2016.

Hassaine, R. and K. Barling, *Abu Hamza: Guilty, the Fight against Radical Islam*, Faringdon: Redshank Books, 2014.

Lambert, R., *Countering Al Qaeda in London: Police and Muslims in Partnership*, London: Hurst, 2011.

Lowles, N. and J. Mulhall, 'Gateway to Terror', *Hope Not Hate*, 25 November 2013.

Nesser, P., *Islamist Terrorism in Europe: A History*, London: Hurst, 2016.

O'Neill, S. and D. McGrory, *The Suicide Factory: Abu Hamza and the Finsbury Park Mosque*, London: Harper Perennial, 2010.

Silber, M.D., *The Al Qaeda Factor: Plots against the West*, Philadelphia: University of Pennsylvania Press, 2011.

Simcox, R., et al., *Islamist Terrorism: The British Connections*, London: Henry Jackson Society, 2011.

Storm, M., P. Cruickshank, and T. Lister, *Agent Storm: A Spy inside Al-Qaeda*, London: Penguin, 2015.

Stuart, H., *Islamist Terrorism: Analysis of Offences and Attacks in the UK (1998-2015)*, London: Henry Jackson Society, 2017.

Verkaik, R., *Jihadi John: The Making of a Terrorist*, London: Oneworld Publications, 2016.

Wiktorowicz, Q., *Radical Islam Rising: Muslim Extremism in the West*, Oxford: Rowman & Littlefield, 2005.

25 SUCCESSES AND FAILURES OF THE UK'S COUNTER-TERRORISM, COUNTER-RADICALIZATION AND PREVENT STRATEGY AGAINST JIHADIST TERRORISM SINCE 1998

John Gearson

Introduction

Despite more than thirty years' experience of countering terrorism, at the start of the twenty-first century the UK entered the era of jihadist terrorism with a poor understanding of the nature of the newly emerging threat; a siloed approach to inter-agency co-operation; fragmented intelligence structures and a policy approach ill-suited to the delivery of a national effort in response to the threat. The following eighteen years saw considerable success in disrupting many planned terrorist attacks; the arrest and conviction of hundreds of people for terrorism-related offences; the development of a cross-sector multi-agency counter-terrorism (CT) strategy – CONTEST; the creation of an effective intelligence-sharing and analytical function – since copied elsewhere – in the Joint Terrorism Analysis Centre (JTAC); and a dramatic expansion in the size and capabilities of the key CT bodies, notably the Security Service, MI5 and the Police's Counter-Terrorism Command.

Nevertheless, this period also saw the UK suffer its first suicide terror attacks on home soil, repeated attempts to breach the increased security structures, limited success in reducing the scale of the threat, the handing over of the terrorist baton from one group of jihadist extremists to another and an uncertain approach to community relations and the challenge of radicalization/extremism. As Britain approaches twenty years of trying to contain jihadist terrorism, the recent review of CONTEST was a missed opportunity for policy makers to reflect on how far existing approaches to countering jihadist terrorism are fit for purpose in the coming decades.[1]

Jihadist terrorism's looming threat

The UK was slow to see the emerging threat from jihadist terrorism in the 1990s as one that was likely to involve or indeed threaten the country, not least as most UK counter-terrorism officials remained focused on Irish-related terrorism. The decade had begun with two of the largest bombs in peacetime detonated in the financial district of the city of London. International terrorism seemed peripheral and jihadist extremists, including what became Al-Qaeda (AQ) and Bin Laden himself, dismissed as primarily concerning the UK in the realms of fund raising and political propaganda.

This approach came in for sustained criticism at home and abroad, for apparently allowing the development of extremism in what had become 'Londonistan'.[2] The French in particular believed Algerian terrorists were using the UK as a base of operations against France, although criticism went further with claims of a 'covenant of security' implicitly making the UK safe for extremists as long as no attacks were mounted on UK soil. The evidence for this claim is circumstantial to say the least, but it continues to be repeated.[3] A mistaken belief that these people were dissidents from political repression, as in the 1970s, is another possible explanation.[4] A more prosaic one is that state security organizations are primarily focused on threats to their homelands and defending their own interests before those of others.[5] Until the end of the 1990s no active jihadist-inspired terror plots against the UK were identified and consequently limited effort or resource was devoted to such threats – not a covenant of security, then, but possibly a dangerous oversight, revealing bureaucratic inertia, a poor grasp of the nature of the emerging challenge and an assumption that it would not be the UK that would be most at risk.

When the first apparently AQ-linked/inspired bomb plot in the UK was disrupted in 2000 with the arrest (and later conviction) of a Birmingham man, the effect was not instantaneous – MI5 still devoted more of its resources to Irish-related terrorism as late as 2002.[6] This was all the more surprising since a succession of terrorist spectaculars, including the first attack on the World Trade Centre in 1993, the Khobar Towers barracks attack in Saudi Arabia, the bombing of two US embassies in East Africa and the attack on the USS *Cole* in Aden had led many terrorism scholars and commentators – but crucially few in the UK CT community – to believe that further attacks against the West on home soil by jihadist terrorists (and especially by Al-Qaeda) was only a matter of time.[7]

After 9/11, the UK responded very differently to the United States despite it being one of the most serious terrorist events in history in terms of British casualties, preferring to avoid a war paradigm in official statements or policy. UK practitioners had decades of experience of facing terrorism and had a continuing preference for dealing with the challenge as a criminal justice matter. There was limited appreciation of the potential for indigenous jihadist recruitment as the threat was seen as primarily coming from foreign nationals based abroad.

Furthermore, the UK was still not seen as the primary target of this 'new' terrorism.[8] When a London-born convert to Islam attempted to bring down a trans-Atlantic aircraft in December 2001 it still appeared that the threat was not domestically focused.[9] Many in the UK CT community felt that, while threats to US interests were significant, direct targeting against the UK and its interests was less clear – a view which prevailed until 2004.[10] In that year the plot to explode an enormous fertilizer bomb in a night club or shopping centre, investigated by Operation Crevice, and the arrest and later conviction of Dhiren Barot, who had planned attacks in the United States and also reconnoitred key London landmarks for attacks possibly using a 'dirty bomb' (Operation Rhyme), changed thinking.

Debates over CT legislation

CT legislation has seen vociferous debates since 1998. The UK had reviewed counter-terrorist legislation some time before 9/11, as it became clear that the nature (if not the scale) of the threat was changing. A high-profile review recognized the future centrality of international terrorism: 'Once lasting peace has been established in Northern Ireland, there will continue to be a need for permanent counter-terrorist legislation to deal with the threat of international and domestic terrorism.[11] Lord Lloyd's 1996 report led to the Terrorism Act 2000, which included the proscription of Al-Qaeda and brought terrorism legislation into permanent statute.[12] Further legislation followed with the UK struggling with the security versus liberty question for many years after the 2000 Act, with five major pieces of legislation.

Notwithstanding the coming into force of the Human Rights Act 1998 in 2000, the UK kept the option of derogation from the Act under Article 15 and used this in December 2001 under Pt4 of the Anti-Terrorism, Crime and Security Act 2001.[13] The emerging transnational threat of jihadist terrorism challenged the criminal justice approach, which struggled to provide an effective response to this, or to the challenge of radicalization, a tension which has remained unresolved. A form of detention without trial was introduced from 2001 primarily to deal with individuals who could not be deported or brought to trial, but this eventually collapsed following a decision by the House of Lords.[14] New legislation also sought to allow prosecution for wider offences attached to the earlier stages of terrorist conspiracies and for the freezing of terrorist assets.[15] Following the 2005 London bombings the government brought in an offence of the 'preparation of terrorist acts' with a lower evidential requirement, which has been used numerous times since 2006.[16] This reflected a desire within the British CT approach to bring criminal prosecutions whenever possible, rather than adopt executive action as in some countries and the changed nature of the threat from terrorists.[17]

The use of Pt4 Powers saw a special court, in the form of SIAC (Special Immigration Appeals Commission) which had pre-dated the Terrorism 2000 Act, coming into public consciousness. SIAC used exceptional measures, including closed sessions, the consideration of intelligence material and lower standards of proof. Controversially, the use of intelligence material in its deliberations, unlike in normal courts, led to the appointment of government-sponsored 'Special Advocates' to represent defendants, who, while able to see the classified material presented against their clients, could not share the information with them, hindering an effective defence as a number of special advocates pointed out and the House of Lords agreed in 2009. The fact that these measures had been used sparingly did not change the fact that the legislation was facing repeated criticism and challenge in the courts and more widely. The fact that the UK did not go much further in reforming and adapting the courts system to deal with the 'new' terrorist threat had much to do with the experience of Northern Ireland, where the use of internment and other special measures such as non-jury trials were deemed to have been huge mistakes.

Pre-charge detention powers were another highly controversial area of policy. These had been raised from seven to fourteen days in 2004, but proposals to allow the police the power to detain people for up to ninety days pre-charge were controversial. After defeats on ninety days under Tony Blair (which led to a compromise of twenty-eight days' detention), his successor Gordon Brown attempted to bring in fifty-six days' detention and then settled for forty-two days. It found little support, despite officials claiming that the need to decrypt electronic media and collaborate with international partners lengthened the time needed to build cases. Privately, operational CT police were taken by surprise when the forty-two days proposal emerged, and some thought it impractical and flawed to seek to introduce an element of parliamentary process into live operational work.[18] Other critics included the former head of MI5, Dame Eliza Manningham-Buller, who stated that she could not support the measure when it came to the Lords for approval. The proposals were dropped and the coalition government, which followed Gordon Brown's tenure, returned the pre-charge detention limit to fourteen days.[19] In 2016 most of those arrested for terrorism offences were held for less than seven days, with sixteen people held beyond a week, and only six for fourteen days.[20]

For many, including some within the security community, these various initiatives were flawed by being outside of what the public saw as established judicial process and ran the risk of being seen as aimed at particular communities. Control Orders, in particular, were regarded as not having been thoroughly thought through in terms of how they were to be delivered operationally, which led to the many legal challenges and lack of confidence in them as an effective counter-terrorist measure.[21]

CT strategy

CONTEST was drawn up in secret in 2003, under the stewardship of Sir David Omand, the then Cabinet Secretary for Security and Intelligence, based around four 'Ps' – Prepare, Protect, Prevent and Pursue. The simple and clear structure of the four Ps made the strategy an enduring brand in CT policy for over fifteen years and was made public in 2006. A central idea within CONTEST was to try to dispense with the traditional home/away distinction associated with different forms of terrorism and introduce a genuinely 'joined-up' and 'fully integrated' approach. In 2006, the first of three published editions made this clear: 'the threat has grown and it has changed in character. It has both domestic and international dimensions.'[22] At the centre of CONTEST was the objective 'to reduce the risk to the United Kingdom and its interests overseas from international terrorism, so that people can go about their lives freely and with confidence', which ultimately led to a risk management approach with a focus on resilience and a perhaps unintended operationally and sometimes tactically focused approach.[23]

The Prevent strand of CONTEST, focused on stopping people becoming terrorists, proved the most controversial area – perhaps unsurprisingly as it was also the most difficult. It attempted to involve communities in the goal of countering terrorism through counter-radicalization and even de-radicalization but struggled with the diverse nature of Muslim communities in the UK, a shortage of representative leaders to call upon to support the initiative and a problematic grey zone between extremism, violent extremism and terrorism – for both political and conceptual reasons. By the later years of the 2000s Prevent began to come in for sustained criticism for employing former extremists and funding programmes with poor oversight, vague objectives and unproven outcomes.

Following the election of 2010 Prevent was refreshed and the focus on violent extremism was replaced with an emphasis on extremism more generally and its alleged links to terrorism. The aspect of Prevent concerned with supporting individuals vulnerable to being drawn into terrorism, Channel, was expanded to cover the whole of England and Wales and Prevent became a statutory duty for local authorities. While it received a better press, even Channel struggled to demonstrate its effectiveness, lacking evidence or rigorous data to assess outcomes and was challenged by contested notions of radicalization and extremism. As noted above, the suicide attacks of 7 July 2005 in London confirmed a shift in the focus of CT from foreign terrorists attacking the UK from abroad to British citizens/residents inspired by foreign terrorist networks, which had begun in 2004 – increasing the importance of Prevent in policy and security terms.[24] A focus on counter-radicalization was at variance to previous policy which had never attempted to de-radicalize the enemy – many recommended that de-radicalization be abandoned in favour of de-operationalizing those intent on carrying out terrorist acts.

Structural changes

Resources devoted to counter-terrorism increased dramatically with the emergence of jihadist terrorism. The Single Intelligence Account (SIA), at just under £2 billion since 2011, will reach £2.3 billion in 2020–2021 – a greater than threefold increase on the pre-9/11 figures. Along with policing and other counter-terrorism activity the total spend is over £3 billion per year and is set to continue.[25] MI5 has tripled in size since before 9/11, to roughly 4,000 people with over 80 per cent of its budget now allocated to CT, [26] but most of this expansion came after 2004.[27]

After 'almost 100 years of competition' the Security Service and Police Service are managing to work well together.[28] One key to this change was MI5 procuring the strategic lead for intelligence on Irish-related terrorism in the 1990s, with the police leading on investigations (although the Metropolitan Police Special Branch remained an intelligence organization for all types of terrorism).[29] Most important was the changing nature of the terrorist threat as the jihadist-inspired terrorist era began, with a transnational threat, unclear boundaries compared to previous campaigns against Irish nationalists, and, for Britain, the novel danger of no-notice mass casualty attacks as revealed by Operations Crevice and Rhyme and, eventually, suicide attacks, leading to emphasis on the prioritizing of public safety. The relationship in British CT between evidence and intelligence had to fundamentally change to allow for earlier intervention and prosecution – a process accelerated by wider events. Scepticism about the use of intelligence following the invasion of Iraq saw a desire emerge in official circles to be more open about the nature of the terrorist threat to the UK (in the face of some public scepticism), and a pressure for intelligence to be gathered if at all possible in ways that were admissible in court and therefore open to public understanding. Eventually these trends led to the creation of Counter Terrorism Command,[30] which, like MI5, expanded significantly, doubling to over 1,700 staff. It increasingly worked closely with MI5 as the threat evolved and the need for evidential approaches and intelligence gathering to converge was accepted.[31] As an example of British success in CT, the working relationship between the domestic intelligence agency and the police services now stands as an international example, if not an international rarity.

The slow appreciation of the emerging jihadist terror threat in the 1990s led to another important reform with the creation in 2003 of JTAC, an inter-agency body tasked with assessing intelligence on the terrorist threat. JTAC has proven to be one of the more successful innovations bringing together officials from across sixteen government departments and agencies to produce all-source analysis. The officials are seconded into the Centre for several years but retain links with their home departments. The decision to take the analytical capability from the individual departments and place them together in JTAC, rather than create a competing agency with its own analysts, had the effect of forcing the various parts of CT intelligence assessment to work together. JTAC was later given responsibility for setting the national terrorist threat level in an attempt to meet criticism that ministers might be tempted to use the terrorist threat assessment for political ends, such as the expansion of legal powers. The threat-level system has weathered these storms but remains of questionable relevance to the public which is not really empowered or informed sufficiently to meaningfully respond to changes in the threat level, not least as it has not fallen below the second highest level for many years. The problems in this area speak to the wider challenge of involving partners across communities and the public more generally in counter-terrorism – an area of policy that has seen limited development in the fifteen years of CONTEST's operation.

The transfer of CT policy responsibility from the Cabinet Office to the Home Office with the establishment of the Office for Security and Counter-Terrorism (OSCT) in 2007 placed CT policy firmly in a department concerned with domestic issues. The author has argued elsewhere that this may have held back the evolution of Britain's counter-terrorism approach as 'CONTEST was excluded by design from developing into a comprehensive military and security strategy for CT, the focus being on developing civilian structures for coordination'.[32] Thus from ambitious beginnings in CONTEST's early years, an unintended effect of placing OSCT in the Home Office may have been that it effectively evolved into a strategy for 'homeland security', not one for countering the jihadist terrorist threat more broadly, despite rhetoric to the contrary. For example, it was only thirteen years after the creation of JTAC that a cross-Whitehall organization was established to work on international terrorism policy and delivery.[33]

Other elements of state power have also been slow to integrate with CT machinery. Notwithstanding long established powers for military support to the civil authorities in terrorist emergencies under MACP and other doctrinal structures, or occasional high-profile deployments such as the deployment of armoured vehicles to Heathrow airport in 2003, the Ministry of Defence (MoD) was slow to evolve its approach to countering terrorism.[34] Despite repeated reviews and internal debates, the MoD only very reluctantly embraced a domestic role to reinforce the police during high levels of threat, with the development of Operation Temperer, which saw the short-term deployment of uniformed personnel following terror attacks in 2017.[35] The MoD, perhaps surprisingly given the threat, has eschewed any significant doctrinal development of its counter-terrorism thinking in the past twenty years – surprising as the equipment and tactics of the UK CT police forces were found to compare poorly with those of their military counterparts in certain key areas as late as July 2005. The creation of a more capable armed policing function, through elite CT police units, has resulted – as well as an expansion in armed police officers, planned to be 11,500 by 2018.[36] Such changes represent another change in the 'normality' sought by CONTEST's approach.

Targeted killing

The UK has displayed limited ambition in respect of ever attempting to 'destroy' terrorism (or even effectively degrading terrorist networks) overseas other than through the intervention in Afghanistan and limited activity in Iraq/Syria.[37]

Many policy makers would suggest that any other stated aim would be senseless given UK experience of terrorism – but, in effect, the UK left this aspect of the campaign to others, notably the United States and its controversial 'drone' campaigns. As such the UK has had little, if any, obvious influence on how that campaign has evolved. The use of drones in 2015 to kill two British citizens in Syria, one of whom was allegedly plotting attacks in the UK on behalf of the Islamic State group, took the UK into new territory in targeted killing.[38] Despite this strike, the UK has been reluctant to embrace the US chosen policy of vigorously degrading jihadist networks through targeted killings, not least as its long-term utility (even accepting short-term tactical gains) remains unproven, but the UK has also had no strategic or conceptual basis from which to proffer any alternative.

Limitations

The oversight of counter-terrorism has also seen limited evolution given the scale of bureaucratic effort, the controversial nature of aspects of its implementation and the significant sums of public money involved. While the position of Independent Reviewer of Terrorism Legislation was put on a statutory basis in 2006 and has developed into an influential voice in CT matters, oversight of counter-terrorism as a cross-cutting policy issue encompassing education, home affairs, transport, intelligence, foreign affairs, local government and the regions, and even defence, has proven difficult to achieve and remains siloed in the select committee structure of parliamentary oversight. Controversies have tended to focus on rendition, intelligence sharing, electronic surveillance, pre-charge detention, Control Orders and Terrorism Prevention and Investigation Measures (TPIMs), and the Prevent brand, not the effectiveness of CONTEST as a national strategy.

It has also proven difficult to frame an effective counter-narrative to jihadism's simple and compelling language, notably backed by graphic images of violence under the Islamic State group – governments are in any case perhaps the worst agency to deliver such messages. Jihadist terrorists have been adept in embracing social media in ways that governments have struggled to emulate or keep pace with – not least as official spokespersons must be sure of their facts. Partnering with communities has proven essential in this work but it is not a panacea and remains difficult unless governments are prepared to accept criticism as well as issue edicts. The lack of community engagement and understanding also partly explains the slow response to two waves of foreign terrorist fighters – in the 1990s with UK nationals passing through mostly Pakistan-based training camps and in the past decade with some 800 UK-based persons responding to the Islamic State group's mobilization, albeit at a far lower level in per capita terms than other European countries.[39]

The operational challenge

The range of threats over the past twenty years has proven particularly demanding – from sophisticated foreign-inspired or -directed conspiracies, to unsophisticated actions which can still prove deadly. The pressures on intelligence and policing were demonstrated most acutely by the 7/7 suicide bombings in London which were followed on 21st July by another attempted series of attacks by four more suicide bombers whose devices failed to detonate. Two of the 7/7 attackers had been linked to another major CT investigation[40] and MI5 was criticized for failing to follow up all leads.[41] The shooting dead of an innocent Brazilian electrician, Jean Charles de Menezes, on 22 July by armed police officers, who mistook him for one of the 21/7 suspects, brought the procedures for dealing with suicide bombers, Operation Kratos, into public discourse, along with the role of the armed forces in supporting counter-terrorist operations in the UK.[42] A year later came one of the biggest terrorist conspiracies of the decade and one of the most successful CT operations – the Liquid Bomb plot to destroy up to ten trans-Atlantic aircraft in an attempt to bring commercial aviation to a standstill.[43]

As understanding of the domestic threat developed, so did the publicly reported number of MI5's persons of interest which rose steadily: from less than 300 in 2001, to hundreds more before the 7/7 attacks and up to 1,600 by 2006. The following year that number had increased to over 2,000, with another 2,000 people potentially of interest.[44] As the challenge moved to Islamic State group-linked terrorism from 2013, MI5 still talked of several thousand people being of interest to them. The Islamic State group mobilization led to another huge spike in activity, with MI5 reporting that twenty-two plots had been thwarted since 2013, nine of which were since March 2017. As of 2018, it lists 500 ongoing terrorist investigations, involving 3,000 persons of interest and, remarkably, a wider pool of over 20,000 individuals who have previously been subjects of investigation.[45] The Islamic State group's mobilization brought into sharp relief the need for closer international co-operation, even amongst close allies such as EU members.

Conclusion

The success in disrupting most terrorist conspiracies over the past eighteen years is for many policy makers what really counts and it is undeniable that at an operational level counter-terrorism in the UK has been broadly successful. Strategically, things are less clear-cut. Given CONTEST's stated central aim to 'reduce the risk to the United Kingdom and its interests overseas from international terrorism', any belief that CONTEST has succeeded is a narrow reading of the aim – the threat of terrorism can hardly be said to have reduced and public concerns about terrorism remain high. The UK has not adopted wider emergency measures such as seen in France, but it has stretched any definition of normality through a series of significant changes in how the state is secured in response to the jihadist terror challenge.

Tellingly, 2017 saw five attacks and nine major plots against the UK foiled – the deadliest year since the 7/7 attacks of 2005. Of particular concern has been the difficulty in addressing continuing radicalization of UK nationals and residents. While the Islamic State group appears to have lost the initiative it so spectacularly possessed during the height of its mobilization of foreign fighters, this does not mean that the potential for further radicalization of UK citizens does not remain high, or that jihadist terrorist ideology is about to disappear. As a leading scholar of radicalization points out: 'Salafi-Jihadism remains an extremely resilient soteriology … it has endured and survived more than three decades of forceful repression.'[46] The Islamic State group's increased focus on a far enemy, as it loses its foothold in Syria and Iraq and scatters across the Middle East and beyond, is possible but not inevitable.

The planned focus on extremism in forthcoming policy reviews is likely to hit up against the continuing challenge of breaking down the barrier in conceptual terms between home and away, and between existing definitions of domestic extremism and international counter-terrorism. Such a distinction, according to a former reviewer of terrorist legislation, 'may have made sense when Islamist plotters were assumed to sit in Afghan caves, but is hard to sustain in the age of the home-grown Islamist terrorist and the emergence of a digital world without borders'.[47] Furthermore, a workable definition of extremism remains elusive. The CONTEST review of 2018 disappointingly did not provide clarity on how the operational successes of twenty years of counter-terrorism can be matched strategically. It is to be hoped that future policy developments will quickly provide this guidance.

Notes

1 Containment of the threat has never been officially identified as an objective, although is implied by the aim of Contest discussed below.

2 See M. Phillips, *Londonistan*, London: Gibson Square, 2008; and F. Foley, *Countering Terrorism in Britain and France*, Cambridge: Cambridge University Press, 2013, pp. 245–251.

3 For example, anonymous interviews by former CT officials and reported remarks by the radical preacher Omar Bakri in 2005.

4 R. Pantucci, '*We Love Death as you Love Life*': *Britain's Suburban Terrorists*, London: Hurst, 2015, pp. 45–49.

5 Although never admitted, British intelligence agencies have also tended to prefer to monitor threats in plain sight rather than force them underground. A number of radical preachers reported being approached by the security services in these years as sources of information – any such approaches could have been for various reasons.

6 Moinul Abedin, who had moved to the UK from Bangladesh in the 1980s as a child with his family, had amassed 100 kilograms of chemicals believed to be in preparation for a major bomb attack – his alleged accomplice was found not guilty.

7 The British Government listed the 1993 World Trade Centre attack as one of AQ's first attacks in a chronology published after 9/11, although many scholars now believe the attack was not AQ related or inspired, despite the connection between the bomber, Ramzi Yousef, and Khalid Sheik Mohammed (his uncle) but who was not yet believed to be part of AQ. For a number of years the Khobar Towers attack in Saudi Arabia was also attributed to AQ, but is now believed to have been the work of a Saudi affiliate of Hezbollah.

8 See P. Neumann, *Old and New Terrorism*, London: Polity Press, 2009.

9 Richard Reid, aka the Shoe Bomber – arguably the UK's first attempted suicide terrorist. An accomplice, Saajid Badat, chose not to carry out his attack and dismantled his device. Two Britons, Omar Sharif and Asil Hanif, launched suicide attacks in Israel in April 2003, but named George W. Bush and Tony Blair as deserving of punishment in videos released later by Hamas.

10 Most activity that was seen was believed to be focused on raising money for organizations/operations abroad. Even the 2002 investigation into a suspected plot to produce ricin, Operation Springbourne, did not change this belief, with the direct threat to the UK questioned. Kamal Bourgass had been sentenced in 2004 to life imprisonment for killing a police officer during his arrest, but in 2005 was further convicted of conspiracy to commit a public nuisance by using poisons or explosives.

11 The Rt Hon Lord Lloyd of Berwick, 'Inquiry into Legislation against Terrorism, Volume I', *Cm 3420*, October 1996, p. xii.

12 The Terrorism Act 2000 came into force in early 2001. Previous legislation required annual approval by Parliament. The Act broadened the definition of terrorism to include religious motivation and included the disruption of electronic systems as qualifying as acts of terrorism.

13 C. Walker, 'Decennium 7/7: The United Kingdom Terrorist Attacks on July 7, 2005, and the Evolution of Anti-Terrorism Policies, Laws, and Practices', *Zeitschrift für Internationale Strafrechtsdogmatik*, vol. 10, no. 11, 2015, pp. 545–555.

14 Control Orders in the 2005 Prevention of Terrorism Act and, later Terrorism Prevention and Investigation Measures Act (TPIMs) in 2011 followed.

15 Walker, *Decennium 7/7*, pp. 547–548.

16 Foley, *Countering Terrorism in Britain and France*, p. 210.

17 Operations Springbourne and Rhyme had revealed the need for offences within the criminal law that would allow for the prosecution of an evolved terrorist threat within the criminal justice system, which did not rely on the Victorian common law offence of 'conspiracy to cause a public nuisance' (which had to be used against terror suspects in earlier cases), but still with a criminal burden of proof. Former senior CT official.

18 I am grateful to an anonymous reviewer for clarifying this point.

19 With a technical possibility to extend this to twenty-eight days in exceptional circumstances of multiple and simultaneous investigations.

20 M. Hill QC, *The Terrorism Acts in 2016: Report of the independent reviewer of terrorism legislation on the operation of the Terrorism Acts 2000 and 2006*, London: HM Stationery Office, 2018, para 6.11, available here: https://

terrorismlegislationreviewer.independent.gov.uk/wp-content/uploads/2018/01/Terrorism-Acts-in-2016.pdf.

21 Former UK security official.

22 HM Government, *Countering International Terrorism: The United Kingdom's Strategy*, Cm 6888, July 2006, p. 3.

23 HM Government, *Pursue Prevent Protect Prepare: The United Kingdom's Strategy for Countering International Terrorism*, Cm 7547, March 2009, p. 56.

24 In early 2004, Operation Crevice, the investigation into a plot to explode a fertilizer bomb at a nightclub or shopping centre, had led to the arrest of Omar Khyam's AQ-inspired network, beginning the shift of focus. The investigation was one of the most extensive and complex in CT history.

25 The 2015 Spending review set a figure of £15.1 billion for counter-terrorism for 2016–2021, up 30 per cent on the previous plans.

26 MI5 website, 'Allocation of Resources by Core Business', 2015/16.

27 S. Hewitt, *The British War on Terrorism*, London: Continuum, 2008, p. 98.

28 Former intelligence official. There was frequent rivalry between MI5 and Special Branch. See also D. Anderson QC, *Attacks in London and Manchester March-June 2017 – Independent Assessment of MI5 and Police Internal Reviews*, 2017, available here: https://www.gov.uk/government/uploads/system/uploads/attachment_data/file/664682/Attacks_in_London_and_Manchester_Open_Report.pdf.

29 The Ascribe arrangements of around 1993. While the Metropolitan Police Anti-Terrorist Branch carried out evidential investigations, intelligence was fed through to evidential investigators at the discretion of intelligence operatives, were they Special Branch or MI5. There was frequent rivalry between MI5 and Special Branch according to insiders.

30 In 2006 Special Branch and the Anti-Terrorist Branch amalgamated to form the new Counter Terrorism Command.

31 Foley, *Countering Terrorism in Britain and France*, pp. 148–154. This along with the creation of regional counter-terrorism units (CTUs) and Counter-Terrorism Intelligence Units (CTIUs) added over 1,500 more counter-terrorism employed police officers around the regions to CTC. MI5 had similarly also established a number of regional offices around the country helping avoid the impression that sharing was only at a national/London level.

32 J. Gearson and H. Rosemont, 'CONTEST as strategy: Reassessing Britain's Counter-Terrorism Approach', *Studies in Conflict and Terrorism*, vol. 38, no. 12, 2015, pp. 1038–1064 esp. section: 'CONTEST isn't broken, so why fix it?'

33 The Joint International Counter-Terrorism Unit was formed in April 2016, based in the Home Office but staffed by FCO and HO officials.

34 David Blunkett, the then Home Secretary, has since written about the 'counter-productive' nature of such deployments unless 'fundamental to the protection of the British people' (Letters to the editor, *The Guardian*, 09072012). Security officials involved in the operation regard the 2003 deployment as a textbook intelligence-led preventative deployment, which deterred a possible attack. The differing perspectives reveal the policy tensions that continue in this area.

35 The successful deployment of troops in support of the London Games in 2012, as well as a desire to avoid a French-style solution of mass mobilization following a series of attacks, may have helped change minds.

36 The Counter-Terrorist Specialist Firearms Officers have special equipment, grey uniforms and, in a significant departure for the UK community-based policing model, often deploy with their faces covered. The 11,500 figure is made up of 7,000 armed police from the forty-three forces in England and Wales, and 3,500 from other forces, including the Civil Nuclear Constabulary.

37 The intervention in Libya was not predicated on countering terrorism, nor was action in Iraq initially, although later releases of JIC papers revealed that the latter was expected to increase the threat domestically.

38 Reyaad Khan and Ruhul Amin were killed in a strike carried out on 21 August 2015 by a Royal Air Force remotely piloted aircraft while travelling near Raqqah in Syria.

39 Some early assessments likened them to British citizens who travelled to Spain in the 1930s to join the International Brigade. Powers to prevent people from leaving the UK and to prevent them returning and even losing their rights of citizenship have followed, which along with more effective monitoring by the Turkish authorities and the loss of initiative by the Islamic State appears to have slowed this mobilization considerably.

40 Operation Crevice.

41 Hewitt, *The British War on Terrorism*, pp. 86–88, 97–98.

42 The operation was criticized for allowing him to leave his flat, board a bus and then enter an underground station and board a train, before he was then shot, despite no positive ID being made. It was later revealed that police officers had been called to over 250 suspected suicide incidents between 7/7 and the shooting of de Menezes. The armed forces are believed to have provided operational support as part of these operations.

43 Operation Overt of 2006. Links between the plotters and an alleged British AQ operative, saw his attempted extradition from Pakistan, which failed, although convictions of a number of conspirators were secured in British courts. Rashid Rauf later disappeared from sight before being reported killed in a US drone attack in 2008.

44 More than three quarters of the conspiracies involving persons of interest were linked to Pakistan's tribal areas in the middle part of the 2000s – by 2010 this was down to less than 50 per cent, as the threat broadened to Somalia, Yemen and eventually Iraq and Syria.

45 While the Westminster and Manchester attackers had both been subjects of interest and one of the London Bridge attackers was under active investigation, the perpetrators of the majority of the twenty Islamist plots foiled since mid-2013 were under active investigation. See Anderson, *Attacks in London and Manchester March-June 2017*, para 2.78 & 5.27.

46 S. Maher, *Salafi-Jihadism: The History of an Idea*, London, Hurst, 2016, p. 211.

47 Anderson, *Attacks in London and Manchester March-June 2017,* para 3.46, and fn44.

Recommended Readings

Anderson QC, D., *Attacks in London and Manchester* March-June *2017 – Independent Assessment of MI5 and Police Internal Reviews*, London: H.M. Stationery Office, 2017.

Foley, F., *Countering Terrorism in Britain and France,* Cambridge: Cambridge University Press, 2016.

Gearson, J. and H. Rosemont, 'CONTEST as Strategy: Reassessing Britain's Counter-Terrorism Approach', *Studies in Conflict and Terrorism*, vol. 38, no. 12, 2015, pp. 1038–1064.
Hill QC, M., *The Terrorism Acts in 2016: Report of the Independent Reviewer of Terrorism Legislation on the Operation of the Terrorism Acts 2000 and 2006*, London: H.M. Stationery Office, 2018.
Hewitt, S., *The British War on Terrorism*, London: Continuum, 2008.
HM Government, *Countering International Terrorism: The United Kingdom's Strategy*, Cm 6888, July 2006.
HM Government, *Pursue Prevent Protect Prepare: The United Kingdom's Strategy for Countering International Terrorism*, Cm 7547, March 2009.
Lord Lloyd of Berwick, 'Inquiry into Legislation Against Terrorism, Volume I', *Cm 3420*, October 1996.
Maher, S., *Salafi-Jihadism: The History of an Idea*, London: Hurst, 2016.
Neumann, P., *Old and New Terrorism*, London: Polity Press, 2009.
Pantucci, R., *'We Love Death as You Love Life': Britain's Suburban Terrorists*, London: Hurst, 2015.
Phillips, M., *Londonistan*, London: Gibson Square, 2008.
Walker, C., 'Decennium 7/7: The United Kingdom Terrorist Attacks on July 7, 2005, and the Evolution of Anti-Terrorism Policies, Laws, and Practices', *Zeitschrift für Internationale Strafrechtsdogmatik*, vol. 10, no. 11, 2015, pp. 545–555.

26 AN INDEPENDENT ASSESSMENT OF THE UK'S CAPACITY AND CAPABILITIES DEVOTED TO COUNTERING JIHADIST TERRORISM: GOVERNMENT, POLICING, INTELLIGENCE AGENCIES AND CIVIL SOCIETY

Richard Walton

Introduction

This chapter aims to provide an independent assessment of the capacity and capabilities of UK government, police, intelligence agencies and civil society in relation to countering jihadi terrorism which is defined for the purpose of this work as 'Islamist terrorism which justifies the incitement, threats or acts of violence around the world in the name of Islam'.

Assessments of the capacity and capabilities of the UK's resources devoted to countering jihadi terrorism have been limited to date to irregular scrutinies and reviews undertaken by the Home Affairs Select Committee (HASC), Intelligence and Security Committee (ISC), National Audit Office (NAO) and minimal published academic papers.[1] There is a clear need for further research and assessment methodology to be applied in this field. With information held by the police and intelligence agencies remaining necessarily limited and governed by Official Secrets Act legislation, there is an understandable absence of accessible data. This scarcity is countered, however, by an ever-increasing number of academic research institutions embracing the topic and generating mainstream and widespread interest in the field. It remains critical and core to the value of any independent assessment that a reasonable balance between these two ends of the spectrum is maintained.

The UK's strategy for Counter-Terrorism (CT), CONTEST, is now in its fifteenth year. It has been subject to regular revision since its inception in 2003 and the most recent version was presented to Parliament in June 2018. CONTEST is rooted in the fundamental principle that terrorism is most successfully defeated through a Rule of Law CT strategy, which I refer to in this chapter as the UK CT Rule of Law Model. This model is predicated on the understanding that terrorism is first and foremost a criminal offence and that perpetrators must therefore face justice in a court of law and penalties, where awarded, commensurate with their crime.[2] In so doing, supporters of extremism and terrorism lose their legitimacy, extremist narratives are countered and the confidence of citizens in the rule of law is upheld. This model places high value on the fundamental rights and freedoms enshrined in the Human Rights Act 1998, in particular Right to Life (Article 2), Right to a Fair Trial (Article 6) and No Punishment Without Law (Article 7).

The UK's Counter-Extremism (CE) Strategy,[3] published on 19 October 2015, defined extremism for the first time as 'vocal or active opposition to our fundamental values, including democracy, the rule of law, individual liberty and the mutual respect and tolerance of different faiths and beliefs' and set out strategic objectives to counter-extremist ideology, build and establish partnerships with those who oppose extremism, disrupt extremists and build more cohesive communities. The strategy was instigated by the then Prime Minister David Cameron who wrote that 'the fight against Islamist extremism is … one of the great struggles of our generation' and that 'terrorism is really a symptom; ideology is the root cause'.[4]

UK government's CT capacity and capabilities

The UK government's focus on tackling terrorism has been sustained at a consistently high level over the past twenty years. Terrorist threats are debated extensively by all political parties with terrorism remaining '*one of the highest priority risks to the UK's national security*' and a designated priority within the National Security Objectives set out in the National Security Strategy.[5]

The threat from jihadist terrorism in the UK has consistently risen over the past twenty years; being described recently as 'multi-dimensional, evolving rapidly and operating at a scale and pace we've not seen before'.[6]

The CONTEST strategy (with its four pillars of Prevent, Pursue, Protect and Prepare) is considered world-leading, with many nation states replicating its approach. This is evidenced by the Council of the EU initiating its first CT strategy in 2005[7] with the four almost identical pillars of Prevent, Protect, Pursue and Respond, the UN instigating its own CT strategy in 2006[8] along very similar lines and, more recently, the Australian/New Zealand National Counter-Terrorism Plan of 2017 setting out similar pillars of Preparedness, Prevention, Response and Recovery.[9]

The revised CONTEST[10] strategy published in June 2018 takes account of the learning from the five terrorist attacks in London and Manchester in 2017. In particular: new legislation is being introduced that will underpin an approach to disrupt terrorism threats earlier; intelligence available to MI5 and Counter-Terrorism Policing will be shared 'with a broader range of partners, including government departments' using 'multi agency approaches' (similar to those that currently exist within the field of sex offender management); a more integrated relationship with the private sector will be sought; the UK will continue to lead on campaigns on aviation security and preventing terrorist use of the internet; and, of particular note here, the resilience of local communities will be strengthened. The strategy acknowledges that Counter-Extremism strategies are emerging (both within the UK and globally) but are not yet as widely established within government departments and civil society structures.

The Home Secretary is the lead Minister for the UK's CONTEST and CVE strategies which are now executed across multiple government departments. For instance, the Ministry of Justice (MOJ) has created a new Security, Order and Counter-Terrorism Directorate that leads on the 'development and delivery of a plan for countering Islamist extremism in prisons and probation';[11] the Department of Education has introduced a range of CVE measures, including publishing advice on the Prevent Duty[12] and a guide to help schools better understand the techniques terrorist groups use across social media[13] and the Charities Commission (overseen by the Department for Culture, Media and Sport (DCMS)) has engaged in reviews of UK-registered charities where there are identified concerns about abuse and mismanagement linked to extremism.

There is empirical evidence that the Prevent strategy has resulted in a significant number of referrals to police.[14] Various agencies made 7,631 referrals in 2015/16, resulting in 1,072 individuals being subsequently assessed for inclusion in Channel, the government's de-radicalization programme.[15] Of those referred, '36% left the process requiring no further action, 50% were signposted to alternative services and 14% were deemed suitable, through preliminary assessment, to be discussed at a Channel panel'. The effectiveness of the Prevent strategy is, however, reliant on people and professionals referring individuals of concern to the police and the subsequent triage and response by police and other agencies to such referrals.

A raft of CT legislation has been enacted over the past twenty years to address the increasing threat from jihadist and other terrorist threats, resulting in the UK having one of the largest suites of counter-terrorism legislative measures of any country in the world, legislation which is subject to continuous review and scrutiny by the UK's Independent Reviewer of Terrorism Legislation.

Unprecedented levels of spending on CT have been supported by the UK government in response to growing jihadist terrorism threats,[16,17] including substantial increases in the CT policing budget and the budgets of the UK intelligence agencies MI5, MI6 and GCHQ.[18] Cross-government spending on security and CT rose from £9.2 billion in 2007–2008 to £10.3 billion in

2010–2011.[19] Over the current spending review period (2015–2019) cross-government spending is expected to increase by 30 per cent from £11.7 billion in 2015 to £15.1 billion in 2021.

The UK is, therefore, assessed as having one of the most respected CT strategies ('CONTEST') of any country in the world with successive UK governments led by all three major political parties having repeatedly enacted new legislation to address the shift in jihadist and other terrorist threats. It has also delivered a pan-government strategic approach and increased spending on CT and CVE. Its CVE strategy, whilst relatively new, is seeking innovative approaches across a range of platforms.

Intelligence agencies and CT policing capacity and capability

The UK's intelligence agencies MI5, MI6 and GCHQ, together with the National Police CT Network (NPCTN), have joint responsibility to gather intelligence against and disrupt jihadist terrorist threats through the application of the UK CT Rule of Law Model.

Over the past twenty years, as the threat from jihadist terrorism has increased, investment in all four organizations has risen substantially with the overall budget for the three intelligence agencies increasing from £1.95 billion in 2011 to £2.373 billion in 2016–2017 and projected to rise to £2.584 billion in 2019–2020.[20] The overall CT Grant for policing counter-terrorism has risen from £579 million in 2010–2011 to £707 million in 2017–2018 (plus an additional £24 million in extra support) and is projected to increase to £757 million in 2018–2019.[21]

In June 2013, the government announced (in the spending review) that the annual budget for the three intelligence agencies, MI5, MI6 and GCHQ, would see a 'real terms increase of 3.4 per cent' in 2015–2016.[22]

The three intelligence agencies and NPCTN have substantially increased in size accordingly. Following the attacks in Paris in November 2015 the then Prime Minister David Cameron announced a significant increase in spending of 15 per cent for MI5, MI6 and GCHQ and an increase of 1900 'security and intelligence staff'.[23]

In 1991 the UK government instructed MI5, an organization that employed approximately 2,000 people, to regard terrorism as a threat to national security.[24,25] By 2004, its budget having grown in the intervening years and faced with an increasing jihadist terrorist threat, both at home and overseas, it was reported that MI5 was increasing the number of employees from 3,500 to 4,100 by early 2011.[26] In his speech in 2017 the Director General of MI5 Andrew Parker confirmed that the organization was growing its number of employees again: 'the women and men of MI5, growing from 4,000 to 5,000 over the next couple of years.'[27]

MI5 acknowledges that 'the resources of all three of the UK's intelligence agencies have been significantly increased since 2001' and that it has 'nearly doubled the number of its staff over the last decade' with '63 per cent of MI5's resources now used to support international counter-terrorism work'.[28]

Specialist police personnel resources in the UK devoted to international terrorist threats (which included Sikh, Tamil, Kashmiri and Palestinian as well as Islamist terrorism) numbered in the low hundreds in 1998, when the jihadist terrorist threat first emerged as a global concern following the Al-Qaeda terrorist attacks against the US embassies in Tanzania and Kenya on 7 August 1998. At this time New Scotland Yard had around 1,200 officers and staff devoted to all security, terrorism and extremism threats, approximately 400 of whom were in the Anti-Terrorist Branch and approximately 800 of whom were in the Metropolitan Police Special Branch (MPSB) (units which were subsequently merged in 2006 to create the Counter Terrorism Command (SO15)). The vast majority of these officers and staff, however, were focusing their efforts on the ongoing threat from Irish terrorism. Today, the National CT Police Network (NCTPN), which was created following the terrorist attacks on 7 July 2005, has over 4,000 specialist CT police officers and staff, including approximately 2,000 in SO15 in London and internationally (working in seventy-six different specialist units), in addition to four regional Counter-Terrorism Units (CTUs) across the country in Leeds, Manchester, Birmingham and Thames Valley. The network also has a National CT Police HQ in London that co-ordinates the national police response to terrorism threats and a National Policing CT Operations Centre responsible for running covert pro-active police surveillance operations against terrorist suspects in collaboration with the intelligence agencies.

The UK CT Rule of Law Model has evolved over many decades to become a highly effective system facilitating a uniquely collaborative interaction between the police and intelligence agencies, allowing for pre-emptive identification and disruption of terrorist threats leading to arrests, convictions and prison sentences.[29]

The high number of disrupted plots and resulting convictions for terrorist offences over the past twenty years (the vast majority of which were jihadist terrorism cases) is evidence of the success of the UK CT Rule of Law Model and strategy against jihadist terrorist threats[30,31]. For example, in 2013, the Head of MI5 informed the Intelligence and Security Committee (ISC) that since the suicide bomb attacks in London on 7 July 2005 'intervention by counter-terrorism agents and police officers had foiled one or two terror attacks a year aimed at creating mass casualties'.[32] In 2014, the then Home Secretary Theresa May stated that 'the Security Service believes that since the attacks on 7 July 2005 around 40 terrorist plots have been disrupted'.[33] In an acknowledgement that jihadi terrorist attack plotting has become more prevalent, it was revealed in November 2017 that twenty-two terrorist plots had been thwarted since November 2013 and nine since the Westminster terrorist attack on 22 March 2017.[34] In December 2017, in confirmation that the vast majority of these were jihadist attack plots,

David Anderson, the former Independent Reviewer of Terrorism Legislation, wrote, 'MI5 and CT Policing have thwarted 20 Islamist terrorist plots in the past four years, resulting in 10 life sentences from the seven plots that have so far come to trial.'[35]

It must be acknowledged, however, that limitations of the UK CT Rule of Law Model have been periodically exposed, with 2017 recognized as the most challenging year since the four separate terrorist attacks on 7 July 2005. The 2017 attacks, that resulted in the deaths of thirty-four people, exposed two notable limitations to the model: firstly, it is heavily geared and funded towards dealing with an identifiable presentation of jihadist terrorism such as radicalized Islamic extremists with intent and capability to carry out a terrorist attack, rather than the root causes such as tackling proponents of warped interpretations of Islamic ideology, with resources allocated accordingly. Secondly, despite substantial increases in resources, police and intelligence agencies executing the 'Pursue' pillar of the UK CT Rule of Law Model are struggling to monitor the increasing number of Islamist extremists within the UK, thereby increasing the potential risk of an attack. The new CONTEST strategy attempts to address this challenge by introducing greater sharing of intelligence by MI5 and CT police with a wider number of agencies via newly created multiagency panels, a policy change introduced in response to David Anderson's 'Independent Assessment of MI5 and Police Internal Reviews' into the terrorist attacks in London and Manchester in 2017.[36]

The recent surge in the jihadist terrorist threat, described by Andrew Parker as a 'dramatic upshift' in 2017 and with 'more threat, coming at us more quickly, and sometimes harder to detect', has placed increasing demands on the UK CT Rule of Law Model, requiring government, police, intelligence agencies and civil society to adopt increasingly collaborative approaches.[37] The surge has resulted in MI5 and NCTPN now 'running well over 500 live operations involving 3,000 individuals known to be currently involved in extremist activity in some way … and a growing pool of over 20,000 individuals that we have looked at in the past in our terrorist investigations'.[38] These mostly pro-active operations are necessarily covert with intelligence agencies and the NCTPN needing to obtain evidence of terrorist offences using a range of lawful techniques such as the interception of communications and mobile surveillance of extremists.

These statistics confirm what CT professionals have long known and witnessed: that jihadist extremism has continued to rise within the UK as well as globally over the past twenty years. To a large extent this form of extremism is a domestic challenge from within the UK with the majority of terrorism-related arrests having been of individuals who were born and educated in the UK as opposed to having entered as immigrants or visitors.[39] Since 11 September 2001 ('9/11') 2,001 UK nationals have been arrested for terrorism offences in the UK equating to 57 per cent of the total number arrested (i.e. including non-UK nationals). This trend is not unique to the UK. Research of the 51 terrorist attacks carried out between June

2014 and June 2017 in Europe and North America reveals that 73 per cent of the perpetrators were citizens of the country in which they committed the attack.[40]

UK's capacity and capability to counter jihadist terrorism in civil society

The population of the UK has become significantly more diverse and cosmopolitan over the past twenty years, with the number of people identifying themselves as Muslim having also significantly increased.[41,42] The UK has experienced a simultaneous increase in Islamist extremism and jihadist terrorism over the same time period.

Academic research indicates that extremists perpetrating acts of terrorism have ties to relatively few vocal, often charismatic, extremist leaders from a small number of extremist groups[43] (e.g. the proscribed organization Al-Muhajiroun), and recent research and reviews provide evidence that some UK Muslim communities are insufficiently resilient to openly advocate tolerance and to resist, expose and confront extremist narratives. Muslim civil society within the UK appears to some degree to be insecure in its ability to support the UK government's counter-terrorism strategy and to confront extremists when they propagate extremist narratives, thereby, albeit inadvertently, allowing extremism to flourish. A review of integration in 2016 found 'a growing sense of grievance among sections of the Muslim population'.[44] A more recent commission concluded that 'the increasing absence of Muslims from British civil society is a growing problem in the UK'.[45] This absence can create vacuums for extremists to fill within institutions and communities – for instance, as witnessed in the 'co-ordinated, deliberate and sustained action … to introduce an intolerant and aggressive Islamic ethos into a few schools in Birmingham'.[46]

When Muslim communities are not appropriately integrated and their civil societies are weak or insecure, they can be, as a consequence, less self-aware and vulnerable to victimization by racist individuals and politically far-right groups (whose numbers have increased in the past three to five years), and to radicalization by individuals and organizations who support an extremist violent form of Islam, potentially resulting in a phenomenon referred to by some as 'reciprocal radicalisation'.[47]

Furthermore, there is a scarcity of effective UK civil society umbrella organizations that impartially represent a diversity of Muslim interests and organizations in the UK. By way of example, the Muslim Council of Britain (MCB) claims to be a broad-based, representative organization of Muslims in Britain, with over 500 Muslim-affiliated organizations, but has historically been controversial and criticized by government ministers from the two main British political parties for a lack of support of the UK Prevent Strategy and a reluctance to engage in counter-extremism projects. The recently appointed Home Secretary Sajid Javid recently supported this view when he said: 'The MCB does not represent Muslims in this country.'[48]

Against this backdrop, a small number of increasingly vocal Muslim campaigning pressure groups have emerged, some of which openly condone or actively promote jihadist extremism – for example, CAGE, whose Director was convicted of a terrorist offence in 2017,[49] and Islamic Education and Research Academy (IERA), which was subject to a Charity Commission investigation that concluded that their trustees 'needed to consider how they address any views which promote extremism.'[50] Neither of these groups express explicit support for any aspect of the government's CT strategy.

Conclusion

The UK has a robust and coherent counter-terrorism strategy (CONTEST) that promotes a UK CT Rule of Law model and which is replicated and respected across the world. It has a less-well-developed CVE strategy that is not yet seen as an international benchmark for countering extremism but which is fast undergoing significant developments.

The NCTPN works closely and effectively with the UK intelligence agencies and both regularly disrupt terrorist plots through implementation of the CT and CVE strategies. A high number of successful prosecutions for terrorist offences have resulted in escalating numbers of prisoners in UK prisons with sentences directly related to jihadist terrorist activity.

Despite this highly effective prevention of terrorism through the disruption of terrorist plots and conviction of terrorist offenders, jihadist terrorism in the UK continues to grow. It appears that the root causes of this extremism and associated extremist narratives are not being adequately addressed, despite key parts of the UK Prevent strategy being effective. It is significantly less equipped to identify or deal with the root causes of radicalization within some Muslim families, schools and communities.

Some Muslim communities in the UK are particularly vulnerable to jihadist terrorism owing to a lack of integration and under-developed civil society organizations. A small number of vocal and active Muslim pressure groups, some of which endorse extremist jihadist terrorist narratives (either openly or subliminally), are competing with more moderate voices across a range of media platforms. Muslim role models and Muslim civil society need to be more broadly empowered and supported.

The recent appointment of an Extremism Commissioner and the publication of an Integrated Communities Strategy Green Paper[51] are opportunities for a more direct approach which is open and transparent about the growth of jihadist extremism in the UK. Counter-extremism measures need to be normalized and mainstreamed within UK institutions and civil society if the growth in Islamist extremism is to be countered. Muslim communities, Muslim civil society organizations and Muslim role models need to be strengthened and supported, with extremists confronted and marginalized. The UK government has historically invested heavily in counter-terrorism; there is arguably a need to invest substantially more in counter-extremism measures, extremism being a significant component of the root causes inherent within the jihadist terrorist threat in the UK.

Notes

1 For example, E. Brady, 'An Analysis of the UK's Counter-Terrorism Strategy, CONTEST, and the Challenges in Its Evaluation', *Sicherheitspolitik-Blog*, [web blog], 10 October 2016, available here: https://www.sicherheitspolitik-blog.de/2016/10/10/an-analysis-of-the-uks-counter-terrorism-strategy-contest-and-the-challenges-in-its-evaluation/.

2 M. Cancio Melia and A. Petzsche, 'Terrorism as a Criminal Offence', in A. Masferrer and C. Walker (eds.), *Counter-Terrorism, Human Rights and the Rule of Law: Crossing Legal Boundaries in the Defence of the State*, Cheltenham: Edward Elgar Publishing, Inc, 2013, pp. 76–16.

3 HM Government, *Counter-Extremism Strategy*, Cm 9148, London, The Stationery Office, 2015.

4 HM Government, *Counter-Extremism Strategy*.

5 HM Government, *National Security Strategy and Strategic Defence and Security Review 2015: A Secure and Prosperous United Kingdom*, Cm 9161, London, The Stationery Office, 2015..

6 Security Service MI5, 'Being MI5', *Security Service MI5*, [Transcript], 2017, available here: https://www.mi5.gov.uk/who-we-are-video-transcript.

7 European Council of the European Union, 'EU Counter-Terrorism Strategy –2005', *European Council of the European Union*, [Online], 2005.

8 United Nations Counter-Terrorism Implementation Task Force, *UN General Global Counter-Terrorism Strategy*, 2006.

9 Australia-New Zealand Counter-Terrorism Committee, *National Counter-Terrorism Plan 4th Edition*, 2017.

10 HM Government, *Counter-Terrorism Strategy (CONTEST) 2018*, available here: https://www.gov.uk/government/publications/counter-terrorism-strategy-contest-2018.

11 *Government Response to the Review of Islamist Extremism in Prisons, Probation and Youth Justice*, 2016, available here: https://www.gov.uk/government/publications/islamist-extremism-in-prisons-probation-and-youth-justice/government-response-to-the-review-of-islamist-extremism-in-prisons-probation-and-youth-justice.

12 *Protecting Children from Radicalisation: The Prevent Duty*, 2015, available here: https://www.gov.uk/government/publications/protecting-children-from-radicalisation-the-prevent-duty.

13 *Preventing Extremism in the Education and Children's Services Sectors*, 2015, available here: https://www.gov.uk/government/publications/preventing-extremism-in-schools-and-childrens-services/preventing-extremism-in-the-education-and-childrens-services-sectors.

14 HM Government, *Individuals Referred to and Supported through the Prevent Programme, April 2015 to March 16*, 9th November 2017. Home Office Statistical Bulletin 23/17.

15 HO News Team, 'Security Minister Statement on Today's Publication of Prevent and Channel Data', Home Office in the media, 9 November 2017, available here: https://homeofficemedia.blog.gov.uk/2017/11/09/security-minister-statement-on-todays-publication-of-prevent-and-channel-data/.

16 *Government Published Strategic Defence and Security Review*, [website], 2015, available here: https://www.gov.uk/government/news/government-publishes-strategic-defence-and-security-review.

17 B. Wallace, [website], *Home Office Written Question, Answered on 9 November 2017*, available here: https://www.theyworkforyou.com/wrans/?id=2017-11-02.111196.h..

18 *'Being MI5'*, [online video], 2017; T. May, *Home Affairs Select Committee: The Security Context and Counter-Terrorism*, 2016, available here: https://publications.parliament.uk/pa/cm201617/cmselect/cmhaff/135/13507.htm

B. Wallace, *Counter-Terrorism: Police: Written Question – 111941*, 2017, available here: http://www.parliament.uk/business/publications/written-questions-answers-statements/written-question/Commons/2017-11-07/111941/; '*Home Office Press Release: "Multi-Million Pound Boost for Counter-Terrorism Policing"*', 2017, available here: https://www.gov.uk/government/news/multi-million-pound-boost-for-counter-terrorism-policing.

19 *Meeting the Aspirations of the British People, 2007 Pre-Budget Report and Comprehensive Spending Review*, 2007, available here: http://news.bbc.co.uk/1/shared/bsp/hi/pdfs/09_10_07_pbr_report.pdf.

20 *Security and Intelligence Agency Financial Statement 2015–2016 (for the year ended 31 March 2016*, 2016, available here: https://www.gov.uk/government/uploads/system/uploads/attachment_data/file/540815/56308_HC_363_WEB.pdf,.

21 *Home Office Fact Sheet: Police Funding for 2018/19 Explained*, 2018, available here: https://homeofficemedia.blog.gov.uk/2017/12/19/fact-sheet-police-funding-for-2018-19-explained/.

22 *Spending Review: UK's Spying Agencies win 3.4% Real-Term Increase*, 2013, available here: https://www.ft.com/content/27f63d10-de81-11e2-b990-00144feab7de.

23 *Lord Mayor's Banquet 2015: Prime Minister's Speech*, 2015, available here: https://www.gov.uk/government/speeches/lord-mayors-banquet-2015-prime-ministers-speech.

24 K. Clarke, *Home Secretary, House of Commons Announcement, 8 May 1991*, available here: https://www.mi5.gov.uk/fa/node/311.

25 *MI5 Edges out of the Shadows: 42% of Elite Security Service Officers Are Women – Terrorists are the Main Target – Bugging of Royal Family Denies – Booklet Outlines Organisation*, 1993, available here: http://www.independent.co.uk/news/mi5-edges-out-of-the-shadows-42-of-elite-security-service-officers-are-women-terrorists-are-main-1485397.html.

26 BBC, 'MI5 "Slashing Staff" to Boost Overall Computer Skills', 2010, available here: http://news.bbc.co.uk/1/hi/uk/3509869.stm.

27 *'Being MI5'*, [online video], 2017.

28 Security Service MI5, *MI5's Response to the Threat*, 2018, available here: https://www.mi5.gov.uk/international-terrorism.

29 K. Weston, 'Counter-Terrorism Policing and Rule of Law: The Best of Friends', in A. M. Salinas de Frias, K. Samuel and N. D. White (eds.), *Counter-Terrorism: International Law and Practice*, Oxford: Oxford University Press, 2012, pp. 323–351.

30 *'Being MI5'*, [online video]2017.

31 G. Allen and N. Dempsey, 'Terrorism in Great Britain: The Statistics', *House of Commons Library Briefing Paper*, Number CBP7613, 2017.

32 S. Laville, 'MI5 Chief Says 34 Terror Plots Disrupted since 7/7 Attacks', *The Guardian*, 7 November 2013, available here: https://www.theguardian.com/uk-news/2013/nov/07/mi5-chief-34-uk-terror-plots-disrupted.

33 L.M. Eleftheriou-Smith, 'Theresa May: British Security Services Foiled 40 Terror Plots Since 7/7 Attacks', *The Independent*, [Online], 24 November 2014.

34 *'Being MI5'*, [online video], 2017, available here: https://www.mi5.gov.uk/who-we-are-video-transcript (accessed 1 January 2018).

35 D. Anderson QC, *Attacks in London and Manchester March – June 2017, Independent Assessment of MI5 and Police Internal Reviews, Annex 2*, December 2017, available here: https://www.gov.uk/government/uploads/system/uploads/attachment_data/file/664682/Attacks_in_London_and_Manchester_Open_Report.pdf (accessed 26 January 2018).

36 D. Anderson QC, *Attacks in London and Manchester March-June 2017 Independent Assessment of MI5 and Police Internal Reviews*, December 2017, available here: https://assets.publishing.service.gov.uk/government/uploads/system/uploads/attachment_data/file/664682/Attacks_in_London_and_Manchester_Open_Report.pdf.

37 *'Being MI5'*, [online video], 2017.

38 *'Being MI5'*.

39 Allen and Dempsey, '*Terrorism in Great Britain: The Statistics*', 2017.

40 L. Vidino, F. Marone, and E. Entenmann, *Fear Thy Neighbour – Radicalisation and Jihadist Attacks in the West*, Milano: Ledizioni LediPublishing, 2017.

41 L. Casey DBE CB, *The Casey Review – A Review into Opportunity and Integration*, 2016, available here: https://www.gov.uk/government/uploads/system/uploads/attachment_data/file/575975/The_Casey_Review_Executive_Summary.pdf (accessed 26 January 2018.

42 Pew Research Center, *'Europe's Growing Muslim Population'*, 2017, available here: http://www.pewforum.org/2017/11/29/europes-growing-muslim-population/.

43 R. Bryson, *For Caliph and Country – Exploring How British Jihadis Join a Global Movement*, The Tony Blair Institute for Global Change, 2017, available here: https://institute.global/insight/co-existence/caliph-and-country-exploring-how-british-jihadis-join-global-movement (accessed 26 January 2018).

44 L. Casey DBE CB, *The Casey Review – A Review into Opportunity and Integration*, 2016, available here: https://www.gov.uk/government/uploads/system/uploads/attachment_data/file/575975/The_Casey_Review_Executive_Summary.pdf (accessed 26 January 2018.

45 E. Jeraj, 'The Citizens Commission on Islam, Participation and Public Life', in *The Missing Muslims – Unlocking British Muslim Potential for the Benefit of All*, Citizens UK, [Online], 2017.

46 P. Clarke CVO OBE QPM, *Report into Allegations Concerning Birmingham Schools Arising from the 'Trojan Horse*, 2014, available here: https://www.gov.uk/government/uploads/system/uploads/attachment_data/file/340526/HC_576_accessible_-.pdf (accessed 26 January 2018).

47 S. McGarry, *'The Far Right and Reciprocal Radicalisation*', Centre for Research and Evidence on Security Threats, 2018, available here: https://crestresearch.ac.uk/comment/mcgarry-far-right-reciprocal-radicalisation/.

48 S. Javid, 3rd June 2018, appearing on the BBC Andrew Marr Show.

49 D. Casciani, 'Why Cage Director Was Guilty of Withholding Password', BBC News, 25th September 2017, available here: https://www.bbc.co.uk/news/uk-41394156; H. Stuart, 'Understanding Cage: A Public Information Dossier', Centre for the Response to Radicalisation and Terrorism Policy Paper No.5 (2015) available here: http://henryjacksonsociety.org/wp-content/uploads/2015/04/Understanding-CAGE.pdf.

50 Charity Commission, *Islamic Education and Research Academy (IERA): Inquiry Report*, 2018, available here: https://www.gov.uk/government/uploads/system/uploads/attachment_data/file/565354/islamic_education_and_research_academy_iera.pdf.

51 Department for Housing, Communities and Local Government, '*Integrated Communities Strategy Green Paper*', March 2018, available here: https://assets.publishing.service.gov.uk/government/uploads/system/uploads/attachment_data/file/696993/Integrated_Communities_Strategy.pdf.

Recommended Readings

Allen, G. and N. Dempsey, 'Terrorism in Great Britain: The Statistics', *House of Commons Library Briefing Paper*, Number CBP7613, 2017.

Anderson QC, D., *Attacks in London and Manchester* March – *June 2017, Independent Assessment of MI5 and Police Internal Reviews' Annex 2*, 2017, available here: https://www.gov.uk/government/uploads/system/uploads/attachment_data/file/664682/Attacks_in_London_and_Manchester_Open_Report.pdf.

Australia-New Zealand Counter-Terrorism Committee, *National Counter-Terrorism Plan 4th Edition*, ANZCTC, [Online], 2017.

BBC, 'Mi5 "Slashing Staff" to Boost Overall Computer Skills', 2010, available here: http://news.bbc.co.uk/1/hi/uk/3509869.stm.

'Being MI5', [online video], 2017, available here: https://www.mi5.gov.uk/who-we-are-video-transcript.

Brady, E., 'An Analysis of the UK's Counter-Terrorism Strategy, CONTEST, and the Challenges in Its Evaluation', *Sicherheitspolitik-Blog*, [web blog], 10 October 2016, available here: https://www.sicherheitspolitik-blog.de/2016/10/10/an-analysis-of-the-uks-counter-terrorism-strategy-contest-and-the-challenges-in-its-evaluation/.

Bryson, R., *For Caliph and Country – Exploring How British Jihadis Join a Global Movement*, The Tony Blair Institute for Global Change, 2017, available here: https://institute.global/insight/co-existence/caliph-and-country-exploring-how-british-jihadis-join-global-movement (accessed 26 January 2018).

Cancio Melia, M. and A. Petzsche, 'Terrorism as a Criminal Offence', in A. Masferrer and C. Walker (eds.), *Counter-Terrorism, Human Rights and the Rule of Law: Crossing Legal Boundaries in the Defence of the State*, Cheltenham: Edward Elgar Publishing, Inc, 2013.

Casciani, D., 'Why Cage Director Was Guilty of Withholding Password', *BBC News*, 25th September 2017, available here: https://www.bbc.co.uk/news/uk-41394156.

Casey, L., DBE Cb, *The Casey Review – A Review into Opportunity and Integration*, 2016, available here: https://www.gov.uk/government/uploads/system/uploads/attachment_data/file/575975/The_Casey_Review_Executive_Summary.pdf.

Charity Commission, *Islamic Education and Research Academy (IERA): Inquiry report*, 2018, available here: https://www.gov.uk/government/uploads/system/uploads/attachment_data/file/565354/islamic_education_and_research_academy_iera.pdf.

Clarke, K., *Home Secretary, House of Commons Announcement*, May 1992, available here (from Column 297): https://publications.parliament.uk/pa/cm199293/cmhansrd/1992-05-08/Debate-2.html.

Clarke, P., CVO OBE QPM, *Report into Allegations Concerning Birmingham Schools Arising from the 'Trojan Horse*, 2014, available here: https://www.gov.uk/government/uploads/system/uploads/attachment_data/file/340526/HC_576_accessible_-.pdf (accessed 26 January 2018).

Eleftheriou-Smith, L.M., 'Theresa May: British Security Services Foiled 40 Terror Plots Since 7/7 Attacks', *The Independent*, [Online], 24 November 2014.

European Council of the European Union, 'EU Counter-Terrorism Strategy –2005', *European Council of the European Union*, [Online], 2005.

Government Response to the Review of Islamist Extremism in Prisons, Probation and Youth Justice, 2016, available here: https://www.gov.uk/government/publications/islamist-extremism-in-prisons-probation-and-youth-justice/government-response-to-the-review-of-islamist-extremism-in-prisons-probation-and-youth-justice.

HM Government, *National Security Strategy and Strategic Defence and Security Review 2015: A Secure and Prosperous United Kingdom*, Cm 9161, London, The Stationery Office, 2015, available here: https://www.gov.uk/government/news/government-publishes-strategic-defence-and-security-review.

HM Government, *Individuals Referred to and Supported through the Prevent Programme, April 2015 to March 16*, November 2017, Home Office Statistical Bulletin 23/17

HM Government, *Counter-Extremism Strategy*, 2015,

HM Government, *Integrated Communities Strategy Green Paper*, March 2018, available here: https://assets.publishing.service.gov.uk/government/uploads/system/uploads/attachment_data/file/696993/Integrated_Communities_Strategy.pdf.

HM Government, *National Security Strategy and Strategic Defence and Security Review*, 2015.

HM Treasure, *Meeting the Aspirations of the British People, 2007 Pre-Budget Report and Comprehensive Spending Review*, 2007.

Home Office Press Release: 'Multi-Million Pound Boost for Counter-Terrorism Policing, 2017, available here: https://www.gov.uk/government/news/multi-million-pound-boost-for-counter-terrorism-policing.

Home Office Fact Sheet: Police Funding for 2018/19 Explained, 2018, available here: https://homeofficemedia.blog.gov.uk/2017/12/19/fact-sheet-police-funding-for-2018-19-explained/.

HO News Team, 'Security Minister statement on today's publication of Prevent and Channel data', Home Office in the media, 9 November 2017, available here: https://homeofficemedia.blog.gov.uk/2017/11/09/security-minister-statement-on-todays-publication-of-prevent-and-channel-data/.

Jeraj, E., 'The Citizens Commission on Islam, Participation and Public Life', in *The Missing Muslims – Unlocking British Muslim Potential for the Benefit of All*, Citizens UK, [Online], 2017.

Kirby, T., 'MI5 Edges out of the Shadows: 42% of Elite Security Service Officers Are Women – Terrorists Are the Main Target – Bugging of Royal Family Denies – Booklet Outlines Organisation', *The Independent*, 17 July 1993, available here: http://www.independent.co.uk/news/mi5-edges-out-of-the-shadows-42-of-elite-security-service-officers-are-women-terrorists-are-main-1485397.html.

Laville, S., 'MI5 Chief Says 34 Terror Plots Disrupted since 7/7 Attacks', *The Guardian*, 7 November 2013, available here: https://www.theguardian.com/uk-news/2013/nov/07/mi5-chief-34-uk-terror-plots-disrupted.

Lord Mayor's Banquet 2015: Prime Minister's Speech, 2015, available here: https://www.gov.uk/government/speeches/lord-mayors-banquet-2015-prime-ministers-speech.

May, T., *Home Affairs Select Committee: The Security Context and Counter-Terrorism*, 2016, available here: https://publications.parliament.uk/pa/cm201617/cmselect/cmhaff/135/13507.htm.

McGarry Samantha, 'The Far Right and Reciprocal Radicalisation', Centre for Research and Evidence on Security Threats, 2018, available here: https://crestresearch.ac.uk/comment/mcgarry-far-right-reciprocal-radicalisation/.

Pew Research Center, *Europe's Growing Muslim Population*, Pew Research Center, [Online], November 2017, available here: http://www.pewforum.org/2017/11/29/europes-growing-muslim-population/.

Preventing Extremism in the Education and Children's Services Sectors, 2015, available here: https://www.gov.uk/government/publications/preventing-extremism-in-schools-and-childrens-services/preventing-extremism-in-the-education-and-childrens-services-sectors.

Protecting Children from Radicalisation: The Prevent Duty, 2015, available here: https://www.gov.uk/government/publications/protecting-children-from-radicalisation-the-prevent-duty.

Security and Intelligence Agency Financial Statement 2015-2016 (for the Year Ended 31 March 2016, 2016, available here: https://www.gov.uk/government/uploads/system/uploads/attachment_data/file/540815/56308_HC_363_WEB.pdf.

Security Service MI5, *MI5's Response to the Threat*, 2018, available here: https://www.mi5.gov.uk/international-terrorism.

Spending Review: UK's Spying Agencies Win 3.4% Real-Term Increase, 2013, available here: https://www.ft.com/content/27f63d10-de81-11e2-b990-00144feab7de.

Stuart, H., *'Understanding Cage: A Public Information Dossier'*, Centre for the Response to Radicalisation and Terrorism Policy Paper No.5, 2015, available here: http://henryjacksonsociety.org/wp-content/uploads/2015/04/Understanding-CAGE.pdf.

United Nations Counter-Terrorism Implementation Task Force, *UN General Global Counter-Terrorism Strategy*, 2006.

Vidino, L., F. Marone, and E. Entenmann, *Fear Thy Neighbour – Radicalisation and Jihadist Attacks in the West*, Milano: Ledizioni LediPublishing, 2017.

Wallace, B., [website], *'Home Office Written Question, Answered on 9 November 2017'*, available here: https://www.theyworkforyou.com/wrans/?id=2017-11-02.111196.h.

Wallace, B., 2017, *Counter-Terrorism: Police: Written Question – 111941*, available here: http://www.parliament.uk/business/publications/written-questions-answers-statements/written-question/Commons/2017-11-07/111941/.

Weston, K., 'Counter-Terrorism Policing and Rule of Law: The Best of Friends', in A. M. Salinas de Frias, K. Samuel,and N. D. White (eds.), *Counter-Terrorism: International Law and Practice*, Oxford: Oxford University Press, 2012, pp. 323–351.

27 COMPARISON OF EXPERIENCES AND BEST PRACTICE DRAWN FROM OTHER RESEARCH IN OTHER COUNTRIES: COUNTERING VIOLENT EXTREMISM IN EUROPE*

Peter R. Neumann

Introduction

Since the mid-2000s many European countries have adopted Countering Violent Extremism (CVE) programmes that seek to counter not terrorism but processes of radicalization. In contrast to counter-terrorism, which aims to thwart terrorist plots and dismantle terrorist networks, CVE involves no coercive measures (such as prosecutions, arrests or threats of force) and seeks to mobilize actors that are not traditionally associated with national security, for example local governments, educators, social workers, families and community groups. The objective of CVE is not to reach active terrorists, but to create resilience among populations that are seen as potentially vulnerable ('prevention') or assist individuals who are open to turning away from extremism ('de-radicalization').[1]

Following the 7 July 2005 attacks Britain became one of the first European countries to develop a comprehensive CVE strategy. This strategy was called Prevent and formed one of the four pillars of the country's counter-terrorism approach. Though pioneering in its scope and ambition, it quickly became clear that countering

* This chapter uses excerpts from, and partially reproduces, the author's recent report for the Organisation for Security and Cooperation in Europe (OSCE); see P. R. Neumann, 'Countering Radicalisation and Violent Extremism That Lead to Terrorism: Ideas, Recommendations, and Good Practices from the OSCE Region', *OSCE*, 28 September 2017, available here: http://icsr.info/wp-content/uploads/2017/09/Countering-Violent-Extremism-and-Radicalisation-that-Lead-to-Terrorism-2.pdf.

radicalization was neither as easy nor as uncontroversial as it might have seemed. Indeed, as other countries were starting to formulate their own strategies, they looked towards the 'British experience' not just as a model and source of inspiration but also – and increasingly – in order to avoid its contradictions and failures.

At the time of writing, 17 of the 28 European Union member states had national CVE programmes and action plans.[2] While not all of these strategies can easily be compared or ranked,[3] they offer a vast pool of relevant approaches. Based on years of research[4] and the author's work as Special Representative on Countering Violent Extremism for the Organisation for Security and Cooperation in Europe (OSCE),[5] this chapter will present case studies from Norway, Germany, the Netherlands, Belgium and Austria. This chapter argues that these countries' experiences offer valuable lessons which may help to address the problems with Britain's Prevent strategy, especially the lack of trust and participation by British Muslims.

The trouble with Prevent

Since its public launch in 2006 Prevent has been controversial among the very communities whose participation and involvement it was meant to promote. While opinion polls have consistently shown that British Muslims want the government to play an active role in '[combating] extremism',[6] this has not translated into widespread support for Prevent. In 2015/16 just 8 per cent of the referrals into the government's de-radicalization programme resulted from reports by family, friends or members of the community.[7] Many mosques and community institutions, as well as practically all major Islamic organizations, refuse to collaborate with Prevent. Senior police officers have described the policy as 'toxic'.[8]

For Prevent supporters, this is mainly the fault of 'Islamic extremists' and far-left activists – the so-called 'anti-Prevent lobby' – whose aggressive campaigns have created an atmosphere of panic and paranoia around Prevent.[9] While this may be true, it ignores the extent to which the policy itself has played into their hands.

One of the principal flaws has been its lack of consistency and clarity. Over the course of a decade the meaning of Prevent has changed so many times that it has become hard to speak of a unified policy. Different government agencies have, at times, pursued contradictory objectives. Community groups that received government support under one version of the policy were seen as 'part of the problem' under another. Most significantly, no government has been able to formulate a clear-cut definition of 'extremism', resulting in overreach as well as accusations of 'thought police' and religious meddling.[10]

Related to this has been a lack of transparency. Unlike other CVE programmes, Britain's Prevent was conceived by intelligence officers and police officers, for whom the sharing of information with the public was not a priority. Until three years ago, for instance, the government provided virtually no public information about its de-radicalization programme Channel. Although its existence was widely known, official documents and government websites contained no references, mentions or figures, with the consequence that nearly all the information that was publicly available was based on rumours and scare stories.[11]

Undoubtedly the biggest problem with Prevent, however, has been its heavy-handedness. Contrary to the idea of mobilizing non-traditional actors, Prevent has excessively relied on security agencies. Unlike other countries, many of the most visible aspects of Prevent have been implemented by the police, which has allowed the policy's opponents to argue that the government sees Muslim communities primarily as a 'security issue' and that community engagement is little more than a euphemism for spying.[12] The recent introduction of a legal obligation to report signs of radicalization (the so-called Prevent duty) has reinforced these suspicions, especially as it was done without adequate guidance and training, and has resulted in many instances of over-reporting.

National Action Plans

As mentioned earlier, Britain's Prevent has served as an inspiration for many countries' national strategies and action plans. There is now a consensus among scholars and practitioners that policy frameworks such as Prevent are essential to ensuring the success of CVE, because they enable governments to define their aims, establish priorities, allocate roles and responsibilities as well as hold agencies accountable and show communities how their activities and programmes fit into the bigger picture. Not least, they compel officials to make realistic statements about the nature of the threat and carefully consider the drivers of extremism in their societies.[13]

One of the most convincing examples for how these objectives can be accomplished is Norway's 2014 Action Plan. It resulted from an extensive process of consultation and was led by a working group consisting of representatives from all relevant ministries. Over a period of several months it met with stakeholders from the police and security services, different parts of the administration, local government, researchers, community organizations, civil society and other European governments.

The resulting document defines extremism, highlights threats from far-right extremists and violent jihadists and explicitly recognizes the risk of cross-community polarization.[14] In the main part it describes thirty concrete measures in five areas of activity: 'knowledge and expertise', 'co-operation and co-ordination', 'preventing the growth of extremist groups and helping to promote re-integration', 'preventing radicalization and recruitment through the Internet', and 'international cooperation'.

All commitments in the Action Plan are transparent and targeted. For each measure it identifies the government departments that are responsible and obliges them to publish updates and progress reports via a public website (www.

radikalisering.no).[15] Through the website new measures and activities can be added, allowing the document to evolve and reflect changes in the nature of the threat.

Referral mechanisms

Many practitioners regard (early) interventions as the most promising element of CVE, as they offer opportunities for dealing with individuals who have exhibited potentially problematic changes in behaviour but have not committed any chargeable offences. Such interventions seek to 'turn people around' and support their voluntary exit from extremism, typically through individually tailored packages of measures, which may include psycho-social support, housing, theological debate or assistance with employment and education.

For interventions to work, however, intervention providers need to receive high-quality referrals. While in Britain most of the referrals into the Channel de-radicalization programme come from public bodies, such as the police, educational institutions and the National Health Service, other countries see significantly higher rates of voluntary reporting, especially from members of communities and families.

Germany, for example, created a nationwide hotline, which is maintained by the Federal Agency for Migration and Refugee's *Advice Centre Radicalisation*. This hotline aims to reach members of communities, in particular families, by offering an uncomplicated and voluntary way of reporting cases and receiving support. Following an initial evaluation, cases are either dismissed or referred to a nationwide network of local intervention providers and civil society organizations that have specialized in assisting vulnerable individuals and their families.

The Advice Centre currently receives between 80 and 100 calls a month, of which an estimated 20 per cent are referred to local providers for further consultation and support.[16] The model is seen as effective because it has created a low threshold for reporting cases, which means that cases are reported earlier and interventions have a higher chance of success. Parents or family members use it because the emphasis is on support rather than sanctions, and neither the Advice Centre itself nor the network of social workers and community organizations are directly linked to the police. Meanwhile, all intervention providers have adopted strict protocols for involving law enforcement if interventions are unsuccessful.

Coordination

Interventions usually require contributions from multiple actors and, therefore, necessitate channels of coordination between different government agencies and non-governmental organizations, such as community groups or religious leaders. In Britain this responsibility often falls to the police, giving rise to accusations of spying and increasing the threshold for community referrals (see above).

In the Netherlands, by contrast, CVE programmes empower local governments. Each major city runs a so-called Safe House – a place where local government, street workers and the police can sit at the same table and discuss individuals who have come to their attention. This makes it easier to mobilize local resources, such as housing and social welfare, and lowers the threshold for reporting cases. It also facilitates close relationships with religious communities, street workers and youth centres, who may be less reluctant to work with local officials than with security agencies. Most significantly, instead of singling out radicalization and treating it as an entirely different problem, it creates synergies with combating non-ideological crimes such as gangs, which recent reports have shown are often precursors for radicalization.[17]

Dutch officials are convinced that the Safe House concept, which is central to the country's counter-radicalization efforts, is a major reason why the Netherlands have been less affected by foreign terrorist fighters and domestic terrorism than its European partners.[18]

Schools

Family and school are the two social environments in which young people spend most of their time. Schools are particularly important because they are places where young people make their first friends and begin to shape their ideas on society and the world around them.

Some of schools' most significant contributions to countering radicalization require no new content or activities that are explicitly linked to countering radicalization. When schools teach critical thinking, make students reflect and question or help them understand nuances, they create resilience against the uncritical acceptance that is demanded by extremist groups. Likewise, when schools counter-stereotypes, create belonging and make young people understand differences, they protect students against extremist narratives, which rely on 'us versus them'.[19]

Even so, schools can also be places in which the first signs of radicalization become obvious. Rather than creating 'checklists', which are often too rigid to capture a complex social phenomenon, many countries have chosen to offer teachers training on how to detect and respond to radicalization, while making schools establish procedures for dealing with potential cases swiftly and appropriately.[20]

The Royal Atheneum in Antwerp, Belgium, is a good example. A secular state school with a large number of Muslim students, it experienced rising tensions over issues such as the wearing of the headscarf. At the beginning of the decade extremist groups were starting to recruit in the school's neighbourhood. In addition to a security response, the school launched a four-year programme which focused on creating a 'common base of shared human values and rights', and involved 'making practical agreements [among the students as well as between students and teachers,] and setting clear limits'[21] in relation to what was acceptable.

The programme included rigorous intercultural dialogue, projects on identity and citizenship, systematic training for teachers in all subjects as well as arts projects in which students were able to express delicate issues without having to articulate them verbally.

From an institution that was, according to its headmistress, on the verge of a 'clash of cultures',[22] the Royal Atheneum has gradually recovered and has yet again become a functional and successful school.

Prisons

Prisons are frequently described as 'hotbeds' of radicalization because they are places in which (predominantly) young men experience personal crises and are cut off from traditional social relationships, such as family and friends. There is evidence that Al-Qaeda and the so-called Islamic State consider prisons to be 'fertile grounds' for radicalization and recruitment and that terrorist plots have been forged by individuals who met behind bars. At the same time, prisons can offer opportunities for de-radicalization and disengagement, and enable terrorists to re-integrate into society.[23] With increasing numbers of returnees from Syria and Iraq, they are likely to become focal points for counter- and de-radicalization efforts.

One of the principal – and near-universal – lessons is to avoid overcrowding because it provides terrorists and radicalizers with opportunities to spread their messages. Other important measures include the systematic provision of spiritual advisors (such as mainstream prison imams), staff training and the creation of adequate systems for reporting and intelligence.[24]

In addition, several European countries have experimented with prison-based interventions and de-radicalization programmes. A good example is *Derad*, an Austrian initiative which works in prisons and assists individuals who have become radicalized or have been convicted of terrorism-related offences. This has also involved a number of returnees from the Syrian conflict. Like similar initiatives, *Derad* provides individual counselling and mentoring, and seeks to address people's personal and psychological needs as well as theological and ideological issues.

What makes *Derad* different from similar initiatives is that the mentoring continues after people have been released. When individuals have served their sentences *Derad* facilitates their re-integration into society, which may involve assistance with seeking employment, getting education as well as dealing with the many challenges that are associated with exiting from an extremist milieu.[25]

Recognizing its success, *Derad* has recently been asked to be part of a new nationwide network for extremism prevention, bringing together civil society organizations with government departments and agencies and setting up effective channels of communication and coordination.[26]

Conclusion

The list of examples and good practices in this chapter is by no means exhaustive, nor should Britain – or any other country – simply 'copy and paste' other countries' experiences. Like in any other policy field, all the programmes and initiatives that have been presented reflect, to a certain extent, their own local, cultural and legal contexts as well as the people and communities for whom they have been designed.

At the same time, other countries' experience can be a source of ideas and inspiration, and help British policymakers be more systematic and open-minded in thinking about its current problems with Prevent. They demonstrate, first and foremost, that there is not just one way of doing things and that other countries have found new and innovative ways for dealing with issues that, in the British context, often seem intractable. They also show that over-securitization as well as the absence of transparency and consistency, and the resulting lack of trust from British communities in CVE approaches, are not inevitable but have resulted from mistakes, which other countries have managed to avoid.

In the end, the 'toxicity' of Prevent may indeed make it necessary to re-brand the entire strategy, as suggested by the Home Affairs Select Committee.[27] It will be equally important, however, to fix the problems that have resulted in Prevent becoming 'toxic' in the first place. Learning from the experiences of other countries is one of the easiest – and most promising – ways of doing so.

Notes

1 See P. R. Neumann, 'Preventing Violent Radicalization in America', *Bipartisan Policy Center*, [Online], 2011, pp. 17–19.

2 See OSCE, 'Inventory of Policy Documents and Legislation Adopted by OSCE Participating States and Partners for Co-operation on VERLT', *OSCE*, [Online], 14 December 2016, available here: http://www.osce.org/secretariat/289911?download=true.

3 Measuring success and/or effectiveness remains one of the great challenges for all types of prevention programmes. See P. Romanjuk, 'Does CVE Work? Lessons Learned from the Global Effort to Counter Violent Extremism', *Global Center on Cooperative Security*, September 2015.

4 For an overview of my publications, see http://icsr.info/about-us-2/staff/peter-neumann-director/.

5 The author served as special representative during Austria's 2017 Chairmanship. All views expressed in this chapter are his own and do not necessarily represent those of the OSCE or the Austrian government.

6 M. Frampton, D. Goodhart and K. Mahmood, 'Unsettled Belonging: A Survey of Britain's Muslim Communities', *Policy Exchange*, [Online], 2016, p. 59.

7 'Individuals Referred to and Supported through the Prevent Programme, April 2015 to March 2016', *Home Office Statistical Bulletin 23/17*, 9 November 2017, p. 8.

8 D. Babu, cited in J. Halliday and V. Dodd, 'UK Anti-radicalisation Strategy Prevent a "Toxic Brand"', *The Guardian*, 9 March 2015.

9 See, for example, R. Sutton, 'The Campaign against Prevent Is Based on Myths and Distortions', *The Telegraph*, 7 December 2016.

10 For a summary of this debate, see 'Supplementary Written Evidence Submitted by David Anderson QC (Independent Reviewer of Terrorism Legislation)', Submission to the Home Affairs Select Committee, 29 January 2016; available here: http://data.parliament.uk/writtenevidence/committeeevidence.svc/evidencedocument/home-affairs-committee/countering-extremism/written/27920.pdf.

11 'Supplementary Written Evidence Submitted by David Anderson QC'.

12 'Supplementary Written Evidence Submitted by David Anderson QC'.

13 'Guidelines and Good Practices: Developing National P/CVE Strategies and Action Plans', *Hedayah Center*, September 2016, available here: http://www.hedayahcenter.org/Admin/Content/File-1792016192156.pdf.

14 'Action Plan against Radicalisation and Violent Extremism', *Norwegian Ministry of Justice and Public Security*, 2014, p. 10, available here: https://www.counterextremism.org/resources/details/goto_url/679/8923.

15 'Action Plan against Radicalisation and Violent Extremism', p. 13.

16 'FAQ: Beratungsstelle Radikalisierung', *Bundesamt für Migration und Flüchtlinge*, available here: http://www.bamf.de/DE/Infothek/FragenAntworten/BeratungsstelleRadikalisierung/beratungsstelle-radikalisierung-node.html.

17 R. Basra and P. R. Neumann, 'Criminal Pasts, Terrorist Futures: European Jihadists and the New Crime-Terror Nexus', *Perspectives on Terrorism*, vol. 10, no. 6, 2016, pp. 25–40.

18 Conversations during official visit to the Netherlands, April 2017.

19 Radicalisation Awareness Network, 'The Role of Education in Preventing Radicalisation', *RAN Issue Paper*, December 2016, available here: https://ec.europa.eu/home-affairs/sites/homeaffairs/files/what-we-do/networks/radicalisation_awareness_network/ran-papers/docs/role_education_preventing_radicalisation_12122016_en.pdf.

20 'Preventing Violent Extremism through Education: A Guide for Policy-Makers', *UNESCO*, 2017, available here: https://reliefweb.int/sites/reliefweb.int/files/resources/247764e-2.pdf. See also 'A Teacher's Guide on the Prevention on Violent Extremism', *UNESCO*, 2016, available here: http://unesdoc.unesco.org/images/0024/002446/244676e.pdf.

21 K. Heremans, 'How to Counter Jihadist Radicalisation in Schools', presentation at the *European Policy Center Policy Dialogue*, 4 July 2017.

22 Quoted in 'Antwerp's Muslim Headscarf Row, the Story on the Ground', *The Economist*, 17 September 2009.

23 See P. R. Neumann, *Prisons and Terrorism: Radicalisation and De-Radicalisation in 15 Countries*, London: ICSR, 2010..

24 Neumann, *Prisons and Terrorism*, pp. 32–3.

25 For more information, see 'Derad – eine Initiative für sozialen Zusammenhalt, Prävention und Dialog', *Derad;* available here: http://www.derad.at.

26 E. Winroither, 'Der Kampf gegen den Extremismus soll effizienter werden', *Die Presse*, 8 February 2017.

27 'Radicalisation: The Counter-Narrative and Identifying the Tipping Point', *House of Commons Home Affairs Committee, Eight Report of Session 2016–17, HC135*, 25 August 2016, available here: https://publications.parliament.uk/pa/cm201617/cmselect/cmhaff/135/135.pdf.

Recommended Readings

'Action Plan against Radicalisation and Violent Extremism', *Norwegian Ministry of Justice and Public Security*, 2014, available here: https://www.counterextremism.org/resources/details/goto_url/679/8923.

'Antwerp's Muslim Headscarf Row, the Story on the Ground', *The Economist*, 17 September 2009.

Babu, D., J. Halliday, and V. Dodd, 'UK Anti-Radicalisation Strategy Prevent a "Toxic Brand"', *The Guardian*, 9 March 2015.

Basra, R. and P. R. Neumann, 'Criminal Pasts, Terrorist Futures: European Jihadists and the New Crime-Terror Nexus', *Perspectives on Terrorism*, vol. 10, no. 6, 2016, pp. 25–40.

'Derad – eine Initiative für sozialen Zusammenhalt, Prävention und Dialog', *Derad*, available here: http://www.derad.at.

'FAQ: Beratungsstelle Radikalisierung', *Bundesamt für Migration und Flüchtlinge*, available here: http://www.bamf.de/DE/Infothek/FragenAntworten/BeratungsstelleRadikalisierung/beratungsstelle-radikalisierung-node.html.

Frampton, M., D. Goodhart, and K. Mahmood, 'Unsettled Belonging: A Survey of Britain's Muslim Communities', *Policy Exchange*, [Online], 2016.

'Guidelines and Good Practices: Developing National P/CVE Strategies and Action Plans', *Hedayah Center*, September 2016, available here: http://www.hedayahcenter.org/Admin/Content/File-1792016192156.pdf.

Heremans, K., 'How to Counter Jihadist Radicalisation in Schools', presentation at the *European Policy Center Policy Dialogue*, 4 July 2017.

'Individuals Referred to and Supported through the Prevent Programme, April 2015 to March 2016', *Home Office Statistical Bulletin 23/17*, 9 November 2017.

'Inventory of Policy Documents and Legislation Adopted by OSCE Participating States and Partners for Co-operation on VERLT', *OSCE*, 14 December 2016, available here: http://www.osce.org/secretariat/289911?download=true.

Neumann, P. R., *Prisons and Terrorism: Radicalisation and De-radicalisation in 15 Countries*, London: ICSR, 2010.

Neumann, P. R., 'Preventing Violent Radicalization in America', *Bipartisan Policy Center*, [Online], 2011.

Neumann, P. R., 'Countering Radicalisation and Violent Extremism that Lead to Terrorism: Ideas, Recommendations, and Good Practices from the OSCE Region', *OSCE*, 28 September 2017, available here: http://icsr.info/wp-content/uploads/2017/09/Countering-Violent-Extremism-and-Radicalisation-that-Lead-to-Terrorism-2.pdf.

'Preventing Violent Extremism through Education: A Guide for Policy-Makers', *UNESCO*, 2017, available here: https://reliefweb.int/sites/reliefweb.int/files/resources/247764e-2.pdf.
Radicalisation Awareness Network, 'The Role of Education in Preventing Radicalisation', *RAN Issue Paper*, December 2016, available here: https://ec.europa.eu/home-affairs/sites/homeaffairs/files/what-we-do/networks/radicalisation_awareness_network/ran-papers/docs/role_education_preventing_radicalisation_12122016_en.pdf.
'Radicalisation: The Counter-Narrative and Identifying the Tipping Point', *House of Commons Home Affairs Committee, Eight Report of Session 2016-17, HC135*, 25 August 2016, available here: https://publications.parliament.uk/pa/cm201617/cmselect/cmhaff/135/135.pdf.
Romanjuk, P., 'Does CVE Work? Lessons Learned from the Global Effort to Counter Violent Extremism', *Global Center on Cooperative Security*, September 2015.
'Supplementary Written Evidence Submitted by David Anderson QC (Independent Reviewer of Terrorism Legislation)', Submission to the Home Affairs Select Committee, 29 January 2016, available here: http://data.parliament.uk/writtenevidence/committeeevidence.svc/evidencedocument/home-affairs-committee/countering-extremism/written/27920.pdf.
Sutton, R., 'The Campaign against Prevent Is Based on Myths and Distortions', *The Telegraph*, 7 December 2016.
UNESCO, *A Teacher's Guide on the Prevention of Violent Extremism*, UNESCO, [Online], 2016. No author., available here: http://unesdoc.unesco.org/images/0024/002446/244676e.pdf.
Winroither, E., 'Der Kampf gegen den Extremismus soll effizienter werden', *Die Presse*, 8 February 2017.

28 COMPARISON OF EXPERIENCES AND BEST PRACTICE DRAWN FROM RESEARCH IN OTHER COUNTRIES: WHAT ACCOUNTS FOR THE LACK OF A CVE STRATEGY IN THE USA?

Lorenzo Vidino

Introduction

Over the last few years the United States has been one of the most enthusiastic proponents of the introduction of Countering Violent Extremism (CVE) activities worldwide. It has spearheaded countless global initiatives, from a high-profile global summit hosted by the White House in February 2015 to the formation of permanent initiatives like the Abu Dhabi-based Hedayah. It has also been providing substantial financial support to counter-radicalization programmes implemented in countries throughout the world through various state department or US Agency for International Development (USAID)-funded initiatives.

Yet, this CVE enthusiasm abroad has not been matched domestically. Efforts on this front, in fact, have been timid, underfunded and haphazard. Technically, the United States possesses a domestic counter-radicalization strategy. In August 2011, in fact, the White House issued a paper, entitled *Empowering local partners to prevent violent extremism in the United States*, which was later followed by various programmatic papers providing further details.[1] Yet none of these documents outlines initiatives that are even remotely as ambitious and far-reaching as those long implemented in many European countries.

With a few limited exceptions, most initiatives are in fact limited to funding research on the radicalization process and engaging the American Muslim community (laudable activities, to be sure). The few initiatives aimed at de-radicalization and disengagement take place only in a handful of geographical areas and are generally underfunded. Counter-narrative initiatives aimed at a domestic audience pale in terms of resources when compared to those funded overseas.

Arguably nine concurring reasons have caused the reluctance on the part of American authorities to devise anything more ambitious. They are as follows.

The delay in the emergence of a domestic jihadist threat

American-based jihadist sympathizers possessing quintessential homegrown characteristics had been detected before 11th September 2001 and in relatively larger numbers after it.[2] Yet the widely held assumption among American policymakers and counter-terrorism professionals was that radicalization did not affect American Muslims except in sporadic cases. Tellingly, for many years following 9/11, in American political parlance the term 'homegrown terrorism' was reserved solely for anti-government militias, white supremacists and eco-terrorist groups. Jihadists, even if possessing quintessential homegrown characteristics, were excluded from this category. This perception started to change around 2010 in the wake of various attacks by, and arrests of, homegrown jihadists. And it has definitely been internalized with domestic Islamic State-related mobilization, which has been unprecedented in numbers and quintessentially homegrown in nature.[3] Yet this delayed perception has been a key factor in determining the late development of a CVE strategy.

Belief that American Muslims' good integration serves as an antidote to radicalization

During the 2000s it was widely argued in American counter-terrorism circles that homegrown terrorism of jihadist inspiration was a uniquely European problem, a direct consequence of Europe's failed integration policies. Radicalization, argued this narrative, is the inevitable by-product of the marginalization and discrimination plaguing European Muslim communities. Despite some notable exceptions, American Muslims, on the other hand, tend to enjoy economic and educational achievements that put them in the top tier of American society.[4]

To some degree, these assumptions have been shattered, as few still believe that American Muslims are 'immune' to radicalization. Yet the perception that radicalization is largely caused by social ills to which most American Muslims are not subject is widely held in many quarters and has caused a delay in the development of CVE programmes.

Faith in 'Hard' counter-terrorism tactics

Although only rarely applying the military and extrajudicial tools they have used overseas, since 9/11 American authorities have adopted a remarkably aggressive posture towards individuals and clusters associated with terrorism of jihadist inspiration operating on American soil.[5] The 2001 Patriot Act granted them extensive surveillance powers and significantly decreased the separation between investigators and intelligence agencies. The catch-all 'material support to a terrorist organization' charge has proven a formidable legal tool. And authorities have often employed the so-called Al Capone law enforcement technique, arresting suspected terrorists for immigration, financial or other non-terrorism-related offences in order to neutralize them when they did not possess enough evidence to convict them for terrorism offences.[6]

Most controversially, they have increasingly resorted to using *agents provocateurs*. Operating under the assumption that certain individuals espousing jihadist ideology are likely to eventually carry out acts of violence, US counter-terrorism officials have sometimes resorted to triggering the passage from the radicalization phase to action themselves. Therefore, since 9/11, the FBI has approached known radicals, many of whom were unaffiliated wannabes, with *agents provocateurs*. Under the strict direction of authorities such individuals approach their targets; lead them to believe they belong to Al-Qaeda or, more lately, the Islamic State; and 'accompany' them as they either plan attacks or provide material support to terrorist organizations.

These tactics, employed with similar enthusiasm by both the Bush and the Obama administrations, have been extensively criticized by many who argue they infringe on civil liberties and create tensions with Muslim communities.[7] Yet their effectiveness, at least in terms of incarcerating targets, is undisputable. A deep belief in the effectiveness of these measures has led many in the US counter-terrorism community to argue that other 'softer' measures are not necessary.

Massive bureaucratic structure

The size of the country and of its bureaucratic apparatus, with the overlap of federal, state and local jurisdictions, creates an additional obstacle to the implementation of a comprehensive counter-radicalization strategy. Coordinating the activities of the over 17,000 law enforcement agencies working on terrorism-related matters throughout the country is an understandably daunting task.[8] Various agencies, such as the National Counterterrorism Center (NCTC) and the Department of Homeland Security, have over time taken key roles in shaping a domestic CVE strategy. But inter-agency rivalries, bureaucratic issues and the sheer size of the country have made that task particularly hard.

Separation of church and state

Deep political, cultural and constitutional issues have also played an important role in determining the American reluctance to experiment with domestic counter-radicalization. The constitutionally sanctioned principle of separation of church and state is arguably one of the main ones. The concept, in fact, is so revered and politically sensitive that US authorities tend to be extremely reluctant to engage in any activity that could give the impression that they are blurring that line and dealing with religion, even in an indirect way.

First amendment issues

A similar dampening of American authorities' enthusiasm for counter-radicalization initiatives is the country's sacrosanct tradition of respect for freedom of speech. America has traditionally provided a degree of protection to all kinds of extreme discourse that is unparalleled in virtually all European countries. This tradition is not just enshrined in the constitution but deeply entrenched in the American political psyche. Consequently, American authorities tend to be reluctant to engage in counter-radicalization activities that can be perceived as limiting free speech.

Little political/public pressure

In most cases, European counter-radicalization programmes were established after a catalyst event – generally a successful or failed attack carried out by homegrown jihadist militants. None of these dynamics seem to have taken place in the United States. Over the last few years several attacks with quintessential homegrown characteristics have been carried out or attempted in the United States. Hundreds of American militants have been arrested on American soil or reported fighting with various jihadist groups overseas. Yet this has not triggered a widespread perception among the American public and policymaking community that homegrown jihadism is a major problem that requires actions other than a traditional law enforcement approach.

Political opposition

The debate over the introduction of CVE measures has often been a highly polarized one. Various critics, both in and outside Congress, have frequently argued that CVE measures unfairly target the Muslim community and/or are ruses designed to spy on it. Similarly, many have argued that right-wing extremism represents a comparable, if not bigger, threat to the United States and that CVE measures should also target that form of militancy. This heated debate, which often leads to political grandstanding, has been one of the main brakes on the development of a domestic CVE strategy.

Reluctance to tackle ideology

While all these factors are unquestionably important, it is arguable that none of them are as important in determining the shyness of the US government in developing extensive counter-radicalization programmes as its reluctance to enter the field of ideology. The Obama and, in its last years, Bush administrations have largely avoided dealing with the ideological underpinnings of radicalization, particularly on the domestic front. While there is no question that various elements within the US government fully acknowledge the role jihadist ideology plays in the process, there is no government-wide consensus on the matter. Since a comprehensive counter-radicalization programme entails tackling the ideological element as one of the main components, albeit not the only one, of radicalization, this indecision leads to the inability to draft extensive programmes like those implemented in Europe.

Recent developments

During the last years of the Obama administration and due largely to the rise of the Islamic State on the global scene, authorities witnessed a rise in the number of American Muslims attracted to jihadist ideology. This development has led authorities to shed some of their previous hesitations about delving into domestic CVE and to develop various initiatives. While still not amounting to the level of commitment seen in many European countries, these efforts represent a clear break from the past.[9]

One CVE approach that has recently attracted the interest of US authorities is targeted interventions. While some of its field offices had been occasionally carrying out some mild forms of intervention below the radar, the FBI formally entered the field in April 2016 through the creation of the so-called Shared Responsibility Committees (SRC). SRCs were meant to get communities more involved in CVE and help 'potential violent extremists' to disengage.[10] SRCs were to be 'multidisciplinary groups voluntarily formed in local communities' at the request of the communities themselves and 'sometimes with the encouragement of the FBI'. The Bureau would have referred at-risk individuals to SRCs and communities would have built a personalized intervention programme to address the issue.[11]

The programme encountered severe criticism. Many critics saw SRCs as the FBI's attempts to create a network of community-based informants. Such a network, they argued, would have infringed upon the civil rights of Muslim communities and created mistrust between community members.[12] Influenced by the negative feedback, the FBI eventually decided against launching SRCs.

Intervention programmes at the local level appear to have had better luck. The Los Angeles Police Department (LAPD) has been operating the so-called RENEW (Recognizing Extremist Network Early Warnings) initiative, an early intervention programme that seeks to bring together law enforcement, Joint Terrorism Task Force officials and mental health professionals.[13] While many of its dynamics have not been made public, the scheme appears to be similar to Channel and other European intervention programmes, allowing for a RENEW coordinator to determine what kind of intervention (such as involvement of mental health professionals or social services) is most likely to interrupt an individual's radicalization trajectory.

Small de-radicalization initiatives have also been set up in other areas. Boston had been identified as a 'pilot city' to work on de-radicalization at the 2015 White House Summit. Since then local and federal authorities, under the leadership of the US Attorney's Office, have been working on devising intervention schemes. And, in what represents a first in the country, in 2016 a Minneapolis judge ordered a de-radicalization intervention for six young Somali-Americans convicted of attempting to join the Islamic State in Syria.[14]

In the last years of its mandate the Obama administration also seemed to reverse the trend that saw CVE efforts plagued by a chronic dearth of funds. In December 2015 Congress passed the Department of Homeland Security Appropriations Act 2016, allocating $10 million for CVE. In July 2016 the DHS announced a CVE Grant Program providing financial support to organizations working on one of the five focus areas identified by the department. FEMA, which is part of the DHS, was responsible for allocating the grants. The five focus areas were selected based on what current research on extremism 'has shown are likely to be most effective' in addressing violent extremism.[15] The five areas included: (a) developing resilience, (b) challenging the narrative, (c) training and engaging with community members, (d) managing intervention activities and (e) building the capacity of community-led non-profit organizations active in CVE.[16] The organizations selected to receive the funds were announced on 13th January 2016, a week before the then president-elect Donald Trump's inauguration.[17]

It is difficult to forecast at this stage what the change in administration will mean for domestic (and, for that matter, international) CVE in America. The Trump administration has been cryptic and vague on many policy issues, including CVE.

What can be said at the moment about its future intentions can, therefore, be little more than speculation, educated guesses made by interpreting rumours and the attitudes of individuals involved in the administration. As of early June 2018, in fact, there has been no CVE-related official decision.

Uncorroborated reports that surfaced in February 2017 indicated that the administration was planning an overhaul of the federal CVE strategy. They also suggested that CVE would be renamed either Countering Islamic Extremism or Countering Radical Islamic Extremism. As the names indicate, the strategy was supposedly to focus solely on Islamist extremists – in that sense, not different in substance from Obama's strategy, albeit with more direct naming.[18] A much more muscular focus on Islamist ideology has also been hinted at by various individuals close to the administration who have been involved in terrorism-related matters.

These rumours spread at a time when the administration's controversial decision to preclude individuals originating in several Muslim-majority countries from entering the country (what came to be known as the 'Muslim ban') was made public. These dynamics led at least four organizations that had been selected by the Obama-promoted CVE Grant Program to state that they were considering rejecting the funds if the administration reshaped CVE according to certain modalities.[19] Ka Joog, a Minnesota-based organization that had been awarded $500,000 under the programme, announced that because of the new administration's 'policies which promote hate, fear, uncertainty', they were not accepting the money.[20] A similar decision was also reached by Bayan Claremont, an Islamic graduate school in California, which turned down an $800,000 grant, the second-largest amount awarded.[21] In an official statement the school announced that they would continue to work with the government when needed but 'given the anti-Muslim actions of the current executive branch, we cannot in good conscience accept this grant'.[22]

Domestic CVE, which in the final years of the Obama administration seemed to have finally managed to be seen by many American policymakers and law enforcement agencies as useful, finds itself the victim of the current extremely polarized political climate. It is difficult to foresee, a year into the Trump administration (at the time of writing) what will happen to CVE. It might be completely scrapped, as some within the Trump camp see it as a pointless and politically correct approach to a problem that needs more muscular solutions. Or it might be revamped, but possibly in ways that differ substantially from past iterations and likely with much more emphasis on ideological components.

It is also likely that, in this chaotic environment, various actors will develop their own initiatives that function at the local level. There are, in fact, indications that an increasing number of community groups and NGOs are engaging in the CVE space. Similarly, various police forces and even federal agencies have been quietly starting their own projects, running small initiatives that, while attracting (intentionally) little attention, have given some initial good results.[23] This localized and low-key approach might be the direction of CVE at times of extreme confusion and polarization in Washington DC.

Notes

1 The Department of Homeland Security, 'Empowering Local Partners to Prevent Violent Extremism in the United States', *The Department of Homeland Security*, [Online], August 2011, available here: https://obamawhitehouse.archives.gov/sites/default/files/empowering_local_partners.pdf.

2 L. Vidino, 'Homegrown Jihadist Terrorism in the United States: A New and Occasional Phenomenon?', *Studies in Conflict & Terrorism*, vol. 32, no. 1, 2009; and W. Rosenau and S. Daly, 'American Journeys to Jihad: U.S. Extremists and Foreign Conflicts during the 1980s and 1990s', *CTC Sentinel*, vol. 3, no. 8, 2010.

3 L. Vidino and S. Hughes, *ISIS in America: From Retweets to Raqqa*, Program on Extremism, George Washington University, [Online], 2015.

4 'Muslim Americans Middle Class and Mostly Mainstream', Pew Research Center, 22 May 2007, 24–25, available here: http://assets.pewresearch.org/wp-content/uploads/sites/12/2007/05/muslim-americans.pdf.

5 Cases like those of Ali al-Marri, a Qatari national arrested in Peoria in the wake of 9/11, and Jose Padilla, a US citizen linked to Khalid Sheikh Mohammed, who was detained without charges for years in a military prison before being tried in the civilian court system, have been exceptions. The vast majority of terrorism suspects apprehended within the United States since 9/11 have been granted due process rights.

6 The term, commonly used by US law enforcement practitioners, owes its origin to the fact that infamous 1920s Chicago mobster Al Capone was never convicted for his well-known criminal activities, of which authorities never possessed enough evidence to stand in court, but, rather, simply for tax evasion.

7 See, for example, J. Markon, 'Mosque Infiltration Feeds Muslims' Distrust of FBI', *Washington Post*, 5 December 2010.

8 J. P. Bjelopera and M. A. Randol, *American Jihadist Terrorism: Combating a Complex Threat*, report for the Congressional Research Service, 20 September 2010, p. 42; Government Accountability Office (GAO), 'Managing for Results: Barriers to Interagency Coordination', GAO-06-15 and GAO/GGD-00-106, Washington, D.C., 29 March 2000, pp. 6–7, p. 14, available here: http://www.gao.gov/archive/2000/gg00106.pdf (accessed February 2, 2011).

9 The author wishes to thank Program on Extremism Research Fellow Katerina Papatheodorou for her help on this section of the chapter.

10 'FBI Shared Responsibility Committees Letter', available here: https://assets.documentcloud.org/documents/2815794/FBI-SRC-Letter.pdf.

11 'FBI Shared Responsibility Committees Letter', available here: https://assets.documentcloud.org/documents/2815794/FBI-SRC-Letter.pdf.

12 'FBI Shared Responsibility Committees Must Pass Privacy Test', Committee on Homeland Security Democrats, 29 April 2016, available here: https://democrats-homeland.house.gov/news/correspondence/fbi-shared-responsibility-committees-must-pass-privacy-test.; H. Murtaza and J. McLaughlin, 'FBI's "Shared Responsibility Committees" to Identify "Radicalized" Muslims Raise Alarms', *The Intercept*, 9 April 2016, available here: https://theintercept.com/2016/04/09/fbis-shared-responsibility-committees-to-identify-radicalized-muslims-raises-alarms/.

13 M. Downing, 'The RENEW Program, a New Approach to Identifying Early Warnings of Potential Violent Behavior', Presentation at the forum on Medical and Public Health Preparedness for Disasters and Emergencies, The National Academies of Sciences, Engineering, Medicine, September 7–8, 2016, available here: http://nationalacademies.org/hmd/~/media/Files/Activity%20Files/PublicHealth/MedPrep/2016-SEPT-7/Presentations/DOWNING.pdf.

14 B. I. Koerner, 'A Controversial New Program Aims to Reform Homegrown ISIS Recruits Back into Normal Young Americans', *Wired*, 24 January 2017, available here: https://www.wired.com/2017/01/can-you-turn-terrorist-back-into-citizen/.

15 Homeland Security, *Fact Sheet: FY 2016 Countering Violent Extremism (CVE) Grants* [website], 6 July 2016, available here: https://www.dhs.gov/news/2016/07/06/fy-2016-countering-violent-extremism-cve-grants.

16 Homeland Security, *Fact Sheet.*

17 Homeland Security, *Statement by Secretary Jeh Johnson Announcing First Round of DHS's Countering Violent Extremism Grants* [website], 13 January 2017, available here: https://www.dhs.gov/news/2017/01/13/statement-secretary-jeh-johnson-announcing-first-round-dhss-countering-violent#.

18 J. E. Ainsley, D. Volz, and K. Cooke, 'Exclusive: Trump to Focus Counter-Extremism Program Solely on Islam – Sources', *Reuters*, 1 February 2017, available here: http://www.reuters.com/article/us-usa-trump-extremists-program-exclusiv-idUSKBN15G5VO.

19 R. Nixon, A. Goldman and M. Apuzzo, 'Pointing to Trump, Groups Reject U.S. Aid to Fight Extremism', *The New York Times*, 2 February 2017, available here: https://www.nytimes.com/2017/02/02/us/politics/trump-muslim-groups-aid-extremism.html?_r=0.

20 https://www.facebook.com/kajoog.org/posts/1561873447164107.

21 D. Bharath, 'Trump Plan Leads to Uncertain Future for Countering Violent Extremism Program', *The Orange County Register*, 24 February 2017, available here: http://www.ocregister.com/2017/02/24/trump-plan-leads-to-uncertain-future-for-countering-violent-extremism-program/.

22 B. Claremont, *Bayan Claremont Declines $800,000 Federal Grant* [website], 10 February 2017, available here: http://www.bayanclaremont.org/dhsgrant/.

23 J. Walters, '"An Incredible Transformation": How Rehab, Not Prison, Worked for a US Isis Convert', *The Guardian*, 4 January 2018, available here: https://www.theguardian.com/us-news/2018/jan/04/american-isis-abdullahi-yousuf-rehabilatation.

Recommended Readings

Ainsley, J. E., D. Volz, and K. Cooke, 'Exclusive: Trump to Focus Counter-Extremism Program Solely on Islam – Sources', *Reuters*, 1 February 2017, available here: http://www.reuters.com/article/us-usa-trump-extremists-program-exclusiv-idUSKBN15G5VO.

Bharath, D., 'Trump Plan Leads to Uncertain Future for Countering Violent Extremism Program', *The Orange County Register*, 24 February 2017, available here: http://www.ocregister.com/2017/02/24/trump-plan-leads-to-uncertain-future-for-countering-violent-extremism-program/.

Bjelopera, J. P., and M. A. Randol, *American Jihadist Terrorism: Combating a Complex Threat*, report for the Congressional Research Service, 20 September 2010.

Braniff, W., S. Hughes, S. Batten and M. Levitt, "From CVE to 'Terrorism Prevention': Assessing New U.S. Policies," *The Washington Institute for Near East Policy*, 17 December, 2017, available here: http://www.washingtoninstitute.org/ policy-analysis/view/from-cve-to-terrorism-prevention-assessing-new-u.s.-policies.

Claremont, B., *Bayan Claremont Declines $800,000 Federal Grant* [website], 10 February 2017, available here: http://www.bayanclaremont.org/dhsgrant/.

Downing, M. 'The RENEW Program, A New Approach to Identifying Early Warnings of Potential Violent Behavior', Presentation at the forum on Medical and Public Health Preparedness for Disasters and Emergencies, The National Academies of Sciences, Engineering, Medicine, 7–8 September, 2016, available here: http://nationalacademies.org/hmd/~/media/Files/Activity%20Files/PublicHealth/ MedPrep/2016-SEPT-7/Presentations/DOWNING.pdf.

'FBI Shared Responsibility Committees Must Pass Privacy Test', Committee on Homeland Security Democrats', 29 April 2016, available here: https://democrats-homeland.house.gov/news/correspondence/fbi-shared-responsibility-committees-must-pass-privacy-test.

Geltzer, J.A. and S. Tankel, 'Whatever Happened to Trump's Counterterrorism Strategy?' *The Atlantic*, 1 March 2018, available here: https://www.theatlantic.com/international/archive/2018/03/trump-terrorism-iraq-syria-al-qaeda-isis/554333/.

Government Accountability Office (GAO), 'Managing for Results: Barriers to Interagency Coordination', GAO-06-15 and GAO/GGD-00-106, Washington, D.C., 29 March 2000, available here: http://www.gao.gov/archive/2000/gg00106.pdf (accessed 2 February 2011).

Homeland Security, *Fact Sheet: FY 2016 Countering Violent Extremism (CVE) Grants* [website], 6 July 2016, available here: https://www.dhs.gov/news/2016/07/06/fy-2016-countering-violent-extremism-cve-grants.

Homeland Security, *Statement by Secretary Jeh Johnson Announcing First Round of DHS's Countering Violent Extremism Grants* [website], 13 January 2017, available here: https://www.dhs.gov/news/2017/01/13/statement-secretary-jeh-johnson-announcing-first-round-dhss-countering-violent#.

Koerner, B. I., 'A Controversial New Program Aims to Reform Homegrown ISIS Recruits Back into Normal Young Americans', *Wired*, 24 January 2017, available here: https://www.wired.com/2017/01/can-you-turn-terrorist-back-into-citizen/.

Markon, J., 'Mosque Infiltration Feeds Muslims' Distrust of FBI', *Washington Post*, 5 December 2010.

Murtaza, H. and J. McLaughlin, 'Fbi's "Shared Responsibility Committees" to Identify "Radicalized" Muslims Raise Alarms', *The Intercept*, 9 April 2016, available here: https://theintercept.com/2016/04/09/fbis-shared-responsibility-committees-to-identify-radicalized-muslims-raises-alarms/.

Nixon, R., A. Goldman and M. Apuzzo, 'Pointing to Trump, Groups Reject U.S. Aid to Fight Extremism', *The New York Times*, 2 February 2017, available here: uhttps://www.nytimes.com/2017/02/02/us/politics/trump-muslim-groups-aid-extremism.html?_r=0.

Rosand, E. 'Fixing CVE in the United States Requires More Than Just a Name Change', *Brookings Institute*, 16 February 2017, available here: https://www.brookings.edu/blog/order-from-chaos/2017/02/16/fixing-cve-in-the-united-states-requires-more-thanjust-a-name-change/.

Rosenau, W. and S. Daly, 'American Journeys to Jihad: U.S. Extremists and Foreign Conflicts during the 1980s and 1990s', *CTC Sentinel*, vol. 3, no. 8, 2010.

"Threats to the Homeland," Testimony of Acting Secretary of Homeland Security Elaine C. Duke, Senate Committee on Homeland Security and Government Affairs, 27 September 2017, available here: https://www.hsgac.senate.gov/imo/media/doc/Testimony-Duke-2017-09-27.pdf.

Vidino, L., 'Homegrown Jihadist Terrorism in the United States: A New and Occasional Phenomenon?', *Studies in Conflict & Terrorism*, vol. 32, no. 1, 2009.

Vidino, L. and S. Hughes, *ISIS in America: From Retweets to Raqqa*, Program on Extremism, George Washington University, [Online], 2015.

Walters, J., "'An Incredible Transformation': How Rehab, Not Prison, Worked for a US Isis Convert," *The Guardian*, 4 January 2018, available here: https://www.theguardian.com/us-news/2018/jan/04/american-isis-abdullahi-yousuf-rehabilatation.

29 CONCLUSIONS AND SUMMARY

Anthony Richards

Through this collection of chapters from leading experts, this edited volume has sought to enhance our understanding of the causes of, and most appropriate responses to, acts of terrorism carried out against the UK by those claiming to be acting on behalf of Islam. It has aimed to, from an evidence-based perspective, identify gaps in research – in other words to determine what we know, what we don't know and what we need to know when addressing the challenge of jihadist terrorism.

A number of themes have emerged from these contributions. These have not all, of course, been unanimously identified as of importance (indeed, there is, unsurprisingly, disagreement on the extent that some of them are significant or even relevant). A broad observation that Maher makes is that it is post-9/11 conflicts 'that have shaped so many of the destructive tendencies we ascribe to *salafi-jihadism* today'. One should certainly not overlook, nor underestimate, the impact of developments in the international environment on domestic radicalization towards violence. Nesser, for example, also suggests that the most significant factors underpinning the jihadist threat to Europe can be traced 'to conflict zones in the Muslim world – rather than internal European affairs'. He further notes the prominence of networks and the role of ideological and resourceful entrepreneurs, and contends that counter-terrorism effort should primarily focus on severing both their offline and online connections. Klausen also emphasizes what she calls the process of 'networked social contagion', the effect of which is to drive patterns of recruitment 'that are best described as neighborhood effects, highly localized real-world clusters or hubs of extremists'. As such, she contends that counter-terrorism should target the hubs and should fight 'further network growth'.

Stenersen raises the specific concern that terrorists will continue to use encrypted communication applications for recruitment and operational planning, increasing the risk of them 'developing more innovative and dangerous attack methods', and she suggests that more research is needed in this area and on terrorist online learning in general. Notwithstanding terrorist use of encryption, however, it seems doubtful that encryption intervention could be adopted as a counter-measure. Miller, for example, argues that encryption is now a necessary part of modern life, that it doesn't just protect the terrorists but everyone else too and that intervention would 'harm the basis of much of cybersecurity'.

In relation to social media more broadly, Braddock usefully proposes eight recommendations for the content of counter-narratives along with three suggestions as to how these might be distributed (emphasizing, not least, the importance of the credibility of the messenger), while on conspiracy theories, Amarasingam suggests that there are no easy solutions in countering them and that confronting such theories may do little more than reinforce belief in them. He calls for further research in order to understand how conspiracy theories take hold in communities, including in the online space, where theories are often 'hatched', with a need for digital ethnography research and social network analysis.

One clear point of divergence within the volume is over the impact or otherwise of socio-economic factors behind violent radicalization. Abbas argues that socio-economic and equality issues are fundamental factors in understanding the reasons behind radicalization towards violence. Yet, conversely, Nesser counters the idea that terrorism is the product of such issues, and Klausen also contends that there is 'no compelling evidence that social alienation is the root cause of terrorist extremism'.

At the individual level, Taylor outlines the methodological constraints in trying to generate a 'terrorist profile' (noting that 'the literature is replete with failures' in generating such a profile), but he argues that 'it does not follow that meaningful or useful accounts can't be developed' and suggests that it may be more worthwhile to assess potential psychological *patterns* for terrorist engagement instead. While there are obstacles in trying to develop a terrorist profile, Hill and Pantucci, in their contributions, have observed an emerging theme relating to terrorist offenders – that there have been many instances where perpetrators have moved from common criminality into terrorism. Pantucci draws on the research of Hannah Stuart and her dataset covering the period 1998–2015, noting that 'overall 38 per cent of the individuals included had a previous conviction for a variety of issues'. Hill, therefore, argues that 'whether or not this is their route into terrorism, we need to consider whether our existing precursor offences are effective', although any such consideration would need to pass the 'stiff test' of complying with ECHR principles and applying domestic jurisprudence. A further potential legal avenue that Anderson has contemplated (when considering cases such as that of Anjem Choudary) is the need for some legislative provision for those 'hate preachers' who encourage the radicalisation of others.

On responses to jihadist terrorism, if there is one theme that resonates across many of the chapters, it is the importance of community engagement and that trust is paramount in such engagement. Choudhury argues that Muslim perceptions of, or lack of, fair treatment can correspondingly represent both an opportunity and a hindrance in relation to Muslim cooperation against terrorism. Spalek and El-

Awa note that the 'research literature places a large emphasis upon community engagement as a critical way of building and maintaining trust', without which 'community members will not pass on information to policing, security and other statutory agencies'. They argue, however, that Muslim communities have become stigmatized, which, along with 'hard' policing and security practices, can have a detrimental impact on community engagement.

This is, according to Sobolewska, against a backdrop of existing literature that 'converges on a picture of deteriorating [public] attitudes towards Muslims in the UK, and on Muslims being the most prejudiced-against group compared to other minority groups'. She contends that the media uses particular frames to discuss Muslims and that there is a need for research on the social responsibility of media reporting. She also raises concerns as to how Muslims are represented and, drawing on Shamit Saggar's work, argues that 'without a widely accepted and respected Muslim leadership, coming from the more compromise-seeking rather than the religiously radical quarters, the situation of British Muslims is unlikely to improve'. In his contribution, Walton argues that some Muslim communities lack the resilience to deal effectively with extremism, that there is a lack of Muslim civil society organizations and that Muslim role models and Muslim civil society need to be more broadly empowered and supported.

Barrett also emphasizes the importance of community engagement if (foreign fighter) reintegration programmes are to be successful, without which 'the task of identifying, assessing, reintegrating and subsequently monitoring returnees is simply impossible' and Clarke, too, underscores the value of community engagement in underpinning the intelligence-led approach to policing (ILP). Notwithstanding the importance of such engagement, Gearson notes, however, that the 'wider challenge of involving partners across communities and the public more generally in counter-terrorism' is 'an area of policy that has seen limited development in the 15 years of CONTEST's operation'.

The Prevent strategy is, of course, intimately bound up with this theme, but it has not been without its controversies, prompting two of the authors (O'Toole and Neumann) to contemplate the possibility of re-branding the strategy altogether. O'Toole notes that there are 'ongoing concerns that the requirements of the Prevent Duty are having discriminatory effects' and the negative implications that this has for Muslim civic engagement. Not all the perceptions of Prevent are negative. Walton, for example, suggests that key parts of the strategy have been effective, with a 'significant' number of referrals made to the police, although he argues that the strategy has been less effective in tackling the 'root causes of radicalization'. Clarke also notes that, although it may have had some negative effects on community relations, Prevent has proved successful in contributing to intelligence-led policing and has 'headed off likely incidents'.

O'Toole suggests that an independent review of Prevent and the counter-extremism agenda should be established. Indeed, one of the proposals to have emerged from the September 2018 conference was that there should be an independent reviewer of Prevent, perhaps modelled along the same lines as the Office of the Independent Reviewer of Terrorism Legislation, which, according to Blackbourn and Walker in their chapter, has worked well and 'adds value to the other devices of accountability'.

One of the challenges for Prevent and counter-terrorism is how to deal with the relatively decentralized nature of the threat, including 'lone-actor' terrorism. On this particular phenomenon, Gill identifies a number of general conclusions from the literature, including that there is no socio-demographic profile of a lone-actor terrorist, that motivation does not revolve entirely around ideology, that mental health problems are common and complex, that 'online radicalization' is a misnomer and that managing the problem will entail interdisciplinary and multi-agency approaches. He also identifies areas for further research in this area, such as how the ecology and pathways of lone-actor terrorism might differ from group-based terrorists.

In his assessment of the contemporary jihadist terrorist threat, Pantucci argues that 'what has noticeably changed … is the number of people with mental health issues emerging in attack plans, as well as a more prominent role from very recent converts', while 'the overall pattern of distant forces stirring homegrown groups has now shifted more to homegrown groups connecting with foreign ideologies.' In confronting this challenge, Walton has argued that the UK has one of the most respected counter-terrorism strategies of any country in the world (though a less-developed counter-extremism strategy), outlining increased resources devoted to countering terrorism and the high number of disrupted plots over the past twenty years. Gearson also notes 'the success in disrupting most terrorist conspiracies over the past 18 years' but that operational/tactical successes need to be matched by a more effective strategic approach.

In relation to comparisons with other countries, Vidino notes how underdeveloped a countering violent extremism (CVE) strategy is in the United States for a number of reasons, while Neumann suggests that the experiences of other European countries 'offer valuable lessons which may help to address the problems with Britain's Prevent strategy, especially the lack of trust and participation by British Muslims' and that one of the best ways to understand how Prevent has become 'toxic' is to learn from these other states. He identifies examples of good practice through National Action Plans (Norway), referral mechanisms (Germany), CVE empowering local government (the Netherlands), school approaches (Belgium) and prison deradicalization (Austria).

Other themes identified as requiring further research include deeper exploration that would enable a more nuanced appreciation as to whether or not, and to what extent, non-violent extremism should be culpable for acts of terrorism. To what extent should non-violent extremist groups be seen as potential partners (and as 'firewalls') in dissuading those who would resort to violence or are such groups part of the terrorist problem (as potential 'conveyor belts')? Spalek and El-Awa argue that 'in the UK considerable research highlights that non-violent extremists can play an important preventative and divertive role' against violent extremism. El-Badawy contends in her chapter that, while at the individual level, there may be informal ties between violent and non-violent groups, at the group level, in cases of *principled* non-violence, such groups are likely to be regarded as firewalls against terrorism, whereas *strategic* non-violence is open to future adaptation and hence the possibility that groups adopting this approach could serve as conveyor belts to terrorism. However, there is, she suggests, a need to generate a more sophisticated and empirical understanding in this area and move beyond the rather simplistic firewall/conveyor belt dichotomy.

A further theme that has emerged is the need to empirically measure the impact of counter-terrorist initiatives. Brown argues that 'evaluations of countering radicalization programmes are generally poor' and that, further, there is a real need for consideration of gender in the analysis of such programmes. For example, she argues that very few CVE programmes address or include women as 'designers, leaders, practitioners or deliverers', that they are treated rather as 'passive targets of these programmes and policies rather than as co-producers'. Gill has emphasized the need for evaluations of interventions in relation to lone-actor terrorists, while Braddock calls for the need for effective measurement of the impact of counter-narratives against terrorism. Walton also argues for further research into, and assessment of, the capacity and capabilities of the UK's resources devoted to counter-terrorism.

Also useful are those research findings that undermine what may be popularly believed – Silke's chapter in particular notes that, while the notion that prisons and madrassas have been incubators of radicalization has had 'considerable influence' on government policy, 'the evidence supporting such a link is often anecdotal and is usually much more conceptual than empirical'. He concludes that, although there have been cases where radicalization in these two settings has 'clearly happened or has been seriously attempted, … successful radicalization is rare in both settings … and that physical setting alone appears to be a poor predictor for radicalization.'

We hope that this volume has provided a broad and useful coverage of many of the key issues in understanding and responding to jihadist terrorism. The editors are grateful to all the authors for their thoughtful and erudite contributions. The terrorist threat from those claiming to be acting on behalf of Islam unfortunately appears to be an enduring one, and so it is imperative that we continue to endeavour to enhance our understanding of it and its evolution in the years ahead. The suggested avenues for future research will lay the basis for Phase 2 of the CoJiT project, and it is discussions around these that will form part of the national conversation that the initiative is seeking to encourage in 2019 and beyond.

INDEX

Lightning Source UK Ltd.
Milton Keynes UK
UKHW010649021019
350824UK00003B/207/P

9 781788 315531